CDC 70
Investment works / 1948-2018

Imagine. Build. Change.

First published by CDC Group plc in 2008

Second edition published in 2018

© 2018 CDC Group plc

ISBN: 978-1-5272-2865-8

Written by Christopher Brain and Michael Cable.

Designed and produced by Honey Creative, London.

Printed in the UK by CPI Colour.

As CDC celebrates its 70th anniversary and looks back over its achievements during seven decades of pioneering development in many of the world's most impoverished countries, it has every reason to be proud of its heritage as the longest-established international development finance institution of its kind. Its longevity and success are due in no small part to the adaptability of CDC as it has faced changes in the political, economic, and social environments over the decades.

Today's CDC Group plc is certainly very different from what started in 1948 as the Colonial Development Corporation, and yet its mission has remained fundamentally and steadfastly the same throughout – to make a lasting impact to people's lives in some of the world's poorest and most neglected places by encouraging, supporting and sustaining responsible economic development.

In the early post-war years of widespread austerity and deprivation in Britain and overseas, CDC's projects were often quite literally groundbreaking. Teams would be dispatched to remote locations, often so far off the beaten track that it would take days, weeks and sometimes even months of travel just to get there, before then starting from scratch in establishing agricultural and industrial enterprises in areas where little if anything of the kind had previously been attempted. In those days, some of CDC's more adventurous staff, often accompanied by their spouses, not only had to endure considerable hardship but also, in some of the more extreme locations, occasionally found themselves risking life and limb. Still continuing to operate in some of the world's hardest places, including regions struggling with the aftermath of armed conflict, the passionate commitment of its dedicated staff and those working for its investee companies remains one of CDC's greatest strengths.

At various points in its history, the strategies through which CDC has sought to achieve maximum development impact have been radically, and sometimes controversially, realigned. In recent years CDC's geographic focus has narrowed to focus on transforming economies, businesses and lives exclusively in sub-Saharan Africa and the poorest parts of South Asia. And as the world's focus moves towards the achievement of the Sustainable Development Goals, CDC's role in the United Kingdom's overall development strategy has become even more important, symbolised through the CDC Act of 2017.

So, while CDC can look back with justifiable pride as a world leader amongst development finance institutions it can also look forward with renewed confidence and an even greater sense of purpose. Our hope is that all stakeholders, in particular UK tax payers, also share in that pride. As Lord Reith our second chairman said, CDC's role is to "do good without losing money". This mandate is by definition challenging, but there is still much good to be done, and the CDC team is determined to do just that.

Graham Wrigley
Chairman
CDC Group plc

1948–1950

Prior to a logo being introduced, CDC uses its CDC Coat of Arms, Seal or the Royal Coat of Arms as the occasion requires.

1951–1963

The Imperial State Crown, similar to Queen Victoria's Crown used when Empress of India, represents CDC when it is the Colonial Development Corporation.

1964–1972

St Edward's Crown replaces the Imperial State Crown shortly after CDC is renamed Commonwealth Development Corporation. The official crown of Queen Elizabeth II, it is also the crown used as a symbol of royal authority in the Commonwealth realms. Towards the end of this period, CDC uses the slogan, 'Finance plus Management'.

1973–1985

Peter Meinerzhagen's arrival as general manager in 1972 prompts a revamp of the logo, encircling it and embossing 'CDC' in a new copperplate font. At the same time CDC introduces a consistent house style in its stationery and publications. Its tag lines includes 'Partners in Development'.

1986–1999

The crown is dropped and a contemporary logo introduced as part of the new chief executive John Eccles' drive to change CDC's culture. The 'D' for Development is highlighted, but the chairman Lord Kindersley seeks to calm fears by stating that investments in the Commonwealth would still be sought whenever the opportunities arise. CDC advertises itself using 'Britain Investing in Development' and 'Investing in Development'.

2000–2003

In 1999, CDC ceases to be a statutory corporation, becoming CDC Group plc. To mark the change of status and CDC's private equity focus it launches a new logo and introduces 'CDC Capital Partners' as its trading name.

2003–2016

The flourish on the D is resurrected by chief executive Richard Laing, re-emphasising CDC as the UK's development finance institution once more. 'CAPITAL for DEVELOPMENT' is in use.

2016–present

Through a new assertive strapline and a bold, black logo, CDC shows renewed confidence in its ability to maximise development impact.

Contents

06

Chapter 1

Visions and ventures

1948–1950

34

Chapter 2

Reith and the battle for the future

1950–1959

64

Chapter 3

Getting better all the time

1959–1972

104

Chapter 4

More help for the poorest

1972–1982

138

Chapter 5

Culture change

1982-1994

174

Chapter 6

Journey to private equity

1994–2004

208

Chapter 7

Fund of funds

2004–2011

242

Chapter 8

An ambition for impact

2012–2017

Visions and ventures

1948–1950

Visions and ventures
1948–1950

1947

World events...

- *Marshall Plan is established.*
- *India and Pakistan gain independence from Britain.*

CDC events...

- Legislation passes through Parliament for the formation of the Colonial Development Corporation. The Overseas Resources Development Bill is put to Parliament with its first reading on 23 October.

- Lord Trefgarne occupies temporary offices in Dover House, Whitehall, bringing together a shadow board on 13 November.

Right: Lusaka, Zambia. Located near Lusaka, CDC's first industrial project, Chilanga Cement, was supported and at times managed from 1949 to 2001, the cement from Chilanga's plants continuing to be used to build Zambia's economy. Over the years, CDC has been active in many other sectors in the country, ranging from agribusiness, mining and hotels to financial services and real estate. These included direct debt investments of $66 million made in 2015 and 2017 in IHS Zambia Limited, the sole and leading independent telecommunications tower operator in Zambia, owning and operating over 1,700 towers that have significantly improved accessibility and reliability of coverage.

1948

Communists complete the division of Berlin, installing the government in the Soviet sector.

The Western European Union (WEU) is founded as a defensive arm for postwar Europe. It leads to the formation of NATO.

Ceylon gains independence from Britain, becoming Sri Lanka in 1972.

The Overseas Resources Development Act 1948 receives Royal Assent on 11 February, establishing CDC as a statutory corporation.

Lord Trefgarne is appointed chairman and assumes the chief executive role. CDC's first board meeting is held on 2 March. CDC moves its head office into 33 Dover Street, London.

CDC's first regional offices open in Kenya, Nyasaland (now Malawi), Nigeria and Singapore.

CDC's first commitments are made: in British Guiana (now Guyana), Turks and Caicos Islands, St Lucia, Falkland Islands, the Gambia, Nyasaland (now Malawi) and North Borneo

1949

• Almost four years after the end of World War II, clothes rationing in Great Britain ends.

• The Communist People's Republic of China is proclaimed under Mao Tse Tung with Chou En-Lai as Premier.

• In Dominica, CDC develops a small hydroelectric power station: CDC goes on to invest in and manage small power utility companies throughout the Caribbean islands.

• CDC makes its first industrial investment, the construction of a cement plant at Chilanga, in Northern Rhodesia (now Zambia). CDC establishes Tanganyika Wattle Estates (Tanwat, in what is now Tanzania). Work starts on growing pines at Usutu, which establishes the pulp industry in Swaziland.

• The forerunners of the Malaysia Building Society and Singapura Finance are established by CDC. A loan finances a new power station near Kuala Lumpur, which is suffering from a major shortage of electricity.

1950

• United States military involvement in Vietnam begins.

• The Korean War starts as forces from the communist North invade the South. It lasts till 1953.

• The first transatlantic jet passenger flight is made.

• Lord Trefgarne submits his resignation in August, and on 1 November Lord Reith takes over as chairman and the role of chief executive. At year-end, CDC already has 340 staff.

• CDC's first hotel project in the Caribbean is to develop and manage Fort George Hotel in Belize City. It is now a Radisson.

• CDC's first investment in oil palm involves the takeover of Kulai Oil Palm Estate, Johor, Malaya (now Malaysia). It is to become a training ground for other oil palm projects, including BAL Plantations in Sabah.

• Swaziland Irrigation Scheme is set up by CDC.

Housewives queuing for rationed food in Catford, London during the terrible winter of 1947 put on a brave face for the camera. With Britain suffering from acute food shortages at the time, it was estimated that, on average, every woman in the country had to spend an hour-a-day in such queues.

Chapter one
Visions and ventures

Britain, during the bleak mid-winter of 1947, was locked in the icy grip of a mounting post-war economic crisis. Victory over Hitler and the forces of Nazi Germany had come at a very high price. Vast numbers of houses, factories, shops and warehouses lay in ruins, destroyed along with the infrastructure that supported them. At the same time, the merchant shipping fleet had been reduced to a third of its pre-war strength.

Despite income tax of fifty per cent and compulsory national savings, the government had been forced to sell its foreign investments in order to pay for the war effort. It also had to borrow heavily abroad and the trade deficit in July 1945, when Clement Attlee's Labour government took office, was the largest in the nation's history.

Economist John Maynard Keynes warned of "a financial Dunkirk" while Hugh Dalton, the chancellor of the exchequer, talked of the threat of "total economic ruin". This was only narrowly averted with the help of a substantial loan from the United States that was not fully and finally repaid until as recently as 2006.

Even with this lifeline to tide the country over the situation deteriorated still further in 1947, identified by Dalton as the nation's "annus horrendus". This was largely due to the worst winter weather of the entire century. Snow blanketed the country continuously from January until March, temperatures were the lowest recorded for one hundred years and February included the longest period without sunshine since records began. When the thaw eventually set in during March the melting snow resulted in widespread flooding that caused further devastation, wiping out twenty per cent of the country's sheep as well as several hundred thousand head of cattle. Winter crops failed, there was a fuel crisis and industrial production halved. Britain faced bankruptcy, mass unemployment and even starvation, the government going so far as to draw up plans for a 'famine food programme'.

"Britain faced bankruptcy, mass unemployment and even starvation, the government going so far as to draw up plans for a 'famine food programme.'"

It was against this background of deepening economic gloom that the creation of the Colonial Development Corporation was formally proposed. As a matter of policy, Attlee's forward-thinking socialist government was keen to develop the economic resources of Britain's remaining colonies, first and foremost for the benefit of the colonies themselves. However, given the worldwide scarcity of goods and supplies of every kind, there could also be advantages for Britain, the British Commonwealth and the world as a whole in any such development. Most importantly, the colonies, rich in so many different natural resources, clearly had the potential to make a significant contribution towards the production of the food supplies and raw materials that were so urgently needed both here at home and elsewhere. And for Britain, there was the further consideration that if the colonies could be helped to create their own income streams through assisted economic development, this would have the effect of reducing their reliance on subsidies.

The general idea had first been mooted as early as August 1943 by Sydney Caine, then financial adviser to the secretary of state for the colonies. As the tide of the war started to turn in favour of the Allies, he was already thinking ahead to possible post-war development strategies and produced a memo for the secretary of state in which he suggested that what Britain would need would be a body to undertake the overall planning of development and "to conceive and carry out major projects".

Caine foresaw problems if the proposed body were to be "a semi-political Colonial Development Board" that would duplicate and compete with the Colonial Office; at the same time, he couldn't see the Colonial Office itself taking a new initiative. What he envisaged instead was "a company clothed in commercial form... working as an agent of Government... not intended to be operated in a commercial spirit" but acting "with the comparative freedom of a commercial concern", freed from the "portentously heavy machinery" of government.

His recommendations were considered by the newly-formed Colonial Economic Advisory Committee when it met for the first time a month later, in September 1943. Its academic and industrialist members presciently noted that, among other things, the memo raised "the important and urgent question of the relation of public to private investment".

In 1946, Caine was brought in to head up the Development Division of the Colonial Economic and Development Council and in March 1947, just as the winter snows were melting, he wrote another memo, entitled 'The Proposed Formation of the Colonial Development Corporation'. He pressed hard for the corporation to be established by Act of Parliament and succeeded in having it included in the legislation that also established the Overseas Food Corporation. The Overseas Resources Bill passed through its first and second readings in the autumn of 1947 before gaining the Royal Assent on 11 February 1948.

The debates in both Houses were overwhelmingly supportive of the proposals. In the House of Lords, one peer declared that he could not recall anything with which the House had been in more complete agreement. Understandably, with just about every basic commodity in short supply in the UK, any proposals that offered relief were most welcome. There was concern in some quarters that it was the British consumer, rather than the colonies, who would benefit most, but the far left-wing minister for food, John Strachey, was quick to quash that idea. "Oh no, I think the primary benefit...will go to the Colonial peoples," he said. "Surely, the Colonial territory in question will be most benefited by producing the commodity of which there is the greatest world shortage."

By the terms of the Act, the corporation was committed to 'investigate, formulate and carry out projects for developing Colonial resources'. To this end, it would be allowed to borrow up to £100 million (equivalent to £3.5 billion in 2018) and although the primary objective would not be to make profits, it would be expected to pay its own way. In general, its aim would be to expand the production of foodstuffs and raw materials as well as assisting in other agricultural, industrial and trade development. In particular, it would be expected to focus much of its effort on the development of agricultural production, since agriculture was basic to the economies of the majority of the countries in which it would be operating.

Sir Sydney Caine

Sydney Caine was financial adviser to the secretary of state for the colonies when, in August 1943, he wrote the memo that first conceived CDC.

He was deputy under secretary of state in the Colonial Office in 1947 when the second of his key CDC memos was drafted. He started his career in the Inland Revenue and transferred to the Colonial Office in 1926, serving in Hong Kong as financial secretary from 1937-40.

In his later career he became chief of the World Bank Mission to Ceylon, vice-chancellor of the University of Malaya and director of the London School of Economics. He was knighted in 1947 and his son Michael, later Sir Michael, went on to become deputy chairman of CDC. Sir Sydney died in 1991. Someone who knew him well, Arthur Seddon, described him as "a persuasive leader in unorthodox ideas and diverse enterprises".

Above: Attracted by William Rendell's camera, children in Lagos jostle to get into this picture taken by the general manager in an area just behind the Mainland Hotel during an official visit to Nigeria in 1958.

Above: A typical street scene elsewhere in Lagos, taken by Rendell during the same visit.

Lord Trefgarne, a left-wing Labour peer, was appointed as the first chairman and an office was provided at Dover House, an elegant mid-eighteenth century building overlooking Horse Guards Parade in Whitehall, now the Scotland Office.

The setting up of an undertaking such as CDC, for which there was no real precedent, presented an enormous challenge, but Trefgarne poured his heart and soul into the job. He was not the sort of man to think small and, in tune with the spirit of the age, he also felt the need to deliver results as quickly as possible. At the same time, he went to great lengths to do things properly, to take advice, to set up an appropriate organisation, to recruit the right staff and to make the correct investments.

As a first step he pulled together a board of non-executive directors whose individual backgrounds and experience he thought would bring the most benefit to the organisation. They included mostly former colonial servants and businessmen used to dealing overseas.

At its first full meeting in March 1948, the board then approved the organisation's structure. This was to be based on five regional corporations – in East, West and Central Africa, the West Indies and the Far East – which were to act as holding companies for the investments in their own particular regions, with the general managers of the local managed businesses reporting to them. In London, there was to be one department responsible for appraising new investments (plans) and another for managing them (operations). The heads of these two departments (joint controllers) would be able to call upon the services of a string of sector and function-oriented operating divisions for advice and delivery. An Executive Council consisting of the chairman, the deputy chairman, the joint controllers and the director of finance would manage the business.

At the same time, Trefgarne arranged for CDC's headquarters to be moved from Dover House to more spacious and rather splendid premises at 33 Dover Street. Located on the north side of Piccadilly, close to Green Park tube station, the elegant building there had originally been divided into half-a-dozen luxurious self-contained apartments.

The senior members of staff who were rapidly recruited to fill these offices came from an unusual variety of backgrounds, although quite a high proportion of the men were ex-army officers, ranking from Major Dickinson (the travel officer) to Lieutenant-General Sir Ernest Wood (controller of operations), with a liberal sprinkling of colonels and brigadiers in between, quite a few of whom would come to work impeccably attired in traditional fashion with bowler hat and rolled umbrella.

Trefgarne, meanwhile, had made sure that CDC hit the ground running by circulating a memo to colonial governors as early as December 1947, several months before the corporation had been formally established, inviting them to propose ideas for projects. The proposals duly came pouring in and having been carefully reviewed, sifted and graded 'A', 'B' or 'C' in terms of feasibility, no less than fifty-seven 'A's had already been identified by the end of 1948. Altogether, thirty-nine were up and running by September 1950. They were located in seventeen territories as far flung as the Falkland Islands in the freezing South Atlantic (the Falkland Islands Freezer Company and South Atlantic Sealing Company), the hot and steamy jungles of Borneo (Borneo Abaca Ltd, later BAL Plantations) and the extremely remote island of Tristan da Cunha (Tristan da Cunha Development Corporation).

Lord Trefgarne

George Morgan Garro-Jones was born in 1894 in Trefgarn, a small village near Haverfordwest in West Wales, the only son of a minister in the local Congregational Church who was also active in Liberal politics.

His career was full and extremely varied. In his early twenties he served as an Air Corps pilot during the First World War, later writing about his experiences in a book entitled *Ventures and Visions*, published in 1935. After the war, he qualified as a barrister while working as London editor of the *Daily Despatch*, but then changed tack completely and decided to go into politics.

He entered Parliament as a Liberal MP in 1924 but stood down five years later and went into business before returning to politics as a Labour MP in 1935. During World War II he acted as a parliamentary secretary at the Ministry of Production and was also private secretary to a Labour peer. When the war ended he went back into business, becoming a director of Barclays Overseas Development Corporation while at the same time acting as chairman of the Television Advisory Committee.

He was elevated to the House of Lords in 1947, taking the title 1st Baron Trefgarne of Cleddau in the County of Pembroke, one of a number of new hereditary Labour peers elevated on merit. Secretary of State for the Colonies Arthur Creech Jones recommended him for the job as chairman of CDC on the grounds that 'his approach to Colonial development accords with that of the Party, he has first-hand knowledge of Colonial conditions, has general commercial experience and knowledge of public policy and administration, and he has age, health and experience on his side'. He served as chairman of CDC from 11 February 1948 to 31 October 1950. He resigned primarily because of the criticism levelled at the Gambia Eggs Scheme, about which he felt compelled to make a personal statement in the House of Lords. He died in 1960, aged sixty-six.

THE COLONIES

SHOWING AREAS, POPULATION AND DENSITY OF POPULATION

1 BAHAMA IS.
Area 4,404 square miles
Population 75,000
Density 17 per square mile

2 BARBADOS
Area 166 square miles
Population 198,000
Density 1,192 per square mile

3 BRITISH GUIANA
Area 83,000 square miles
Population 390,000
Density 4.6 per square mile

4 BRITISH HONDURAS
Area 8,867 square miles
Population 62,000
Density 7 per square mile

5 JAMAICA
Area 4,411 square miles
Population 1,350,000
Density 306 per square mile

6 WINDWARD IS.
Area 821 square miles
Population 256,000
Density 312 per square mile

7 TRINIDAD
Area 1,980 square miles
Population 590,000
Density 297 per square mile

8 LEEWARD IS.
Area 422 square mile
Population 108,500
Density 257 per square mile

9 BASUTOLAND
Area 11,720 square miles
Population 556,000
Density 47 per square mile

10 BECHUANALAND
Area 275,000 square miles
Population 294,000
Density 1 per square mile

11 GAMBIA
Area 4,033 square miles
Population 251,000
Density 62 per square mile

12 GOLD COAST
Area 91,843 square miles
Population 4,100,000
Density 44 per square mile

13 KENYA
Area 224,960 square miles
Population 5,180,000
Density 23 per square mile

14 NIGERIA
Area 372,674 square miles
Population 25,000,000
Density 67 per square mile

15 NORTHERN RHODESIA
Area 290,323 square miles
Population 1,720,000
Density 6 per square mile

16 NYASALAND
Area 47,404 square miles
Population 2,150,000
Density 45 per square mile

17 SIERRA LEONE
Area 27,925 square miles
Population 2,000,000
Density 71 per square mile

18 SOMALILAND
Area 68,000 square miles
Population 700,000
Density 10 per square mile

19 SWAZILAND
Area 6,700 square miles
Population 187,000
Density 28 per square mile

20 TANGANYIKA
Area 362,688 square miles
Population 7,080,000
Density 19 per square mile

21 UGANDA
Area 93,981 square miles
Population 5,000,000
Density 53 per square mile

22 ZANZIBAR
Area 1,020 square miles
Population 265,000
Density 260 per square mile

23 BRUNEI
Area 2,226 square miles
Population 41,000
Density 18 per square mile

24 MALAYA
Area 50,850 square miles
Population 5,000,000
Density 98 per square mile

25 NORTH BORNEO
Area 29,387 square miles
Population 332,000
Density 11 per square mile

26 SARAWAK
Area 50,000 square miles
Population 550,000
Density 11 per square mile

27 SINGAPORE
Area 282 square miles
Population 950,000
Density 3,369 per square mile

28 CYPRUS
Area 3,572 square miles
Population 460,000
Density 128 per square mile

29 GIBRALTAR
Area 2½ square miles
Population 22,000
Density 9,770 per square mile

30 MALTA
Area 122 square miles
Population 307,000
Density 2,516 per square mile

31 ADEN
Area 112,080 square miles
Population 731,000
Density 6 per square mile

32 FIJI IS.
Area 7,040 square miles
Population 270,000
Density 38 per square mile

33 SEYCHELLES
Area 157 square miles
Population 35,000
Density 223 per square mile

34 MAURITIUS
Area 809 square miles
Population 456,000
Density 563 per square mile

35 FALKLAND IS.
Area 4,618 square miles
Population 2,250
Density 0.48 per square mile

UNITED KINGDOM
Area 93,053 square miles
Population 50,049,000
Density 537 per square mile

Above: A map showing the full extent of the British colonies in 1949.

Below: Lord Trefgarne (centre, holding glasses) conducts a CDC press conference in 1950 flanked by (left) Sir Robin Cook, board member from 1948-53 and deputy chairman from 1949-53 and (right) Frederick Winterbotham, external relations officer from 1949-52.

33 Dover Street

The elegant offices at 33 Dover Street (top left) into which CDC moved in 1948 were located in the heart of Mayfair, in an historic street where a number of famous gentlemen's clubs are still to be found. It is also where P.G. Wodehouse placed his fictional Drones Club.

As the CDC staff expanded to 340 by the end of 1950, they spread out into satellite offices next door and directly behind in Berkeley Street, to which they were connected by a bridge.

Further office space was later commandeered at 19 Curzon Street, once the home of Benjamin Disraeli, where Britain's secret services were also based until the 1970s. This was the location that Ian Fleming no doubt had in mind when he wrote about James Bond's visits to 'M' and Miss Moneypenny. Joyce Osborne (bottom left) started work as a secretary at Dover Street in October 1948, on a salary of £6 5s 0d a week. In 2008 she recalled:

"The Dover Street building had been designed as self-contained flats – two on each floor on either side of a landing on which the tea lady appeared with her trolley every morning and afternoon. Some of the rooms had fireplaces. One of the more important secretarial tasks was to get the fire going – a skill not included in the secretarial college syllabus.

"Office life was very formal. It was unusual for an executive to call a secretary by her first name and for a secretary to use an executive's first name was unheard of.

"The social event of 1950 was Lady Trefgarne's girls' tea party for the staff. For those of us who were young and unaccustomed to taking tea with titled ladies in Mayfair hotels, this presented serious problems of etiquette. Should one wear a hat? Gloves? Did one speak before one was spoken to?

"Lady Trefgarne was young and attractive. She joined each table in turn for a friendly chat. It was all very civilised and enjoyable. Later in the year, we all crowded into Browns Hotel for Lord Trefgarne's farewell. On 1 November Lord Reith took over as chairman. CDC would never be quite the same again."

One of the earliest projects was located in the Caribbean, where a CDC team of architects and engineers supervised the rebuilding of the St Lucian capital, Castries, the heart of which had been almost totally destroyed in 1948 by a fire as devastating in its way as the Great Fire of London of 1666.

A local workforce of 1,200 men and women having first been recruited and trained for the job, a new Castries rose phoenix-like from the ashes, including not only houses, flats and shops, but a Parliament building, government offices, city hall, law courts, customs house, warehouse, post office, telephone exchange, city hall, fire station, police station and barracks. And much of the extra specially hard, long-lasting and water-resistant greenheart timber used in the reconstruction came from British Guiana Timbers, another CDC project in the region in which it made a major investment.

In terms of the geographical spread and the wide range of activities involved, all this might seem to add up to a very impressive start. And yet, despite having recognised in advance that one of the pitfalls CDC would have to be careful to avoid was "the error of swallowing more plans than it can digest", Trefgarne nevertheless allowed it to do

just that in those first two or three years. Although the corporation turned down many projects, it still took on more than it could chew, let alone digest.

Part of the problem was the inexperience of the staff, especially the analysts. Many of them had been in the military or in government departments during the war and although they were well aware of the difficulties of estimating costs, timescales and markets they still, quite understandably, had little idea about where to start when it came to some of the more unusual circumstances and remote locations that they suddenly found themselves having to consider.

However, as well as several well-meaning but misconceived schemes and one or two wonderfully gung-ho adventures the many projects set up during that initial two-year flurry of activity also included a number of notable long-term successes, some of which proved over time to be among the most interesting, important and long-lasting investments in CDC's history.

Above: Architects study a model showing the planned reconstruction of Castries, the capital of St Lucia, the centre of which was completely destroyed by fire in 1948. One of CDC's earliest projects, the extensive re-building was completed in two years, between 1949 and 1951.

Above: The new town centre as it was some years later in 1965.

In Africa, where much of CDC's early effort was concentrated, Tanganyika Wattle Estates (Tanwat) and Kenya's East Africa Industries, in particular, provided two of the more outstanding examples.

Both set up in 1949 with the help of CDC money and management expertise, they made a slow start but diversified and expanded steadily over the years and are still flourishing today, having brought far-reaching economic, social, cultural, infrastructural and welfare benefits locally and nationally. East Africa Industries – managed by Unilever from 1953 onwards, although CDC retained an interest until 1977 – manufactures a wide range of well-known brands from Blue Band margarine to Omo washing powder and is still thriving as Unilever Kenya. Tanwat, when CDC finally disengaged in 2006, encompassed 18,000 hectares of wattle, tea and forestry plantations, employed 3,000 people and had provided housing, medical, educational, sporting and cultural facilities for the community while also supporting many local shops, businesses and institutions.

In southern Africa, Swaziland, a country not much bigger than Wales, became the focus of much long-term sustainable CDC activity, thanks largely to the early influence of the high commissioner, Sir Evelyn Baring. An enthusiastic supporter of CDC right from the start, Sir Evelyn later went on, as Lord Howick, to become its longest-serving chairman.

In the highveld area of the country work started in 1949 on establishing Usutu Forest, the softwood pine plantations on which the country's thriving pulp and paper industry came to be founded. Covering 75,000 hectares at one time, this was one of the world's largest man-made forests.

Meanwhile, in the lowveld region, the Swaziland Irrigation Scheme was to prove one of CDC's most significant long-term successes. It began in 1950 with the purchase of 42,000 hectares of land between the Komati and the Black Mbuluzi rivers, an area bordered by the spectacular scarp of the Lebombo Mountains. But it wasn't until the late fifties that the scheme really got under way with the construction of a weir across the Komati river and the creation of a long canal, in a project that came to be known as Mhlume Water, that brought irrigation to an area of 26,000 hectares.

This was first used for growing rice, becoming the largest rice farm in southern Africa before a switch was then made to sugar and the establishment of Swaziland's sugar industry through the Mhlume Sugar Company. A major managed project, this included setting up a pioneering smallholder settlement, Vuvulane Irrigated Farms, with more than 250 smallholdings of between three and seven hectares owned by local Swazi farmers. In addition, a 500-hectare area of the irrigated land was set aside for the establishment of the Mananga Agricultural Management Training Centre and trial farm, where the three-month agricultural training courses came to be attended by staff from CDC projects around the world. By the sixties, SIS later Inyoni Yami SIS (IYSIS), had become one of CDC's largest single direct investments.

As well as Swaziland, the three so-called High Commission Territories for which Sir Evelyn was responsible as governor also included the Protectorate of Bechuanaland (Botswana) and Basutoland (Lesotho) and he encouraged CDC to get involved in both those countries, too. In Bechuanaland it ventured into the meat industry, first rebuilding, modernising and extending the derelict Lobatse Abattoir and then investing in its own 120,000-hectare Molopo Ranch. Wholly-owned and managed by CDC over five decades, Molopo went on to become one of the largest cattle ranches in southern Africa and provided the foundation for a meat industry that, until diamonds were discovered, was the most important business in the country.

In Basutoland early investigations into the possibility of a hydroelectric scheme on the Malibamatso river with the aim of exporting power and water to the neighbouring Orange Free State were abandoned at that time, but were successfully revived many years later in the 1990s when CDC helped to finance the Lesotho Highlands Water Project. A hugely ambitious scheme, this involved the construction of a system of dams and massive underground aqueducts through the mountains in order to harness the water that is the country's major natural asset and re-channel it to provide a valuable export to the Free State and Gauteng Provinces.

Elsewhere in Africa, the Chilanga Cement works in Northern Rhodesia (Zambia) became the first cement works to be built in any of Britain's colonies outside of Hong Kong, providing the cement for the Kariba Dam, built with the help of a major CDC loan, while in Uganda CDC agreed to take a controlling equity and management interest in the newly-built and spectacularly-sited Lake Victoria Hotel.

Top: Cattle leaving CDC's Molopo Ranch in Bechuanaland (Botswana). The ranch on the north bank of the Molopo river and south of the Kalahari desert became one of the biggest cattle ranches in southern Africa (148,500 hectares by the mid 1980s) and was wholly-owned and managed by CDC for five decades, improving the quality of the national herd and demonstrating best practice.

Above: The first consignment of meat from CDC's Lobatse Abattoir in Bechuanaland goes on sale at London's Smithfield meat market in 1958. The sign at the back on the right reads 'Direct from Lobatsi, the most modern abattoir in the world'.

Right: An aerial view of the modern abattoir and meat processing plant at Lobatse, now the centre of the Botswana meat industry.

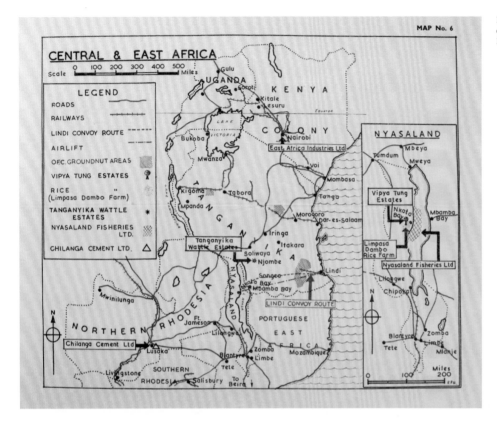

Left: A map of Central and East Africa, showing the location of various early CDC projects and the route of the legendary Lindi Convoy.

Operation Ploughshare and the Lindi Convoy

Nothing was too difficult for the military men recruited by CDC in the early years. By 1949, only four years after the end of the war, many of them were itching to get involved in a good campaign and the opportunity came in Nyasaland (Malawi) with the urgent need to import several hundred tonnes of heavy-duty equipment for use in clearing land at two of the earliest CDC projects, Viphya Tung Estates and its associated farm at Limpasa Dambo, where food for the Viphya Tung workers was to be grown. Both were located in an area west of Lake Nyasa (Lake Malawi), some 1,000 kilometres from the nearest large port of Beira on the coast of Mozambique.

Famine in the south following the failure of the maize crop meant that the only road up from Beira was clogged with traffic bringing in relief food supplies. The nearest railhead was 240 kilometres away and a collapsed bridge anyway ruled out that possibility.

CDC's radical response was to go in via Lindi, a tiny port due east on the coast of Tanganyika (Tanzania) that consisted of little more than a wharf that could take no more than one or two small boats. This meant that the transport ships had to anchor offshore while the equipment was ferried ashore on landing craft.

With no time to waste, the most urgent items – including over 100 tonnes of ploughs, harrows, seed planters, winches, brick-making and other essential equipment – were then transported from Lindi to Lake Malawi in a flying boat chartered from the British Overseas Airways Corporation, the first time a flying boat had ever landed on the lake.

The rest of the equipment went overland in a convoy of fourteen tractor-towed trailers and one 4.5-tonne truck under the command of Major-General Thomas Wynford 'Tiger' Reece. In a graphically written report, engineer Stan Phipson recorded how the 800 kilometre route mostly followed a narrow dirt track through a remote and sparsely populated region, through rivers that had neither bridges nor even proper fords and down the steep Great Rift Valley escarpment where German engineers had cut a track during the First World War. The convoy then crossed Lake Malawi from Mbamba Bay to Nkhata Bay in a lake steamer, having first had to construct special loading and unloading jetties at each end, and then went on to complete the final stage of the journey up to CDC's headquarters at Mzuzu and on to Viphya Tung. The entire operation took several weeks and was heralded in the British press under the headline: '508-mile Trail Blazed In Africa To Aid Colonial Development'.

Above: The Lindi Convoy moving down one of the more user-friendly stretches of road en route to Mzuzu via Mbamba Bay.

Above: Members of the CDC team at Lindi assembling one of the two-wheeled trailers, which, pulled by tractors and Thames trucks, formed part of the Lindi Convoy.

Above: The flying boat that was chartered from the British Overseas Airways Corporation pictured at Nkhata Bay on Lake Malawi where it dropped off cargo, some of which is visible in the foreground, that was transported onward to Mzuzu by the Lindi Convoy.

Lake Victoria and Fort George Hotels

CDC realised early on that if development was to take off anywhere at all, visiting business people and government officials needed decent places to stay.

In 1949 its Hotels Division investigated twenty separate hotel projects around the world, a couple of investigative tours having confirmed that the standard of colonial hotels was sadly lacking. In Uganda, the government had already come to the same conclusion and when no private sector investment was forthcoming it had started to build a sprawling white crescent-shaped sixty-bedroom hotel that benefited from a spectacular setting on the Entebbe peninsula that jutted out into Lake Victoria. Lake Victoria Hotel (top) opened its doors for business on 1 August 1949, by which time CDC had agreed to take the controlling interest. A year later, CDC took over the management.

In 1953, after three profitable years, CDC sold its shares to the Uganda Development Corporation at a twenty-five per cent premium to cost, at the same time relinquishing its management responsibilities.

Taking into account the dividends received by CDC, this was an early example of a financially successful exit that also met its development objectives. Today, an internet search describes it so: "Spacious and elegant, entirely refurbished and redecorated, this classic colonial style four-star property is a true oasis of tranquillity. It nestles in lush tropical gardens, amidst majestic Royal palm trees, while its verandas and terraces overlook the calm beauty of Lake Victoria".

Elsewhere, CDC built and managed the Fort George Hotel (left) in British Honduras, now Belize. Located on Fort George Island, the site of an old British fort, and opened in 1953, the Fort George was the country's first hotel. Aimed at attracting tourists as well as business visitors it got off to a slow start and was never quite as busy in the early years as had been hoped.

A few tourists, mostly Americans, would stay there in the months between January and April and otherwise it catered mainly for visiting businessmen, oil prospectors, loggers and the like. Princess Margaret, Her Majesty Queen Elizabeth II's late sister, dined there a couple of times during a visit to the colony in 1958 and nearly thirty years later, in 1986, Harrison Ford stayed there while filming *The Mosquito Coast*, an event commemorated with a plaque in the bedroom he occupied.

The entire film crew were also accommodated there and for six months the hotel enjoyed full occupancy as a result. What's more, the publicity helped to put Belize on the tourist map, giving the Fort George a new lease of life. Paul Hunt, who had been CDC's manager there for fifteen years, then bought ownership and, having expanded the accommodation with the help of a loan from CDC, continued to run it until 1990 after which it became the Radisson Fort George Hotel and Marina. CDC's remaining association ended in 1994 when its last loan was repaid.

Guyana Timbers

Greenheart timber, found mostly in Guyana's tropical rainforest, is one of the world's rarest and toughest hardwoods, much in demand at one time for use in building jetties, wharves and docks because of its unique salt water-resistant qualities. It also provided the foundation for one of CDC's earliest and, at the time, largest investments.

British Guiana Timbers was formed in 1951 and, managed for CDC by Steel Brothers, a British conglomerate based in Burma, (now Myanmar). It started by harvesting greenheart, purpleheart and other hardwoods from 38,000 hectares of forest at Manaka (see left), later moving on to the 130,000-hectare Bartica Triangle. The project also involved the construction of what was to be the biggest sawmill in South America at Houston, near Georgetown (see above).

By 1953, BGT was exporting 16,000 tonnes of timber annually and, to this day, greenheart can be found in old docks from the US to the UK.

Two years later, CDC took over the management of the business from Steel Brothers, who dropped out following political unrest and uprisings against British rule. Shortly after that, CDC refocused the business and, in 1959, began manufacturing pre-fabricated wooden houses that were sold not only in Guyana itself but all over the West Indies.

BGT became Guyana Timbers following independence in 1966 but CDC continued to provide management until 1971 when the socialist government started nationalising businesses, at which point it was transferred to the Guyana State Corporation.

Meanwhile, CDC had also been involved in developing housing estates through two other managed businesses – the Guyana Housing and Development Co Ltd and the Guyana Mortgage Finance Co Ltd. Between 1967-76 it was responsible for several new estates in Georgetown and New Amsterdam (see below left), that altogether featured nearly 2,000 of the famous pre-fabricated homes. Elsewhere in Guyana it also built an apartment block and several other smaller housing developments.

Other investments around the world included the rehabilitation of the abaca plantations in North Borneo. After early problems, Borneo Abaca Ltd went on, as BAL Plantations, to become one of CDC's largest and most successful long-term managed businesses, eventually sold on after fifty years for a good return. In Singapore, the Federal and Colonial Building Society, the predecessor of the Malaysia Building Society and Singapura Finance, started making home loans available in those regions for the first time, catering primarily for the needs of aspiring clerical and professional people and thereby helping to encourage not only home ownership but also political stability. In neighbouring Malaya (now Malaysia), a large loan was made to the electricity board at a time when few financial institutions were lending to the state, due to the ongoing Malayan Emergency.

Despite quite a few such positive and commendable achievements and several other investments that were to survive and go on after early setbacks to become significant long-term successes in the future, these early years were written off as pretty much of a disaster and came to be recalled with horror even by CDC itself. At the time, Prime Minister Clement Attlee declared himself 'unhappy' with the progress that had been made; there were debates in Parliament, an official government inquiry was launched and Trefgarne was eventually put in a position where he felt he had no option but to resign.

The reasons for much of the negativity that eventually overwhelmed this honourable man were rooted in two conspicuously disastrous failures that coloured everybody's perception of CDC and what it was trying to achieve – this despite the fact that CDC had nothing to do with the more notorious of the two failed enterprises.

Above: An aerial view of the Chilanga Cement factory in Zambia. CDC's involvement with Chilanga lasted from 1948 to 2001 – one of its longest-lasting investments during which it took over management on three separate occasions at various stages of the company's development.

Right: Workers inside the factory stacking bags of cement as they come off the production line. At its peak, production ran at 500,000 tonnes per annum.

Chilanga Cement

CDC's involvement with Chilanga Cement lasted fifty-three years and spanned seven decades between the late 1940s and the New Millennium – a long-running saga with many ups and downs and twists and turns leading eventually to a happy ending.

The story began way back in 1948 in what was then Northern Rhodesia when the CDC board under Trefgarne agreed to provide seventy-five per cent of the equity of the new company and to construct and manage the plant at Chilanga, in the limestone hills south of Lusaka.

The plant was officially declared opened for business by the colonial governor in 1951, with the general manager, Brigadier Clifford Brazier, sitting behind a desk draped with the Union Jack, the event covered on the radio by the Central African Broadcasting Services.

After some early operational teething problems, Chilanga got off to a good start, making an annual profit in its first full year, and was soon looking to expand with the construction of a second kiln. However, Lord Reith, who had taken over from Trefgarne by this time, didn't have great confidence in CDC's management capability generally and decided that if the expansion was to go ahead, then private sector partners would have to be sought. As a result CDC, in 1954, duly reduced its equity stake to forty per cent and relinquished management control, which passed to the Premier Portland Cement Company (Rhodesia), based in Bulawayo in Southern Rhodesia.

Boosted by winning the contracts to supply the cement for the construction of the Kariba Dam wall in 1957 and 1959, Chilanga went from strength to strength until the mid-sixties when independence for Northern Rhodesia as Zambia, followed by Ian Smith's Unilateral Declaration of Independence (UDI) in Southern Rhodesia, caused major political problems. Zambia could not allow Southern Rhodesia-based Premier Portland's management to continue and bought out its shares.

Anxious to protect its own substantial investment, CDC then stepped in and offered to take over the management itself once again. This arrangement lasted from 1966 until 1969 when President Kenneth Kaunda arbitrarily appointed his own executive chairman. CDC took a back seat, although continued to second financial staff and to provide financial consultancy, and encouraged nationalisation in 1973. Even then, with its own holding further diluted to twenty-four per cent, CDC continued to provide financial support through a twenty-year period of steady decline that was caused mainly by a general economic slump.

Then, in 1993, following the fall of Kaunda and his replacement by President Frederick Chiluba, the new Zambian government embraced the trend towards privatisation and offered to sell its shares to CDC, which took over management for the third time, installing an ex-Blue Circle man as general manager.

Two years later, Chilanga became the first company to be listed on the newly-opened Lusaka Stock Exchange. CDC went on to refurbish Chilanga's plant over the next five years, operating to high environmental and social standards and providing a role model for other large Zambian businesses. It initiated community programmes such as HIV/AIDS prevention and treatment while also sponsoring eleven university undergraduates.

Having also taken control of two other privatised cement companies – Malawi's Portland Cement and Tanzania's Mbeya Cement – CDC then combined the three to form the Pan African Cement group in 2000 and this was bought by Lafarge (now LafargeHolcim) in 2001, yielding a good return on investment. Fifteen years later CDC then re-established its connection with the new owners, launching a joint venture in Malawi – 14Trees – to produce affordable low carbon housing materials.

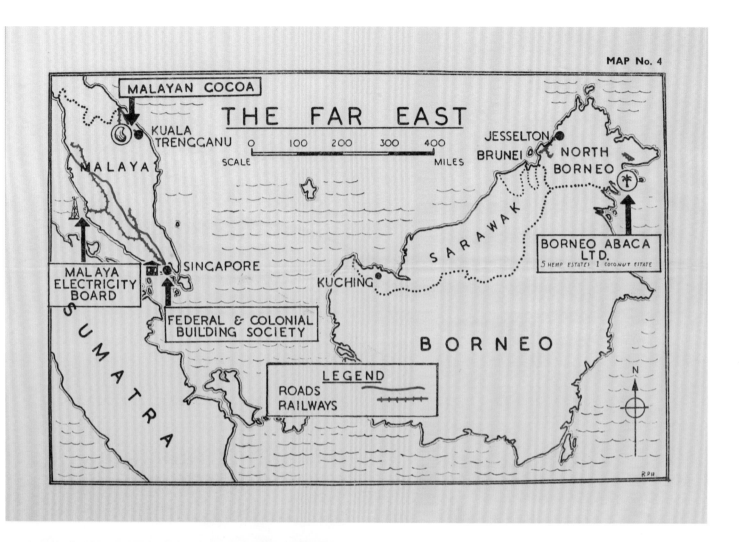

THE FAR EAST

MALAYAN COCOA

KUALA TRENGGANU

SCALE 0 100 200 300 400 MILES

MALAYA

JESSELTON
BRUNEI
NORTH BORNEO

SARAWAK

MALAYA ELECTRICITY BOARD

SINGAPORE

KUCHING

BORNEO ABACA LTD.
5 HEMP ESTATES 1 COCONUT ESTATE

FEDERAL & COLONIAL BUILDING SOCIETY

S U M A T R A

B O R N E O

LEGEND
ROADS
RAILWAYS

N

R.P.H.

Top: A map showing the location of CDC's investments in the Malay Peninsula and Borneo at the end of 1949.

Above: Abaca stems being loaded onto a train at BAL Plantations for transportation to the mill.

Borneo Abaca Ltd (BAL Plantations)

Tawau in North Borneo (Sabah) was about as remote a place in the 1940s as one could imagine. Until operations started in the South Pacific there was nowhere in CDC's world further away from London, apart from the Falkland Islands.

The small town of Tawau was tucked away in the south east corner of the colony, facing the Celebes Sea, close to Dutch-controlled Kalimantan and the westernmost Philippines. It existed to support the few large rubber, hemp and coconut plantations in the area, developed originally by the Japanese but then severely damaged during the war. Outside the town of Tawau all was sea and virgin rainforest. No roads led across the interior to the capital, Jesselton (Kota Kinabalu). A letter from Singapore could take nineteen days to arrive.

CDC heard about the five hemp estates put up for sale by the Custodian for Enemy Property and, in 1948, bought a stake with another partner, the Hong Kong Transportation Co. The estates were neglected and diseased but manila hemp, also known as abaca, was in short supply around the world. Most of it was produced in the Philippines, which meant that dollars were required to buy it – and dollars were also in short supply. From what were very unpromising beginnings, CDC developed an extraordinarily successful, pioneering managed business. Borneo Abaca Ltd, which became BAL Plantations, planted primarily with oil palms, was only sold nearly fifty years later in 1996.

Above: Processes involved in the production of manila hemp from the abaca plant include first stripping and 'decorticating' (cleaning) the fibres from the large leaves of the plant, which can be up to four metres long.

Right: The fibres are then hung across drying poles in the open air.

The infamous Groundnuts Scheme was actually down to the Overseas Food Corporation, but confusion arose partly because the OFC had been created by the same Act of Parliament that created CDC. Originally conceived by Unilever in 1946 and then passed on to the OFC by the Ministry of Food, the idea of the Groundnuts Scheme was to cultivate one million hectares of land in central Tanganyika (Tanzania) to grow peanuts and other crops, the peanuts to be used to produce much-needed vegetable oil for Britain. The government earmarked £25 million for the project, a huge sum at the time, while demobbed soldiers volunteered to join the 'Groundnut Army'.

However, a lethal combination of poor infrastructure, inadequate planning and growing trials, inappropriate equipment for land development and cultivation, natural disasters, inexperience, unrealistic targets and rising costs ensured that it was a mighty failure, with losses rising to a staggering £49 million. It turned out to be the only major project ever undertaken by the Overseas Food Corporation, which had disappeared altogether by the mid-fifties.

CDC almost inevitably found that it was tarred with the same brush, especially after its own first grand design – Gambia Eggs – then turned out to be just as much of a fiasco. The idea, which came from Trefgarne himself, was to set up a large-scale poultry farm in Africa's smallest country, with 200,000 chickens producing twenty million eggs a year that would mostly be shipped back to the UK for consumption by a grateful public who had been starved of their favourite breakfast food for nearly a decade. This would meet CDC's aims of developing the economies of the colonies while at the same time producing much-needed food for Britain.

Trefgarne had seen a smaller but similar scheme in operation in the Bahamas during a visit there in the early months of 1948 and thought it would be ideal for the Gambia, whose governor had been one of those who responded most keenly to the circular sent out shortly before CDC was formally established, calling for project suggestions. On a wave of unbridled enthusiasm, the plan was cleared in principle at the very first CDC board meeting in March 1948 and approved two months later.

Just like the Groundnuts Scheme, it foundered on inexperience and lack of proper planning and trials. There was a host of unforeseen problems – land clearance causing erosion, pests affecting the crops that were to provide feed for the birds, disease killing the poultry, reproduction difficulties, refrigeration breakdowns and maintenance and marketing disasters, with the UK market rejecting 'dirty' eggs that resulted from faults in the nesting system. The press got hold of the story and put the boot in. *The Financial Times* was especially damning: "The Colonial Development Corporation is busily trying to turn the colony of Gambia into an egg farm but it would be easier and less costly to raise poultry on the pavements of Piccadilly than on the sour soil of Gambia."

"Trefgarne's energy, enthusiasm and commitment to CDC were never in doubt. He had been 'immersed continuously and without leisure in all its affairs, great and small, for three years', travelling 100,000 kilometres on CDC business worldwide at a time when the scheduled airline flight from London to Singapore took an exhausting fifty-one hours."

The scheme was soon abandoned with losses of over £1 million and shortly afterwards the entire flock was wiped out by an epidemic of Newcastle Disease. Only the large and well-built abandoned hen houses were left, to be converted later into barracks-style residential accommodation. The level of criticism, ridicule and widespread bad publicity that this unfortunate debacle attracted effectively drew attention away from the good work that had been done elsewhere. It could easily have led to the demise of CDC almost before it had got off the ground, just as the Groundnuts Scheme had done for the Overseas Food Corporation. As it was, it hastened the resignation of Trefgarne who left in October 1950, so shattered by the bitter attacks made on him and CDC that he felt compelled to make a personal statement to the House of Lords.

Trefgarne's energy, enthusiasm and commitment to CDC were never in doubt. In his letter of resignation he wrote that he had been 'immersed continuously and without leisure in all its affairs, great and small, for three years', travelling 100,000 kilometres on CDC business worldwide at a time when the scheduled airline flight from London to Singapore took an exhausting fifty-one hours. If anything, he had been guilty only of trying to do too much too quickly. He had also been perhaps too bold in his approach, preferring venture to caution.

Above: The front cover of the Overseas Food Corporation Annual Report for 1951-52.

Below: A map showing the distance and journey times involved in getting to various CDC operations around the world in 1949. Even by air, it could take days to get to some of the more remote destinations in those early days.

Above: A picture of the Nyika forestry plantation trials at Chilinda in 2007.

Above: The remote Nyika Plateau in the far north of Malawi where, with the help of Laurens van der Post, CDC investigated the possibility of setting up a forestry project in the fifties, to serve a pulp and paper industry, only to abandon the idea when it became clear that it was just too far off the beaten track to be a practical proposition. The building shown in the picture is now used for eco-tourist accommodation, while the trees planted experimentally by CDC remain as a lasting monument.

Below: Another shot of the wonderfully remote Nyika Plateau, Malawi's first National Park, photographed in 1983 and showing the trial plantations.

Laurens van der Post and the Lost World of Nyika

Above: Laurens van der Post's book *Venture To The Interior*, which helped to make his name as an explorer, writer and philosopher and which was based on the recce of the Nyika Plateau and also of Mount Mulanje, in the south of what was still then Nyasaland, that he carried out for CDC in 1949.

One of CDC's more fanciful proposed ventures in the very early years revolved around the 'lost world' of the Nyika Plateau in what was then Nyasaland (now Malawi) and also involved the South African writer, explorer, thinker and friend of HRH The Prince of Wales, Laurens van der Post.

A cool grassland plateau, 2,600 metres high and often shrouded in clouds, the Nyika was uninhabited and regarded superstitiously by the local people. The governor suggested that it might be suitable for a livestock project of some kind and CDC asked van der Post to do a recce and report back. He spent three weeks exploring the area and was fascinated by it, describing it as having "a sort of Rider Haggard, a King Solomon's Mines, a Queen of Sheba touch about it..."

In his report he said that it reminded him of the English Cotswolds, the moors of Devon and the fells of Northumberland all rolled into one and he was very positive about its potential for development. Later, a CDC team of experts went out to have a look and decided that rather than livestock, it would be better suited to forestry.

A Nyika Forestry Development Syndicate was put together with Albert E. Reed & Co and Imperial Tobacco, two companies involved respectively in paper production and paper use, but in the end the project was abandoned. This was partly because no practical ways could be found for a pulp mill to be sited nearby but also because van der Post, in his book *Venture To The Interior*, focused public attention on the conservation of flora, fauna and natural environments which led to the formation of the country's first National Park. A trial patch of forest plantation the size of Hyde Park remains there to this day in what is otherwise an unspoilt eco-tourist attraction.

Following his visit to Nyika, van der Post went on to carry out other missions for CDC, in northern Bechuanaland (Botswana), where he was an enthusiastic supporter of CDC's Bechuanaland Cattle Ranch. His famed book *The Lost World of the Kalahari*, published in 1958, was as influential on public opinion as his 'Venture To The Interior', helping to inspire the creation of the Central Kalahari Game Reserve in what is now Botswana in 1961.

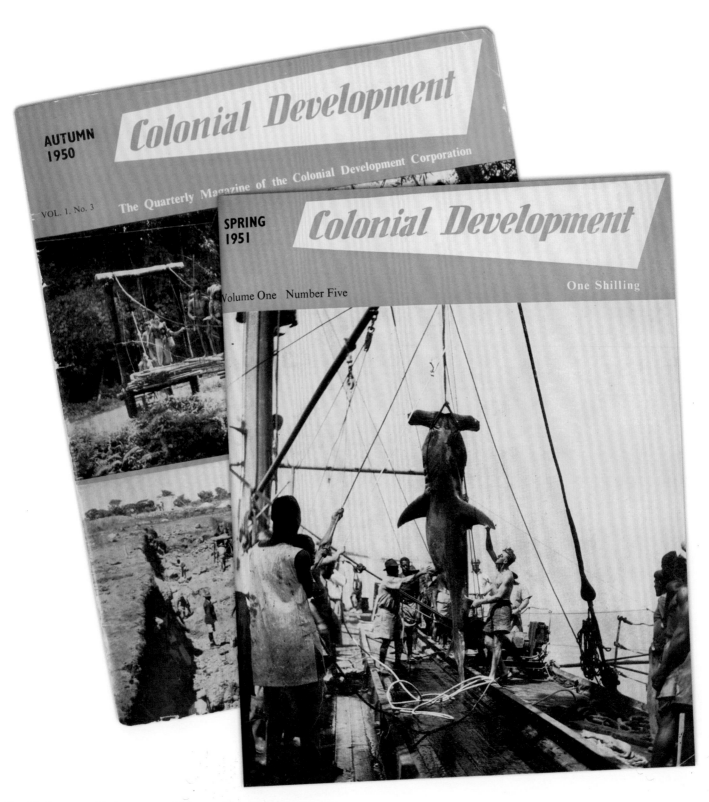

Above: The front covers of the Autumn 1950 and Spring 1951 editions of 'Colonial Development' magazine, the latter showing shark fishing off the coast of the Gambia aboard the factory ship that was rather romantically named 'The African Queen'. The project was not a success.

Under his direction, CDC had entered into a lot of often grandiose schemes at a fast pace, trying to run before it could walk while operating with a staff that was just as enthusiastic as he was, but lacking in experience in many areas. Although the Gambia Eggs debacle stood out as by far the most seriously damaging and heavily publicised mistake, there had been plenty of other false starts and failures. Money had been wasted and criticism had mounted.

The Financial Times of 17 April 1950, for instance, commented scathingly: "Their crazy experiments (in timber production in British Guiana) are worthy of the Groundnutters. This is but one of their many follies." As it happens, although a great deal of money was invested in British Guiana Timbers without any great initial return, which was the reason for the FT's scorn, that particular project did eventually establish itself as a very solid and sustainable venture with which CDC remained involved for more than twenty years.

The same could not be said about some other so-called 'follies' such as the Falkland Island Freezer Co Ltd (processing and freezing for export Falkland Islands sheep and cattle that were reared solely for hides, wool and sheepskin and that were otherwise discarded after slaughter), the South Atlantic Sealing Company (processing seals and sea lions for oil) and Atlantic Fisheries.

The latter, also based in the Gambia, involved a factory ship, romantically renamed the *African Queen*, which was to process sharks, tuna and crawfish caught off the west coast of Africa. The 2,000-tonne vessel was bought in Denmark before being towed across the North Sea to Grimsby to be fitted out with facilities for quick freezing, cold storage, canning, oil extraction, fillet drying and fish meal production, the fish meal to be used as feed in the ill-fated poultry farm.

Launched in 1950, the project went under a year later just as the film The African Queen, based on the C.S. Forester novel and starring Humphrey Bogart and Katharine Hepburn, was released. The problem was that the 1951 fishing season turned out to be disastrous; although shark catches were above what had been expected, the price of vitamin A oil, which is extracted from sharks' liver and which was to have been the main source of revenue, fell sharply. At the same time, tuna and crawfish proved elusive. Faced with this double whammy CDC decided to cut its losses, which by then already amounted to over £1 million.

Gambia Rice Farms, meanwhile, produced yet another embarrassing failure in the Gambia. The plan was for a large scale 5,700-hectare paddy field development on two swamps at Pachari and Kudang on the Gambia river that was to include an irrigation scheme. Delays and problems with the irrigation works and heavy flooding in the wet season of 1950, when an initial rice crop was washed away, led to the whole operation being scaled down and then abandoned altogether two years later. Again, losses ran into seven figures.

In the end, the barrage of criticism that came CDC's way as a result of these and other failures – 'abuse' was the word used by the editor of CDC's quarterly magazine, *Colonial Development* to describe the relentless sniping – brought about Trefgarne's resignation in October 1950 after he had served his minimum term. He had simply worn himself out in the cause. And although he had undoubtedly presided over mistakes, it is also a fact that during his time in control a string of major undertakings had been initiated that were to become some of CDC's greatest long term developmental and financial success stories.

Above: A map of the Gambia, showing the locations of the equally ill-fated Gambia Poultry Farm and Gambia Rice Farms.

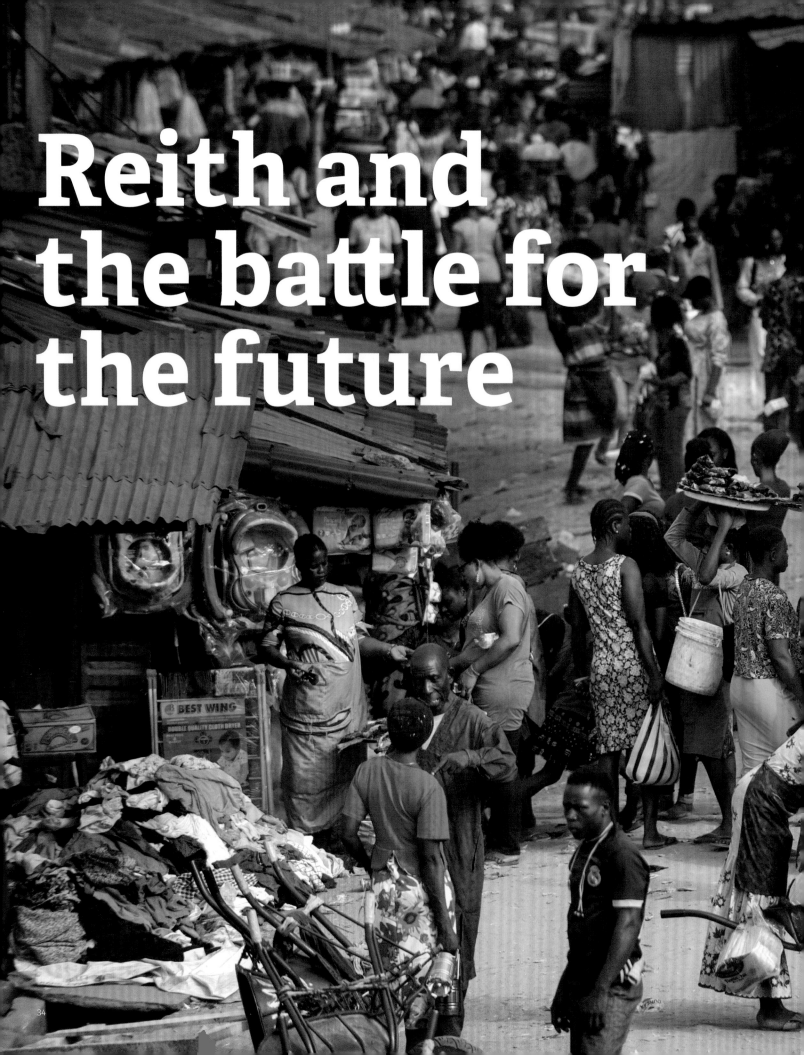

Reith and the battle for the future

1950–1959

Reith and the battle for the future 1950–1959

World events...

1951

- Sir Winston Churchill takes over from Clement Attlee. It is Churchill's second time as British prime minister.

1952

- Britain's King George VI dies of lung cancer. His daughter, Elizabeth II, succeeds him.
- Killer fogs in London from coal fires lead to the coining of the word 'smog' and the appreciation of the need to clean up London's air.

1953–54

- Mt. Everest is climbed by Sir Edmund Hillary and Tenzing Norgay in 1953.
- Britain creates the Central African Federation in 1953, consisting of Southern Rhodesia (Zimbabwe), Northern Rhodesia (Zambia) and Nyasaland (Malawi).

1955

- Anthony Eden becomes British prime minister.
- The Warsaw Pact is formed.

CDC events...

- CDC's regional office for Central Africa transfers to Salisbury, Rhodesia.
- Singapore Factory Development Ltd is set up to establish and finance industrial estates: managed by CDC, it is successful and is sold in 1973.
- The CDC Engineering Ltd depot is established at Eynsham in the British Midlands, occupying a disused sugar beet factory with a railway siding connected to the Fairford branch line. Here it marshals purchases of heavy equipment and other supplies before despatching them to the ports and their destinations overseas.

- Molopo Ranch, Bechuanaland (now Botswana) started by CDC: it will become one of the largest cattle ranches in southern Africa.

- William Rendell is appointed as general manager in 1953.
- CDC's regional office for High Commission Territories in Southern Africa opens in Johannesburg in 1954. CDC is not given permission to work in South Africa until 1994.

- In its accounts, CDC declares a surplus for the first time. It continues to do this, 'doing good without losing money', every year until 1998.
- CDC's regional office for the Caribbean opens in Bridgetown, Barbados, transferred from Kingston.

Right: A market in urban Nigeria. In 1959 CDC set up the Development Finance Co Ltd in Nigeria. This was one of the first of many local development finance companies established between then and 1972 in the Northern and Eastern Regions of Nigeria, and elsewhere in Sierra Leone, Borneo, Malaya, Fiji, Tanganyika, Kenya and Uganda. Controlled by local boards, with ownership shared with the local governments, and with participation also from other newly-formed national DFIs, Devcos enabled support to be given to the establishment and expansion of hundreds of small and medium-sized businesses. CDC was among the first of the foreign institutions to provide finance for SMEs, a pioneering initiative later extended to include support for the millions of low-income but would-be entrepreneurs through the provision of microfinance.

1956

- *The International Finance Corporation is established by the World Bank, itself set up in 1946.*
- *The first transatlantic telephone cable system from Newfoundland to Scotland is inaugurated.*
- *The Suez Crisis erupts after Egypt's nationalisation of the Suez Canal.*

- The Colonial Office tells CDC not to look for new investments in colonial countries due to become independent, introducing a period of uncertainty ending only in 1963.
- CDC helps to establish FELDA, the Federal Land Development Authority, Malaya (now Malaysia) which will become one of the world's most successful settlement schemes.

1957

- *Harold Macmillan takes over as Britain's prime minister.*
- *Malaya achieves independence from Britain.*
- *Gold Coast and British Togoland achieve independence from Britain as Ghana.*

- Swaziland Irrigation Scheme's Mhlume Water is opened by King Sobhuza II - a weir and canal bringing water from the Komati River to irrigate Swaziland's lowvelt.

1958

- *Treaties establishing the European Economic Community come into effect.*

- Office opens in Kuala Lumpur, Malaya.
- Development Finance Co Ltd set up in Nigeria: it is one of many development finance corporations managed by CDC, focussing on encouraging smaller businesses.
- Borneo Development Corporation is set up by CDC: it will develop and finance residential, commercial and industrial developments in Sarawak and Sabah.

1959

- *The Inter-American Development Bank is formed to assist in promoting social and economic development in Latin America and the Caribbean, from its base in Washington.*
- *Russia's unmanned spacecraft, Lunik II, reaches the moon.*

- Lord Reith retires as chairman and is replaced by Sir Nutcombe Hume.
- Office opens in Dar es Salaam, Tanganyika.

Chapter two

Reith and the battle for the future

CDC under Lord Trefgarne had come to be perceived with increasing alarm by the mandarins at the Colonial Office as being out of control. Fearing that they had unwittingly created a free-spending monster that was in danger of running loose, they were in no doubt at all that with Trefgarne out of the way, a strong and trusted pair of hands was needed to rein it in and keep it on a tight leash. The man appointed by Attlee to impose the required discipline was Lord Reith.

Reith, who had made a legendary name for himself as the founding managing director and later director-general of the BBC, was just about as different from Trefgarne as it was possible to be. At a craggy six-foot-seven-inches tall (two metres), the great Scot was a larger-than-life figure in a very literal sense, a towering, glowering, humourless son of the manse who arrived at Dover Street with a fearsome reputation as a ruthless and unbending disciplinarian, prone to terrible rages and almost childish sulks but with a rigid commitment to the highest ideals of enlightened public service.

The Observer newspaper greeted his appointment with the comment: "Where in our mild, modern community could one find a man possessing the technical and social standards of today and the peculiar caste of mind of the great imperial pioneers? In selecting Lord Reith to be chairman of the CDC, Mr Attlee has shown great insight of the man and the job."

"Reith, who had made a legendary name for himself as the founding managing director and later director-general of the BBC, was just about as different from Trefgarne as it was possible to be."

Above: Boats on the Kuching River. CDC opened the offices of the Borneo Development Corporation in Kuching in 1958.

Lord Reith

Reith truly was a legend in his own lifetime, the adjective 'Reithian' having already become part of the language to describe high moral public service values to enlighten and educate, while the annual Reith Lecture was established in his honour as early as 1948.

Born in 1889, the son of the Very Reverend George Reith DD, moderator of the Free Church of Scotland, John Charles Walsham Reith had a stern and austere upbringing that formed his character.

Severely wounded and very nearly killed in the trenches in 1916, he survived to establish the BBC in 1922 – some say in his own image – and ran it for sixteen years with structures redolent of the Free Church of Scotland. After leaving in 1938 he was briefly chairman of Imperial Airways before going into politics as MP for Southampton in 1940 and then serving as minister of works in Churchill's wartime government.

Those who worked with him in CDC recall him with a mixture of awe, wonder, trepidation and admiration. William Rendell, who worked closely with him as general manager wrote: "Reith did not encourage overt expressions of affection". By all accounts, that was something of an understatement. His long-standing PA was one of the few people able to penetrate the steely and rather intimidating exterior, which she did by treating him rather like a pet.

He revealed to one senior colleague that he believed in 'timor parentis' – fear of the parent – and that seemed to dictate his attitude to most of those who worked for him. There are endless anecdotes about him from his time at CDC. David Fiennes who was regional controller in the Far East under Reith, recalled asking him once whether he had enjoyed a particular function that they had attended together.

"Mr Fiennes, I never enjoy" he growled. Some time later, they were again together on a tour of the Far East and after an especially pleasant evening in Kuching, Sarawak, including a memorable sampan trip across the Kuching River during which Reith appeared unusually animated, Fiennes commented that he was glad to see that he had enjoyed it after all. "Mr Fiennes, I will admit I was interested," he conceded.

As well as rages, tantrums and a tendency towards puritanical excess, he was also occasionally given to childish sulks. Returning earlier than expected from an overseas visit, he was apparently so devastated to find that his secretaries had not had time to provide the customary 'Welcome Home' cake that he retreated into a state of high dudgeon, pointedly refusing his regular morning coffee. And when he walked into a senior manager's office to be confronted by a sketch portrait hanging on the wall of Winston Churchill, with whom he had fallen out badly while serving in the wartime government, he reacted as if he had suffered a sudden seizure, sinking into a chair and pointing to the offending artwork with a hoarse cry of: "How dare you do this to me!" The picture had to be turned to the wall and its immediate destruction promised before he was able to regain his composure.

Widely credited, despite such eccentricities, as the man who rescued CDC from early extinction during his nine years as chairman, he went on to take up a number of company directorships as well as the vice-chairmanship of British Oxygen, later becoming rector of Glasgow University and Lord High Commissioner of the General Assembly of the Church of Scotland. He died in 1971 at the age of 81.

Reith started work on 9 November 1950 and having had a look through the books, as it were, declared himself to be utterly horrified by what he found. He accused his predecessor of "shocking bad management", his contempt for Trefgarne further reflected later on when he pointedly omitted to mention him by name at any point in his annual report for the year 1950. In a diary entry in January 1951 he expressed his "considerable disgust and concern about the state of affairs in CDC". Management controls were "farcical", he wrote, going on later to complain: "Each day I seem to come on some new sickness in CDC – some new underestimate, disloyalty, grumble or failure. I wish I could find occasional things to praise or even to feel relatively easy about."

Based on these damning assessments, he then embarked in characteristically rigorous fashion on a comprehensive root and-branch reform of the entire CDC set-up, streamlining the management structure, reducing the workforce, closing down unprofitable operations within the business and generally getting rid of any dead wood.

Starting at the top, he separated the functions of the board and general management and launched a new organisational structure that delegated power to regional controllers and laid an emphasis on individual accountability and responsibility while at the same time introducing rigid financial and overall policy controls at the centre. The board was to decide policy and give formal approval to investments but would leave the rest to management. The chief executive would not be a member of the board but would have delegated powers to manage day-to-day operations, advised by his Executive Management Board, known as EMB.

As well as the chief executive and the deputy chairman, EMB included the four head office controllers (administration, commercial, finance and operations) and five regional controllers (the Caribbean, West Africa, East Africa, Central Africa and the Far East).

At the same time, the earlier Commercial Operating Divisions were scrapped. They had been headed by technical experts whose abilities to run a business enterprise were scathingly dismissed by Reith with the comment that "in general, the more technically expert people are, the less commercially and managerially experienced or even intelligent they tend to be". These experts were therefore put firmly in their place, relegated to purely advisory roles under the commercially-minded controllers.

As ever with Reith, who acted as both chairman and chief executive of CDC for the first three years of his reign, control was everything. Nothing went to the board except through EMB. Its deliberations were recorded in detail, becoming the case law of CDC, widely circulated to the staff in offices throughout the organisation in such a way that everybody gradually absorbed management thinking. In what was a far-flung organisation this was an effective means of communication, although it did tend to encourage toeing the line rather than blue skies thinking.

The rationalisation of the management structure contributed towards the cost-cutting that was also high on Reith's agenda. Within four years of him taking over, the head office staff had been more than halved, down from 340 to 168, thereby reducing annual costs by forty per cent from £340,000 to £200,000. At the same time, seventeen of the projects that had been started under Trefgarne were dropped, most of them in the Caribbean and West Africa.

First to go, not surprisingly, was the Gambia Eggs Scheme, swiftly axed in February 1951. Even this prompt action wasn't enough to stem the tide of criticism of CDC's early performance that came mainly on two counts: its failure to undertake experimental or pilot schemes before launching full-scale undertakings and also the sheer variety and apparently random selection of the businesses in which it had chosen to invest – "Tropical Allsorts" as one member of the House of Lords colourfully and disparagingly referred to them.

"Within four years of Lord Reith taking over, the head office staff had been more than halved, down from 340 to 168, thereby reducing annual costs by 40 per cent from £340,000 to £200,000."

Reith responded by sending out teams worldwide to conduct thorough investigations into the prospects of all the less promising enterprises, the board then weeding out the no-hopers. 'Redding up' – the Scottish equivalent of 'spring cleaning' – was the term Reith himself used to describe this process of clearing out and tidying up the portfolio.

As far as any new investments were concerned, strict criteria for acceptance were introduced. Small-scale trials were to be mandatory wherever possible and these were to be monitored as closely as any full-scale undertaking, the Nyika Forestry Development Syndicate being one of the first examples of this new procedure in action.

Experienced management was to be an essential requirement and, in practice, this normally meant going to the private sector, those involved being encouraged to take a small stake in ownership as a demonstration of their commitment. For the same reason, colonial governments would also be urged to invest financially alongside CDC or at least to provide aid in support of basic infrastructure such as roads and bridges.

Having successfully re-structured the management, slimmed down the staff, cut costs and got rid of fanciful and loss-making projects, Reith turned his attention to CDC's finances. A report at the end of 1951 by auditors Peats (now KPMG) had confirmed the importance of setting up a better system of financial control within the new-look organisation.

After a lengthy search, accountant William Rendell was finally identified as the right man for the job and was appointed controller of finance in August 1952. However, he so impressed Reith that he was promoted to be chief executive a year later. Preferring the title general manager, he was to hold that position for the next twenty years.

Rendell was strong and capable with a personality every bit as forceful as that of Reith himself and a manner that could be equally abrasive, and yet instead of clashing, as might have been expected, the two men almost immediately established a mutual trust and respect. Sharing the same vision for CDC, they complemented each other perfectly to become a formidable double act – Reith setting the overall political agenda and Rendell supplying the commercial and financial expertise.

Sir William Rendell

William Rendell was more than a match for Lord Reith when it came to being fearsomely abrupt.

It is said that when he was being interviewed for the job of controller of Finance at CDC he was asked by Reith what sort of salary he was looking for.

"£7,000-a-year," came the firm and instant response.

"But I only get £5,000 as full-time executive chairman!" exclaimed Reith, obviously somewhat taken aback.

"What has that got to do with it?" snapped Rendell.

Although anecdotal and possibly apocryphal, this story rings true to people who knew him well.

A chartered accountant and partner at Whinney, Murray and Co, he had been recommended as a likely candidate for the job by CDC's auditors, Peats. A tough, hard and sound businessman, blessed with vision and a good head for figures, he was also full of energy and had a very strong personality.

Passionate about the CDC mission, he was a serious individual whose forthright manner was by no means the only personality trait that he shared with Reith.

Among the ranks, neither of them was known for joviality and both could be very abrasive. And just like Reith, Rendell could be very intimidating, fixing people with a steely gaze from under thick black eyebrows.

It seems surprising that two such forceful characters should have been able to get along, but they did. And once Reith had left, Rendell then dominated the organisation until his retirement in 1973. Always keen to be one step ahead of his senior managers, he travelled the CDC world extensively so that he would know exactly what was going on.

Following his retirement, he wrote *The History of The Commonwealth Development Corporation* published in 1976. Knighted in 1967, his interests included fishing and duck-hunting, pursuits in which he indulged enthusiastically when on tour with CDC. He was always on the lookout for something to shoot – not just with a gun but also with a camera, being a keen photographer. He died in 1995, aged 86.

Left: The painted ceiling by James 'Athenian' Stuart that graced one of the rooms at CDC's offices at 33 Hill Street, part of which was once owned by the celebrated 18th century London socialite and intellectual Mrs Elizabeth Montagu, 'Queen of the Bluestockings'.

33 Hill Street

Shortly after Lord Reith's arrival, CDC moved its headquarters from 33 Dover Street to 33 Hill Street in Mayfair, another splendid location just off Berkeley Square and to the east of Park Lane. CDC later expanded into the neighbouring buildings, Grade II listed premises that boast a colourful history dating back to 1744, when one of the original houses was built for a wealthy socialite named Mrs Elizabeth Montagu. Mrs Montagu's intellectual and artistic soirees, attended by the likes of Dr Johnson, Boswell, Carrick, Walpole and Sir Joshua Reynolds, gained her a reputation as 'the Queen of the Bluestockings'. Clearly a woman of taste as well as substance, she commissioned both Robert Adam and his great rival James 'Athenian' Stuart as interior designers and Stuart's striking Zephyr ceiling painting still survives in what was originally her bedroom, used in CDC's time as the chairman's office.

The floors of the different houses were all on different levels so that the offices spread through a veritable rabbit warren of corridors, passages and stairways in which it was very easy to get lost.

Some of the ground and first floor rooms made magnificent offices for those in power but the rest of the staff often had to make do with partitioned rooms that had originally been servants' bedrooms, sculleries and the like.

Outside, the front door was guarded by William Blackman (right), the commissionaire, resplendent in his immaculate Corps of Commissionaires' uniform. Bill, who had been on duty with CDC since the day it opened for business at Dover Street in 1948 and who remained a permanent fixture on the door until 1975, was a real character, remembered by staff and visitors alike, all of whom would always invariably be welcomed with a courteous and professional greeting as they crossed his threshold.

Although very punctilious and correct, he was not afraid to speak his mind. Lord Reith was very fussy about the appearance of the building and hated untidy passageways. Bill, who would don his full uniform only when he reached the office used to hang his cap on the hat stand outside the boardroom. When asked to remove it as an 'unbecoming object' he declined, saying: "you wouldn't ask me to do this if it was a bowler!" And there it continued to hang.

Above: 33 Hill Street as it was in 1963, an illustrated
picture taken from the CDC Staff Bulletin front cover.

Top and above: The Kariba Dam under construction in 1958 (top). Most of the one million cubic metres of cement used in the dam wall was supplied by CDC-managed Chilanga Cement from its manufacturing plant near Lusaka (bottom).

Together, they steered CDC through a very tricky transitional period during which they successfully completed the major overhaul initiated by Reith that put it on a firm financial footing while simultaneously being subjected at almost every stage to increasingly hostile and malicious attacks from Whitehall.

Elements in the Colonial Office, in particular, remained steadfastly anti-CDC, regretting that it had ever been allowed to come into existence, jealous of its independence and convinced that they themselves could do a much better job. Given all this, the fact that Reith and Rendell were so conspicuously clever and effective only served to stoke up further resentment. Meanwhile, the change of government in 1951 didn't help CDC's cause either, since the Conservatives were naturally inclined to be unsupportive of anything that had been started by Labour. The situation here was made worse by the ill-feeling that existed between Churchill and Reith, Reith having held various posts in Churchill's wartime government before being sacked for being difficult to work with, prompting a later reference in his diary to "that bloody shit, Churchill".

Seeming to be constantly on the look-out for any opportunity to undermine and discredit CDC, the Colonial Office even seized on the new-found financial stability that had been achieved under Reith and Rendell and tried to turn this against them. In his annual report of 1955 Rendell was able to announce that CDC was into profit for the first time, showing a surplus after servicing its own loans from government and thereby satisfying one of the mandates set by its founding Act of Parliament. "Doing good without losing money" was the proud boast that became Reith's guiding maxim.

What the Colonial Office immediately found fault with here was the investment policy change that had made all this possible, namely a substantial switch from equity investments to loans. Mostly supported by guarantees from colonial governments, these loans had the twofold advantage of being less risky while also guaranteeing regular income. By the end of 1955 CDC had made nine such loans amounting to £12.4 million – a third of its entire portfolio – and earning more than enough in interest to cover the annual cost of servicing its own government loans.

For Reith and Rendell to have turned things around and balanced the books so soon after taking over an organisation that was in considerable disarray was a notable achievement, but the Colonial Office chose to take a less positive view, laying into CDC for becoming a 'finance house', no better than a bank, and accusing it of reneging on other elements in its mandate to do with the more hands-on developmental approach of initiating ideas, undertaking feasibility studies, establishing trials and generally setting up and managing fledgling greenfield enterprises.

This fundamental and often bitter dispute over exactly what CDC's role should be and where its priorities should lie in deciding how to go about satisfying the two often competing demands of doing good and making money is one that has raged on and off throughout much of the organisation's history, with the pendulum swinging to and fro at different times between the safety first of loans and the riskier, more adventurous option of managed projects and equity investments, although the portfolio has always contained a mixture of the two.

Despite the sniping from the Colonial Office, Reith and Rendell ably supported by controller of finance, Gren Totman, actually achieved a sound balance that looks even better with the benefit of hindsight. Major loans, most notably the enormous £15 million that went to finance the building of the Kariba Dam and its hydroelectricity power station (the equivalent of £340 million today and in real terms still one of CDC's biggest-ever loans) brought in the sort of income over many years that helped to support other, longer term developmental projects. With Kariba there was the added bonus that it also provided a hugely valuable spin-off for another, truly pioneering CDC enterprise, Chilanga Cement, which won the contract to supply the one million cubic metres of cement that went into the construction of what was, at the time, the largest-ever man-made dam wall. Chilanga went on to become one of CDC's longest-lasting industrial ventures.

The Kariba Dam

One of the largest dams in the world, Kariba was a truly massive project that took five years to complete and cost the lives of a hundred construction workers. Complicated from the start by the fact that one end of the dam was on the south bank of the Zambezi in Southern Rhodesia (Zimbabwe) and the other on the north bank in Northern Rhodesia (Zambia), the situation became politically and financially even more fraught following the end of the Central African Federation in 1963. At that point the assets and liabilities of Kariba had been transferred to the Central Africa Power Corporation, jointly-owned by the Rhodesian and Zambian governments. However, following Ian Smith's declaration of UDI in 1965, the Rhodesian government refused to pay CDC any interest on its loans or to make any repayments, a major problem considering the huge amount of the loan. It took considerable ingenuity to come up with a solution that involved a subtle recycling of the debt.

Above: Her Majesty Queen Elizabeth the Queen Mother inaugurates the Kariba hydroelectric scheme on 15 May 1960. Here Sir Duncan Anderson presents personnel associated with the underground power station to Her Majesty in the lift access gallery.

Above: The dam in operation in 1980, with the 600KW Kariba North Bank hydroelectric power station visible on the right.

Left: Inside one of Kariba's underground turbine halls.

Left: Alan Lennox-Boyd, MP, Secretary of State for the Colonies, inspecting the Mbeya Exploration Co Ltd's niobium mining operation at Panda Hill near Mbeya in Tanzania in October 1957 after officially opening the pilot mill there.

Mining in East Africa

At around the time in the early fifties when cinema audiences were flocking to see Stewart Granger and Deborah Kerr in the film version of Rider Haggard's 'King Solomon's Mines', CDC was busy conducting some adventurous mining and prospecting activities of its own in Africa.

During the three years between 1949 and 1952, exploratory teams were sent out into remote areas of what was then still Tanganyika to carry out mapping, drilling and sampling of the geological resources, mostly in the Ruhuhu river basin, with a view to exploiting the country's coal and iron ore deposits and possibly creating an industrial zone to rival those in Rhodesia. Some of these surveys involved the opening up of new roads through dense forest and other major logistical challenges. CDC's reports established that commercial mining was feasible, but only if a railway was built into the region. The government wasn't in a position to provide the railway at the time so the whole plan was shelved and was not revived until quite recently, with a new rail link now once again in prospect.

By 1955, CDC did nevertheless have a number of other mining interests in East Africa. These included Tangold Mines at Musoma in Tanganyika (gold) and Macalder-Nyanza Mines Ltd in Kenya (gold and copper), both of which were CDC-managed. There was also an investment in copper and cobalt-producing Kilembe Mines in Uganda and an exploration at Panda Hill, near Mbeya in Tanganyika – a joint venture with Billiton aimed at opening a niobium mine there, niobium, at the time, having been identified for use in a revolutionary range of new lightweight and heat-resistant super-alloys for airframes, jet engines and nuclear reactors.

The Tangold and Macalder-Nyanza mines were both in very isolated, arid areas on the shores of Lake Victoria and contact with the outside world was maintained partly through the shared use of a single-engined Cessna light aircraft. This was piloted by the Macalder manager's wife, Mrs Loretto, who also doubled as Matron of the mine hospital.

CDC's John Taylor, company secretary at Macalder-Nyanza Mines in the sixties, recalled a famous occasion when the general manager of Kilembe Mines made a flying visit to Macalder-Nyanza, accompanied by his secretary. It was on the way back that a classic situation arose. "As the aircraft was making its taxi run after landing at Entebbe, the general manager, who was nicknamed 'Uncle Alf' glanced out of the window to see one of the landing wheels running out at an angle before the aircraft came to a very lop-sided and sudden halt on the runway, fortunately without injury to the occupants. According to mine folklore, the secretary was still casting a few stitches on her knitting when she realised what had happened."

Mining generally fell out of favour with the CDC board in the early sixties, Rendell dismissing it in 1961 as being "in principle objectionable and in practice unprofitable". After that, no new investments were made for about twenty years until the 1980s when attitudes changed.

Although Reith and Rendell relied heavily on loans to bolster CDC's finances, they were also responsible for a number of other shrewd and very significant long-term investments in CDC-managed businesses and development schemes for which they deserve much more credit than they were given at the time. This applies both to those projects inherited from Trefgarne that they chose to continue as well as to some that they initiated themselves.

With regard to the former, the two outstanding examples were Borneo Abaca Ltd in North Borneo and the Swaziland Irrigation Scheme. BAL came near to closure early in its history owing to a number of factors including the ravages of 'bunchy top' disease on the abaca plants and the remote location of the plantations in Tawau, a sparsely-populated area where there was consequently a severe shortage of local labour. Management of the estate had already been subcontracted to a long-established regional plantation company in 1951 and by 1954, with losses mounting steadily, CDC wanted out altogether. However, a stay of execution was granted after a dynamic young executive named Peter Wise, sent out from CDC's Singapore office to assess the situation, reported back that the operation could be made to work with good management, diversification into other crops plus the provision of attractive housing and other facilities aimed at making Tawau an attractive place in which to settle, thereby attracting a resident labour force. Wise, aged just twenty-nine, was told to go ahead and prove it – and he proceeded to do just that. Within five years, regional controller and BAL chairman David Fiennes was able to report that BAL was by far the biggest agricultural enterprise in the Borneo Territories and that it compared in efficiency with the best anywhere.

"Many thousands benefit directly through wages paid, houses provided and the company's medical and social services" he stated at the 1959 AGM. "Many thousands more benefit indirectly through the spending of those wages, which brings prosperity to a multitude of trading enterprises and minor industries in Tawau. Many hundreds of thousands benefit at third-hand through the export duties and other levies paid by the company and its workers to the government for the general benefit of all the people of North Borneo."

Just as importantly, he added, BAL was providing disciplined training in agricultural techniques that would be of great benefit to development elsewhere in the territory. One way and another, it had turned into a model CDC project. And it was to become an even more significant success in future years. Peter Wise, meanwhile, went on to become CDC's regional controller in East Africa and a prospective general manager of CDC before contracting hepatitis and dying, tragically, at the age of forty-two.

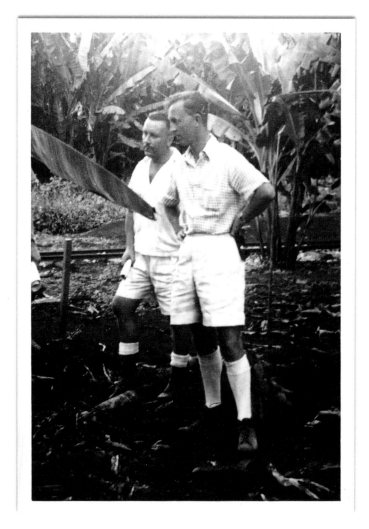

Above: Peter Wise (foreground) pictured at Borneo Abaca Ltd in 1955 with John Reidy who went on to plant the first trial plot of forty-seven oil palms at Mostyn in 1957, leading to the establishment of the first commercial oil palm estate in Sabah.

The Swaziland Irrigation Scheme was another Trefgarne initiative that might well have been dropped in the wake of his departure and Reith did indeed put the project on hold at first, the 42,000 hectares of land having been bought only three months before Trefgarne resigned and he took over. He ordered new surveys from irrigation consultants and extensive trials were then carried out over the next few years during which everything from bananas to barley, jute to lupins and peas to peppers was grown experimentally before the scheme was eventually given the green light in 1955, allowing work to start on the construction of the 245-metre weir and 67-kilometre canal. This positive decision in favour of the project possibly owed something to the special personal interest taken in it by William Rendell, who developed a particular liking to the lowveld region with its ample opportunities for the hunting and photography that he so much enjoyed.

Known as Mhlume Water, SIS's canal and weir were officially opened in 1957 by King Sobhuza II, the Paramount Chief of Swaziland, laying the foundation for another pioneering and long-lasting agribusiness venture that was to expand steadily over the next fifty years to qualify as one of CDC's greatest success stories, dominating the economy of the entire region and already providing employment for some 15,000 people by the 1960s.

Opening of Mhlume Water

(Opening of Mhlume Water from an article by Miss K.M. Hunt in the Staff Bulletin, October 1957)

The opening of the Mhlume Canal on 14 August 1957 was a red letter day in the history of SIS. For several weeks beforehand there had been a hum of activity in and around Mananga Township and the project had taken on a new look. One member of the staff was heard to mutter: "You might as well be on a battlefield!" However, the result when the great day dawned was a very pretty township with neat gravel roads and park-like surroundings, showing the beauty of the trees scattered over them to great advantage.

A great deal of planning, naturally, went into the reception of guests and the accommodation for visitors but there was considerable anxiety when the caterers from Johannesburg, who were providing luncheon for over one hundred guests, did not turn up the day before as planned. Search parties were sent out in all directions until late into the night and it was 3am when they finally arrived. They had taken a wrong turning and had to traverse some of the worst mountain roads in Swaziland.

We were blessed with a beautiful day on the 14th. A platform and awnings had been erected over the sluice gates, and the curving weir in the background, with the sun glinting on the water that was foaming over it, was a wonderful sight. To add gaiety and colour to the scene were Swazi warriors with their scarlet scarves, ox-hide shields and coloured ornaments; a smart contingent of the Swaziland police with their band; and last but not least, the fashion plate attire of the ladies present, many of whom, despite the fact that they have lived in the bush for months, would have done credit to Ascot.

On arrival at the weir site soon after 10am, the Paramount Chief, Sobhuza II, CBE, with his councillors and HE the acting high commissioner and the acting resident commissioner and their party were met and conducted to the weir house where Mrs Townsley, wife of our weir-keeper, provided refreshments. The party then inspected the Police Guard before proceeding to the platform above the sluice gates. Here, Mr William Rendell read a cable of good wishes from the chairman in which he expressed the hope that Mhlume Water would bear prosperity and production in its spread. Archdeacon Martin then said a prayer for God's blessing on the fruits of his work, reading part of Psalm 65. Mr Wishart briefly explained the intention to grow sugar under irrigation now that gravity water was available.

The Paramount Chief Sobhuza II compared the canal to a child which has to be tended with great care during the first years. After his speech, he walked to a ribbon stretched across the canal above the sluice gates and cut it and at the same moment two Swazis stationed on the sluice gate platform started to raise the gates and a fountain of water gushed into the empty channel. Little Ann Davidson, looking demure in a light muslin frock with a big bow presented a bouquet to Mrs Scrivenor, wife of HE the acting commissioner.

Cars bearing the guests to the luncheon then proceeded to drive the thirty-odd miles along the canal road to Mananga. At one point, a herd of impala obligingly stationed themselves only a short distance from the road. That evening, the club, tastefully decorated and hung with coloured lights and balloons, was the setting for the dance and once again the women came up to scratch with their party frocks. The scene was truly elegant and there were very many lovely dresses. Thanks to an excellent and most co-operative band, brought up from Mbabane for the occasion, the dancing went with a swing until the early hours of the morning.

Above: Swazi warriors at the ceremonial opening of the Swaziland Irrigation Scheme on 16 September 1957 by King Sobhuza II.

Above (right): SIS's 67-kilometre-long Mhlume irrigation canal.

Right: A worker alongside the irrigation canal in the cane fields of Mhlume Sugar.

"The Mhlume canal and weir were officially opened in 1957 by King Sobhuza II, the Paramount Chief of Swaziland, laying the foundation for another pioneering and long-lasting agribusiness venture that was to expand steadily over the next fifty years to qualify as one of CDC's greatest success stories."

Left: A view of the canal and spillway on the Komati river at SIS.

Of the new projects that were launched under Reith and Rendell between 1950 and 1959, one of the most significant was the Federal Land Development Authority in Malaya. Aimed at reducing rural poverty by providing land and support for landless Malayan nationals to farm, the organisation of FELDA was largely the brainchild of David Fiennes, another key figure during this period of CDC history. A dynamic and inspiring character – a scion, incidentally, of the family that also includes explorer Sir Ranulph and actors Ralph and Joseph – Fiennes was constantly on the lookout for ways and means to promote Malaya's development after becoming CDC's regional controller for the Far East in 1955 and the idea of FELDA developed out of discussions initiated by Tunku Abdul Rahman, the leading Malay politician and thinker who became Malaysia's first prime minister following independence in 1957.

FELDA's aims were set out at the end of 1956 in a ten-page booklet entitled 'No Need To Be Poor' that is now exhibited in a display case in the authority's impressive museum in Kuala Lumpur. The idea outlined by Fiennes in this manifesto was to encourage poor farmers to create more wealth both for themselves and for the country through the development of government-owned land.

With Fiennes as chairman and part-time chief executive, FELDA's initial purpose was simply to channel funds from the Federal Government to land development boards in the Malay states such as Kelantan, Pahang and Johor. By 1960, however, its role had been vastly expanded, largely at the instigation of Tun Abdul Razak, the deputy prime minister at the time, later prime minister, and it was carrying out developments in its own right. Located in remote areas and devoted exclusively to rubber production at first, these developments came to be set up on a grand scale that was beyond the resources of the individual states, involving the mass transfer of people, the creation of whole new communities and the establishment of public services.

The earliest example was at Ayer Lanas in the northern state of Kelantan in 1957. At that stage FELDA merely provided the loan to finance the project, which was then managed by the Tanah Merah Land Development Board. Once the location of the new village had been identified, 400 landless settlers were transported by convoy to a transit camp on the site where they lived while working in gangs to build their own houses, moving in with their families a couple of months later. Each house occupied a plot measuring twenty metres by fifty that allowed sufficient space for a vegetable garden.

Above: A smallholder settler working on his own house plot at the Ayer Lanas scheme of the Federal Land Development Authority in the Federation of Malaya.

"Aimed at reducing rural poverty by providing land and support for landless Malays to farm, the organisation of FELDA was largely the brainchild of David Fiennes, another key figure during this period of CDC history."

In addition, each of the settlers was allocated four hectares of land for planting with rubber, rice, and fruit trees whilst also being given a subsistence allowance to tide them over until they were able to earn income from what they produced. The village included shops, a school, a mosque, a playing field and other facilities.

The first project to be set up and run directly by FELDA itself was in the Bilut valley of Pahang, a very isolated and inaccessible area that was particularly well suited for rubber production. The pioneer settlers, recruited from a village on the outskirts of Kuala Lumpur, arrived in a convoy of Land Rovers and wagons that often had to be pulled out of the mud by tractors. Again, they built their own houses before bringing in their families to join them. They were then followed by other settlers from every state in the Federation, a total of 623 that included a diverse ethnic mix of Malays, Chinese and Indians.

By the end of 1959 ten schemes were up and running, all of them built around rubber plantations. In 1961 there was then a move into oil palms in Kulai, with CDC's neighbouring Kulai Oil Palm Estate, already well-established by this time, able to make a major contribution by providing expertise and staff training as well as practical help.

Over the next thirty years or so no less than 120,000 families totalling more than a million people were resettled in 322 new communities. Most of the settlers had been poor rubber tappers, rice planters or labourers, while others had been unemployed. In return for hard work, they received a monthly income and once their loans from FELDA had been repaid they were able to receive title to the land they had developed.

They took pride in their homes, often extending and rebuilding them. Some, lucky enough to have land in the right place, later went on to become millionaires through property development.

However, it was their children and grandchildren who were, arguably, the greatest beneficiaries. FELDA can point to thousands of teachers and managers and hundreds of doctors, lawyers, architects and accountants who came through the village schools that were built in these communities, forming part of the new generation of middle class professionals that has transformed the economy of Malaysia. Meanwhile, rural poverty has been effectively eradicated and, again, it is no exaggeration to claim that this achievement is in no small part attributable to the phenomenal success of FELDA.

Above: Members of the first group of settlers at Ayer Lanas, brought together for a reunion many years later.

Left: The Connaught Bridge Power Station at Port Klang, near Kuala Lumpur in Malaya. To help the Malayan Electricity Board to finance the construction of this much needed facility at a time when few if any other financial institutions were willing to lend to the Malayan Government as a result of the ongoing Malayan Emergency, CDC agreed in 1949 to make a long-term loan of £3.75 million, a quarter of its entire committed capital for that year and an exceptional sum of money at the time, equivalent to £130 million in today's terms. It was the start of a very long relationship to finance the expansion of public sector power generation capacity in Malaysia lasting into the 1990s.

Borneo Development Corporation

The Borneo Development Corporation (BDC) was launched in 1958 with the opening of an office in Kuching, the capital of Sarawak and in the view of Ivan Ho, a locally-recruited BDC manager who went on to work with CDC in the region for thirty-five years from 1963 to 1999, its long-lasting impact upon the peoples of Malaysia ranks equal to that of the Malaysia Building Society and second only to that of FELDA.

Malaya's independence as the Federation of Malaya in 1957 did not include Sarawak or North Borneo, so CDC was free to carry on operating in the two colonies. BDC and its sister company, Borneo Housing Mortgage Finance Ltd, which CDC also managed and which shared the same offices for the first few years, became the most prolific developers and financiers of commercial, industrial and residential estates throughout what were later the Malaysian states of Sarawak and Sabah.

Having rapidly expanded, with the opening of offices in Sibu, Miri, Jesselton (Kota Kinabalu) and Sandakan and with a succession of talented, locally-recruited managers, BDC built and/or financed the largest developments in both states.

It developed industrial estates and boat-building yards and provided loan finance both for the construction of industrial and commercial buildings by others and also for those wishing to buy factories that it had built itself. It also encouraged entrepreneurs with equity and loan finance. Most notably, it was responsible for building Sarawak's largest integrated housing scheme, with 1,500 houses, shops, offices and small factories and the seven-storey Electra House office and retail block in Kuching (left).

Borneo Housing Mortgage Finance worked hand-in-hand with BDC and with local governments. It, too, expanded to operate throughout both Sabah and Sarawak, attracting funding from local banks, insurance companies, government and other pension funds as well as provident funds. By the time CDC passed ownership of both companies into state hands in 1975, BDC was a highly profitable business and BHMF was operating seven thousand active mortgage accounts, with mortgage assets of £23 million.

Above: General Manager William Rendell (centre of the group of three) and new regional controller David Fiennes (on his right) with military guards in the background, visiting Kulai estate in 1955.

Top and bottom (left): CDC South East Asia regional controller Peter Gregoire (top left) and Kulai Oil Palm Estate General Manager William Gibson (bottom left) who were murdered by communist terrorists in 1954 while touring the Kulai estate in the southern Malay state of Johor.

Terrorists attack the Kulai Oil Palm Estate

Working for CDC in the field was not without risk, as the fate of Peter Gregoire and William Gibson in the southern Malay of Johor demonstrated only too clearly.

Peter Gregoire, handsome, grey-haired and intelligent, was the Far East regional controller based in Singapore while William 'Gibby' Gibson – tall, bulky, immaculate and imperturbable – was the general manager of the Kulai Oil Palm Estate, the first of what were to be many successful CDC palm oil businesses around the world.

The factory and the estate at Kulai had been badly damaged during fighting between the British and the Japanese in 1942 and in 1950 CDC launched a project to repair the mill and expand the planted area from 700 to 3,500 hectares. Oil palm was a minor commercial crop in Malaya at the time and the idea was that the enlarged estate and new factory would act as a nucleus, encouraging smallholders in the area to grow oil palms.

The project got off to a good start. Twelve hundred hectares having been cleared and planted and the first crop successfully harvested, palm oil and palm kernels were trucked off to a bulking station in Singapore some thirty kilometres away and the produce then sold to Britain's Ministry of Food. However, despite its proximity to Singapore, Kulai was a very dangerous place in which to work for the first few years of its operation due to the fact that communist terrorists were using the nearby rainforest and villages for cover

and support. As a result, 'Gibby' Gibson and his team found themselves having to work behind barbed wire defences in what were described as 'wartime conditions'. CDC's 1951 report noted: "Bandit activity in the Kulai neighbourhood is serious; manager and staff are in continual danger." This was borne out in horrific fashion in July 1954 when Gibson and Peter Gregoire were ambushed and killed as they toured the plantation in an armoured car along with the British MP Geoffrey Shawcross, who survived the attack.

A memorial was erected on the site but this did not impress Reith when he visited Kulai four years later, escorted by two armoured Land Rovers full of troops. "The memorial I thought awful," he confided to his diary, adding in characteristically blunt critical style that it resembled "about twenty cubic feet of concrete, like an enormous piece of cheese, with two names and the date of the murder – nothing to tell what happened; no symbolism; no imagination".

Gibson and Gregoire were the first but by no means the last to lose their lives in CDC's service. In their case, the fact that the regional controller was targeted suggested that the terrorists knew what CDC was about and saw it as a legitimate economic and perhaps political target.

In 1958, shortly before Reith's visit, Operation Tiger effectively ended communist activity in the area, with security forces killing fifteen terrorists and capturing nine more in their first exercises. This represented a quarter of those operating in the local forest and the

rest were cleared out by the end of the year, bringing to a close what the 1958 Annual Report described as "ten weary years of barbed wire and curfew, bombs and armoured cars".

A year earlier, CDC had set up a separate factory company, Johore Palm Processing Ltd, to take in crop from the surrounding area and between them the two businesses provided training for both Malayan nationals and aspiring CDC plantation managers. Kulai was a significant project for CDC because it was there that it learned its palm oil business while also gaining useful experience in working with smallholders, all of which could be passed on and used in other, similar CDC projects.

It was in this respect that FELDA in particular, was able to benefit when it first started diversifying from rubber into oil palms in 1961, Kulai providing agronomic advice and the training of thirty-five Malaysian undergraduates as managers and supervisors as well as supervisory help with the planting and maintenance of the first 1,600 hectares of oil palms, the plants supplied from its nursery. The CDC factory then processed the fruit from the first smallholdings until yields were high enough for FELDA to build its own.

CDC eventually sold the estate and its assets as a going concern to publicly-listed Benta Plantations, receiving payment in shares that were not finally sold until many years later.

In addition to BAL Plantations, FELDA and Kulai, CDC's notable Far East successes in the fifties also included the Federal and Colonial Building Society – later the Malaysia Building Society and Singapura Finance – which between them financed major housing developments in Malaya and Singapore.

Home ownership helps to foster a flourishing middle class, underpinning economic growth and creating greater political stability. In the 1950s, settling the professional and clerical workers – especially the Chinese, many of whom were supporters of the communists – played a part in dealing with some of the root causes behind the Emergency in Malaya and laid the bedrock of future economic progress.

The moving force behind the success of the Malaysia Building Society – and many other of CDC's other mortgage finance companies thereafter – was Jack Burgess. A suave, nattily-dressed and silver-tongued product of the Abbey National, Jack's ability to raise finance became legendary. Described by one admiring colleague as 'a confidence trickster without the tricks he would smother all doubts in dulcet words, and come out of a room with a million quid'. As general manager, and later managing director, of the Federal and Colonial Building Society, later the Malaya Borneo and then the Malaysia Building Society, he made a fact of the trite phrase, a property-owning democracy. In 1955, in Singapore, he had proved his point that Chinese, Malays and Indians would, if given the chance, buy and look after bungalows and terrace houses provided with all mod cons. During the next ten years this lesson was exploited throughout all the towns of Malaya so as to transform urban life for thousands and thousands of families.

Having established itself in housing finance and estate development, it was a logical step for CDC to provide the same financial support for factories and industrial estates through Singapore Factory Development Ltd. The first of several industrial estates was on a twenty-one-hectare site at Alexander Road in Singapore in 1951 and featured a textile mill, an edible oil refinery and a rope factory, as well as a Kiwi shoe polish manufacturing plant.

Managed by Lee Ek Hua, one of the first local recruits to manage a CDC business, Singapore Factory Development soon went on to become highly successful and by 1960 had set up a second estate in Alexander Road for light industries and a further one in Bukit Timah for heavy industries.

However, the main key to success was the provision of small loans to Chinese back street entrepreneurs, enabling them to move into purpose-built workshops. As the Singapore government cleared slum areas, SFDL purchased and developed the land, building little factories of only 300 square metres in area, which could be bought as single, double or triple units, using ten-year loans for small amounts, usually between £5,000 and £10,000. These sold very fast and were soon turning out great quantities of noodles and mosquito coils, scent and hair-cream, envelopes and kerosene cans, paint and print. CDC later used the same approach to finance small factories in Borneo, Hong Kong and Malaysia while the Singapore government also used it as a model when, in 1968, it established the Jurong Town Corporation, which became Singapore's national developer of industrial infrastructure.

In 1963 CDC sold half its equity in SFDL to Singapore's Economic Development Board, building a long-term mutually-beneficial relationship while continuing to manage the company. By the mid 1960s the newly-independent country was people-rich but resource-poor, and as a result was gearing up its efforts at industrialisation. Therefore, in 1968, when the government sponsored the Development Bank of Singapore (DBS) to take over certain functions from the EDB, with the aim of increasing still further the pace and scale of industrial development, CDC was a natural partner. CDC became a founder shareholder and helped start-up what has since expanded and diversified to become Singapore's largest bank and one of the largest regionally.

Above: An artist's impression of Kiwi Polish Company's impressive-looking factory, prior to its construction.

Left: Employees sealing and packing tins of shoe polish at the end of the production line at the Kiwi Polish Company's factory in Singapore in 1955. This was built on one of Singapore Factory Development Ltd's industrial estates.

Reading through the list of investments made under Reith and Rendell, it is clear that CDC had built up a fairly impressive and well-balanced overall portfolio, yet it nevertheless found itself having to face a concerted campaign of disruption by the Colonial Office which appeared determined to clip its wings and restrict its activities, with the underlying but undeclared aim of killing it off altogether. In 1956, for instance, Colonial Office lawyers suddenly decided that the investments CDC had been making for some years in road construction in West Africa and housing in Southern Rhodesia were not covered by the terms of the original Act of Parliament. Supported by the Attorney General, CDC successfully fought against this and a new Overseas Resources Development Act provided the necessary clearance.

The Colonial Office nevertheless managed to get a clause slipped into the Act stipulating that CDC could only invest in projects when alternative finance was unavailable, arguing that a newly formed private sector competitor, the Commonwealth Development Finance Company, should otherwise have first option. This was another real threat to CDC, which had to point out that, almost by definition, alternative credit worthy candidates for investment would be hard to find.

At the same time, the Colonial Office also informed CDC that it would not be allowed to invest in any country once that country had gained independence and warned that a clause would be added to each Independence Act expressly forbidding any such investment. To CDC's shock and dismay, the Ghana Independence Bill did contain such a clause. It read: "Without prejudice to the continuance of any operations commenced by the Colonial Development Corporation in any part of Ghana before the appointed day (of independence), as from that day the expression 'colonial territories' in the Overseas Resources Development Acts 1948 to 1956 shall not include Ghana or any part thereof". The breeze that was to become British prime minister Harold Macmillan's famous 'wind of change' was already starting to blow and CDC was beginning to feel the chill.

Reith instantly recognised not only the threat to CDC's future, but also the worrying implications for the newly independent countries, arguing that the loss of access to new finance and, just as importantly, the technical and management skills that CDC had to offer, could well contribute to political instability down the line. At the same time, he pointed out that the stifling of CDC's ability to expand would undermine staff morale and over time, with fewer and fewer colonies in which to work, would lead to its demise. For CDC's adversaries, who couldn't see any future for a body with 'Colonial' in its title, that was all part of the plan.

Usutu

Usutu Forest was among CDC's earliest ventures, initiated in 1949. Over the next ten years, the first 45,000 hectares of softwood pine were planted in the highveld grasslands of western Swaziland. In the late fifties CDC then invited Courtaulds, a UK-based industrial group, to join it in a partnership to build a pulp mill on the banks of the Great Usutu river at Bhunya. The first bales of high quality kraft pulp, used in the manufacture of paper and board, were produced in 1961, when the picture (left) was taken.

The Usutu Pulp Co began exporting to markets throughout the world via the newly constructed Swaziland Railway to Maputo, establishing a reputation for low-cost, high-quality kraft pulp. Both forest and mill expanded; the forest became one of the world's largest man-made forests, covering 75,000 hectares, and by the 1990s the mill was responsible for an eighth of the world's total production. When Courtaulds decided to exit the sector, Sappi, Africa's largest forest-products company, took over control and management in 1990 and CDC then sold part of its equity, retaining a small investment until 2000.

Subsequently, after forest fires and citing market conditions, Sappi closed the pulp mill in 2010 and sold the company to the Swazi-owned and operated diversified timber products company Montigny in 2013, which continues to manage the forests sustainably, producing a range of innovative products.

Despite Reith's best efforts and regardless of representations from the likes of Tunku Abdul Rahman, who praised CDC's efforts in Malaya and expressed disappointment that it would no longer be able to initiate projects there in future, the government confirmed that newly-independent Commonwealth countries should look to the World Bank or the Commonwealth Development Finance Company for investment, rather than CDC. CDC, it suggested, could make use of its experience by offering advice as long as no finance for new projects was involved.

Faced with this, CDC invested heavily in countries next in line for independence, notably Nigeria, in an effort to build its credibility. It also set up a number of local development companies, mini CDCs that would be able to carry on its work when it was no longer able to do so itself – Northern Nigerian Investment Ltd and the Development Finance Company (Eastern Nigeria) Ltd being two prime examples. And it sidled up to the Commonwealth Relations Office, established in 1947 at the time of India and Pakistan's independence, in the hope of making friends and influencing people there – a shrewd move that was to pay off later.

In the meantime, the Colonial Office dealt what they may well have thought would be a killer blow to CDC's chances of survival by persuading Macmillan not to reappoint Reith for a third term as chairman. Reith was furious. He most definitely did not want to go and was even more enraged when his deputy Sir Nutcombe Hume – "that wretched man" as he described him in his diary – was appointed as a stopgap replacement. A former investment banker who had won the Military Cross in the First World War and was director of commercial finance at the Ministry of Supply in World War II, Hume had joined CDC under Trefgarne in 1948 and was given responsibility for the Far East before becoming deputy chairman in 1953.

Relations between him and Reith had always been somewhat strained and Reith was convinced that 'Nut Hume', as he was known to friends and colleagues, would be outwitted by CDC's enemies at what was clearly a critical time. The story is told that when Reith reluctantly left the building at Hill Street he gave instructions that an axe was to be taken to his office chair just to stop Hume sitting in it.

Reith's anger and frustration at being removed with the job half done, as he saw it, is understandable and outweighed any satisfaction he may have felt with what had been achieved. His place in CDC's history was nevertheless assured. As William Rendell later commented in his 1976 book: "It is hard to believe that the Corporation would still have been in existence, except possibly as a captive appendage of the Colonial Office, if it had not been for Reith".

And, as it turned out, his legacy was not to be wasted. Rendell, a powerful kindred spirit, was still there as general manager to carry on the good work. And waiting in the wings to take over as chairman was a man who was destined to prove a more than worthy successor to Reith, using diplomatic skills rather than confrontation to secure CDC's future, expand its operations and establish its international reputation.

"The story is told that when Reith reluctantly left the building at Hill Street he gave instructions that an axe was to be taken to his office chair just to stop Hume sitting in it."

CDC's investments in 1959

- Despite Reith and Rendell's caution, project numbers double in the 1950s, with agricultural developments dominating.

- Two-thirds of the projects are in Africa but the single largest country portfolio is Malaya.

- CDC managers are seconded to two in every five of its projects.

Global investment (£m)

- Americas
- Africa
- Asia

Sector of investment (£m)

- Basic development
- Primary production & processing
- Commerce & industry

- # 88 investments
- # £60 million invested

(£1.35 billion in 2018 terms)

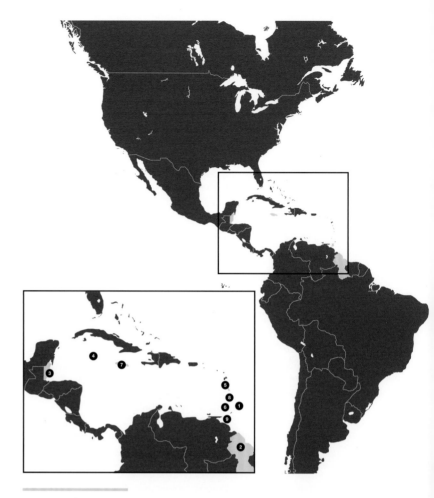

Americas

1. **Barbados (Regional Office)**
   Power
2. **British Guiana** (*Guyana*)
   Agribusiness
3. **British Honduras** (*Belize*)
   Agribusiness, Hotels and Tourism
4. **Cayman Islands**
   Transport
5. **Dominica**
   Power, Agribusiness
6. **Grenada**
   Power
7. **Jamaica**
   Power, Property and Housing
   Finance, Agribusiness
8. **St Vincent**
   Power
9. **Trinidad & Tobago**
   Manufacturing and Commerce

Africa

10. **Bechuanaland** *(Botswana)*
    Agribusiness
11. **Ghana**
    Transport
12. **High Commission Territories**
    (Botswana, Swaziland and Lesotho)
    (Regional Office)
13. **Kenya (Regional Office)**
    Power, Property and Housing
    Finance, Transport, Minerals,
    Oil and Gas, Manufacturing and
    Commerce, Hotels and Tourism
14. **Nigeria (Regional Office)**
    Property and Housing Finance,
    Transport, Agribusiness,
    Manufacturing and Commerce,
    Hotels and Tourism, Devcos and
    Financial Institutions
15. **Northern Rhodesia** *(Zambia)*
    Power, Manufacturing
    and Commerce

16. **Nyasaland** *(Malawi)*
    Property and Housing Finance,
    Agribusiness
17. **Sierra Leone**
    Hotels and Tourism
18. **Southern Rhodesia** *(Zimbabwe)*
    (Regional Office)
    Property and Housing Finance,
    Devcos and Financial Institutions
19. **Swaziland**
    Agribusiness, Manufacturing
    and Commerce
20. **Tanganyika** *(Tanzania)*
    (Territorial Office)
    Agribusiness, Minerals, Oil and Gas
21. **Tristan da Cunha**
    Agribusiness
22. **Uganda**
    Minerals, Oil and Gas

Asia

23. **Borneo Territories** *(East Malaysia)*
    Property and Housing Finance,
    Agribusiness, Devcos and Financial
    Institutions
24. **Malaya** *(West Malaysia)*
    (Regional Office)
    Power, Property and Housing
    Finance, Agribusiness
25. **Singapore (Territorial Office)**
    Devcos and Financial Institutions

Getting better all the time

1959–1972

Getting better all the time
1959–1972

1960–61

World events...

- In February 1960, British prime minister Harold Macmillan delivers his Wind of Change speech in Cape Town, heralding an accelerated policy towards giving independence to its colonies.
- Côte d'Ivoire gains independence from France in August 1960.
- Southern and French Cameroons gain independence from Britain and France in 1960.
- Nigeria and Tanganyika gain independence from Britain in October 1960.

CDC events...

- Lord Howick is appointed as chairman in 1960.
- CDC forms and manages the Caribbean Housing Finance Corporation in Jamaica in 1960.
- In 1960, CDC helps to form Malaya (renamed Malaysia) Industrial Development Finance, now one of Malaysia's premier development finance institutions.

1962–63

- Kenya, Jamaica, Trinidad and Tobago, and Uganda gain independence from Britain.
- President John F Kennedy is assassinated in November 1963.
- The Africa Development Bank is formed, with its headquarters in the Ivory Coast (Côte d'Ivoire).
- Federation of Malaysia formed between Malaya, Singapore, Sarawak and Sabah (formerly North Borneo).

- Commonweath Development Act passed in 1963, changing CDC's name to Commonwealth Development Corporation and giving it powers to operate in newly independent territories.
- Chilanga Cement is nationalised by the Zambian Government in 1963.

1964

- Harold Wilson becomes British prime minister.
- Tanganyika and Zanzibar unite to become Tanzania.
- Northern Rhodesia gains independence from Britain, becoming Zambia.
- Nyasaland gains independence from Britain, becoming Malawi.

- Minister of Overseas Development takes responsibility for CDC.
- St Lucia Electricity Services (Lucelec) is incorporated as a CDC subsidiary.
- CDC supports the establishment of Kenya Tea Development Authority. Development Finance Co of Uganda (DFCU) is established.

1965

- The Gambia gains independence from Britain.
- Singapore leaves the Federation of Malaysia to become a sovereign state.
- Southern Rhodesia declares independence unilaterally from Britain, as Rhodesia, leading to 15 years of isolation and conflict.

- Regional office for Central Africa moves to Lusaka, Zambia.
- Regional office for East Africa moves into Commonwealth House, Nairobi.
- Total amount invested tops £100m at year-end, at £105m.
- Housing Finance Co of Kenya is launched by CDC and the Kenya Government.

Dar es Salaam, Tanzania. CDC opened an office in Tanganyika in 1959, but had already been investing there since 1949, when it established Tanwat – which, when eventually sold in 2006, encompassed 18,000 hectares of wattle, tea and forestry plantations. Nearly seventy years later, in 2015, CDC and IFC together invested $12 million each to acquire a 5 per cent holding in CRDB, the leading provider of financial services in Tanzania, with operations in both Tanzania and Burundi operating through its network of 120 branches. The funding is being utilised by the bank to support continuing growth, enabling it to provide extended access to financial services in under-served markets.

1966–67

- *British Guiana gains independence from Britain in 1966, becoming Guyana.*
- *Bechuanaland gains independence from Britain, in 1966, becoming Botswana.*
- *Basutoland gains independence from Britain in 1966, becoming Lesotho.*
- *The Asian Development Bank is established in 1966, headquartered in Manila, Philippines.*

- King Sobhuza II opens the Sand River Reservoir of Swaziland Irrigation Scheme in 1966, enabling the extension of its irrigable area.

1968–69

- *Swaziland gains independence from Britain in 1968.*
- *The Boeing 747, the world's largest airplane, makes its first commercial flight in 1969.*
- *Neil Armstrong and Edwin Aldrin become the first men to land on the Moon in 1969.*

- CDC participates as a founder shareholder of DBS in 1968, now Singapore's largest bank.
- Overseas Resources Development Act 1969 extended CDC's area of operations to outside the Commonwealth, subject to Ministerial approval.
- Regional office re-opens in Kingston, Jamaica, in 1969, transferred from Barbados.

1970–71

- *The Conservative Party's Edward Heath becomes British prime minister in 1970.*
- *The Dutch development finance institution, FMO, is established in 1970.*
- *Britain joins the EEC.*
- *In 1971, Bangladesh (East Pakistan) gains independence from West Pakistan, which becomes Pakistan.*

- Work starts on the conversion of malarial swamplands into a world-class marina and resort at Rodney Bay, St Lucia in 1970.
- CDC finances Modern Terminals, in 1970, one of the first custom designed container ports in Hong Kong.
- Offices open in Jakarta and in Bangkok in 1971.
- A loan to Merpati Airlines, Indonesia, in 1971, is CDC's first investment outside the Commonwealth.

1972

- *Idi Amin expels Asians living in Uganda.*

- Lord Howick retires as chairman and is replaced by Sir Eric Griffith-Jones.
- Office opens in Addis Ababa.
- The number of projects at year-end tops the 200 mark - at 205.
- CDC founds and runs Mananga Agricultural Management Centre, Swaziland, which as Mananga Management Centre is still respected throughout Africa for its management courses.

Chapter three
Getting better all the time

Lord Reith's worst suspicions about the Colonial Office's ulterior motives in getting him out of the way and replacing him with a less combative chairman in Sir Nutcombe Hume seemed to have been confirmed when, on the very day that Hume succeeded him on 1 April 1959 a letter arrived announcing the formation of a new committee to review CDC's activities and make recommendations for its future.

Made up of an industrialist, a banker and an auditor, the Sinclair Committee duly met and deliberated with CDC over its function and its capital structure. Not for the first, or for the last time, CDC found itself in the position of having to justify its existence.

By now, however, it had complete confidence in the effectiveness of its systems and organisation as well as pride in its achievements and in the face of some fairly hostile questioning from the committee, including the suggestion from some quarters that 'colonial development' seemed to have been invented for the benefit of CDC rather than the other way round, William Rendell was able to make out a very strong, positive case in its favour.

Above: A meeting of CDC's Executive Management Board, unusually attended by the chairman, at Head Office in 1965 with (round the table, left to right): Andrew Goode, OBE (HO controller), Alan Belsham (regional controller, East Asia and Pacific Islands), David Fiennes, CBE (HO controller), Robert Prentice, CA (HO controller), Gordon Firmston-Williams (RC, Caribbean), William Rendell. FCA (general manager), Lord Howick of Glendale, GCMG, KCVO (chairman), Peter Meinertzhagen (RC, West Africa), Guy Caunce, MC (solicitor), Douglas Fairbairn (RC, Central Africa), Gren Totman, OBE FCA (controller of finance), Roger Swynnerton, CMG, OBE, MC (agricultural adviser), Peter Wise (RC, East Africa).

Swaziland Railway

The Swaziland Railway, providing a vital rail link between the Usutu region and the nearest seaport at the Mozambiquan capital of Lourenço Marques (Maputo), was another great example of CDC's can-do approach at its best.

Although Usutu Pulp used the line to move its product to Maputo for export, the original motive for its construction was the need to transport high grade haematite ore from the 'Iron Mountain' at Ngwenya, north of Usutu, down to the port. The Swaziland colonial government liked the idea but had neither the money nor the expertise to set it up and approached CDC for help. The British government gave the go-ahead on condition that CDC vouched for the commercial and technical viability of the entire integrated mining and transport project.

CDC was willing, but it was a massive and complex task that involved confirming the estimated Iron Mountain reserves of 27 million tonnes and checking the plans for everything from the operation of the mine, the construction of the railway and the establishment and management of the railway operating authority to the improvement of the facilities at the port in Mozambique – which involved building a new dock and deepening the channel – the building of three new 77,500-tonne ore-carrying ships in Norway and all the contractual arrangements between the various parties, including a ten-year contract with the Japanese importers.

As a reward for putting it all together, CDC negotiated a 7.5% equity stake in the mine company, Swaziland Iron Ore Development. Lord Howick, who had become CDC chairman in 1960,was instrumental in making it all happen, flying out to handle the negotiations personally, pleased to be back in his old stamping ground.

The 220 kilometre railway from Kadake, near the mine, to Goba, where it joined up with the main line to Maputo, carried its first consignment of ore in September 1964, having opened on time and on budget. As well as providing essential infrastructural support for both the mining and the wood pulp industry, it helped the economic development of Swaziland as a whole. From CDC's point of view, it was a successful project in almost every respect.

The Swaziland Railway was officially opened by King Sobhuza II on 5 November 1964.

As he pointed out, CDC worked closely with the governments and the people of the various countries in which it was operating in order to establish exactly what was wanted – and then actually delivered. It was able to do this because of its regional organisation, with well-respected regional controllers taking a proactive role in identifying local needs. It made projects happen and it didn't just set them up, get them going and then wave goodbye; it remained with them long-term, helping them to develop and adapt to changes in the economic and technical environments. And, of course, it provided finance too.

The committee had come looking for reasons to limit CDC's operations, so a long list of attributes was not what it really wanted to hear. But when it then moved on to consider the government's funding of CDC, Rendell and his talented controller of finance Gren Totman was even more bullish, reiterating the need for greater financial support. Loans with fixed interest rates and rigid repayment schedules was not the way to finance risky, long-term ventures in distant locations. What was really required was some substantial equity investment.

With regard to loan repayments, Trefgarne had already managed to wring a relatively minor concession from the government insofar as it had been agreed that interest due on loans was to be rolled up for the first seven years and then spread over the following thirty-three years, giving new projects a chance to get off the ground and start earning some income out of which to make the repayments. Rendell now called for the waiving of all debt relating to the failures of the early years, so-called 'special losses' that amounted to £8.8 million by 1958.

The force of his arguments was reflected in the fact that the committee went away and came up with a report that was very positive in almost every respect. It accepted that CDC was running a highly professional business and on the subject of funding it went a fair way towards including Rendell's entire wish list in its recommendations.

This was definitely not what the Colonial Office had anticipated. After considering the report for several months, it eventually came back with a flat statement to the effect that the government was unable to accept most of the recommendations apart from one or two relating to minor aspects of the financing arrangements. Basically, no further funding would be made available and terms would remain the same. The idea of an injection of permanent equity was rejected out of hand. CDC would have to live within its existing means. The only concession was that if it failed to repay its loans in the future, the government would help to pick up the pieces in the bankruptcy courts.

Invited to respond, CDC rejected the proposals wholesale, believing that it was actually better off as it was. In doing so, it underlined the need for greater financial support by reminding the Colonial Office that it had been set up to undertake risky ventures, mainly in primary production, of a sort that private enterprise was not prepared to take on because the risks outweighed the potential rewards. In answer to criticism that it had got away from its original brief by opting to make loans rather than initiating and managing its own projects, it explained that while it had indeed made some large, lower-risk loans, this was simply in order to produce the cash flow from interest that was needed to keep it solvent while it was setting up long-term sustainable businesses of its own and that this departure from the norm had only been intended as a temporary measure. Now it seemed there was a real danger that it would have to recycle its funds by selling off these companies without completing their development.

At this difficult juncture, with CDC's whole future increasingly on the line, several significant new factors combined to save the situation. The first of these was Lord Howick's arrival at Hill Street in April 1960 as deputy chairman and chairman designate. As diplomatic and charming as Reith had been awkward and abrasive, the former Sir Evelyn Baring played a key role behind the scenes in making friends and influencing people on CDC's behalf.

"By the time he arrived at CDC, Howick had already established a reputation as a distinguished man of great character, commitment, influence, achievement and modesty."

Lord Howick

Lord Reith may be the more famous name, but Lord Howick was the longer-serving and more popular of the two CDC chairmen. While Reith preached the virtues of discipline and organisation, Howick's patrician diplomatic skills helped to secure CDC's future, expand its operations and establish its international reputation.

Evelyn Baring was born into the wealthy banking family of the same name and entered the Indian Civil Service straight from Oxford in 1926 at the age of twenty-three. However, it was not in India but in Africa that he made his name, his first post there being as a representative of the Indian government in Durban where Indians were suffering under apartheid.

Later, back in India, he suffered a severe bout of amoebic dysentery that affected his health for the rest of his life, restricting his diet and causing him periods of extreme exhaustion. It ended his career in the ICS and also rendered him unfit for active military service during the Second World War.

Joining the Foreign Office instead, he became governor of Southern Rhodesia from 1942-44 and then British High Commissioner in South Africa and in the High Commission Territories of Basutoland, the Bechuanaland Protectorate and Swaziland between 1944 and 1952. It was during this time that he first came into contact with CDC, being the one who initially suggested the possibility of the pine plantations at Usutu that led directly to the establishment of Swaziland's valuable pulp industry and, indirectly, to the start of the Swaziland Irrigation Scheme, which went on to become CDC's largest project in the 1960s. From 1952 to 1959 he was governor of Kenya, dealing with the Mau Mau rebellion and again became involved with CDC and its work there. Knighted during this time, Sir Evelyn Baring became 1st Baron Howick of Glendale in 1960. Having already been earmarked to succeed Reith as chairman, he was made deputy chairman on 1 April 1960 and took over the chair on 1 December of the same year. He retired on 30 June 1972 and died eight months later on 10 March 1973, aged sixty-nine.

By the time he arrived at CDC, Howick had already established a reputation as a distinguished man of great character, commitment, influence, achievement and modesty. His career as an outstanding colonial administrator of the best sort had coincided with the last years of the British Empire; a biography by Charles Douglas-Home, published in 1978, identified him as *The Last Proconsul*.

CDC staff at every level had enormous respect for Howick. His successor as chairman, Sir Eric Griffith-Jones, an old friend from his Kenya days, wrote a tribute upon his death in which he mourned the fact that CDC had lost "one of the best friends it ever had and one of the greatest men who have ever devoted their lives to its service".

At his memorial service in Westminster Abbey, Bishop Trevor Huddleston gave an address that included the words: "He was, without question, and by any standards, one of the greatest colonial administrators of our age; in his years of office as chairman of the Commonwealth Development Corporation he deployed all his gifts, energies and talents to the single most urgent task confronting the world – the bridging of the widening gulf between the affluent and the hungry nations of the earth".

Indeed, Howick had always been an advocate for the rural poor in the poorer countries of the developing world, stressing that development was about people, especially those depending on the land for their livelihoods.

Very much a people person, he always carried a little black book with him wherever he went on overseas tours with CDC and in it he would makes notes about everybody he met, from general managers to the smallholder farmers. When he then returned on his next visit, sometimes years later, he would utterly charm them by asking after their wives and children by name.

He also had a masterful command of languages; on one occasion, while visiting a CDC project in Kenya, he surprised a group of East African Asians by joining in their conversation in Urdu. Perhaps rather paradoxically, his hobbies included both bird-watching and pheasant-shooting and his secretaries could occasionally be glimpsed plucking a brace or two on the balcony of his office in Hill Street.

A commemorative plaque that was put up after his death on the wall of the community hall at Bhunya, Swaziland, in the heart of the Usutu Forest that he was so instrumental in creating, provides a poignant and fitting tribute to this great and much respected man. It reads: "In memory of the late Lord Howick, better known to all Swazi people as Evelyn Baring. His contributions to the forest industry in Swaziland were timely and vital. He will be remembered in this land as long as pine forests flourish on the Swazi hills."

Even before he moved up from deputy chairman to chairman, Howick, a brilliant communicator and diplomat, had been quietly lobbying behind the scenes on CDC's behalf. In particular he had been leading the campaign to have its remit extended to cover the Commonwealth, successfully drumming up support for such a move from the governments of a number of countries that were coming up for independence. Quite by chance, CDC then managed to score vital points at the highest level by helping to get the Colonial Office and the government out of a hole in East Africa.

Independence was about to come much sooner than expected for Kenya, Tanganyika and Uganda. However, the accelerated timetable introduced at the Lancaster House conference in 1960 had sparked widespread nervous apprehension among ordinary men and women on the street in all three countries as to what might happen once African politicians were in control, especially with regard to local financial institutions such as savings banks.

In Kenya, which was first in line for independence and where 50,000 people had deposits totalling £6 million in three building societies, mostly in accounts with very small balances, panic set in and there was a classic run on the banks. Thousands of anxious investors started queuing outside branch offices to withdraw their money, causing a major cash flow crisis and bringing several institutions close to collapse. Most at risk were those whose business was primarily mortgage finance and who relied on short-term savings to fund their long-term loans.

The British government was extremely worried by this development – and with good reason. Having finally made up its mind to relinquish control of its colonies sooner rather than later it didn't want anything to upset its plans for rapid and orderly progress towards independence. A major loss of confidence in the financial systems could easily undermine the whole process and might even lead to serious economic recession. In these circumstances the government rather surprisingly turned to CDC for assistance.

This was unexpected for two reasons. Not only did it seem to be awkwardly if not hypocritically at odds with the government's continuing insistence that CDC could not operate in any country after independence; apart from that, CDC had regularly been criticised by the Colonial Office in the past for getting involved in housing finance, which was seen as being an inappropriate use of the funds at its disposal.

Perhaps partly because of this, the initial response from Hill Street when first approached by Kenya's minister of finance was hesitant, Rendell sucking air between his teeth and making the point that CDC was supposed to be in the business of backing new development, not refinancing debt to others. However, it was agreed that Jack Burgess, the man behind the success of CDC's housing finance operations in South East Asia, would be dispatched to Nairobi to review the situation. He duly reported back that it was indeed serious. Meanwhile, the government had confirmed that they would like CDC to do whatever it could to sort things out, at which point Howick and Rendell, not about to look a gift horse in the mouth, became determinedly positive and helpful, making the most of what was to prove another pivotal juncture in CDC's history.

Above: CDC's Annual Report and Accounts for the years 1961, 1962 and 1963. In 1962, CDC avoided using 'Colonial' on the cover, preferring just its initials. In 1963, the new name 'Commonwealth' was proudly highlighted.

The institutions that were struggling to survive were the First Permanent Building Society, Savings and Loan and the Kenya Building Society, all three of which were close to bankruptcy. CDC first made some relatively small loans to shore them up but these were not sufficient except in the case of Savings and Loan, where a major shareholder, Pearl Assurance, stepped in to provide extra support. With the other two still in trouble, CDC made its big move, forming two subsidiary companies to take over their assets while also providing enough funding to meet their obligations. No new mortgages were agreed, the existing portfolio was allowed to run down, new deposits were safeguarded and the situation gradually stabilised. Independence came without any problems and everyone breathed a sigh of relief. It was a job well done. For CDC, whose reputation was greatly enhanced, the wider implications were immense.

By coming to the rescue of the government and the Colonial Office in their hour of need, CDC changed attitudes among some of the key decision makers who were in the process of debating its future. The Treasury, for one, almost immediately became more sympathetic, with the result that some revised funding proposals were put forward which, although they still did not go nearly far enough, were more acceptable than those put forward by the Colonial Office after the Sinclair Committee review and angrily rejected by CDC. The new proposals allowed for much longer-term borrowings to finance the riskier equity-type projects while other loan arrangements were also altered in CDC's favour.

Howick then capitalised on the more favourable political climate by turning up the pressure even further in the campaign for CDC to be allowed to invest in the Commonwealth. Missing no opportunity to point out that the rescue operation in Kenya would not have been possible post-independence under the existing rules, he also stressed that newly-independent countries would undoubtedly need support for enterprises that were too risky to attract private investors. As typical examples of such enterprises, Howick cited the smallholder agricultural schemes and housing finance companies, which had the added virtue of tending to encourage political stability.

Other points in CDC's favour included the fact that it was flexible in ways that other financial institutions were not at the time. For instance, the International Finance Corporation did not invest in equity or alongside government money, which ruled out Africa altogether; nor did any other institution have the same extensive regional organisation at its disposal. Armed with a pile of letters from the leaders of countries coming up for independence, all of them in support of CDC being allowed to continue its operations, Howick also stressed the potential advantages to Britain itself. Even though CDC participation was not tied to British procurement of equipment, the British economy generally stood to gain because of the opportunities created by its projects. And British economic influence could be maintained in the independent countries.

By 1962, the situation was getting ever more desperate from CDC's point of view. With more and more territories becoming independent, the potential for new developments was declining rapidly. If CDC couldn't get things changed, its days were numbered.

In the end, the success of the financial salvage operation in Kenya and Howick's well-argued case did the trick and in July 1962 the Cabinet made the decision, confirmed in the 1963 Commonwealth Development Act, that CDC would be allowed to operate in the Commonwealth. As an added bonus, it now had a new master, the Commonwealth Relations Office replacing the Colonial Office, which had been such a thorn in its side over the years.

"In the end, the success of the financial salvage operation in Kenya and Howick's well-argued case did the trick and in July 1962 the Cabinet made the decision, confirmed in the 1963 Commonwealth Development Act, that CDC would be allowed to operate in the Commonwealth."

The only slight frustration was the Cabinet's arbitrary decision to change CDC's name to the Commonwealth Development Corporation. Although this conveniently allowed the continuation of the CDC initialised branding, it was to cause a certain amount of confusion in the years ahead when CDC's scope was further extended to include countries outside the Commonwealth. It was also never actually a Commonwealth institution as such and there were those who felt that an opportunity had been missed to free it entirely from any such connotation. Something like the British Overseas Development Corporation would have been preferred. However, that was a minor quibble. The main thing was that the long struggle for survival was over and with CDC's role confirmed the future was more secure than it had ever been before. Given this new lease of life, CDC entered a period of rapid expansion throughout the rest of the sixties so that between 1963 and 1972, when both Howick and Rendell retired, its investment portfolio increased by eighty per cent to £165 million.

Of that worldwide total of £165 million, nearly a quarter (£40.5 million) was invested in the Caribbean, compared with £31.4 million in South East Asia and the Pacific Islands and £28.7 million in East Africa. And in a number of years during the sixties and seventies, new investments in the Americas equalled those in the rest of the world put together. The fifty-five projects and investments that were up-and-running in this region in 1972 included the Fort George Hotel in Belize and handful of enterprises in British Guiana (Guyana) on the South American mainland, but were otherwise dotted throughout the islands of the Greater and Lesser Antilles, from Grand Cayman in the west to Barbados and Trinidad in the east, the main areas of activity being housing developments, mortgage finance companies and managed electricity utilities.

CDC had been helping to light up the Caribbean since the early fifties when the construction, operation and management of hydroelectric power stations in Dominica and St Vincent, both opened in 1953, were numbered among its first ventures. Having set successful precedents with Domlec and Vinlec, CDC and the government of Grenada formed Grenlec in 1960, with CDC managing and implementing an expansion programme to supply power to all the island's townships. This was followed in 1964 by Lucelec in St Lucia and by Monlec in Montserrat in 1968. In 1969 CDC then set up Caribbean Utilities Ltd, based in Barbados, to supply management and technical services to all five Lecs, described by one cynic as 'The Five Eveready Batteries'. And this led on eventually to the formation of the worldwide power generation company Globeleq in 2002.

Above: Overhead cables carry electricity generated by Dominica Electricity Services to public buildings, industries, shops and houses in the capital town of Roseau and surrounding country.

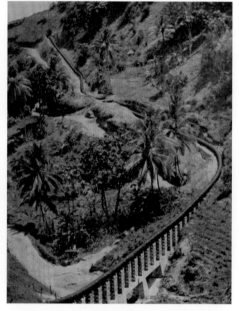

Above: The wooden stave pipe built by CDC to carry water down from the mountains of St Vincent to drive the turbines of the Vinlec power station. A considerable feat of civil engineering, the pipeline ran for several kilometres over difficult terrain.

Below: Up the pole – two linemen working for St Lucia Electricity Services Ltd, another of the 'Five Eveready Batteries'.

The 'Five Eveready' batteries

As a result of its power supply activities in the Caribbean over the years, CDC became synonymous with electricity throughout the islands, as in: "Our dinner was spoiled last night when the CDC went off". And when oil price rises in the seventies had to be passed on as fuel surcharges, causing widespread public protests, a popular calypso included the chorus line "CDC killin' we"!

In St Vincent, Vinlec's first manager was Norbert 'Andy' Andalcio, a Trinidadian known to his men as the 'Black Mussolini' on account of being a burly individual who would stand no nonsense from anyone. He recruited local sailors to be his overhead linemen on the grounds that if they could cling to the swinging yardarm of an inter-island schooner, then climbing a pole to attach power lines would be a piece of cake.

When stealing of electricity by means of tampering with meters became a problem, he adopted the policy of moving the meters from the verandahs of houses to the tops of poles. "Watch it or your meter will climb the pole" was the warning to any suspected offender.

Andy worked well with 'Old Mac' McClean, the civil engineer recruited by CDC to supervise the daunting task of laying a sixty-nine centimetre-diameter wooden stave pipe for several kilometres down steep mountain slopes and across ravines via aqueducts in order to bring water from the head of the Colonarie River valley to drive the power station's turbines. 'Old Mac', who had learned his trade on the London Underground, was as much of a character as 'Andy' and the two of them became a formidable combination.

In St Lucia, the first general manager of Lucelec was known as Alistair 'Engineering' Boyd to distinguish him from Alistair 'Mortgage' Boyd, who ran East Caribbean Housing Ltd at around the same time and who went on to become a regional controller and CDC's deputy chief executive in London under John Eccles in the eighties.

Above: An aerial view of the Duhaney Park estate in Kingston, Jamaica where CDC financed the building of 1,500 low-cost homes in 1963-4. CDC had teamed up with British life assurance company Eagle Star to form the Caribbean Housing Finance Corporation in 1960, taking a two-thirds equity stake in the company and agreeing to finance mortgages in the same proportion.

Above: New homes on the Duhaney Park estate in Kingston, Jamaica.

From the mid-sixties onwards, right up until the mid-nineties, the majority of CDC's Caribbean portfolio was concentrated in Jamaica and involved mostly low-cost housing finance to begin with, before expanding to include development of the island's commercial, industrial, tourist, port, harbour and other infrastructure facilities.

Behind this explosion of activity in Jamaica was the development of a strong and highly successful association between CDC and a particularly dynamic regional private sector partner in the shape of the Matalon family – principally Mayer, Moses, Aaron and Zacchie Matalon – whose business empire was based mostly on construction and property development. The relationship had started when CDC and Edinburgh-based life assurance company Standard Life got together in a joint venture to form the Jamaica Housing Development Company with the aim of providing mortgages for the owners of over seven hundred low-cost, part-prefabricated houses built by the Matalons on the old Mona sugar estate just outside Kingston.

The success of the Mona Estate development led to a second one at Harbour View and this time CDC teamed up with another British life assurance company, Eagle Star, to form and manage the Caribbean Housing Finance Corporation (CHFC) in 1960.

Harbour View featured over eighteen hundred homes, with CHFC offering 90% mortgages repayable over twenty years. A third estate, comprising a further fifteen hundred houses, was then built at Duhaney Park, followed by a fourth one next door at New Haven. Although high interest rates and the devaluation of the Jamaican dollar was to slow the rate of development in later years, CDC went on to manage CHFC successfully until the mid-eighties. In 1985 it celebrated its 25th anniversary by returning to Harbour View, its first scheme, for a service at St Boniface Church that was attended by five hundred people. The following year, CHFC was sold to the Jamaica Mortgage Bank.

During the sixties and early seventies, CDC set up and ran similar housing finance companies throughout the Caribbean – in Trinidad and Tobago (1965), Barbados, Dominica, Guyana and St Lucia (all in 1968) and St Vincent (1972). To get these up and running and to provide technical advice and management, CDC also set up its own management company, East Caribbean Housing Ltd. Based in Barbados and managed by Alistair 'Mortgage' Boyd, ECHL designed and built four prototype show houses as inspiration for local property developers before then going on to develop its own housing estates, thereby offering purchasers a convenient 'one-stop shop' facility.

Above: A house on a government housing scheme in Port of Spain, bought with a mortgage provided through the Trinidad and Tobago Mortgage Finance Company, eighty per cent owned and also managed by CDC.

Meanwhile, CDC had been further expanding its relationship with the Matalons to include an ever more ambitious range of collaborations. In 1962, the year that Jamaica achieved independence, the Matalons established Industrial Commercial Developments (ICD) as a vehicle through which to buy local manufacturing and supply businesses that it then reorganised and built up. CDC agreed to provide a line of credit as well as taking a small equity stake and although this was criticised at the time as simply helping to enrich a small number of individuals, ICD went on to become a huge success and by 1970 could lay claim to having created or protected 2,700 jobs.

Among the larger scale projects in which CDC became involved through its association with the Matalons was a new deep water harbour to serve Kingston at Newport West, the opening of which in 1966 was marked by the docking in the harbour of SS United States, then the world's largest cruise ship.

At around the same time, the Portmore Land Development Co, financed and later managed by CDC, bought a large area of swampland across Hunts Bay, to the west of Kingston, where it created a complete new city, including both residential estates along with shops, hotel and other facilities. The first residents moved into what is now the suburb of Independence City in 1968 and Portmore has since grown into a huge, thriving community, home to 170,000 people.

CDC and the Matalons also teamed up with the local Urban Development Corporation in 1967 to undertake another highly enterprising development at Ocho Rios, turning this former fishing village sixty kilometres north of Kingston into a world-renowned holiday resort, aimed primarily at the North American tourist market. A great success, this would probably never have got off the ground without the support of CDC, which provided the finance for the purchase, reclamation and initial development of the thirteen-hectare waterfront site before going on later to invest in hotels, apartments and a commercial centre that went up as part of the resort.

Above: Newport West docks near Kingston, Jamaica, with Western Terminals Ltd's deep-water berths in the foreground and Western Storage Ltd's cold storage and warehouse facilities and the Newport Holdings Industrial Estate behind. CDC had an equity stake in all three developments.

In addition, it provided loans to finance the construction of the Western Terminals complex and Western Storage and formed a subsidiary, Commonwealth Property Development Services Ltd, to manage the Newport Holdings industrial estate, which went on to become one of the biggest in Jamaica.

Right (top): The successful waterfront resort of Ocho Rios in Jamaica, featuring a beach created artificially with white sand dredged from the bay and with the four Turtle Towers apartment blocks at one end and the 357-bed Inter-Continental hotel at the other. Without CDC's investment, it might never have happened. The resort was initially developed by CDC in partnership with the Matalon family and the local Urban Development Corporation, CDC providing a loan for the original purchase, reclamation and site development of the beach and beachfront plots for sale to developers.

As well as investing in the equity of Turtle Towers, CDC provided construction finance through the Caribbean Housing Finance Corporation that was then converted into mortgages for the individual apartments. CDC provided a loan and held preference equity in the Inter-Continental Hotel and also had a stake in the Ocho Rios Commercial Centre, a complex of shopping units with a 46-room motel and restaurant.

Right (bottom): The resort in the early stages of development, viewed from the other end of the beach. Turtle Towers are under construction in the foreground but work has yet to start on the Inter-Continental.

Above (top, left and above): St Lucia's Rodney Bay marina (top), the centrepiece of an ambitious development that turned an area of mosquito-infested swampland (above) into a popular international sailing and holiday resort (left). At the far end of the beach is historic Pigeon Island. It was here that Admiral Rodney, the British admiral after whom the Bay is named, built a stronghold in the late eighteenth century following a successful operation against the French and it was at the nearby Admiral's House that David Mills lived with his wife while manager of Rodney Bay in the 1970s. The only other resident on the island at the time was the legendary Josset Legh, an elderly and eccentric lady who lived in a cottage on the beach and who had come to be regarded as something of an institution in St Lucia. The island was later given to the nation by the Rodney Bay Development Company and is now a National Park.

In 1970, the CDC/Matalon partnership then turned its attention to St Lucia, where Moses Matalon had conceived yet another grand plan, this time for an integrated tourist and residential development at Rodney Bay. This involved transforming a mosquito-ridden swamp into an artificial saltwater lagoon with a 232-berth yachting marina, while also creating a 1,500-metre beach and building houses, apartments, hotels, water sports facilities, a shopping centre and offices.

Although slow to take off, largely because of the worldwide economic downturn in the mid-seventies, this has since gone on to become very successful, with the harbour regarded as one of the finest in the Caribbean and with a Sandals resort occupying a prime spot at one end of the bay, next to historic Pigeon Island.

The CDC board at the time did not go into tourism projects such as Ocho Rios and Rodney Bay without reservations. Rendell noted disapprovingly that tourists 'in commercial quantities tended to present human behaviour at its worst'. And when so much of what they ate and drank had to be imported, the benefits to a country's external balance of payments from tourist dollars tended to be marginal. Nevertheless, there was no doubt that tourism created plenty of jobs throughout the economy, and for many of the countries where CDC worked, especially the many smaller island nations in the Caribbean, there were precious few other opportunities for stimulating development. Blessed with warm sunshine, beautiful beaches, natural wonders and historic old forts, governments welcomed CDC's promotion of tourism projects as a route to economic development.

As in the Caribbean, CDC's activities in Africa overall expanded rapidly during the sixties and seventies, although military coups (Ghana, Nigeria and Tanzania), war (Eastern Nigeria), political upheavals (Southern Rhodesia, Southern Cameroons), corruption (Uganda) and struggling economies (Sierra Leone and Ethiopia) caused considerable disruption in many areas, ensuring that things were not always straightforward. In Southern Rhodesia, the Unilateral Declaration of Independence in 1965 brought all operations to a complete halt for fifteen years. In Tanzania, Julius Nyerere's introduction of socialist policies that were at odds with CDC's support of private sector enterprises slowed things down. There were problems in Ghana following the military coup of 1966, in Sierra Leone and in the Southern Cameroons, where there was an outbreak of civil strife in 1961 after a UN-organised plebiscite resulted in a vote to join the Republic of Cameroon rather than Nigeria. And in Nigeria itself, the secession of Eastern Nigeria as Biafra and the war that followed made life extremely difficult during the three years from 1967-70, posing a threat to CDC staff, some of whom had to be evacuated.

Up until then, the industrial development finance companies (Devcos) that had been hurriedly set up by CDC just before Nigeria's independence in 1960 had been doing well, proving their worth in supporting small and medium-sized enterprises, backing risky start-ups and helping local entrepreneurs to expand their businesses. A number of these Devcos, or mini-CDCs, had been launched in several West African countries as a last-minute hedge against the situation whereby CDC was barred from making new investments in former colonies post-independence, the idea being that they would be able to carry on CDC's work, passing on its DNA, as it were.

By 1966, the Devcos for Northern and Eastern Nigeria had a portfolio of forty-four investee companies between them, most of them very profitable. They included everything from textile mills, tanneries, metal works and plywood manufacturers to a bakery and, perhaps most colourfully, a recording studio. EMI (Nigeria) hosted a visit from Paul McCartney and Wings in the early seventies while another artist who worked there was Fela Ransome Kuti, the controversial Nigerian musician known as the King of Afrobeat who achieved legendary status worldwide, most notably with his protest song 'Zombie' – a bitter attack on the behaviour of the Nigerian military that became his greatest hit but which also served to make him very unpopular with the government.

Almost as unlikely as a pop recording studio among CDC's Nigerian interests at this time was a railway buffet car! This came about through an investment in Nigeria Hotels Ltd, another of those that were made just prior to independence. By the terms of the deal, CDC acquired just over half the equity in the company. It also agreed to provide a loan to finance the improvement and extension of the existing hotels within the group, including the Central Hotel in Kano and the Ikoyi Hotel in Lagos, plus the leasing and operation of some new ones, the first of these being Lagos's only other international class hotel, the Bristol. In addition to its hotels, the company also provided catering services for Nigerian Railways and Kano Airport, including in-flight meals.

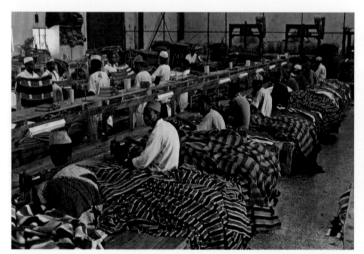

Above: Hand-made blankets being produced in Nigeria at the Kano factory of Northern Textile Manufacturers, one of thirty companies financed by Northern Nigeria Investments Ltd.

Above: Poolside at Lagos's Ikoyi Hotel, managed by CDC-owned Nigeria Hotels Ltd, which continued to flourish throughout the Biafran War. After the war, it was expanded to include 460 rooms, becoming Nigeria's largest hotel.

Below: Eric Hall of Hallway Hotels (left), Alhaji Halilu of Nigeria Customs (centre) and (right) Stanley Allison, general manager of Nigeria Hotels.

Hotelier in war-torn Nigeria

The managing director of Nigeria Hotels Ltd prior to its acquisition by CDC was an experienced hotel professional, Eric Hall. He stayed on and when, in 1964, CDC then found itself left to manage some tourist hotels in the Caribbean after its business associates in the venture withdrew, he was asked to help out. Two years later, with still more hotels having been added to its worldwide portfolio, CDC decided to form its own hotel management company, Hallway Hotels Overseas Ltd, with Eric Hall as a partner and managing director. Hallway took over the management of Nigeria Hotels and by 1969 had development, consultancy or management contracts for thirty-two hotels in Africa, Singapore and the Caribbean, plus the leasing of two more in the Seychelles.

Perhaps rather surprisingly, Nigeria Hotels remained profitable throughout the Biafran War. The Kano Central lost many of its Igbo staff and the Bristol's occupancy rates dropped because businessmen were no longer staying in the centre of Lagos, but the Ikoyi continued to thrive, although the clientele tended to be more mixed and included suspected mercenaries and arms dealers. And after the war it was expanded to 460 rooms, becoming Nigeria's largest hotel.

"Yoruba music was the financial salvation of the Bristol Hotel when the Biafran War decimated its occupancy," recalled John Taylor, company secretary at Nigeria Hotels at the time. "Incorporated in the hotel development was the Koriko Bar; this was not the hotel bar but a separate establishment with its own entrance from the street and its own clientele and the war increased rather than reduced its patronage.

The music, which was a feature of the bar, was the Yoruba 'Juju' music which was popular at the time; traditional music adapted for electric guitars. To the non-Yoruba speaker, the lyrics were not understandable except that most of the compositions seemed to be in praise of particular individuals, but the melodies were enjoyable nonetheless. The bar was reputed to have the highest sales of Guinness per square foot of floor space of any outlet in Nigeria. Eric Hall would often end a dinner party at the quiet Bristol Hotel by a foray with his guests through the humming Koriko Bar from the back door to round off the evening!"

Everything was going fine in Nigeria until the coup by Igbo officers from Eastern Nigeria in January 1966 set in motion the train of events that led to the outbreak of the Biafran War the following year. Inevitably, the local economy in Eastern Nigeria took a battering as a result of the three-year conflict and the Devco DFC (EN) was badly hit. A few of the investee companies survived by moving their operations out of the area and continued to pay dividends, but many disappeared without trace and only a few limped back into production when the war finally ended in 1970. Attempts to find new companies in which to invest failed and the Devco was liquidated.

There was a happier outcome for another CDC investment that came close to being wiped out. The Nigeria Cement Co Ltd, known as Nigercem, of which Biafran leader Ojukwu had been chairman at one time, was located in the area around the Eastern Nigerian capital of Enugu that was worst affected by the fighting during the war and had quickly been abandoned in the face of advancing troops. With cement desperately needed for reconstruction work once the war was over, CDC stepped in, provided a loan for the rehabilitation of the factory, and seconded Adrian Kerwood as general manager to help get the company back on its feet again.

Adrian, who went on to become a regional controller and a deputy general manager at Hill Street, did the job well and by the end of 1973, the factory had been fully rehabilitated, the workforce of 1,100 reinstated and retrained and the workers' housing estate renovated. The company's estate schools and its 100-bed hospital had also been re-opened. Profitability soon exceeded pre-war levels and in early 1974, with the job done, and CDC's rehabilitation loan repaid, CDC handed over the keys of the general manager's office to a Nigerian successor. CDC exited when its shares were sold to the public in 1977 but Nigercem went on to operate very successfully for another thirty years.

Above: A rather spectacular mishap, a bridge on the road to the Nigercem plant at Nkalagu, having collapsed under the weight of a truck.

Above: The Nigercem plant at Nkalagu.

Above: The official opening of the Umuhuali Community piped water supply standpipe at Nkalagu in 1974 by Adrian Kerwood, general manager of Nigercem at the time.

Gabriel Akwaeze

Gabriel Akwaeze (pictured above, centre, with the staff of Development Finance Company (Eastern Nigeria)) became CDC's local hero during the Biafran War. In 1967, as Enugu's hotels filled with war correspondents and expatriate CDC staff were evacuated, Gabriel was left behind as the acting general manager of DFC (EN). When the Biafran government moved out of Enugu to the small town of Umahia he moved his office there, too, and, supported by his board but out of touch with CDC in Lagos, reopened for business, supporting new small enterprises mostly connected with the production of emergency food supplies. As the Nigerian government troops pushed towards Umahia, the beleaguered Biafran government moved twice again with its commercial camp followers and Gabriel and his team went with them. Throughout all this, Gabriel operated by the book, taking his custodianship of the business most seriously.

John Taylor (seen above, fifth from the left), the former company secretary to DFC (EN) who was sent back as general manager after the war in an attempt to revive it, wrote later: "When the end of the war came and the Federal troops stormed into the area where (Gabriel and the team) were living and demanded the handing over of the DFC (EN) vehicle, which Gabriel Akwaeze had carefully kept over nearly three years, he tried to argue that it did not belong to him and that therefore he could not let it go; fortunately, the men with the guns won and took the vehicle without bloodshed.

If ever the integrity of a man needed to be established (and in Gabriel's case it certainly did not) his behaviour in all of the circumstances of that period did just that and I do not think that this has ever been fully recognised since by all of those involved."

However, he did get his just reward when he was head-hunted by the Nigerian Bank for Commerce and Industry, set up in 1973 to promote the development of small and medium size enterprises, going on to become its managing director.

Shortly after that, he rose even higher when President General Gowon appointed him to be Nigeria's federal minister for trade.

Nigeria wasn't the only trouble spot in West Africa during the sixties. There were also problems and unrest in Ghana and Cameroon, where the civil war that followed the independence of French-administered East Cameroon and the Southern Cameroons' plebiscite decision to join it in the Federal Republic of Cameroon in 1960 came close to forcing CDC to pull out and abandon the long-established Cameroon Development Corporation, which it had started managing shortly before. Camdev had actually been set up as a statutory corporation by the British governor of Nigeria as long ago as 1946, in the days before CDC existed and at a time when the Southern Cameroons was treated as a region of Nigeria. After much agonising, CDC, to its credit, decided that it could not leave Camdev's staff and its enormous number of 17,600 employees in the lurch, thereby possibly contributing further to the instability of the region, so it stayed put, issuing guns to selected members of staff and sending expatriate families home until things quietened down.

Because of the rules of engagement that forbade CDC from getting involved in countries outside the Commonwealth, CDC could not go ahead with plans to become a major equity investor in Camdev once the Southern Cameroons opted to become part of the new Republic. However it continued to provide management, technical and marketing services for another fifteen years and, to this day, Camdev remains the largest commercial undertaking in the country and is the second biggest employer after the government. Although CDC gave up corporate management in 1974, its involvement did not end there and it went on to provide loans and staff in the seventies and eighties to help with further development of the tea, rubber and oil palm plantations that now extend to 42,000 hectares.

One way and another, the sixties was a time of frustration for CDC's regional office in West Africa. The portfolio did not grow as hoped and by the end of the decade the amount invested there made it the smallest of all the regions, with only nine per cent of the worldwide portfolio.

Meanwhile, much more significant progress was made in East Africa, where the greater stability that followed independence in Kenya, especially, enabled housing finance, Devcos and agricultural projects – tea production in particular – to flourish.

CDC's rescue of the Kenyan banks and building societies during the period of uncertainty leading up to independence had involved putting a block on new mortgages in order to safeguard savings, leaving would-be house-buyers with nowhere from which to borrow money. The result was that urban housing had become polarised between well-off residential areas and squalid shanties, with little in between.

By 1965, with the situation starting to become critical, CDC suggested to the governments of Kenya, Uganda and Tanzania that new housing finance companies were essential to meet the needs of the lower-middle income groups who aspired to own their own houses, pointing out that owner-occupation helped to encourage political and economic stability. It proposed to set up new mortgage finance companies as joint ventures, with CDC taking sixty per cent of the equity alongside the governments' forty per cent, with both providing loan finance.

The proposals were agreed and CDC delivered. First off the ground was the Housing Finance Company of Kenya Ltd in 1965, followed in 1967 by the Housing Finance Company of Uganda and the Permanent Housing Finance Company of Tanzania.

In Kenya, new housing estates soon started sprouting all around the country. At first, these were mostly built by the National Housing Corporation, but CDC soon became a developer in its own right, starting with the seventeen-hectare Valley Field estate in Nairobi in 1968. This was the first project taken on by the Commonwealth Housing Corporation, set up by CDC earlier the same year, with Jack Burgess at its head, to provide management and consultancy services to all CDC's housing projects.

Above: Bananas being washed and packed for export in the packing house at Ekona Banana Estates in Cameroon, one of the divisions of CDC-managed Cameroon Development Corporation. Being another 'CDC', in CDC it was called 'Camdev' and in 'Camdev', CDC was called 'Comdev'.

The success of Valley Field led to approval in 1971 for what was to become the largest private sector housing estate in Africa. Located on a 270-hectare site on the outskirts of Nairobi, Buru Buru, inspired by CDC's Ian Lane, was an innovative and pioneering development in all sorts of ways, with great attention given to the provision of schools, shops and other facilities such as community halls and playgrounds, and from the moment the first nine hundred of its five thousand houses were offered for sale in 1973 demand vastly exceeded supply. Now absorbed into Nairobi's suburbs, it is remembered with considerable affection by most of those who grew up there as being a wonderful place to live compared with what had been available before.

CDC had hoped to repeat this success in Uganda and Tanzania but was thwarted in each case by political developments. In Uganda, Idi Amin's expulsion of the Asian community just as the first 111 houses on the Nsambya estate came on the market, along with a national shortage of building materials, prompted CDC to halt work on any further expansion. In Tanzania, the promotion of private property ownership didn't sit well with Julius Nyerere's socialist principles. The government bought CDC's shares and absorbed the company into its state-controlled Tanzania Housing Bank, an organisation now defunct.

Although the Devcos that had been set up in Tanzania and Uganda by CDC with government intermediaries and like-minded European Development Finance Institutions were affected by the same political factors, they managed to survive and grow throughout the sixties so that by 1975 the Tanganyika (Tanzania) Development Finance Co Ltd (TDFL) and the Development Finance Company of Uganda (DFCU), along with the Development Finance Company of Kenya (DFCK), had 123 investments between them – fifty-three in Kenya, forty-two in Tanzania and twenty-eight in Uganda.

In Tanzania, the Arusha Declaration of 1967 that resulted in the Nyerere regime's nationalisation of foreign-owned banks, insurance companies and industries, again made life awkward, with some investee companies going out of business and others being nationalised. However, CDC and TDFL hung on and although their aims of supporting private enterprise were blunted, much good development was nevertheless delivered.

In Uganda, Amin's expulsion of the Asians had much more severe repercussions and in the ensuing economic uncertainty all confidence collapsed. CDC withdrew its expatriate staff and effectively closed down its operations. A skeleton staff of an executive, a secretary and a messenger manned the office in Kampala, receiving the occasional dividend from the investee companies that were still functioning, primarily in the food, beverage and textile sectors. In this way, DFCU maintained a low-profile presence until Amin fled the country in 1979 and the return of Milton Obote cleared the way for its gradual revival and its eventual establishment as a major diversified financial institution.

Above: The Annual Report and Accounts for Tanganyika Development Finance Company Ltd (1968), the Development Finance Company of Kenya Limited (1992) and the Development Finance Company of Uganda (2003).

"Located on a 270-hectare site on the outskirts of Nairobi, Buru Buru was an innovative and pioneering development in all sorts of ways, with great attention given to the provision of schools, shops and other facilities such as community halls and playgrounds..."

Right and below: Aerial view of the Buru Buru housing scheme in Nairobi and (below) one of the houses in the Phase IV of the development, with murals painted on the wall. The first houses were offered for sale in 1973 and Buru Buru eventually grew to become the largest private housing estate in Africa, with 5,000 houses.

In Kenya, meanwhile, DFCK had flourished, making mainly loan investments in support of businesses across the whole range of economic sectors from agricultural products and small manufacturing facilities through to beach resorts and, notably, safari lodges. Without this support, many of those businesses would not have got off the ground. CDC remained involved until 2006 when it sold its eleven per cent share to a Kenyan investment group.

The greatest and longest-lasting East African success story to have come out of the sixties is that of the Kenya Tea Development Authority (KTDA). This had its earliest origins in a report put together in 1954 by Roger Swynnerton, later Sir Roger, who was then working for the Department of Agriculture in Kenya, but who later joined CDC as its head of agriculture. The Swynnerton Plan for agricultural development following the Mau Mau rebellion proposed the large-scale development of African-grown cash crops such as tea, coffee, sisal, fruit and sugar cane in Kenya's most fertile areas as a way of helping to rehabilitate people displaced during the state of emergency. A British government loan of £5 million over five years would help to fund the scheme.

At the end of five years, however, only 650 hectares had been planted out of the 4,900 hectares envisaged by the Swynnerton Plan. It was at this point that CDC became involved. In 1959, Chris Walton led a mission to investigate a specific proposal to finance two tea factories to process the expected tea crop and having concluded that managing the necessary increase in smallholder crops production was too big a task for the local government to handle by itself, he reported back that what was really needed was a separate statutory authority to take control. This led to the proposal for a Special Crops Development Authority and CDC's best brains in London and Nairobi were then engaged for the next two years in deciding exactly how that body should operate to ensure the best results.

Renamed the Kenya Tea Development Authority in 1964, following independence, it set about working closely with licensed smallholders at every stage of the production process from the supply of seedlings through to the transport of the green leaf tea to the factories. The farmer would receive a first payment in cash for his crop and a second payment related to the price his tea fetched at auction. At the same time, CDC encouraged the rapid Africanisation of KTDA's top management. The World Bank, which up until this time had not been involved in rural development, was so impressed by what it saw being achieved there that it agreed to work in tandem with CDC from then on.

KTDA went on to become established as Africa's most successful smallholder scheme. A measure of that success is reflected in simple statistics. In 1963 there were 18,000 licensed tea growers with an average of 0.2 hectares of land planted with tea alongside other crops, just 3,300 hectares in all; no factories had been built to process the tea they produced. Twenty years later there were 145,000 farmers with 58,000 hectares of tea being processed in thirty-nine factories. Every fourth cup of tea drunk in Britain at that time came from Kenya, half of it produced by KTDA smallholders, and KTDA could claim to be the largest single tea-growing organisation in the world. By 2006, the figures had increased to 420,000 smallholders growing tea on 90,000 hectares, with fifty-four factories producing 730,000 tonnes per annum, representing sixty per cent of Kenya's tea production, which is the second largest foreign exchange earner after tourism.

When William Rendell retired as general manager at the end of 1972 he asserted that CDC's support for KTDA had "directly raised the standard of living of more families than any other CDC project". That is even truer today when, given an average family of five for each of KTDA's 420,000 smallholders, one could be talking in terms of the livelihood of over two million people. Unfortunately, attempts to replicate this success in Malawi, Uganda, Tanzania and even Ethiopia at various times over the next twenty years or so did not fare quite as well, due mainly to political problems.

Above: A handful of freshly-picked tea leaves, picked by one of Kenya Tea Development Authority's tea growers.

Top and above: Sorting and weighing the tea in the factory. KTDA became Africa's most successful smallholder scheme, producing sixty per cent of Kenya's tea and ranking as the country's second largest foreign exchange earner after tourism.

Top and above: The KTDA factory at Githambo under construction and (top) tea chests being prepared for despatch to Britain, bound for Avonmouth.

Left: The Githambo factory seen from the outside. KTDA regularly needed new factories to match its expansion, and CDC assisted by investing in the equity of the businesses set up to operate them. The first two were at Chinga and Mataara, on the lower slopes of Mount Kenya one hundred kilometres north of Nairobi, and by 1980, CDC had invested in thirteen factories, scattered in the highland areas to the east and west of the Rift Valley.

Top and above: Watched by William Rendell (seated, wearing sunglasses) and other CDC staff, Swaziland's King Sobhuza II pulls a lever to inaugurate the extension of the Swaziland Irrigation Scheme system in 1966 that allowed water from the already existing canal to be channelled to the Sand River valley where a dam created a large storage reservoir. Located in a beautiful, peaceful setting, the reservoir (bottom) became the home of the Sand River Yacht Club.

Elsewhere in Africa, the sugar industry in Swaziland had become firmly established during the years following the opening of the Mhlume Sugar mill in 1960 as part of the Swaziland Irrigation Scheme (SIS) project. In its first year the mill produced 39,200 tonnes of sugar and by 1968 this figure had risen to 83,000 tonnes, making Mhlume the biggest producer in Southern Africa. From 1962, the cane came not only from Mhlume's own fields but also in gradually increasing quantities from the local smallholders who had been settled on the CDC-managed Vuvulane Irrigated Farms in a pioneering smallholder scheme that Rendell described as "the most interesting and significant unit of the SIS group".

By the mid-seventies there were 260 Swazi smallholders at Vuvulane, each with between three and seven hectares of land on which they were growing cane and a variety of rotation crops. This was a social as well as an economic success. The farmers and their families were encouraged to settle in permanent villages and were provided with community services. Health improved as a result and CDC also founded and part-financed a primary school that was soon educating hundreds of children. In 1974, Donald Nxumalo became Vuvulane's first Swazi manager, having been seconded to Kenya for training.

Sadly, Vuvulane was to become embroiled in local politics in years to come and never quite fulfilled the promise that Rendell had seen. Handed over to the Swaziland National Agricultural Development Corporation in the eighties, it went into liquidation ten years later. However, at the last count there were 550 smallholders still growing cane in Swaziland, so it left a worthwhile legacy.

Mhlume and SIS, meanwhile, continued to flourish and expand. By the mid-sixties the area that could be irrigated by the existing system had reached its limit and so it was decided to expand the system. This necessitated another major water engineering project that involved building a pumping station from the main canal to the adjacent Sand River valley, where a dam created a large storage reservoir from which supplementary water could be drawn, when necessary, to meet increasing peak demand.

As with the original weir and canal ten years before, this was opened in 1966 by King Sobhuza II. The start of the ceremony was delayed by His Majesty deciding to take a short cut on the way over, missing the agreed rendezvous with officials at SIS's boundary. He was eventually found sitting calmly and patiently beside a track leading to a stone quarry.

Arriving at the appointed spot, he was greeted enthusiastically by hundreds of Swazi warriors, all dressed in full regalia of skins and brandishing spears and shields, while whistling noisily as a traditional mark of respect. Barefoot and clad simply in a colourful cloth, the King pulled a dummy lever at the same time as a rocket signalled the pump station to pump water down the inlet channel into the reservoir basin. As back-up, in case the rocket failed to go off, the managers had organised a radio link and semaphore flags to alert the pump station. The Sand River reservoir is now a beautiful and peaceful place to walk.

Above: Distillation vats at the Shiselweni Forestry Company in southern Swaziland being filled with eucalyptus leaves as part of the process of extracting eucalyptus oil.

King Sobhuza II and Shiselweni Forestry

A colourful character in every way, King Sobhuza II of Swaziland (1899–1982) was an absolute monarch who, in 1947, had enjoyed the unlikely honour of welcoming the King and Queen of Great Britain to Nhlangano, the remote district headquarters of Shiselweni in the largely inaccessible south of his country. Within a few years of Swaziland gaining independence in 1968, he dispensed with the constitutional parliamentary democracy that came with it, but he was nevertheless always genuinely concerned for the development of his land and the prosperity of his people welcoming CDC's investment in sixteen enterprises between 1949 and 1981.

It was at his instigation that CDC first considered repeating the success of its Usutu Forest plantation at Shiselweni. A CDC team was duly sent out and identified an area of 40,000 hectares in and around the rocky uplands that although unsuitable for agriculture was ideal for forestry plantation, especially eucalyptus. This was initially grown to provide pit props for the South African gold mines but eucalyptus oil, used in various medicinal and pharmaceutical preparations, later became a valuable secondary product. Over the next thirty-five years, Shiselweni Forestry Company grew into a model of sustainable development, a commercial success and also an acknowledged centre of excellence for management training. By the end of the century, CDC deemed the development work at the Shiselweni Forestry Company to have been completed and sold it in 2001. The plantations continue to be managed sustainably, providing employment and income for Swazis living in one of the poorest areas of Swaziland.

In South East Asia and the Pacific, meanwhile, CDC's activities in the sixties and seventies included some adventurous and pioneering agricultural projects in faraway locations such as Sarawak and the Solomon Islands.

Guadalcanal, the scene of fierce fighting between the Americans and the Japanese during one of the most decisive campaigns of World War II in the Pacific, had been selected as the most likely of the seven islands in the Solomons group for development, largely because of the flat Guadalcanal Plains in the north, so in 1963, Dick Johnson was sent out to supervise the first trials to test the feasibility of rice, soya bean and oil palm cultivation. The rice and soya didn't work out for various reasons, but the oil palms, planted on a nine-hectare site between the Ngalimbiu River and Red Beach – the US military codename for its 1942 invasion beachhead – flourished.

However, a major local hazard was then revealed in 1967 when two cyclones hit the island in fairly quick succession, the first blowing out the walls of Dick and Dione Johnson's house and scattering the contents far and wide while the second flattened many of the trial's oil palms. Fortunately, the plants survived after being winched upright and, undaunted, CDC decided to go ahead with the investment. Solomon Islands Plantations Ltd was launched in 1970 as a joint venture between CDC, the Solomon Islands government and the local landowners, with CDC taking seventy per cent of the equity and providing management. SIPL went on to become a solid, long-term success, despite a much more powerful cyclone in 1986 that caused mass destruction and nearly brought about its demise.

There was also plenty of drama at Sarawak in Borneo, a country whose more remote forest hinterland was the haunt of hornbills and hunter-gatherer groups. In 1961, CDC decided to investigate the possibility of planting oil palms in the Limbang Valley, a curious finger of low-lying land which, although belonging to Sarawak, is surrounded on three sides by tiny Brunei and is only just south of the sultanate's capital of Bandar Seri Begawan. Sabri Katon Ali, a Sarawakian who had graduated from BAL's agricultural cadet scheme in neighbouring Sabah, was seconded by CDC to set up and manage a trial planting. This duly went ahead but was then terminally interrupted when, in 1962, during an attempted coup in Brunei, armed rebels fighting for an independent state of North Kalimantan occupied the pilot scheme's offices at Batu Danau. The Sarawak Rangers used the makeshift playing field to land their troops by helicopter, defeating the rebels after a battle among the oil palms.

None of the CDC staff or workforce was hurt but their houses were searched for weapons and, as other government workers elsewhere had been taken hostage and killed, they went into hiding for several days. Some of the palms had been damaged and trial records lost, and the final straw came a month later when violent storms caused the worst flooding for a hundred years. With some areas under five metres of water, three people were drowned and there was widespread damage to the palms and the infrastructure. That was the end of the Limbang Oil Palm Pilot Scheme.

Above: Tending young oil palm plants in a nursery on the Sarawak Oil Palms Bhd estate at Suai in Sarawak, Malaysia.

Above: Watering cocoa seedlings in the BAL Plantations Sdn Bhd nursery in Sabah, Malaysia.

CDC turned its attention instead to a forested location south of the coastal town of Miri. Because the area was almost totally inaccessible by road, the only way in which equipment could be delivered to the site was by using an old tank landing craft to beach a D6 Caterpillar tractor that then drove a path inland to connect up with a long-disused oil prospecting road. From Miri, John Foster – the Sarawak government's director of research before joining CDC – went to meet the landing craft by travelling along the beach seated in a deckchair that had been set up on a trailer pulled by a tractor, this unlikely convoy escorted by an armed British trooper and a Malay infantryman as protection in the event of any confrontation with forces involved in the continuing dispute between Malaysia and Indonesia. It was a somewhat bizarre start to what developed into a very successful enterprise, with Sarawak Oil Palms, which was incorporated in 1968, going on to provide CDC with an annualised financial return of twenty six per cent over the twenty-seven years of its involvement, an outstanding result for an agricultural investment. And it didn't end there. SOP currently has 89,000 hectares under oil palm.

In Sabah, the most important development during this period was the decision by Borneo Abaca Ltd to stop growing abaca, which was no longer economic, and to switch instead to cocoa, which it established as a major crop, and, predominantly, oil palm. This opened the way for what was first renamed BAL Estates and then BAL Plantations to develop into one of CDC's greatest successes over the ensuing thirty years. It became its flagship of quality management and exemplary governance, a model plantation business for demonstrating what CDC had done and could do – generating cash, surviving the ups and downs of several commodity cycles and producing world-class research on both cocoa and oil palm cultivation, which it freely shared. When CDC eventually sold the company in 1996, the £100 million price rewarded it with an impressive annualised return of thirteen per cent for each of its forty-eight years of involvement.

"BAL Plantations became its flagship of quality management and exemplary governance, a model plantation business for demonstrating what CDC had done and could do…"

Elsewhere in Malaysia, the founding of Malaya (later renamed Malaysia) Industrial Development Finance was a joint venture with the Malaysian government in which CDC took a leading role. Until then, there had been nowhere for the small businessman to go for development finance in the form of loans and equity with which to expand or start up a small company. The larger businesses were well-served, able to attract finance from the established banks or from overseas. But local people, who could often speak no English and who worked from their homes or backyards, usually had no option but to seek family money or borrow at high rates from moneylenders. MIDF filled this important gap at a time when Malaysia needed it.

By the middle of the sixties it was processing hundreds of loans and also making direct equity investments. A quarter of the businesses supported were in the metal and engineering industries, with wood processing another important sector. Other enterprises included food processing, rubber and leather goods, chemicals and paper products. MIDF effectively kick-started the SME sector in Malaysia and many of these small companies grew into big businesses.

Hong Kong was another new territory in which CDC got involved for the first time in this period. It had previously been out of bounds, considered 'too rich' to need outside help, but at a time when a lot of the colonies were gaining independence, CDC's sphere of operations was reducing since it was still not permitted to work outside the Commonwealth, and so there was a need to look round for things to do wherever legitimately possible. CDC's first venture in Hong Kong, in 1961, was to provide finance for a private company to build, own and rent out a ten-storey block of 'flatted factories' in New Kowloon. These properties included a small amount of factory space along with connected residential accommodation and the thirty-eight tenants produced clothing, furniture and electrical goods among other things.

Having established this foothold, CDC persuaded the Hong Kong government to support a housing finance company under CDC management. The Hong Kong Building and Loan Agency was formed in 1964 to meet the demand for private ownership of middle-income apartments, thereby encouraging the building of more such blocks. By the end of 1966, seventy-one blocks had either been built or were in the process of going up and 4,500 flats had been approved for mortgage lending. The company is still providing mortgage finance and is listed on the Hong Kong Stock Exchange.

The only other development that CDC has financed in Hong Kong was a major one. At the end of the sixties, Hong Kong - Europe was the only major commercial shipping route not to have converted to containerisation. An area of unclaimed seabed at Kwai Chung in the New Territories was set aside for development into a container terminal and Modern Terminals was founded in 1969 to construct a deep-water container berth. The company then had difficulty in raising medium-term finance and CDC stepped in with a loan, convertible to a small amount of equity. It did convert and sold its shares to a Chinese port operator in 1992, just as Hong Kong was starting to get ready to be handed back to China in 1997, making a significant financial return.

In Fiji, CDC initially established its presence through the Fiji Development Co. This started off by managing the Fiji government housing authority's operations and also provided secretarial and accounting services to the local Cathay Hotels group. Later, the Home Finance Company exploited CDC's growing expertise in mortgage finance to provide loans for middle-income workers, going on to become a long-lasting commercial success despite initial scepticism from Hill Street, where it was doubted that it would ever find a large enough market to make it viable. CDC continued to manage it until 2001. Apart from that, CDC's main investments in Fiji were to support forest products, power supply and sugar sectors.

Back in London in the late sixties, CDC's expanding activities and growing list of successes from 1963 onwards had at last won government respect. The permanent secretary at the Ministry of Overseas Development told the Estimates Committee of the House of Commons in 1968 that CDC was "probably as efficient a form of aid as exists in this country or anywhere in the world, a view which I know the World Bank also holds".

The committee recommended that CDC receive a larger share of the aid budget and as a result the Overseas Resources Development Act of 1969 announced that borrowing limits were to be raised from £150 million to £225 million. More importantly for its future development, CDC was cleared to work outside the Commonwealth. At the same time, the lifting of the restriction that limited its operation even within the Commonwealth to those countries that were dependent territories in 1948 opened the way to working in India and Pakistan.

Concern in some quarters that CDC might suddenly neglect the Commonwealth as a result of this new freedom was calmed by the inclusion of a clause that required the minister for overseas development to approve each new country. And Parliament received assurances that approval would be given sparingly.

"The permanent secretary told the House of Commons that CDC was 'probably as efficient a form of aid as exists in this country or anywhere in the world, a view which I know the World Bank also holds'."

A colourful night-time view of the Modern Terminals container berth at Kwai Chung in the New Territories of Hong Kong. The company had had difficulty in raising medium term finance and CDC stepped in with a loan, later converted to a small amount of equity that yielded a high return when sold in 1992.

99

Above: Lord Howick receiving a leaving present from Jill Cunnington on the occasion of his retirement. A keen ornithologist, Lord Howick was also presented with two rare books on British birds and a pair of binoculars on behalf of CDC staff, including Anna Davies (seated) and Angela Weeks.

Above: Sir William Rendell (middle) at his retirement dinner, with Peter Meinertzhagen (right), who succeeded him as general manager, and Sam Hunter (left), regional controller for West Africa.

The first batch of non-Commonwealth countries in which CDC was given permission to work were Cameroon, Ethiopia and Indonesia, followed over the next few years by Thailand, Tunisia, Zaire, Côte d'Ivoire and Costa Rica. The first investment outside the Commonwealth was actually in Indonesia, where a loan was made to the state-owned airline Merpati (known to the more cynical members of the local CDC staff as 'Mersplati' on account of a rather poor accident record), which was operating services between the Indonesian islands and wanted to expand.

Although welcome, this broadening of CDC's horizons brought its own set of problems. The new countries often turned out to be hard going. The governments weren't sure what CDC did and some were understandably suspicious. CDC representatives had to inform, gain the confidence of the local political and business communities, familiarise themselves with different ways of doing business and establish extensive networks. This was often challenging, especially when they were flying in and out from their regional bases. Francophone West Africa and Spanish-speaking Latin America called for different language skills and different attitudes. In Commonwealth countries, there was a good chance one could get away with English, the legal system was based on English Common Law and they usually drove on the left. CDC was moving out of its comfort zone.

Meanwhile, a change of government at home in 1970 saw Ted Heath come to power at the head of a right-wing Conservative administration. Earlier in the same year, the Labour government had set up a Select Committee on Overseas Aid that had encouraged CDC to ask for more money, a disarming approach to which CDC was not accustomed. The new Tory administration then immediately shut down the work of the select committee and also pressured CDC to give priority to the more under-developed countries, especially those in sub-Saharan Africa. CDC saw this as a threat to its new and hard-won independence and flexibility, pointing out that its role had always been to fill the gap between direct government aid, appropriate to the poorest countries, and private sector-led commercial operations in countries that didn't need assistance, stressing that it relied on the latter to make the financial return needed to service its Treasury loans. In the end, a compromise was reached whereby it was agreed that CDC would indeed give preference to projects in poorer countries as long as they met CDC's other investment criteria.

Lord Howick retired on 30 June 1972 after twelve years as CDC's chairman. In advance of his retirement, he took the opportunity in CDC's Annual Report for 1971 to draw some conclusions and consider lessons learned. Having reviewed CDC's financial successes and development achievements, he turned to external endorsements of the organisation's work. He first quoted two statements made by government officials to parliamentary committees, praising its efficiency and its valuable contribution to developing countries. Then, in what he described as "a last blow of this trumpet", Howick proudly recalled the words of Robert S. McNamara, the president of the World Bank Group and former US defence secretary, who had paid tribute to CDC as "a unique organisation that has shown the way to the rest of us".

Rendell followed Howick into retirement six months later, after twenty years as its first and longest-serving general manager or chief executive to date. Under his management CDC had grown and prospered. In 1950 it had invested £10 million in forty-seven projects in twenty-one countries. In 1972 there was £165 million of investment in 205 projects, including fifty-four managed businesses, in thirty-eight countries. It had made a profit every year since 1955, ploughing its surpluses back into more development. Its future was still very much in the balance when Howick arrived at Hill Street in 1960 and when he left in 1972 it was totally secure.

Reith had established the decentralised regional organisation and decision-making disciplines that had provided a solid foundation for the expansion that took place during the sixties. Reith and Rendell and then Howick and Rendell had managed the threats and had made the most of the opportunities thrown up by a changing world.

All three had strength of character and a sense of what was right for CDC. Tough leadership combined with efficient and disciplined management – a powerful combination.

Their departure truly marked the end of an era. And as a result of their work, the legacy that they were able to pass on was vastly greater than the one they had inherited.

"Howick proudly offered the words of the president of the World Bank Group and former US defence secretary, Robert S. McNamara: CDC was 'a unique organisation which has shown the way to the rest of us'."

CDC's investments in 1972

- After a rapid expansion, over a quarter of the portfolio is in the Caribbean.

- Power and water is the largest sector, but CDC's aptitude for housing finance makes it a close second.

- There are fifty-four businesses run by CDC staff, half in Africa.

Global investment (£m)

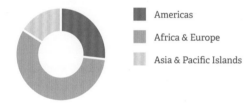

- Americas
- Africa & Europe
- Asia & Pacific Islands

Sector of investment (£m)

- Basic development
- Primary production & processing
- Commerce & industry

- # 205 investments
- # £165 million invested

(£2.1 billion in 2018 terms)

Americas

1. **Antigua**
   Transport, Hotels and Tourism
2. **Barbados (Regional Office)**
   Power, Property and Housing Finance
3. **British Honduras** (*Belize*)
   Hotels and Tourism
4. **Cayman Islands**
   Transport
5. **Dominica**
   Power, Agribusiness, Hotels and Tourism
6. **Grenada**
   Power, Hotels and Tourism
7. **Guyana**
   Power, Agribusiness, Property and Housing Finance
8. **Jamaica (Territorial Office)**
   Power, Property and Housing Finance, Transport, Agribusiness, Manufacturing and Commerce, Hotels and Tourism
9. **Montserrat**
   Power
10. **St Kitts**
    Hotels and Tourism
11. **St Lucia**
    Power, Property and Housing Finance, Hotels and Tourism
12. **St Vincent**
    Power, Property and Housing Finance
13. **Trinidad & Tobago**
    Property and Housing Finance, Manufacturing and Commerce, Hotels and Tourism

Pan Americas
Power, Property and Housing Finance, Hotels and Tourism

Africa and Europe

14. Botswana
Property and Housing Finance,
Agribusiness

15. Cameroon
Agribusiness

16. Cyprus
Hotels and Tourism

17. The Gambia
Hotels and Tourism

18. Ghana
Manufacturing and Commerce

19. Gibraltar
Property and Housing Finance

20. Kenya
Power, Property and Housing
Finance, Water, Agribusiness,
Manufacturing and Commerce,
Hotels and Tourism, Devcos
and Financial Institutions

21. Lesotho
Property and Housing Finance

22. Malawi
Power, Property and Housing
Finance, Water, Agribusiness,
Manufacturing and Commerce,
Hotels and Tourism, Devcos
and Financial Institutions

23. Mauritius
Property and Housing Finance

24. Nigeria (Regional Office)
Property and Housing Finance,
Agribusiness, Manufacturing and
Commerce, Hotels and Tourism,
Devcos and Financial Institutions

25. Seychelles
Hotels and Tourism

26. Sierra Leone
Water, Hotels and Tourism, Devcos
and Financial Institutions

27. Swaziland
Property and Housing Finance,
Transport, Agribusiness, Minerals,
Oil and Gas, Manufacturing
and Commerce

28. Tanzania (Territorial Office)
Power, Agribusiness, Manufacturing
and Commerce, Hotels and Tourism,
Devcos and Financial Institutions

29. Uganda
Property and Housing Finance,
Agribusiness, Minerals, Oil and Gas,
Manufacturing and Commerce,
Devcos and Financial Institutions

30. Zambia (Regional Office)
Power, Property and Housing
Finance, Transport,
Manufacturing and Commerce

31. Rhodesia (Zimbabwe)
Power, Property and
Housing Finance, Devcos
and Financial Institutions

Note: Regional Office for South Africa
is in Johannesburg.

Asia and Pacific Islands

32. Fiji (Territorial Office)
Property and Housing Finance,
Agribusiness, Devcos and
Financial Institutions

33. Hong Kong
Property and Housing
Finance, Transport

34. Indonesia (Territorial Office)
Transport

35. Malaysia (Territorial Office)
Power, Property and Housing
Finance, Water, Agribusiness,
Devcos and Financial Institutions

36. Singapore (Regional Office)
Property and Housing Finance,
Transport, Water, Manufacturing
and Commerce, Devcos and
Financial Institutions

37. Solomon Islands
Agribusiness

38. Thailand (Territorial Office)
Property and Housing Finance

More help for the poorest

More help for the poorest
1972–1982

1975

- *The Labour Government releases a White Paper on aid: "The Changing Emphasis in British Aid Policies: More Help for the Poorest".*
- *Mozambique gains independence from Portugal.*
- *Papua New Guinea gains independence from the Australian-administered UN trusteeship.*

1973–74

- *The world is hit by an oil crisis, following the 1973 Yom Kippur War.*
- *A Labour government is returned to power in 1974, with Harold Wilson as prime minister once more.*

1977–78

- *The French government creates Proparco in 1977 as its catalyst for private sector development in developing countries.*
- *Ethiopia invades Eritrea.*
- *Solomon Islands and Dominica gain independence from Britain in 1978.*

1976

- *Harold Wilson resigns as prime minister and is replaced by James Callaghan.*

World events...

CDC events...

- Sir William Rendell retires in 1973 and is replaced by Peter Meinertzhagen as general manager.
- In 1973 CDC supports the Kenya sugar industry through a founding investment in Mumias Sugar Co Ltd.
- Nava Nakorn, a new town near Bangkok and Thailand's first industrial promotion zone, is developed by CDC in 1973.

- CDC finances the expansion of the Oriental Hotel, Bangkok, in the year Saigon falls to the North Vietnamese.
- Government's first 'quinquennial review'.

- Higaturu Oil Palms in Papua New Guinea is established by CDC and the PNG government.

- Office reopens in Dar es Salaam in 1977.
- Commonwealth Development Corporation Act 1978 consolidates earlier legislation and increases borrowing powers.
- Office opens in San Jose, Costa Rica in 1978.

Right: Lilongwe, Malawi. In 1981, CDC moved its regional office for Central Africa from Lusaka to the new capital city of Malawi. In the decade that followed, it was supporting and managing government authorities in various parts of the country that had been set up to help smallholder farmers grow tobacco, sugar, coffee and tea. Returning to Malawi in a big way in 2015, CDC has made a series of investments totalling $32 million (by the end of 2017) aimed at making significant impact. Of these investments, one was to Lilongwe-based 14Trees, which produces soil-stabilised bricks for use in building low-cost and environmentally-friendly housing (as pictured here at 14Trees' main demonstration site). Bricks produced in this way have the added benefit of saving the trees used to fire traditional clay bricks.

1979

- *Margaret Thatcher becomes Britain's prime minister.*
- *A revolution in Iran followed by Iraq's invasion of Iran precipitates a world oil crisis which continues into the early 1980s.*
- *St Lucia and St Vincent and the Grenadines gain independence from Britain.*

- Lord Grey replaces Sir Eric Griffiths-Jones as chairman. HRH The Prince of Wales joins the CDC board (until December 1987).
- Regional office in Lagos closes and moves to Monrovia, Liberia.
- Offices open in Castries, St Lucia and in Gaborone, Botswana.

1980

- *Finnfund, Finland's development finance institution, is formed.*
- *Zimbabwe-Rhodesia gains independence from Britain, becoming Zimbabwe.*
- *New Hebrides gains independence from Britain and France, becoming Vanuatu.*

- Lord Kindersley is appointed as chairman.
- Government's second 'quinquennial review'.

1981

- *HIV/AIDS is identified.*
- *The Brandt Commission report is released, called 'North-South: A programme for survival'.*
- *Swedfund, Sweden's development finance institution, is formed.*
- *British Honduras gains independence from Britain becoming Belize.*

- Regional office for Central Africa moves to Lilongwe, Malawi, from Lusaka.

1982

- *The Falklands War is fought between Britain and Argentina.*

- Commonwealth Development Corporation Act increases borrowing powers.
- A review of CDC undertaken by John Eccles and Arthur Lewis points to a weakening of CDC's commercial and management sharpness.
- Offices open in Harare and Douala.

Chapter four

More help for the poorest

Lord Howick and William Rendell had both
retired by early 1973 to be replaced as chairman
and general manager by Sir Eric Griffith-Jones
and Peter Meinertzhagen respectively.
Once again, the new regime brought about a
marked change of climate and culture at CDC.

Although sincere and dedicated to the cause, Sir Eric, whose health deteriorated rapidly
towards the end of his time in office, was more of a figurehead and less of a hands-on
chairman than his predecessors, setting the pattern for the future in which the general
manager increasingly took overall control. At the same time, Peter Meinertzhagen
introduced what 1990s board member Sir Michael McWilliam later characterised in his book
on the history of CDC, *The Development Business*, as a 'gentler' kind of leadership than that
which had gone before. Promoted from within, having been a regional controller in both
East and West Africa during his previous fifteen years with CDC, he was not quite such
a hard-headed businessman as Rendell, the trained accountant and economist, but was
more attuned to development than financial viability, more committed to doing good than
to making money. As things turned out, this chimed perfectly with government thinking
following the return to power in 1974 of the Labour Party under Harold Wilson, as reflected
in the publication of a White Paper in 1975 entitled 'The Changing Emphasis in British Aid
Policies: More Help For The Poorest'.

**"The case for promoting agricultural projects
and, in particular, smallholder schemes was very
persuasive at this time."**

Above: Sir Eric Griffith-Jones, CDC's chairman
from 1973-1979.

Meinertzhagen's leadership style, in contrast to that of both Rendell before him and John Eccles afterwards, was consensual. And as the first and only chief executive to have lived and worked overseas for CDC before his appointment he was well-liked and respected by his peers, especially those operating out in the field with whom he shared a certain natural empathy as a result of his own first-hand experience. With his understanding support, the regional controllers became ever more powerful and influential.

The new team got off to a flying start, enabling Meinertzhagen to claim in his first Annual Report that 1973 had been one of the most successful years in CDC's history. Record investments of £48 million had been split between twenty-one new ventures and thirty-one existing projects, with gross income also reaching a new high of £16 million and producing a greater operating surplus than in any previous year.

Whilst taking obvious pride in these achievements, the new boss made it clear where his real priorities lay by stressing that CDC's performance should be judged "not solely, nor even primarily, by its financial results but by its success in promoting and carrying out sound development projects of real value to the greatest number of people in the countries where it operates... also in creating employment and opportunities and in improving the quality of life for the poorer classes of the community."

The case for promoting agricultural projects and, in particular, smallholder schemes was very persuasive at this time. The World Bank had estimated that eighty per cent of the population in developing countries lived in rural areas, often scratching a meagre living through tilling the land or animal husbandry. Opportunities for employment were all too often failing to keep pace with population growth and what jobs there were tended to be mainly in the towns, encouraging urban drift. The most pressing problem facing many governments was therefore how to improve the lives of the majority of their people – the rural poor.

CDC was well-placed to help here, especially so given its unrivalled experience in setting up and running agricultural enterprises in different parts of the world. Roger Swynnerton led the way in promoting the idea of nucleus estates supporting smallholder schemes. As had already been proved by the success of smallholder projects such as the Kenya Tea Development Authority (KTDA) and the Federal Land Development Authority (FELDA) in Malaysia, these schemes had the potential to lift hundreds of thousands of families out of subsistence while at the same time encouraging other local businesses to sprout and flourish.

In 1973, Meinertzhagen's first year in charge, more than half of all CDC's new project approvals – eleven out of twenty-one – had to do with renewable natural resources projects, mostly smallholder agricultural schemes. All of them were in Africa and they ranged from tea in Malawi and Ethiopia and tobacco in Malawi and Zambia to rubber in Côte d'Ivoire and sugar in Kenya.

These well-intentioned CDC-managed ventures enjoyed mixed fortunes. In Malawi, the Lingyangwa Smallholder Tobacco Scheme was set up as part of the already well-established Kasungu Flue-Cured Tobacco Authority, while the Malawi Smallholder Tea Factory was connected to the Malawi Smallholder Tea Authority, both of them doing reasonably well. In Zambia, however, the Mukonchi East Assisted Tenants Scheme, along with the Mukonchi Tobacco Training and Settlement Scheme with which it was associated, was blighted by political interference under Kenneth Kaunda, while the Family Farming Tobacco Project, which involved small family-owned plots growing tobacco and maize in rotation, also failed to establish a Zambian tobacco industry to rival that of Malawi. In Ethiopia, the Gumaro Tea Plantation, a remote estate in the forests of the south-west highlands 650 kilometres from the capital, Addis Ababa, struggled to survive amid the political upheavals that followed the fall of Emperor Haile Selassie in 1974 and in 1977 CDC finally shut up shop for good, closing its office in Addis and clearing out, not to return until 2011.

Sir Peter Meinertzhagen

Born into a family of investment bankers in 1920 and educated at Eton, Peter Meinertzhagen went almost straight from school into the Army to fight in the Second World War. Thereafter, instead of following in the family banking tradition, he joined Albert Booth and Co, a Liverpool-based international import-export group with roots in leather trading and shipping. He worked for them in East Africa for several years, during which time he developed a great attachment to the African people and a strong commitment to making some sort of contribution to their social and economic progress. It was there that he met his wife, Dido. Sharing the same ideals regarding the development of Africa, she became a perfect foil to her husband – as vivacious as he was gentle, quiet and unassuming. Meeting Lord Howick in Kenya and seeing the work of CDC at first hand convinced him that this was where his future lay and he joined CDC in 1958, becoming regional controller first in West and then in East Africa.

He succeeded Rendell as general manager in February 1973. Knighted in 1980, Sir Peter held the post of general manager until his retirement in 1985.

An obituary in *The Independent* following his death in 1999 noted: "It was soon clear that Peter Meinertzhagen would bring his own particular style to the job. In his first message to staff after taking over, he said: 'Behind the figures lie many stories. When you have seen what they mean in terms of improving the lot of peoples living in the developing countries you begin to appreciate that the job we are doing is tremendously worthwhile'. This concern with the effect that the activities of CDC would have on the lives of ordinary people in the poorer countries of the world remained a central tenet of his philosophy."

Below: Family members harvesting tea in one of the tea gardens supported by Malawi's Smallholder Tea Authority.

Smallholder projects in the Land of the Lake

Malawi – formerly Nyasaland – was and is a very poor country, making it a prime candidate for CDC investment at a time when the focus was very much on helping the poorest nations. This resulted in a CDC presence and portfolio that was, for many years, way out of proportion to the size of the country or its economy. It began with Viphya Tung Estates in the late forties, one of CDC's earliest projects, and grew steadily until, by the 1990s, Malawi was one of CDC's largest country portfolios and, in the Sable agribusiness conglomerate, its single largest investment.

In purely developmental terms, it was the smallholder authority projects that were the most successful. Innovative schemes pioneered by Mike Lewis and David Killick, CDC's men in Malawi during this time, provided a source of cash income for poor farmers where none had existed before while also generating foreign exchange for the country through producing a crop for export. The Kasungu Flue-Cured Tobacco Authority (KFCTA), the Smallholder Tea Authority and the Smallholder Coffee Authority establishing models that came to be repeated throughout CDC's world at the time.

KFCTA could trace its origins back as far as 1949 when CDC leased 4,400 hectares from the Nyasaland government and established the Kasungu Tobacco Scheme, which featured a tobacco plantation and the barns in which the leaf was to be cured using smoke and heat from wood-burning stoves.

This developed into a smallholder operation on a minor scale with the arrival of six farmers in 1957 but only really started to expand when KFCTA was set up in 1968 to encourage the training and settlement of smallholders. By 1980, nearly 1,200 farmers were cultivating between one and eight hectares each and producing ten per cent of Malawi's entire tobacco crop, already by then its major export.

The Smallholder Tea Authority was actually set up the year before KFCTA, in 1967, with CDC seconding a secretary/accountant and also providing loans for development, including the construction of a tea factory to process the green leaf. The project grew rapidly until, by 1983, there were 4,800 smallholders tending 2,300 hectares of tea.

The Smallholder Coffee Authority eventually provided a livelihood for even more farmers. Originally set up by the Malawi government in 1971, it was dissolved three years later for want of proper resources but was then revived in 1978 with CDC support. This came in the form of a loan that financed the construction of a headquarters complex at Mzuzu, including processing facilities, workshops and offices. The loan also provided the working capital that enabled farmers to receive credit for materials and services.

As with the other smallholder authorities, the farmers were also supported with a whole range of services that included training, the supply of fertilisers and pesticides and, further down the line, help with processing and marketing. By 1981 3,000 farmers were registered and by 1985 this figure had risen to 8,000.

The last of CDC's managed smallholder authorities in Malawi was the Smallholder Sugar Authority, launched in 1977 and located on the hot, wet, mosquito-infested flatlands bordering the Dwangwa River where the Dwangwa Sugar Corporation, a new cane-growing estate and mill owned by Lonrho and part-financed by CDC, had been established earlier in the same year.

The authority, set up by CDC, encouraged several hundred farmers to settle and produce irrigated sugar cane on two-hectare plots, supported by the usual package of services. Although these projects were eminently successful in fulfilling CDC's brief to help the poorest people in the poorest countries, they came with innate financial problems that were thought to be insoluble. These included fluctuations in commodity prices and the potentially crippling effects of foreign exchange movements. Because no politically and economically acceptable way could be found of persuading the farmers to build up their savings in the good times to tide them over in the lean times, the farmers ended up benefiting when prices were high while the authority took the hit when they were low.

At the same time, the challenges of managing other governments' statutory bodies, with all the potential and reality for political interference that was involved with these so-called parastatals, were wearing. This, combined with a changing, more commercial investment culture within CDC, meant that no further smallholder agricultural authorities were promoted by CDC after the early 1980s. But by then, much had been achieved – and there are still plenty of smallholders growing sugar, coffee and tea.

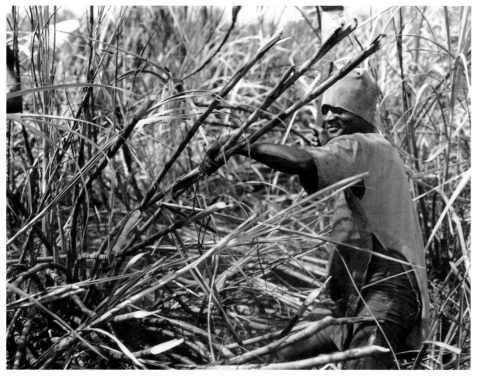

Left: Cutting cane by hand at Dwangwa, a delta bordering Lake Malawi. Managed with the help of Malawi's Smallholder Sugar Authority, the farmers' cane was processed in the mill of neighbouring Dwangwa Sugar Corporation, financed partly by a loan from CDC.

Below (left): Inspecting coffee on one of the Malawi Smallholder Coffee Authority estates in the area around Mzuzu. The five main growing areas were dotted around the blue/green misty hills that stretch for hundreds of kilometres to the north, south and east of Mzuzu, the best quality coffee coming from the Misuku Hills on the Songwe River in the north, close to the border with Tanzania.

Below (right): Tobacco leaf – 'Malawi's Gold' – planted at Kasungu in Malawi, where the Kasungu Flue-Cured Tobacco Authority was launched in 1968 on estates managed by CDC since the early 1950s.

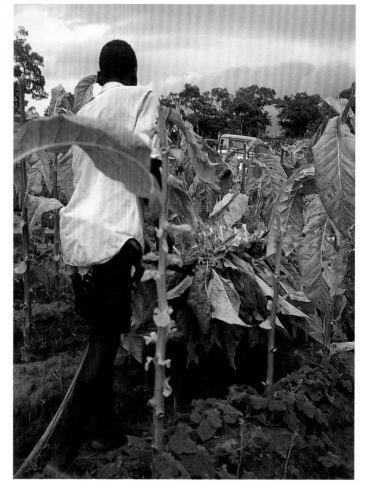

In Kenya, three new tea factories contributed to the continuing and ever-expanding success of the Kenya Tea Development Authority's operations, while involvement in the setting up of the Mumias Sugar Company and the subsequent funding of the Mumias Outgrowers Company proved to be the most significant long-term successes to come out of that clutch of 1973 approvals, helping to lay the foundations of the Kenyan sugar industry. Together with the British government, CDC supported the outgrowers (outgrowers being the term used for farmers who operated independently but who sold their crops to a nucleus estate), providing them with credit, agricultural services, technical assistance and representation in business negotiations as well as other facilities such as a savings cooperative. In addition, it provided finance to MSC for expansion and provided back-up in the shape of advice from the CDC board members and visits by CDC's agriculturalists and engineers. By 2006, when CDC finally sold its fifteen per cent stake in the company, MSC was responsible for half of Kenya's entire 550,000-tonne sugar production.

One of the other successes to come out of the Meinertzhagen team's eleven first year approvals was in Côte d'Ivoire, where CDC's investment in the state-controlled rubber company Societe Africaine de Plantations d'Heveas (SAPH) was its first in what used to be known as the Ivory Coast. The country was stable and relatively advanced, having prospered on the back of post-independence French investment and high cocoa and coffee prices, and the 'Ivorian miracle' was much envied elsewhere in Africa.

The French had immigrated rather than emigrated following independence in 1960 and their influence was reflected in Abidjan's wide boulevards and mouth-watering patisseries. However, the French way of doing business did present new challenges for CDC who therefore decided to focus at first simply on building a small portfolio of loan investments in public sector projects in the agribusiness and forestry sectors, alongside government, the World Bank and other development finance institutions.

These might have seemed relatively safe on the face of it, but the development finance institutions were often the lenders of last resort and lending to state-controlled institutions was not without risk. When the debt crisis came along several of these projects, which were mostly rubber, coconut and oil palm estates farmed by outgrowers and smallholders, got into difficulties. In the case of SAPH, CDC ended up buying and then managing the company through its expansion and listing on the Ivorian stock exchange, going on to retain its small equity stake until 2005, more than thirty years after making its initial small loan.

Later, CDC was to be involved in another much more pioneering, challenging and sometimes downright dangerous rubber plantation project in Côte d'Ivoire when it bought and managed the 2,000-hectare Compagnie Heveicole de Cavally in 1995. This was located in the Western Region of the country, just west of Zagne and close to the border with Liberia in an area that was to be the scene of fierce fighting during the civil war between the rebel-held north and the government-controlled south that lasted from 1999 to 2005. CDC could well have been forgiven for walking away, given the operational difficulties, danger to personnel and periods of poor rubber prices. And yet it persevered, hanging in there right through civil war and the commodity cycle to build and maintain a well-managed plantation that provided some stability in what was otherwise a war zone. And when it did eventually sell the company it received a handsome $74 million return on its $30 million investment.

Back in the seventies, meanwhile, the problem for the countries most in need had suddenly become even more acute as a result of the oil crisis of 1973-74 and the world recession that followed in its wake. The developing countries, with the exception of those that were fortunate enough to be oil producers themselves, suffered proportionately more than anywhere else as foreign exchange reserves dissolved and cash-strapped governments cut their spending.

Meinertzhagen wrote in 1974 that conditions in some of the poorer countries were "no longer tolerable"; by 1975 they were "unspeakably grim". Millions were enduring severe hardship and starvation. As the situation worsened, Meinertzhagen appealed for both developed and developing countries to work together to tackle world poverty and made a point of underlining the mutual benefits this could bring, calling on the prosperous nations to accept the need to provide fair or even favourable terms of trade and trading "if the lot of the poor of the world is to be improved and the stability of the industrialised economies is to be assured". Possibly with the aim of stiffening the aid sinews of the British government specifically in mind, he harped on the same theme when writing that "CDC investment is an investment in international stability".

His pleas, it seemed, did not fall on deaf ears. As its title indicated, the White Paper of 1975 'More Help for the Poorest' undertook to help the poorest, especially in those countries most affected by the oil price increases. And within the poorest countries, the target would be to help the poorest people. This would demonstrate to other governments and international institutions what was achievable and would encourage them to match British aid contributions.

Meanwhile, under the Labour government, the Overseas Development Administration had become the Ministry of Overseas Development (ODM) once again and was generally more supportive of CDC, later increasing its borrowing powers substantially to £500 million, forgiving some of the amounts still outstanding from failed projects in the very early days and pushing through a useful Act of Parliament that consolidated legislation dealing with CDC.

As part of this new spirit of co-operation, ODM also agreed to provide extra financial help in various other useful ways, notably with regard to integrated rural development projects. Here, CDC's investments would, in certain circumstances henceforth, be able to benefit from having vital infrastructure such as roads and bridges paid for separately out of ODM's aid funds. Special ODM grants would also be made available for other situations such as where a project could not afford to pay for expatriate management during its development phase. Again, ODM would provide the extra money. At the same time, CDC happily acceded to ODM's proposal for a joint working party to discuss how CDC might implement the aims identified in the White Paper, this review setting the precedent for regular quinquennial progress evaluations.

With the world in recession, with anti-foreign investment policies adopted in some former colonies that were determined to underline their political independence and with an escalating debt crisis, it is surprising – and much to its credit – that CDC did so well in the years following the oil crisis of 1973. By 1976, it was working on no less than twenty-six major project investigations in fourteen countries. And, true to the aims stated in the 1975 White Paper – and already embraced before that by Meinertzhagen – nearly eighty per cent of its commitments in that same year were in poorer countries and more than seventy per cent in renewable natural resources.

"Meinertzhagen wrote in 1974 that conditions in some of the poorer countries were 'no longer tolerable'; by 1975 they were 'unspeakably grim'. Millions were enduring severe hardship and starvation."

Above: Cylindrical coagulation tanks of rubber latex at the Societe Africaine de Plantations d'Heveas (SAPH) factory in Côte d'Ivoire being sprayed with a chemical as part of the process for converting natural latex into high grade crumb rubber to Michelin's specification.

One of the more ambitious new projects launched in 1976 took CDC to Papua New Guinea for the first time. PNG had become self-governing in 1973 and was granted full independence two years later in 1975, the year in which the British government gave CDC permission to operate there. The new nation's economy was very under-developed, with most of the Melanesian population still living a traditional hunter-gatherer existence in the densely-forested island, the more remote parts of which remained unmapped due to their almost total inaccessibility.

In 1974, the local Department of Finance had invited CDC and the World Bank to consider what might be done in terms of agricultural development. A joint mission duly went out specifically to assess a promising area of land in the Northern Province. The land, at Higaturu, near the provincial capital of Popondetta, was deemed to have considerable potential having previously been the site of a seemingly rather unlikely scheme, long since abandoned, that involved setting up of a settlement project for Australian World War II veterans. The CDC/World Bank team were able to confirm that eruptions in the past from nearby volcanoes had helped to create fertile soils that would be ideal for oil palm cultivation and put forward a proposal for a nucleus estate and mill with an attached smallholder scheme that the World Bank was to finance.

Higaturu Oil Palms was formally established in 1976 as a 50:50 joint venture with the PNG government. Managed by CDC – its first general manager, Richard Beacham, received an OBE in 1980 for his services to British interests in PNG – Higaturu formed the initial building block in what eventually became CDC's largest palm oil group, Pacific Rim Palm Oil Ltd (PRPOL), which it controlled until 2005. By that time, Higaturu comprised an area extending to nearly 9,000 hectares of mature palms on three estates, each producing fresh palm fruit for processing in a large mill with a capacity of sixty tonnes per hour. CDC had also taken the lead in creating a social infrastructure that included housing, shops, sports and entertainment facilities and medical clinics as well as mains power, water and sanitation.

Further extensive oil palm estates were established at Milne Bay in 1985 and at Poliamba on the island of New Ireland in 1988. Milne Bay, which was set up with plans for 3,700 hectares of palms, eventually grew to be almost as big as Higaturu, with 8,200 hectares, while Poliamba was not far behind with 6,000 hectares, making a grand total of over 23,000 hectares.

As well as its very substantial palm oil interests, CDC had gone on to launch a number of other major projects in PNG, its activities there reaching a peak from the late 1980s on. In 1987, it set up its first ever private equity management company, PNG Venture Finance Pty Ltd, another innovative and significant new development with implications for the future. It also supported the PNG Electricity Commission with two loans for power station development and got involved in housing finance.

Above: Her Majesty Queen Elizabeth II and HRH the Duke of Edinburgh during a visit to Popondetta, Papua New Guinea, in 1977, the year of the Queen's Silver Jubilee. The general manager of neighbouring Higaturu Oil Palms, Richard Beacham, and his wife, Judith, were presented to the Royal couple.

Above: Karl Edwards.

Above: The fruit of the oil palm, ripe for harvesting.

Above: A view of Milne Bay in Papua New Guinea, the location for one of CDC's three oil palm estates in PNG.

Tragedy at Milne Bay

Papua New Guinea includes some of the last unexplored places on earth and CDC arrived there in the seventies to find that relief maps of the island still contained blank spaces in the interior marked 'Cloud – Relief Data Incomplete'. Impenetrable on land, these areas of dense tropical jungle are permanently shrouded in low cloud that renders even aerial photography useless to cartographers. During three years of fierce fighting between the Allies and the Japanese in World War II, no less than 325 Allied planes disappeared without trace over the island. The impenetrability of the jungle also accounts for the fact that over seven hundred different languages and dialects are known to have developed on the island – simply because there could be virtually no contact between tribes living in different communities in the jungle even though sometimes separated by only a few kilometres. As a result, Pidgin English became the nearest thing to an official language in the urban centres.

Tribal rivalries based on a system known in pidgin as 'Wantok' – 'one-talk' or 'the same language' – combined with widespread poverty caused by urban drift meant that the towns, especially the capital, Port Moresby, suffered from a serious urban violence problem, with mass brawls and roaming gangs of 'rascals' providing a constant threat.

Expatriates and the wealthier nationals tended to live behind high walls and barbed wire and burglaries at gunpoint were not uncommon. The same threats could be found in the rural areas and armed hold-ups of estate managers, especially on pay-day, were all too frequent.

From a security point of view, Milne Bay, where CDC opened its second oil palm plantation, was considered one of the better places to be posted, with the calm waters of Milne Bay providing facilities for sailing and scuba diving, but it was here, tragically, that general manager Karl Edwards was murdered in 1992 after addressing a gathering of employees.

Having previously worked with Christian Aid in Uganda, Karl had joined CDC as a research agronomist at Tanganyika Wattle Company in 1974, going on to hold a number of senior positions in Africa and the Pacific, working with both the Smallholder Coffee Authority and the Smallholder Sugar Authority in Malawi, the Northern Tanzania Farms project and then Metenesel Estates in Vanuatu before returning to Malawi as managing director of Kawalazi Estates in Mzuzu. He became general manager at Milne Bay in 1992 only a short time before his murder. Married to Gay, he had two daughters, Esther and Sarah, and a son, Luke.

Loading bunches of fresh oil palm fruit bunches onto a truck at Higaturu, CDC's first oil palm estate in Papua New Guinea.

An absolutely straight north-south borderline down the middle of the island of New Guinea divides Indonesian West Papua (known as Irian Jaya until 2002) from Papua New Guinea. And it was there, at a place called Ransiki, that CDC established a cocoa plantation project, PT Coklat Ransiki, that was even more remote and pioneering than those in PNG. When the initial CDC investigation team went out to do a feasibility study in 1976 it took them three days to get there and even when they had blazed a trail and the venture was up and running, it still took twenty-four hours to get there from Jakarta.

CDC had been doing its best to get established in Indonesia since 1971 but had found it tough going. The country, which is made up of more than 13,000 islands, had been a backwater for many years and there was no tradition of foreign investment when General Suharto replaced Sukarno as president in 1968 and set about introducing measures to stabilise the economy and kick-start development. Attracting outside investment was certainly part of his plan, but all sorts of practical difficulties got in the way. English was not well understood, everything was tied up in a tangle of red tape and the local investment law was a nightmare for CDC people to understand, based as it was on Roman-Dutch principles with security for loans somewhat difficult to establish, let alone enforce. Also, sectors for investment were restricted, with agriculture initially being out of bounds. One way and another, doing business was challenging, to say the least.

"**CDC had been doing its best to get established in Indonesia since 1971 but had found it tough going. The country, which is made up of more than 13,000 islands, had been a backwater for many years and there was no tradition of foreign investment...**"

CDC nevertheless persevered. Its loan to Merpati Airlines had been its first investment outside the Commonwealth. Others followed and although none of these early projects was particularly significant they served to teach CDC how to do business in the country. Its first agricultural investment was in PT Tatar Anyar, a group of tea and rubber estates in central and west Java, managed by Anglo-Indonesian. The enterprise needed more finance in order to rehabilitate its plantations and factories and CDC was invited to take equity, provide loan finance and supply technical advice by way of seconding staff and undertaking regular monitoring visits. It maintained an interest in what some called 'Tatty Annie' until 1998.

Meanwhile, the World Bank, which had turned its attention to agriculture, had asked CDC for assistance in developing its expertise in that sector and, to that end, Tom Phillips had been seconded to the bank for twelve months, identifying opportunities for investment in Indonesia agriculture. CDC was then invited by the Indonesian government to participate in their public sector smallholder schemes, making a series of loans in support of World Bank-led settlement projects. This it did to such an extent that Indonesia became CDC's largest country portfolio for a while.

This was fine, especially as these investments provided a significant and relatively risk-free income stream. However, what CDC really wanted to do was to get involved in its own managed project – and it was PT Coklat Ransiki that eventually provided the opportunity, albeit a logistically challenging one. That, in itself, was not a problem. CDC was keen to show the Indonesian government what it was made of and if that meant working in the back of beyond, then so be it.

For reasons completely beyond CDC's control, the project then almost foundered before it got under way when the fast-flowing Ransiki River suddenly changed its course after a heavy storm caused a major flood and started flowing through the middle of the land earmarked for the plantation, reducing the area by half. This all happened in between the project being approved by the CDC board in London and the date when work on its implementation was due to start. Not wanting to abandon the eagerly anticipated development, the project management nevertheless decided to go ahead.

The existing jetty on which supplies and equipment were to be brought ashore had been washed away in the flood so a landing craft had to be used to bring in the first bulldozer, which then pushed logs onto the beach to create a ramp up which it could get itself onto the land. Supervised by manager John Morris, who had come in on the landing craft, the ramp was then built up with gravel so that the other supplies could be offloaded.

To start with, John and his wife lived in a house on the beach, but over the next few months, houses for senior expatriates and a general office were built on some low hills nearby, well above the malaria-carrying mosquito line, and a roadway was laid that connected up with an existing road leading into the small district centre of Ransiki. Later, visitors were able to fly in using a small airstrip that had been built by the Japanese during the war.

Enough plantation land had been cleared and prepared for the first plantings to go ahead in 1980, using plants and seeds from CDC's BAL estates. Seven years later, 900 hectares were under cultivation and 550 local people were employed on the estate while Ransiki itself had grown from little more than a small outpost into a thriving town with a population of 3,500 people.

Above: The jetty at Ransiki, the remote location where CDC established a cocoa estate in the late seventies, its first managed project in Indonesia. The original one was washed away in a flood shortly before the CDC advance team arrived to start clearing the land for planting, necessitating the use of a landing craft to get the first bulldozer ashore.

Mananga Agricultural Management Centre

The Mananga Agricultural Management Centre, established in Swaziland in 1972, represented one of CDC's more innovative and far-reaching initiatives behind the scenes, as it were. The training and subsequent promotion of local indigenous staff had long been a facet of CDC's operations worldwide, but this consisted mostly of training in particular technical skills and depended to a considerable degree on local circumstances and the motivation of CDC's regional and project staff. Mananga took things on a significant stage further, aiming to impart the sort of broad knowledge and experience through residential courses that would turn agricultural managers from all around CDC's universe into competent general managers.

The centre was located within the Swaziland Irrigation Scheme on the lower slopes of Mananga Mountain, its beautiful gardens commanding a fine view over the entire SIS area, from the green irrigated fields immediately below to the parched grasslands in the distance.

In the early years, the centre typically offered courses lasting three months to those already holding responsible positions in agricultural management, with a shorter course for senior managers that addressed strategic management issues. There was accommodation for twenty students per course in individual study bedrooms and this number was increased as time went on. The students had the exclusive use of 485 hectares belonging to MAMC as a practical classroom extension, part of it fully irrigated. Yields for these text-book managed areas were some of the highest in Swaziland and the income was used to subsidise the centre's costs.

CDC and its agricultural projects around the world were not the only ones to benefit. Mananga's reputation as a training centre of excellence spread rapidly and demand for places on its courses soon extended way beyond CDC, with eighty per cent of its students coming from outside by 1980 – most of them sent there independently by African governments. In its first fifteen years MAMC trained several thousand managers from over fifty different countries.

Continuing to develop and expand at a rapid rate, it dropped 'Agricultural' from its name in 1993 to reflect the reality that by then it had widened its teaching and its intake to meet the needs of a changing economic environment.

CDC continued to own it until 1998, by which time it was beginning to look a little out of place among CDC's private equity portfolio, and at that point one of its senior lecturers, Dr Ranga Taruvinga, acquired the intellectual rights to the centre and its library. Rebranded the Mananga Centre for Regional Integration and Management Development, it moved to a new campus near the Swaziland capital of Mbabane. Meanwhile, the old buildings on the slopes of Mananga Mountain were taken over to house a new High School, Mananga College, which is now well established as one of the best schools in the region.

Top and above: Houses and part of the industrial estate (below) built at Nava Nakorn, Thailand's first new town, built to relieve pressure on Bangkok. Today, it is a thriving industrial zone, home to more than two hundred factories and businesses with modern residential estates to house the people who work there.

In addition to Indonesia, the other South East Asian country in which CDC opened up offices as soon as possible after being freed to operate outside the Commonwealth was Thailand. Looking forward to the possibility of a lot of new investments there, it sent in young and energetic staff to do the business.

Thailand in 1971 was a very different country from the ex-British colonies with which CDC was most familiar. The ancient Thai monarchy had never been colonised by any western imperial power and the Thai culture, with its Buddhist roots, Grand Palace and Ayutthaya was distinctly alien and quite unlike that of Malaysia, where the mock-Tudor bungalows and red telephone boxes of the Cameron Highlands, relics of British rule, provided reminders of home for expatriate CDC staff. At a time before Thailand had opened up to mass tourism, English was not widely spoken outside the business and government communities and almost all road signs were in Thai script. It was also easy to cause offence if you hadn't taken the trouble to learn some basic rules of local etiquette. All this made it a fascinating and exciting place to live, but a challenging environment in which to work.

There was a particular Thai way of doing business and getting things done. The Thai business communities were based on long-standing relationships. They worked closely with each other, were very self-confident and took only what they wanted from the West. This was even more the case among the Chinese families who had long thrived in Thailand. It was not going to be easy to break into these circles; it would take time, hard work and patience for newcomers to become accepted. CDC's new office had to work out what it had to offer, where it could be most useful and, just as importantly, with whom it could work. Establishing those relationships with people it could trust was going to be the key to success. If it sent the wrong people to staff its office and if they, in turn, chose the wrong business partners, things could go badly wrong. Alan Belsham, the Singapore-based regional controller at the time described the risks as "traps for new players".

On top of all that, CDC's arrival on the scene coincided with a period of political unrest. Just as the new representative, Christopher Stephenson, was working out how best to operate, the Thai government suddenly established direct military rule. This led, two years later, to demonstrations by students and others in favour of a more democratic system. It took the King's intervention to quell these protests, the first time since 1932 that the monarchy had assumed a direct role in Thai politics. The outcome was a brief period of parliamentary democracy, followed by another coup in 1976. And so it continued – cycles of military interventions and power-sharing, with spells of democracy in between. Given the repressive regimes at the time of Burma (later Myanmar) to the west and, later, Cambodia to the east, it was noteworthy that Thailand managed to survive without succumbing to extreme radicalism. At the same time, CDC succeeded in establishing a presence and, despite the political instability, was able to build a portfolio that was, by the 1990s, one of the five most valuable within CDC anywhere in the world.

CDC's opening venture was the Thailand Housing Finance Co Ltd. Bangkok was teeming with a population of three million people and while there was a strong land-owning tradition among the Thai people, meaning that even the poorer families often had a small plot, few had enough money to develop it and build decent homes. There was no building society culture and the banks did not meet the need. It took two years for CDC and its counsel to set up a workable legal structure, ready to start operations in 1973, with CDC providing management and loan finance while also holding forty-nine per cent of the equity.

It had rightly identified the market demand among low and middle-income earners and by 1979, when it changed its name to Sinkahakan Credit Foncier, it had more than 3,000 loans outstanding. A long-term sustainable business, it was profitable from its second year of operation, paying annual dividends, attracting other finance from banks and insurance companies and, by example, encouraging the Thai banking community to move into mortgage finance. It went public in 1982, and although a Thai had taken over as general manager in 1980, CDC continued to second staff to the company until the late 1990s, when it was sold as a going concern to a local financial institution.

Following the establishment of the Thailand Housing Finance Co Ltd, CDC's next venture in Thailand was another long-lasting, CDC-managed project in the real estate sector. During one of the early reconnaissance missions that had preceded the opening of its office, CDC had been introduced to the Charusorn family by M.L. Usni Pramoj, a shrewd, Oxford-educated barrister who managed His Majesty's Private Property Office. Right from the start, M. L. Usni had been an enthusiastic supporter of CDC and, through him, the Private Property Office, the Crown Property Bureau and a respected Thai bank had become CDC's partners in the Thailand Housing Finance Company.

It was in M.L. Usni Pramoj's office that the introduction was made to Khun Suree, the matriarch of the Charusorn family. She unveiled a map showing a jigsaw of small areas of old rice paddy that she had acquired with ideas of developing Thailand's first new town to relieve the pressure on Bangkok. This was to be ideally located 46 kilometres from Bangkok and just 15 kilometres from the airport. CDC agreed to carry out a feasibility study with the help of its housing experts, who came up with a plan for an integrated development featuring housing, commercial and industrial areas, roads and services. Named Nava Nakorn, this was given the go-ahead and CDC took a small equity stake and managed the project. The Charusorns, the Private Property Office, the National Housing Authority and another investor subscribed the rest of the equity.

Nava Nakorn got off to a slow start. To some extent, this was probably because it was a little too far ahead of its time, while political events also had an adverse knock-on effect on demand for factory space. For whatever reasons, it did not initially attract businesses and families to move out in quite the numbers expected. Today, however, it is a well-established and successful industrial zone, with two hundred factories and businesses, and the idea has been replicated throughout the Great Bangkok area. CDC managed it until 1991 when it sold its shares at a time when demand had taken off and land prices were high, delivering a reasonable financial return on the investment.

The third CDC-managed business in Thailand, the Thai Factory Development Co Ltd, had meanwhile grown out of the need to make the most of development at Nava Nakorn. Given the slow sales of industrial sites there and also CDC's experience in Singapore, Malaysia and Jamaica, the obvious next step seemed to be to build fully serviced, off-the-shelf factories for sale or rental at Nava Nakorn. The idea was that these units would cater specifically for the expansion of small businesses that were operating out of crowded shop/home premises in the central Bangkok area.

With the Industrial Finance Corporation of Thailand (IFCT) as a partner, CDC launched the new company in 1977, handing over management to IFCT three years later but retaining its equity share until 1989. Thereafter, CDC continued to make a number of loans to IFCT, with whom it had developed a mutually beneficial relationship, supporting its work in providing medium to long-term loans and working capital to the Thai private sector.

Other early investments in Thailand included a loan of £800,000 to finance a major extension to the magnificent and luxurious 400-room Oriental Hotel, CDC stepping in where others feared to tread following the fall of Saigon. The loan was controversial, but not because of any perceived domino-effect Communist threat; the local office of the Overseas Development Administration objected strongly on the grounds that it wasn't helping the poor. This, however, was overruled by the ODA in London.

There was also a series of loans to the Office of the Rubber Replanting Aid Fund (ORRAF), with CDC's rubber experts providing further assistance. By the time it closed down in 1991, ORRAF had helped 300,000 smallholders and had replanted 430,000 hectares, contributing to a 300 per cent increase in the country's rubber exports. So nobody could quarrel with the validity of that investment.

Left: The Oriental Hotel in Bangkok. At a time when other investors were wary following the fall of Saigon, CDC made a controversial loan to finance the building of the major new extension that can be seen on the left of the picture.

Right: Shiselweni Forestry Company's Themba Vilane (pictured left) discussing the day's forestry operations. Joining from school in 1988, Themba was sponsored by USAID to take a forestry degree in the United States, returning to become Harvesting Manager. Shiselweni had Swazi estate managers from the start. In the late 1960s CDC sponsored recruits to go to Dedza Forest College in Malawi, and they went on to be the backbone of the estate management. The first Swazi manager was Induna Vilakati, a real character and certainly not to be messed with. He had been in the army during the Second World War and advanced north through Italy. He once met Prince Charles and when asked how he found Italy promptly replied "By sea, Sir". He died in 1994.

Successful careers

Part of CDC's mission has always been to recruit and train up local management staff wherever possible and the roll call of those who went on to build successful careers for themselves includes some colourful and outstanding characters.

The Far East Region set the pace in recruiting and promoting local staff and the honour of being CDC's very first local project general manager goes to Shim Kah Foo.

Educated at Raffles College, Singapore, Shim was one of a cadre of local recruits taken on by South East Asia regional controller David Fiennes under a far-sighted management trainee scheme. He joined the regional office in Kuala Lumpur in 1954 and after a spell in the London office in 1958 was then chosen to be CDC's first manager of the Borneo Development Corporation (BDC) based in Kuching. From the same office, he also managed BDC's sister company Borneo Housing Development Ltd, later renamed Borneo Housing Mortgage Finance Bhd. Together, these were the most prolific developers and financiers of commercial, industrial and housing estates throughout the two Borneo territories that later became the Malaysian estates of Sabah and Sarawak.

A loquacious and engaging personality, Shim used to boast that his classmates at Raffles had included such future luminaries as Dr Goh Keng Swee, deputy to Singapore's first prime minister Lee Kuan Yew, and Hon Sui Sen, the country's first finance minister. A man blessed with a not inconsiderable ego, he took pleasure in his easy command of English and liked to hold sway in conversations, but was also good-natured and kind-hearted.

Shim was the first of a succession of very capable locally-recruited managers in the region that included Lee Ek Hua, Howard Yap and the delightfully named (if you're a fan of Sir Walter Scott!) Ivan Ho. Like

Shim, Howard Yap was educated at Raffles and served his CDC apprenticeship in the Kuala Lumpur office before going on in 1964 to take charge of the newly-opened independent head office of Borneo Housing Development Ltd in Jesselton (Kota Kinabalu).

Lee Ek Hua, a geography graduate from the University of Malaya, was recruited in 1958 and became the manager of highly successful Singapore Factory Development Ltd before migrating with his family to Canada where he studied law and ended up running a law practice in Vancouver. Ivan Ho, who joined CDC in 1963, worked with both Shim in Kuching and Howard in Jesselton before being appointed manager of a new branch of BDC/ Borneo Housing Mortgage Finance in Sandakan. He later worked for CDC in the regional and country offices in Singapore and Kuala Lumpur where he became country manager for Malaysia before retiring in 1999. His even longer-serving colleague, Mrs Tai Yan Yoon, retired in 2000 having been with CDC since 1962, working as personal assistant to a string of CDC heads.

Borneo Abaca Ltd, later BAL Plantations, was also exceptional in the number of local recruits who passed through its agricultural and engineering cadet training schemes to become senior managers. By the mid-1970s all five estate managers at BAL were ex-cadets and with local staff rising through the ranks in all departments, the number of expatriate managers was gradually reduced until, by 1992, there was just one – general manager William Tully. At that time, his seven locally-recruited senior managers could claim to have clocked up over two hundred years of CDC service between them. The longest-serving of the seven was chief accounting manager Mok Thai Yin, with forty-three years under his belt. Mok, a warm, friendly character who, among other things, is remembered by former colleagues for his love of snooker, retired the following year at the age of seventy. He died in 2005.

The West Africa regional office in Lagos also took a lead in training and promoting local Nigerians. One of the first to benefit was Gamaliel Onosode, a graduate of Ibadan University, who joined one of the first intakes to the London-based graduate management scheme in 1957. Returning to Nigeria he worked his way up to a senior position in the Lagos regional office before leaving to become a presidential adviser and candidate, long-time chairman of Dunlop Nigeria, Cadbury Nigeria and, latterly, Celtel Nigeria. He was also pro-chancellor of Ibadan University. He died in 2015.

Emeka Anyaoku was another graduate of Ibadan University who took part in the London graduate management training scheme at around the same time and who then worked in the Lagos office for several years before going on to an illustrious career in the Nigerian diplomatic service and as Commonwealth secretary general from 1990 to 1999. His daughter, Adiba Ighodaro, joined CDC in 1991, reopened an office in Lagos in 2000 and is now a partner at Actis.

Richard Kemoli was the first Kenyan to become a CDC management trainee. Carrying out vacation work in the Nairobi office was what had inspired him to join CDC and he was taken on as a trainee after graduating from Uganda's Makerere University with a degree in Economics. He then remained with CDC until his retirement in 1996. After gaining a Diploma at the School of Management Studies in London as part of his training, Richard returned to the Nairobi office where he worked first as assistant, then as executive assistant and finally as senior executive, with a spell as acting representative in the East Africa regional office. In January 1995 he was appointed an Honorary MBE by the Queen in recognition of "thirty-two years of service with the Kenya Office of CDC". He has continued to be prominent in the Kenyan business community, chairing former CDC investee companies Lafarge Bamburi Cement and Unga Group.

Elsewhere in the Asia Pacific region, CDC was again active in Singapore in the early seventies. In 1968 Britain had announced its military withdrawal, ending its long-term commitment to the island country's defence and leaving a large local workforce unemployed. In order to create new jobs, the far-sighted first prime minister of Singapore, Lee Kuan Yew, formed the Jurong Town Corporation (JTC). Building on the experience of CDC's Singapore Factory Development, its aim was to turn Singapore into a major industrial complex.

In 1969, CDC had supplied finance to the fledgling JTC for the construction of the Gul Channel as the first stage in the scheme, which involved reclaiming land from the sea and the swamps that cover much of Singapore so that shipyards and oil rig repair yards could be built. The new town of Jurong was then developed on an impressive scale, with vast areas of housing and industrial estates, while the Royal Naval Dockyard was taken over and converted into a dry dock capable of accommodating the world's largest tankers, CDC providing a loan for this project in 1973. As its last two investments in Singapore's infrastructure, CDC made a loan to the Public Utilities Board for the building of the new Upper Peirce Reservoir and its associated pipelines, pumping stations and water treatment works, needed to meet the new demand brought about by the Jurong development, and, more spectacularly, partly financed the construction of the Ocean Building skyscraper office block.

Ocean Building, Singapore

To encourage growth in commercial activity, the government declared some central districts of Singapore to be redevelopment zones, making possible much needed regeneration of run-down areas. Ocean Properties acquired a triangular plot next to Raffles Place and fronting onto Collyer's Quay and partly financed by CDC in 1972, the 114m-high, 28-storey Ocean Building mounted steadily and impressively skywards. Upon completion in 1974, CDC's regional office moved into the 22nd floor, its staff enjoying superb views over the harbour.

The building had its own in-built air-conditioning and computer systems, shopping floors and an underground car park – features that are taken for granted now but were very much state-of-the-art at that time. Standing alone on a bare site when it was opened (with a copy of CDC's annual report placed in a time capsule in the foundations) it is now in the thick of the busy harbour front business district. Part of CDC's loan was converted to equity, which it eventually sold for a tidy sum. It continued, intermittently, to have a regional office located in Singapore, although, like Hong Kong, the country was long ago deemed too rich to need CDC investment.

Top: The building under construction.

Left: The impressive 28-storey Ocean Building in Singapore, with a copy of CDC's Annual Report sealed in a time capsule in the foundations!

Back in Africa, CDC again found itself experiencing mixed fortunes during the mid-to-late seventies. In Nigeria, the situation had started to deteriorate as early as 1972 when, increasingly flush with petrodollars, the Nigerian government decided that it no longer needed foreign investment and embarked on a policy of nationalisation. First, it introduced a series of Enterprises Promotion Decrees designed to increase the percentage proportion of the economy owned by Nigerians. Each decree listed by name those businesses that had to achieve majority Nigerian ownership by a given date. These companies were then valued by a commission and shares issued through the Lagos Stock Exchange. The values set were low and bank finance was readily available, so the shares were snapped up.

The first list in 1972 did not include any of CDC's investments, all of which were held through its holding company, CDC Nigeria Ltd, and the government gave assurances that there was no intention of listing it in the future. However, when the decree of 1977 was issued, CDC Nigeria Ltd was nevertheless included. CDC appealed but despite the ruling twice being reconsidered by the government's executive council, it stayed on the list. This was quite regardless of the fact that CDC was actually in the process of developing and managing Savannah Sugar, the largest agribusiness development in Nigeria at the time.

There was no alternative but to go along with the directive and over the next three years CDC gradually ceded control of all its investments. By 1980 it had sold most of its industrial and commercial portfolio to the state-controlled Nigeria Industrial Development Bank, CDC Nigeria Ltd becoming a wholly-owned subsidiary of the bank. At the time, it also closed down its regional office overlooking the bustling waterfront in Lagos. The management of Savannah Sugar was left to struggle on until 1982 when it too packed up and left for home or for other parts. After that CDC was not to have a presence in Africa's most populous country for another twelve years.

It was a disappointing end to thirty years of involvement in Nigeria during which CDC had done much to promote agriculture, industry and hotels within the country. The truth of the matter was revealed much later when General Obasanjo, making a speech on his retirement as Head of State, happened to mention that his time at Sandhurst had included a study of economic conditions in Nigeria that had led him to conclude that foreign investors such as CDC (which he named) were interested only in profit and were little more than exploiters!

Left: An artist's impression of the impressive Kiri Dam, built across the Gongola River to form the reservoir that fed the Savannah Sugar Company's irrigation system via a long, wide canal.

Right: A truck loaded with raw sugar cane heads for the Savannah Sugar Company's mill and refinery at Numan in North Eastern Nigeria, set up and managed by CDC between 1975 and 1982.

Savannah Sugar

It was rather ironic given what happened subsequently that the Nigerian government almost had to twist CDC's arm to secure its involvement in Savannah Sugar. The site for the proposed project was located in a remote area in North Eastern Nigeria, near the small town of Numan, 1,000 kilometres from Lagos. It was generally flat, mainly unused land with clay soils, backed by hills – ideal for growing sugarcane except that it needed drainage in the rainy season and irrigation in the dry season. CDC undertook a pilot scheme to look into the commercial viability of establishing a 12,000-hectare plantation to be irrigated using a long, wide canal from a reservoir created by damming the Gongola River, with a factory to mill, refine and pack 100,000 tonnes of sugar annually.

Agriculturally, the trials went well but with no supporting infrastructure in place and no local workforce available, setting up the project would be a challenge.

It would involve starting from scratch in every respect – including the installation of all the basic infrastructure, including power and water supplies, housing, medical and schooling facilities as well as the construction of the factory itself. The North Eastern Nigeria state government did not have the resources or skills to build the dam so the company would have to handle that as well. At the end of the trial in 1974, CDC concluded that it would not be commercially viable.

At that point, the Nigerian government, benefiting from the rising income it was earning from its oil exports thanks to the hike in prices following the 1973 crisis, stepped in and offered to pay for the dam if CDC would agree to manage the project. In 1975 CDC agreed to manage it for ten years, a period it needed to see the development through.

It went ahead and in the first successful harvesting season in 1981 Savannah Sugar produced 10,000 tonnes from 2,660 hectares of cane and was employing 4,400 people. However, things never ran smoothly. As anticipated, getting anyone to work on the remote estate was not easy at any level. 'Local' Nigerian workers had to be recruited from all over the country and offered packages that included housing and regular travel home. And a Nigerian with a UK Chartered Accountant qualification flatly refused to join the administrative team there, telling financial controller Jim Parrish in no uncertain terms: "I didn't return to this country to go work in the bush!"

At the same time, getting the promised funds out of the Nigerian government proved challenging, involving frequent enforced visits to Lagos. On top of all that, getting dividends repatriated was equally difficult. In the end, CDC ended its management contract in 1982, three years early, by mutual agreement with the government. It had not been one of its happier investments.

Having closed its West African regional office in Lagos in 1979, CDC decamped instead to the Liberian capital of Monrovia. This seemed like a good idea at the time but soon proved to be ill-fated when, in 1980, the Liberian president was killed in a coup led by Master Sergeant (later General) Samuel Doe. This marked the start of a twenty-year period of military rule, disputed elections, civil war and general strife and in 1983 CDC downgraded its regional office in Monrovia to a representative office, having made only three minor investments in Liberia. The region was bottom of CDC's investment leagues both in terms of money and numbers and CDC wasn't really making a huge difference to the development of the countries in which it was working.

There were some much more positive developments in the other regions of Africa. Although Kenneth Kaunda's nationalisation policies together with the worldwide recession combined to make life difficult in Zambia, CDC continued to invest there throughout the seventies, providing finance for the ailing copper mining industry in the form of loans to Nchanga Consolidated Copper Mines and Ndola Lime and supporting the textile sector with loan finance and equity in Kafue Textiles, whose brightly coloured patterned prints, often adorned with the faces of politicians, were a fashionable part of Zambian life during the seventies and eighties. CDC also remained steadfastly committed to Tate & Lyle's Zambia Sugar Company, financing all its expansions over a twenty-year period from 1968 onwards, becoming a thirty-one per cent shareholder when it was re-privatised in 1995 and staying involved through good times and bad for thirty-three years altogether.

CDC's involvement in Zambia's sugar industry was not limited to Zambia Sugar. In 1980 it promoted and developed a successful smallholder settlement scheme based on 1,800 hectares just south of Zambia Sugar's Nakambala Estate. Each of the Kaleya Smallholders Company farmers had to undergo a six-month training course before being accepted for the scheme and allocated a small irrigated plot complete with a foundation slab on which to build a house. Kaleya provided technical assistance, equipment and harvesting while the farmers were responsible for in-field irrigation, weeding and fertiliser application. The cost of the materials and services would then be deducted from the proceeds of selling the cane to Zambia Sugar for processing and the farmers would receive the balance. They did so well that CDC ended up being accused by the socialist Zambian government of creating mini-capitalists, a charge against which CDC successfully defended itself. By 1989, Zambians had taken over most of the management posts from CDC expatriates and soon after that Kaleya was accounting for fifteen per cent of Zambia's entire sugarcane production. It is still thriving today.

Women farmers of Kaleya

One outstanding feature of Zambia's Kaleya Smallholder Company's success was the part played by women. The company's selection committee adopted a policy of accepting applications from women who were on their own, without a husband for one reason or another, and they proved to be among the best of all the farmers.

Agnes Maseko's husband had left her and until she came to Kaleya she had been trying in vain to support her family of five daughters by growing and selling maize and vegetables that she grew on a small plot. At Kaleya, she was not only able to become self-sufficient in food, but also earned enough from her cane sales to build a house and educate all her daughters. Annie Tembo did even better. She had previously been struggling to provide for her eleven children through buying and selling fish, but as a Kaleya smallholder she earned enough from her cane to meet all her expenses, build a house, buy two cars and put all eleven children through school.

Right: A farmer cutting his sugar cane by hand at Kaleya – a picture that captures the dirty, dangerous and physically demanding nature of the job.

Above: De-tasselating maize at Tanwat as part of the process of producing high-yielding hybrid seeds.

Above: Inside the National Seed Company of Malawi factory warehouse in Lilongwe.

As well as the growing number of well-established sustainable investments that continued to flourish and expand in Eastern, Central and Southern Africa and in addition to those smallholder and outgrower schemes that had been started in the early seventies, the more significant new projects to be launched during the decade included the national seed companies that were set up in Tanzania and Malawi.

The Tanzania Seed Company grew out of the development by the long-established Tanzania Wattle Company (Tanwat) of a special high-altitude hybrid type of maize. This had yields and a calorific value that was way above ordinary maize, the main staple, but the seed was logistically and technically difficult to produce. The setting up of a national seed company to exploit Tanwat's expertise and experience in this matter was a logical progression.

The business started in a small way, with Tanwat buying a seed processing unit, along with cleaners, graders and a treatment plant, and began selling certified seeds. In 1973, in a joint venture with the National Agricultural and Food Corporation, CDC then took over the renamed Tanzania Seed Company Ltd, initially providing management and technical advice. And once most of the posts had been localised, it continued to second a financial controller.

Tanseed's headquarters were established in the northern town of Arusha in 1976 and later expanded to include plants at Iringa and Morongoro, while maintaining the original operations at Tanwat. Under CDC management, it produced 5,000 tonnes per annum of seed grown by over seventy-five outgrowers and employed two hundred people.

The experience gained through Tanseed was invaluable in establishing the National Seed Company of Malawi (NSCM). The need for Malawi to become self-sufficient in seed supplies, especially for the maize and tobacco that were its most important crops, had been highlighted by the political upheavals in Rhodesia, which had always in the past been the traditional source of supply. Recognising this, the Malawi government decided to establish a national seed scheme and work began in 1976.

A basic infrastructure was put in place, a modern seed testing laboratory was constructed and laboratory assistants and field inspectors were trained. However, it soon became clear that the local government would be unable to handle the large-scale production that was envisaged, particularly as demand for hybrid and composite seed maize varieties was increasing rapidly along with a large requirement for the different varieties of flue-cured, burley, dark fire western and oriental tobacco.

In 1978 NSCM was set up as a joint venture by CDC and the local marketing organisation ADMARC, with ADMARC holding the majority interest and CDC taking on the management contract. By 1979, a specialised seed farm had been established on the outskirts of the capital, Lilongwe, a modern seed processing factory had been built in the town's industrial zone and a professional CDC seed team plus Malawian staff had been put in place. Production and sales increased steadily over the next few years and by 1984 Malawi was not only self-sufficient in seed supplies for all its major crops but had also developed a thriving export trade. The impact made by NSCM on the country's economy in terms of food supplies, reserves and export earnings was enormous.

"The impact made by NSCM on Malawi's economy in terms of food supplies, reserves and export earnings was enormous."

Expatriate lives

CDC's sense of purpose has always attracted committed and motivated people and staff members working in some of the more remote and politically unstable locations around the world have often found themselves having to endure difficult, dangerous and life-threatening conditions. Over the years, several have actually lost their lives through tropical diseases, terrorism and murder.

In the early years, long before the advent of satellite telecommunications and jet travel transformed the world into the global village, life in the more isolated CDC outposts could be both tough and tedious at times and called for a pioneering and adventurous spirit. The following snapshots convey something of what it was like.

1950s

"Iris and I settled down to life on the estate (Tanwat, in what was then Tanganyika, in the early 1950s). There were tea-time visits to other married couples and bachelors elsewhere within Tanwat and reciprocal visits by them to the estate, but most evenings were spent on our own, with reading and the radio, with crackly short-wave reception, being our main relaxation. Weekends were different in that there was usually some sort of activity at the club, including tennis during the day and a dance or film on one of the evenings. Apart from the regular breaks in the transmission of the 16mm films there were quite often other unscheduled breaks when the film broke so it was quite often a little difficult to follow the story and then there were the odd occasions when the reels were put on out of sequence and had to be changed again."

Excerpt from the memoirs of John Taylor. Having trained as a forester with the Forestry Commission in Scotland, John worked for Harlow New Town before joining CDC in 1953 at the start of a thirty-six-year career. The first ten years were spent in East Africa while he qualified as an accountant, and the last ten in the East Caribbean, as representative, with spells in Nigeria, Swaziland and at Head Office in London in between. Following his retirement in 1989, he stayed on in St Lucia where he undertook voluntary work with the local community association. He died there in 2011.

1960s

"Mostyn (part of BAL in Malaysia) was another experience, a huge adventure. One little anecdote: it took place a year or so before I arrived in 1967, in the local fishing village of Kunak, Mostyn's only outlet to the sea. The village consisted of no more than a few timber shophouses on stilts over the water and a small wooden jetty that extended the laterite road out a few metres into the bay so that small boats could tie up. Ray Shepherd, who was a field assistant at Mostyn at the time, was sitting on the edge of the jetty with new field assistant Monty Woodbridge, who had recently arrived at the estate.

"They were gazing out into the bay, looking at what appeared to be some small fishing boats approaching when Ray urgently yelled: 'Lari! Lari!'. Monty, whose normally keen senses had been dulled by a few Tiger beers, mumbled: 'Who the hell is Larry?' and turned to Ray to seek an answer. But Ray was no longer there. He had slid down the side of the jetty into the water and was taking shelter underneath as the pirate perahus (boat) roared into the harbour, guns blazing, to pillage and so forth. Ray and Monty both survived to tell the tale – and, indeed, it was Ray who told me the tale himself. Pirates were very active in the area in the 1960s. A reader without much Malay would need to know that the English translation of 'Lari!' is 'Run!'"

David Mills, who joined CDC as a management trainee straight from Oxford in 1965 and was with the organisation for the next fifteen years, during which time his postings included East and West Malaysia (Johore Oil Palms, Mostyn and BAL), the Solomon Islands Oil Palm Trial at Ilu), the Caribbean (manager at Rodney Bay, St Lucia), Nigeria (company secretary, regional office in Lagos) and Indonesia (investigations executive). He died in 2010 in Australia.

1960s

"We (Harry and Margaret Alexander) had gone back to the UK from Tanganyika at the end of 1961 intending to settle after being in the Colonial Service. Harry applied for a job with CDC in London, but they apparently had lots of applications for it. However, he was told that if he were willing to return to Tanzania he would be considered. He was then appointed company secretary of Kilombero Sugar in April 1962.

"At that time, the Kilombero managing agents were VKCM, but three of their top brass had been killed in an accident and Kilombero was not doing well. Harry flew out and I followed by sea with our sons and packing cases.

"There was no house for us when we arrived so we were accommodated in two lots of two interconnecting rooms in the Guest House block. The ablutions – showers only – were at the end of the block, not the easiest thing when you have a toddler still in nappies. Our very nice house was duly built and there we entertained numerous guests from CDC, Tate & Lyle, Bookers and an American lobbyist, I remember. A number of the then young CDC types also visited the estate, including Chris Stephenson, Richard Beacham and others from the Dar es Salaam office. Tarquin Olivier (actor Laurence Olivier's son) was appointed to the estate at some stage and there was great excitement when his mother, Joan Plowright, came to visit. I remember we went fishing on the Ruaha."

These recollections came from Margaret Alexander. Born in 1921, Harry Alexander served as an RAF observer during the war before training as an accountant before joining the Colonial Service and being posted to a cotton project in northern Tanganyika near Lake Victoria. It was there that he met Margaret, who was working with the Colonial Nursing Service.

After Kilombero Sugar, he was transferred in 1967 to Mhlume Sugar in Swaziland as company secretary, a post he held until his retirement in 1983. He died in 1990.

[Document on upper left:]

...ACA LIMITED

seventh   day of February
...y seven   BETWEEN BORNEO ABACA
...y situate at TAWAU (hereinafter called
... Richard Home Warton JOHNSON
...er, Hants
...) of the other part.

[Letter document:]

...inafter
...l serv
...   ...loy
...   Emplo
...au, or
...s oe v
...f o
...h
...h
...o d

TELEPHONE: MAYFAIR 8484

COLONIAL DEVELOPMENT CORPORATION

TELEGRAMS: VELOP, AUDLEY, LONDON

Tvl/Trip 3590   33 HILL STREET   CODE: BENTLEY'S SECOND
R.H. Johnson, Esq,   LONDON
                              W 1

14th February, 1957

Dear Mr Johnson,

Subject to the completion of your contract, I confirm that you are booked to leave UK for Singapore by Flight BA.770 on 25th February. You will be required to report to Airways Terminal, Buckingham Palace Road, at 1945 hours on that day. You will arrive at Singapore on 28th February and have a night-stop on the 27th at Colombo. You will travel from Singapore to Sandakan on 1st March and from Sandakan to Tawau on 2nd March. Transit accommodation at Singapore and Sandakan is being arranged by the Airways.

Your passport will be handed to you with your tickets and final movement instructions when you call here next week. Will you please let me have your inoculation certificates when these have been completed. You will be issued with £10 in sterling travellers cheques for expenses on your journey and this will have to be accounted for after your arrival at the project.

The baggage allowance for the journey is 44 lbs. I understand you wish to take advantage of sending a consignment of air freight at the special unaccompanied rate. This must consist of personal clothing only and I shall require a priced inventory of contents and that you will understand you will have a trunk of sea freight and that keys and keys will also be required for the sea freight. Inventory

Yours sincerely,

1970s

"Nkalagu was not an ideal posting for an expatriate family in the immediate aftermath of the Biafran War. The location was 50 kilometres from the nearest town, Enugu, which was the local business centre and capital of the then East Central State; communications had been disrupted during the hostilities and not yet fully restored; imported goods were in short supply even in the foreign-owned shops in Enugu; medical facilities on site were rudimentary at least until the company's hospital had been re-staffed and re-opened; and the locally endemic malaria was debilitating.

"There had also been a spate of armed robberies in the locality – presumably making use of hardware left over from the war – which prompted me to introduce a curfew, restricting all Nigercem staff to the company's estate after nightfall. This had the effect of restricting social life to the estate, unless invitations to dinner included an offer of a bed for the night! John Taylor, who was managing the Development Finance Corporation in Enugu and David Wood, DFC's accountant, were my nearest CDC neighbours and Eileen and I were always happy to accept their hospitality – and overnight accommodation."

Adrian Kerwood, general manager of Nigercem from 1972 to 1974. Adrian, who gained a degree in Engineering and Law at Cambridge University, joined CDC in 1964 as regional engineer for East Asia and the Pacific Islands, based in Kuala Lumpur and then Singapore. Following his two years with Nigercem he was CDC's representative in Indonesia before being appointed regional controller for the Caribbean. Posted back to London as DGM (operations) and later DGM (West Africa and Asia) he retired early in 1988 after a traffic accident.

1970s

"My first posting with CDC was to Housing Finance Company of Uganda in 1970. It was my first time in Africa and I didn't know what to expect.

"I was woken early one morning in Kampala by a telephone call from my boss, Ian Lane, who told me that the BBC World Service had announced that there was a military coup in progress in Uganda. The local Uganda Radio had missed its usual news broadcast and was playing pop music (My Boy Lollipop by Lulu I recollect was played quite a lot that day). The belief that military coups are accompanied by funereal music and military marches does not, as I recall, hold good in Uganda. Ian, as general manager of HFCU kindly invited (i.e. instructed) me to join him on a trip downtown to close down the HFCU office in Kampala (local staff did not normally tune in to BBC World Service and were therefore actually quite unaware that a coup was in progress) and ensure that the local staff were sent or delivered safely home.

"The streets of Kampala that morning were populated mainly by military personnel waving large automatic weapons and occasionally letting them off in various directions. However, the office closure and home delivery of staff was duly completed by Ian and it was time for us to return homewards. Just before where Ian and I lived in our respective homes the road curved round in a gentle bend before going uphill. Approaching this bend I noticed parallel score marks in the road which had not been there when we left earlier. "Tank tracks," said Ian laconically, a bit like James Bond I thought at the time. He then pulled the car off the road as a rumbling sound came from behind the bend in the road. Round the bend, slowly and deliberately, trundled a tank. It was quite small, as tanks go, I believe it had been purchased second-hand by the Ugandans from the Israelis having seen action in the 1948 Arab/Israeli conflict.

"This tank was deeply festooned with Ugandan soldiers, all in military fatigues and carrying lots of heavy calibre weaponry. The soldiers looked sternly at us. We gave them a wave and a 'thumbs up' sign. It seemed like a good idea at that particular moment in time. They waved back (and smiled) and rolled slowly on down the road towards downtown Kampala. It was about that time, I think, that it dawned on me that overseas service with CDC as an accountant could possibly be rather different and potentially more interesting than more conventional career paths!"

George Anderson joined CDC in 1970 as chief accountant for HFCU, moving to CDC's Dar es Salaam office the following year. He was then company secretary to the Tanganyika Development Finance Company for the four years 1971 to 1975 and regional head of finance for West Africa from 1975 to 1979. After a two-year spell as senior finance executive in London (natural resources) he held senior financial posts with Solomon Islands Plantations and Inyoni Yami Swaziland Irrigation Scheme before returning to the London Office for the last thirteen years of his CDC career, retiring in 2001. He died in 2015.

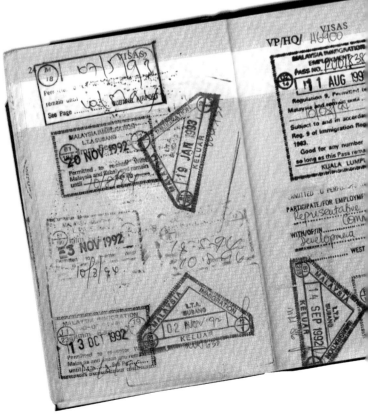

Meanwhile, CDC's universe had been expanded to include Latin America for the first time. The entry point here was Costa Rica, a small country that straddles the isthmus between the Caribbean and the Pacific. CDC was given permission to operate there in 1973 and after an initial assessment of the various possibilities for investment opted for housing mortgage finance, signing a £3 million loan agreement in 1974 with the Banco Central de Costa Rica for on-lending to the government-owned Instituto Nacional de Seguros, the country's principal source of mortgages.

Given CDC's long experience in the mortgage business, this was seen as a safe investment with which to get a foot in the door in the new territory. However, agriculture being very much the top priority at the time, CDC started looking around for possible palm oil projects not only in Costa Rica but also in Colombia and Ecuador. Ecuador was added to CDC's list of approved countries in 1977 but Colombia's reputation for drugs and kidnapping ruled it out.

It was to be another six years after that first Central American investment before CDC found a second – and, as things turned out, it was neither in oil palms nor in any of the countries in which it had originally been looking. Honduras had been cleared for investment in 1979 and almost immediately CDC made a £5 million loan to the state electricity authority, Empresa Nacional de Energia Electrica, towards the cost of the massive El Cajon hydroelectric power project. Aimed at reducing Honduras's reliance on oil imports, El Cajon's first generator came on line in 1985 and set a trend for CDC's future commitments in the region, which tended to be concentrated on large public sector infrastructure projects.

Elsewhere in Honduras, CDC had in the meantime at last found the first of three palm oil investments in the region that enabled it to fulfil its obligations to focus on sustainable agricultural development projects that would benefit poorer people. The Cooperativa Agroindustrial de la Reforma Agraria de la Palma Africana in Honduras, more straightforwardly known as Coapalma, was a cooperative of 4,800 smallholders growing 10,000 hectares of oil palms in the Aguan Valley in the Caribbean coastal region of Honduras, just south of Trujillo. CDC made a £6 million loan through the Honduran government to finance the building of three palm oil mills. Sadly, things did not turn out well in the long run since CDC had no control over the running of the cooperative in which every member had an equal say, with predictable results as the various factions fought for control. However, CDC was not put off and went on to invest in other palm oil ventures in both Costa Rica and Ecuador.

In Costa Rica, a loan of £9 million financed the construction of a mill at another cooperative, Cooperativa Agroindustrial de Productores de Palma Aceitera, where 1,200 families were engaged in tending 3,900 hectares of palm oil plantations. Well-managed, this was said to be one of Costa Rica's five most profitable businesses by the 1990s, bringing prosperity to the area, and it is still flourishing today. In Ecuador, CDC took a fifteen per cent equity stake in family-sponsored Palmoriente's development of a 5,000-hectare estate as well as making a significant loan, providing agricultural and engineering consultancy services and seconding junior staff. Peter Meinertzhagen himself ceremonially planted the first oil palm on the estate, which was located on the banks of the Huashito River at Francisco de Orellano, with distant views of the Andes.

Despite the worldwide economic woes that had been such a feature of the seventies and which continued on into the eighties, and regardless of the political difficulties that arose in many of its territories, CDC under Meinertzhagen's general managership marched on determinedly, expanding its office network and its portfolio – especially the number of businesses owned and managed by CDC – and busily identifying new projects everywhere it could, regularly breaking its own annual records for the value of new commitments. In 1982, for instance, it committed £103 million to an impressive thirty-four projects in twenty countries.

Meinertzhagen and his hard-working team might therefore seem to have had good reason to feel satisfied with what they had managed to achieve. They had certainly met the goals set by the British government regarding the proportion of investment that should be devoted to renewable natural resources and to the poorer countries. And the second quinquennial review of CDC's performance, instigated by the new Conservative government in 1980, was broadly supportive of what it had been doing in the previous five years, recognising, in particular, its special skills in the development of natural resources.

Not everyone was totally impressed, however, being concerned that the record of worthy development seemed to have been achieved at the expense of financial viability. The view had started to take hold that CDC was trying to do too many things and that it had lost focus as a result and questions were being asked in some quarters about its future direction.

Below: A dramatic shot of the dam and the visible part of the mostly underground power station at the El Cajon hydroelectric power project on the Humuya River in Honduras.

Central America's 'Wild West'

Life could occasionally get quite dramatic in untamed Latin America as CDC civil engineering consultant Gavin Grant discovered during one of his many visits to the Coapalma 'cooperative' in Honduras where the members were all too often at each other's throats. Gavin (pictured left with a pack horse and local youngsters) recalled: "I had retired to bed in the guest house when I was awoken by pistol shots ricocheting off the buildings and much drunken shouting. It transpired that one of the Coapalma board members had allegedly murdered the local chief of police in the local bar. The perpetrator escaped into the hills and returned to business some weeks later. I gather there was never a conviction. This really was 'Wild West' territory where the fastest gun ruled."

CDC's investments in 1982

- New estates and smallholder projects make agribusiness by far the largest sector, twice the size of power.

- Most investments are in Africa, the largest portfolios being in Kenya, Malawi, Swaziland and Zambia.

- The first investment has been made in South Asia.

Global investment (£m)

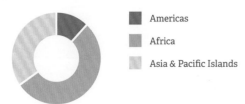

- Americas
- Africa
- Asia & Pacific Islands

Sector of investment (£m)

- Basic development
- Primary production & processing
- Commerce & industry

- **246 investments**
- **£467 million invested**

(£1.6 billion in 2018 terms)

Americas

1. **Antigua**
   Transport
2. **Barbados (Regional Office)**
   Power, Property and Housing Finance
3. **Belize**
   Agribusiness, Hotels and Tourism
4. **Costa Rica (Territorial Office)**
   Property and Housing Finance, Water
5. **Dominica**
   Power, Property and Housing Finance
6. **Ecuador**
   Agribusiness
7. **Grenada**
   Power
8. **Guyana**
   Power, Property and Housing Finance
9. **Honduras**
   Power, Agribusiness, Manufacturing and Commerce
10. **Jamaica (Territorial Office)**
    Power, Property and Housing Finance, Transport, Agribusiness, Manufacturing and Commerce, Hotels and Tourism, Devcos and Financial Institutions
11. **Montserrat**
    Power
12. **St Kitts**
    Hotels and Tourism
13. **St Lucia (Territorial Office)**
    Power, Property and Housing Finance, Agribusiness, Manufacturing and Commerce, Hotels and Tourism
14. **St Vincent**
    Power, Property and Housing Finance
15. **Trinidad & Tobago**
    Property and Housing Finance, Manufacturing and Commerce, Hotels and Tourism

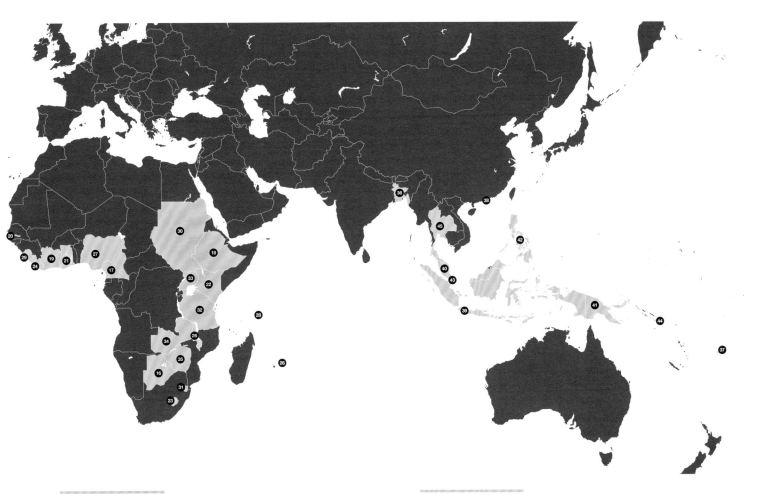

Africa

16. **Botswana (Territorial Office)**
Power, Property and Housing
Finance, Agribusiness
17. **Cameroon (Territorial Office)**
Water, Agribusiness
18. **Ethiopia**
Agribusiness
19. **Ivory Coast (Côte d'Ivoire)**
Agribusiness
20. **The Gambia**
Manufacturing and Commerce,
Hotels and Tourism
21. **Ghana**
Agribusiness, Manufacturing
and Commerce
22. **Kenya (Regional Office)**
Power, Property and Housing
Finance, Manufacturing and
Commerce, Devcos and
Financial Institutions
23. **Lesotho**
Property and Housing Finance,
Manufacturing and Commerce
24. **Liberia (Regional Office)**
Water, Agribusiness, Devcos
and Financial Institutions
25. **Malawi (Regional Office)**
Power, Property and Housing
Finance, Water, Agribusiness,
Manufacturing and Commerce,
Hotels and Tourism, Devcos
and Financial Institutions
26. **Mauritius**
Water

27. **Nigeria**
Property and Housing Finance,
Agribusiness, Manufacturing
and Commerce, Devcos and
Financial Institutions
28. **Seychelles**
Power, Hotels and Tourism
29. **Sierra Leone**
Water, Devcos and
Financial Institutions
30. **Sudan**
Manufacturing and Commerce,
Devcos and Financial Institutions
31. **Swaziland (Regional Office)**
Power, Agribusiness,
Manufacturing and Commerce,
Hotels and Tourism
32. **Tanzania (Territorial Office)**
Agribusiness, Manufacturing
and Commerce, Devcos and
Financial Institutions
33. **Uganda**
Property and Housing Finance,
Agribusiness, Devcos and
Financial Institutions
34. **Zambia (Territorial Office)**
Power, Transport, Agribusiness,
Manufacturing and Commerce
35. **Zimbabwe (Territorial Office)**
Power, Property and Housing
Finance, Devcos and
Financial Institutions

Pan Africa
Property and Housing Finance,
Hotels and Tourism

Asia and Pacific Islands

36. **Bangladesh**
Property and Housing Finance,
Devcos and Financial Institutions
37. **Fiji (Regional Office)**
Power, Property and Housing
Finance, Agribusiness,
Manufacturing and Commerce,
Hotels and Tourism
38. **Hong Kong**
Property and Housing Finance,
Transport, Devcos and
Financial Institutions
39. **Indonesia (Territorial Office)**
Agribusiness, Manufacturing and
Commerce, Hotels and Tourism
40. **Malaysia (Territorial Office)**
Power, Property and Housing
Finance, Water, Agribusiness,
Devcos and Financial Institutions

41. **Papua New Guinea**
Agribusiness
42. **Philippines**
Agribusiness
43. **Singapore (Territorial Office)**
Property and Housing Finance,
Transport, Water
44. **Solomon Islands**
Property and Housing Finance,
Agribusiness
45. **Thailand (Territorial Office)**
Property and Housing Finance,
Agribusiness, Hotels and Tourism,
Devcos and Financial Institutions

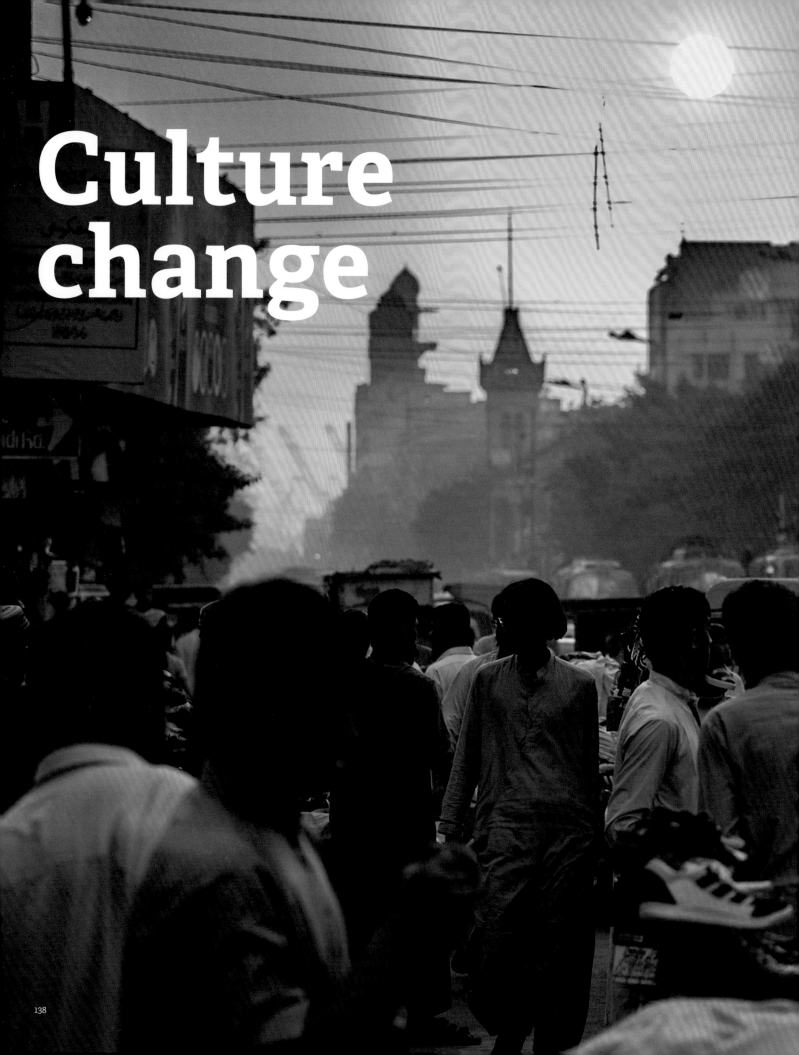

Culture change

Culture change
1982–1994

1983–84

World events...

- 'The Tamil Tigers', insurgents in Sri Lanka, demand independence for the north of the island.
- Indiri Gandhi is assassinated by Sikh members of her household in 1984.

CDC events...

- Total amount invested tops £0.5bn, with £506.5m at year-end in 1983.
- Office opens in Port Moresby, Papua New Guinea in 1984.

1985

- Military rule ends in Brazil.
- Mikhail Gorbachov becomes general secretary of the Soviet Communist Party.
- Live Aid concerts in London and Philadelphia draw attention to the plight of famine-affected regions of Africa.

- Sir Peter Meinertzhagen retires as general manager and is replaced by John Eccles.

1986

- The first cellular phones are introduced into Britain: at the year-end there are 115,000 subscribers.
- The US space shuttle Challenger explodes after lift-off.
- A nuclear disaster at Chernobyl, Soviet Union, leads to the evacuation of several hundred thousand people throughout the region.

- Commonwealth Development Corporation Act 1986 permits CDC to borrow and lend in foreign currency.
- Cyclone Namu hits the Solomon Islands causing major damage to Solomon Islands Plantations Ltd.

1987

- The World Commission on Environment and Development, headed by The Norwegian prime minister, Mrs Gro Brundtland, publishes 'Our Common Future', calling on governments to improve the management of environmental resources in a sustainable way.
- Parts of Ethiopia, Angola and Mozambique suffer famines made worse by guerrilla war.

- First investments in India and Pakistan. CDC's first managed venture capital company, PNG Venture Finance, is open for business.
- Government publishes the results of another 'quinquennial review'.
- Office opens in Abidjan, Côte d'Ivoire.

Right: Karachi, Pakistan. In 1987, CDC started investigating the feasibility of making investments in India and Pakistan, which, because they had achieved independence just before CDC was formed, had been excluded from the original list of countries eligible for investment. CDC went on to back some significant projects in Pakistan, including the power station at Hub River, Engro Chemicals and Fauji Fertilizer. Thirty years later, CDC has a portfolio of investments in a wide range of sectors, the largest by far being a direct equity investment of $121 million made in 2015 to Habib Bank (now HBL), Pakistan's largest private sector bank, where CDC's funds are supporting its financial inclusion strategy aimed at helping Pakistan's poorest peoples.

1990–91

- *Nelson Mandela is freed from prison on Robben Island in 1990, after 26 years.*
- *Namibia gains independence from South African mandate in 1990.*
- *The Gulf War starts in 1990.*
- *The old Soviet Union breaks up in 1991, giving way to the Russian Federation and a number of newly independent states.*

1988–89

- *The process of perestroika starts in the Soviet Union.*
- *Protesters in Tiananmen Square, Beijing, demanding greater freedoms, are fired upon by police and troops, killing two thousand in 1989.*
- *The Berlin Wall comes down in 1989, paving the way for the re-unification of Germany.*

1992–93

- *The war in Bosnia starts in 1992 (continues to 1995).*
- *Benazir Bhutto becomes prime minister of Pakistan in 1993.*
- *The conflict between Israel and the Palestinians intensifies.*
- *Mass starvation rages in Somalia.*

1994

- *Rwandan genocide begins.*
- *The African National Congress attains power in South Africa when the first multiracial, multiparty elections are held.*
- *A sudden devaluation of the peso precipitates the Mexico financial crisis.*
- *The Channel Tunnel linking Britain and France is opened.*

- In 1988, CDC's London Office moves to new open-plan offices at One Bessborough Gardens, Pimlico, reuniting all London-based departments for the first time since 1972.
- Offices open in Delhi, Karachi and Port Louis, Mauritius in 1988.
- The privatisation of Jamaica Telephone Co. is achieved with CDC's finance in 1988.
- In 1989, Sir Peter Leslie takes over as chairman from Lord Kindersley.

- Office opens in Accra, Ghana in 1991.
- In 1991, the number of projects or investments at year-end tops the 300 mark for the first time, at 304. The total amount invested passes £1bn - with £1.017bn at year-end. At the same time, CDC records record realisations of equity investments.
- CDC backs Engro Chemicals, the first management buy-out in Pakistan in 1991.

- Office reopens in Lagos in 1992.
- In 1992, CDC estimates that over 350,000 people are employed in companies in which it has invested; and that 700,000 outgrowers or smallholders are benefiting from CDC's investments.
- In 1992, establishment of Ghana Venture Capital Fund, the first CDC-sponsored private equity fund to attract third party investors.
- CDC becomes a founding member of EDFI, the Association of European Development Finance Institutions in 1992.

- John Eccles retires as chief executive and is replaced by Dr Roy Reynolds.
- Offices open in Manila and Maputo.
- Chilanga Cement plc becomes the first major privatisation in Zambia.

Chapter five

Culture change

The seeds that were to produce yet another major change in CDC's culture, organisation and investment policy under its next general manager were already being sown while Sir Peter Meinertzhagen was still in office.

The process of reappraisal could be said to have begun as early as 1979 with the return of a Conservative government under Margaret Thatcher. CDC's ailing chairman, Sir Eric Griffith-Jones, had finally succumbed to ill health only months beforehand, leaving a void that was filled temporarily by his deputy, Lord Grey. He was already seventy years old by the time he took over from Sir Eric and had only ever been seen as a stop-gap while a suitable long-term successor was sought. He was duly replaced in June 1980 by Lord Kindersley.

In order to decide what CDC's future direction should be and how best to refocus its vision, Kindersley brought in a hard-hitting industrialist, John Eccles, and a retired former CDC Head Office controller, Arthur Lewis, to carry out a thorough internal investigation of the organisation's overall aims, its structure and its operations right across the globe.
To this end, the two men embarked on a world tour of inspection in September 1981, visiting each of the seven regions that were then in existence and putting all the major managed businesses under the microscope.

What they found was a CDC that had become far more widely and thinly spread around the world than in Rendell's day, weighed down with baggage from the past in terms of projects that were past their sell-by date and with its managers divided over many matters relating to what its investment policy and priorities should be. In this respect, the fiercest debate was between those who wanted to give up managed businesses altogether and those who remained equally convinced that it was through managed businesses that CDC could achieve the most effective impact.

At the same time, Eccles and Lewis were also concerned that little thought seemed to have been given to the fundamental question of how to justify CDC's existence. As a small, unusual and often misunderstood public corporation at a time when such bodies were out of fashion and disappearing fast, and with few natural friends even among the aid fraternity, CDC was vulnerable. If it did not come up with a clear and convincing answer to those who questioned its usefulness, there was a danger that it too could be closed down.

"As a small, unusual and often misunderstood public corporation at a time when such bodies were out of fashion and disappearing fast, and with few natural friends even among the aid fraternity, CDC was vulnerable."

Lord Grey

A New Zealander, Ralph Grey had trained as a barrister before joining the colonial administration service in Nigeria prior to the Second World War, going on to hold governorships in British Guiana, the Bahamas, the Turks and Caicos and then, from 1973 to 1979, Northern Ireland. It was during this same six-year period that he was also deputy chairman of CDC. However, his spell as chairman lasted less than a year. Very well-liked and appreciated by the staff at Hill Street, he was already seventy years old by the time he took over from Sir Eric and had only ever been seen as a stop-gap while a suitable long-term successor was sought.

John Eccles

John Dawson Eccles was the first of CDC's general managers to be firmly rooted in commerce and industry. The board, from which he resigned to take over the role, asked him to take the more fitting title chief executive. At the same time, his social background as the only son of 1st Viscount Eccles was as well-connected as any of CDC's top brass over the years. He joined the CDC board as the Hon. J.D. Eccles and became 2nd Viscount Eccles upon his father's death in 1999.

Born in 1931, he was educated, like his father, at Winchester and Oxford but his CV thereafter was quite unusual by the standards of CDC's upper echelons. Having chosen a career in heavy industry, he was still only thirty-seven when appointed managing director of Head Wrightson, a northern engineering group with businesses in steel, nuclear power, and manufacturing for the process and mining industries. From 1972 to 1996 he was also a director of Glynwed International, a company that made Aga cookers and manhole covers, among other things. Other directorships held during the time he was in office at CDC included the British private equity firm Investors in Industry (since renamed 3i) from 1974 to 1988 and the UK Monopolies and Mergers Commission – since renamed the Competition Commission – from 1976 to 1986.

Much more like Reith and Rendell than his immediate predecessor, Meinertzhagen, he soon established a reputation as a forceful and formidable personality who, to put it politely, did not suffer fools gladly. And just as Reith had been horrified by the organisation he inherited from Trefgarne, so Eccles found fault with a lot of what – and who – he found awaiting him when he took over. Very bright and good at getting right to the kernel of a problem, he was absolutely convinced that his sense of direction was the right one for CDC. But although he also proved to be perceptive about individuals and their capabilities, in driving through change he relied just as much on force of argument as on winning over hearts and minds.

Like Rendell, he tended to make all the big decisions himself, often going over a manager's head to get information direct from the man on the ground. He led negotiations that one might have expected others to lead and, holding to his belief that there was an urgent need for transformation at CDC, he didn't hesitate once he had made up his mind on a particular course of action, but simply he went ahead and ordered its implementation.

There were failures among the projects embarked upon during Eccles's tenure, and over these he agonised; however, there can be no denying that he was a highly effective chief executive, starting CDC on the path towards what it is today. After the soft loans and subsidisation of the 1970s, he was determined to enforce rigorous financial and developmental disciplines, sharpening the organisation's analytical capability and emphasising the interdependence of financial viability and development impact. He also initiated the changes that gradually altered CDC's fundamental investment strategy, directing it towards investment with, and in, the private rather than the public sector and also steering it towards equity rather than loans. Under Eccles, CDC also started to think about building value in its investments, and with the future financing of CDC's growth in mind, of selling them when it had achieved all that it could. It was Eccles, too, who introduced CDC's first closed end managed funds.

At the same time, he very effectively defended CDC when it came under official scrutiny. As a former deputy chairman of the Monopolies and Mergers Commission he was ideally positioned to deal with an investigation from that particular body. And there were endless other government reviews, time-consuming occupational hazards faced by every CDC chief executive that he dealt with in masterful fashion.

John Eccles retired in 1994, having indelibly stamped his mark on CDC. As an active member of the House of Lords, Lord Eccles continues to speak out on issues relating to international development, including those concerning the past, present and future of CDC.

Lord Kindersley

Robert Hugh (Hugo) Molesworth Kindersley, 3rd Baron Kindersley, came from a line of investment bankers for whom Lazards was the family firm, he himself becoming a managing director there. He was the first of CDC's chairmen to come from a financial background and it was said that his appointment owed much to Margaret Thatcher's determination to install somebody who would toe her own Conservative party line in terms of introducing a more commercially businesslike approach to CDC's activities. He served as chairman from 1980 to 1989.

The report that Eccles and Lewis subsequently produced came down firmly in favour of continuing to manage enterprises in countries where foreign capital, along with the techniques, technology and management skills necessary for the development of such enterprises were in short supply and this included taking more majority equity stakes.

The proposed reorganisation of CDC that was based on the report's findings signalled the end of an era during which the overseas-based regional controllers had enjoyed growing autonomy within their own patches, 'barons' being a word that was occasionally used to describe them. Eccles and Lewis recommended that those powers that had gradually been devolved to the regional offices over the previous twenty years should revert to the centre, questioning the fundamental effectiveness of the entire regional organisation. With John Eccles appointed to the board in October 1982 and then taking over as general manager when Sir Peter Meinertzhagen retired in March, 1985, there was never much doubt that the report's recommendations were going to be implemented.

The dismantling of the regional organisation involved the downgrading and then the gradual withdrawal of the regional controllers – starting with those in West Africa and the Caribbean – while full responsibility for approving and confirming fresh commitments and for setting up and running new ventures was vested in the beefed up London Office posts of deputy general managers for administration, finance, investigations and operations, all of them reporting direct to an Executive Committee. After some initial teething troubles, this set-up was tweaked slightly for practical purposes so that instead of working independently, investigations and operations were merged, the two respective DGMs, plus a former regional controller, each taking responsibility for one of three separate regions – East Central and Southern Africa; West Africa and Asia; and the Pacific Islands, the Caribbean and Latin America.

This basic reorganisation of the management structure was followed over the next few years by an equally significant sea change in CDC investment policy, with a marked switch from the public to the private sector.

The economic challenges of the late 1970s had continued into the early 1980s. Although the situation in the developed countries was starting to improve by the mid eighties, thanks to gradually falling oil prices, the control of inflation through high interest rates and a generally more confident entrepreneurial spirit, the woes of the developing countries were far from over. For them, those high interest rates simply translated into a higher cost of borrowing. At the same time, the prices of the commodities they sold abroad – mostly agricultural products and metals – were at a low point in their cycles, which reduced export earnings.

The overall result was that currencies were weakened and governments were left without enough foreign exchange to pay off their debts. Some borrowed even more on worse terms, leading to requests for repayments to be postponed. Almost all of them cut imports of manufactured goods, which didn't help the developed countries to pull the world out of recession. It was a vicious cycle that, in Africa especially, was further compounded by drought, famine and other natural disasters, and led Lord Kindersley to describe 1984 as "the most difficult year for development ever experienced".

The lingering world recession in the countries where CDC operated precipitated a crisis. Loans had replaced equity as the main financial instrument used in CDC's investments – the proportion of equity in the worldwide portfolio had fallen from fifty-eight per cent in the mid-fifties to less than twelve per cent by the mid-eighties – and a large slice of these loans were in the public sector, either to government-owned organisations, known as 'parastatals', or direct to governments for lending on to their own schemes. These usually went to finance much needed development projects in the industrial sector or in infrastructure, mainly in the form of power stations and water utilities, and were often on a large scale. It got to the point where many governments were struggling to pay the interest on these loans, let alone meet the repayment schedules on which they had given guarantees. They needed more time to repay and a number of them wanted to include CDC's debt in mass reschedulings – a move that CDC stoutly resisted, although it did later recycle some old debts in new equity investments in some innovative arrangements.

Public sector-led development was thus no longer considered the best way forward. Apart from the fact that governments hadn't got the money to fund new schemes, state-based and state-run projects were also prone to suffer from bureaucracy and interference. There was a movement towards the selling-off of government-owned organisations, through privatisation proposals encouraged by the World Bank's structural adjustment programmes. At the same time the entrepreneurial skills of the private sector were being recognised as most capable of delivering economic growth.

Against this background there was a radical rethink of future investment policy and under John Eccles' management CDC actively sought to increase its portfolio in the private sector. It was a turning point that marked the start of an unstoppable trend and by the end of the decade over half of all new investments were in the private sector, and virtually all by 1994. John Eccles was also determined to increase the proportion of equity from its low base of twelve per cent. This also rose markedly, although not as meteorically. However, by introducing the concept of 'risk capital' CDC recognised that many if not all its loans to private sector enterprises in the poorer countries were sharing a similar risk.

Also significant was a subtle change in the way in which potential investments were to be assessed in future. The Commonwealth Development Corporation Act of 1978 had defined CDC's purpose as being to assist overseas countries in the development of their economies. Although this basic aim remained the same, what altered was the manner in which it was to be achieved. Up until this point, it had been routinely accepted that there would be consultation between CDC's regional offices and the government concerned as to where investment could be best directed. As time went on, this country-needs approach, which had served well under progressive regional controllers such as David Fiennes, was now replaced by a narrower, more focused and businesslike process of selection whereby each proposal was considered purely on its own merits and rigorously appraised; it needed to stand alone financially while satisfying economic, developmental, social and environmental criteria. To this end, a formal handbook was produced that laid down guidelines for carrying out appraisals.

The impact of all this on CDC came to be felt as something of a delayed reaction. Throughout the years of the world recession CDC had managed to carry on pretty much regardless, busily identifying new projects all over its universe and regularly breaking its own records for the value of new commitments. At the same time, income from established investments also continued to reach record levels, benefiting from prevailing high interest rates on loans and substantial dividends from its big owned and managed businesses. However, these figures disguised underlying problems which, by 1984, were starting to cause serious concern.

To go with these organisational and operational changes, CDC's corporate image was also updated and overhauled. After more than thirty-five years at Hill Street, CDC was given a brand new home at One Bessborough Gardens in Pimlico, where modern, open-plan offices with individual work stations were concealed behind a mock classical façade; "A good blend of the old and the new – not a bad description of CDC itself," as Lord Kindersley remarked. At the same time, the CDC logo was redesigned. The crown above CDC was dropped and amid the bright red lettering the D was shadowed in black to give it a 3D effect, emphasising the Development angle.

"At the same time, the CDC logo was re-designed. The crown above CDC was dropped and amid the bright red lettering the D was shadowed in black to give it a 3D effect, emphasising the Development angle."

One Bessborough Gardens

The new London Office at One Bessborough Gardens was officially opened by
Prince Charles on 14 July 1988 and HRH, who had recently retired from the board
of CDC and whose conservative architectural tastes are well documented, would
undoubtedly have approved of the brand new building's neo-classical façade,
which was based on original designs by Thomas Cubitt, the architect and builder
responsible for many of the late Regency/early Victorian houses elsewhere in
Pimlico. Inside, many of the fixtures and fitting were also extremely elegant,
even though the open plan offices themselves were modern and businesslike.
Just around the corner from Tate Britain and not far from MI5, one end of the
building overlooked the Thames, with a view across the river to MI6 on the
other side. In another subtle change to alter old attitudes, John Eccles renamed
it London Office as opposed to Head Office.

Out in the field, meanwhile, one of the most significant new developments during this extended period of reorganisation and change at the London Office was CDC's first involvement in Bangladesh, which opened the way for a belated entry into South Asia. Because India and Pakistan achieved independence just before CDC was formed they were excluded from the original list of eligible countries. And even after CDC was then cleared to work in Commonwealth countries in 1963, and outside the Commonwealth in 1969, priorities elsewhere, a general lack of manpower resources and concern within the organisation as to whether CDC would be able to make any real impact, meant that South Asia continued to be ruled out of contention. But given CDC's worldwide reach and the government's brief to focus on the poorest, the lack of any activity in this region became increasingly difficult to justify. Meinertzhagen was keen to do something, but was struggling to come up with a suitable project until an opportunity eventually arose through an invitation from the Aga Khan to join with Industrial Promotion Services (IPS), a subsidiary of the Aga Khan Fund for Economic Development (AKFED), in investing in a project in Bangladesh.

From its headquarters in Switzerland, IPS had established several offshoots in East Africa and South Asia in collaboration with national governments and financial institutions, providing venture capital, technical assistance and management support for various development schemes and enterprises. The Aga Khan approached CDC in the late seventies with a proposal to set up a similar operation in Bangladesh.

Despite the difficulties that still existed there, the British government gave CDC the go-ahead and an investigative team was dispatched to Dhaka from the regional office in Singapore to assess the possibilities. As a result, CDC agreed to assist managerially as well as financially, seconding Jeremy Rowe as financial controller to help set things up.

The Industrial Promotion and Development Company of Bangladesh (IPDC) was the country's first ever local source of development finance. It was incorporated at the end of 1981, with seventy per cent of the equity shared equally between IPS, CDC and two other international development finance institutions – the International Finance Corporation and Germany's DEG – while the balance was held by the Bangladeshi government.

Jeremy Rowe arrived in Dhaka in 1982 to find a large, empty and rather gloomy office without so much as a pencil anywhere to be seen. The first investment was nevertheless made that same year in Monno Ceramic Industries Ltd, a company producing high quality ceramic and porcelain tableware that went on to become one of the country's largest ceramics manufacturers. A handful of further investments was added to the portfolio in each of the following years, during which time a second CDC secondee took over as managing director. Included among them was Bangladesh's first leasing company – Industrial Development Leasing Company – that is still flourishing today as IDLC Finance, now diversified and claiming to be 'the largest non-banking financial institution in the country'.

CDC also started to make direct investments in a number of private sector companies in Bangladesh. The number of investments there has never been very large, but the outcomes have almost invariably been outstandingly successful, quite remarkable given the political instability and the general economic problems.

The Aga Khan

Famed as one of the world's wealthiest individuals, the Aga Khan, the Imam of the Nizari Isma'ilite sect of the Shi'ite Muslims, was also a far-sighted philanthropist who recognised the value of private initiative in establishing industrial, commercial and agricultural businesses that would help to boost the development of poorer countries. Through AKFED, he had set up IPS in 1963 specifically to work in South Asia and East Africa. It was here that CDC first came into contact with the organisation, helping to finance some of its hotels, tourist lodges and industrial ventures in Tanzania and Kenya. It is a relationship that has endured. In 2017 CDC announced a partnership with the AKFED to bring new power to East Africa.

The establishment in 1990 of the Karnaphuli Fertilizer Co Ltd (KAFCO), utilising Bangladesh's natural gas fields to produce urea fertiliser and ammonia for export, was a major undertaking, with CDC making a loan as well as investing $25 million in the equity of the company, a significant amount at the time. The price charged by Bangladesh for the use of its gas – critical to maintaining KAFCO's financial viability – was subject to regular and extremely difficult negotiations between KAFCO and the government. With CDC's representatives leading the negotiations for KAFCO while the World Bank argued the case for the government, a fair balance was somehow maintained. Even so, KAFCO suffered a severe setback in the second half of the nineties when fertiliser prices halved, and here CDC helped to put together a far-reaching financial reconstruction that enabled the company to pull through and it is now doing well, a major contributor to Bangladesh's foreign exchange earnings and employing six hundred people who are mostly housed on an estate with its own schools, medical and recreational facilities. CDC sold its equity in 2004 and the loan was finally repaid two years later.

It was in the late nineties that CDC, through a mix of equity and loan finance, supported the expansion of mobile phone operator Grameenphone, another great success story. Originally set up in 1997, Grameenphone had 18,000 subscribers at the end of its first year of operations but by 2005 this had risen to 5.5 million and it became Bangladesh's leading GSM mobile phone operator in terms of both coverage and number of subscribers. At the same time, its pioneering village phone programme brought communication with the outside world to thousands of poorer people in outlying areas without access to fixed lines.

CDC's other point of entry into South Asia was in Sri Lanka. Permission to work there had been given in the late seventies but it took a while to find a suitable first investment. This eventually emerged in 1984 in the shape of Pelwatte Sugar, a 4,500-hectare plantation of rain-fed cane in the south-eastern Moneragala district of Uva province, the largest and one of the poorest districts in the country. A loan to fund a hydroelectric power scheme on the Walewa Ganga River followed in 1986 and then, in the early nineties, CDC took a small equity stake in the privatisation of the National Development Bank.

The star investment and high-scoring development project in Sri Lanka was to come later with the substantial expansion and upgrading of Colombo harbour's Queen Elizabeth Quay and the construction there of a new container terminal that opened in 2003, soon turning out to be an extremely valuable addition to the country's infrastructure. In putting together the financial package that made it all possible, CDC took equity in the company, South East Asia Gateway Terminals, and also provided a loan. This was repaid early and when the equity was then sold in 2006 it proved to be highly profitable, returning eleven times the original investment.

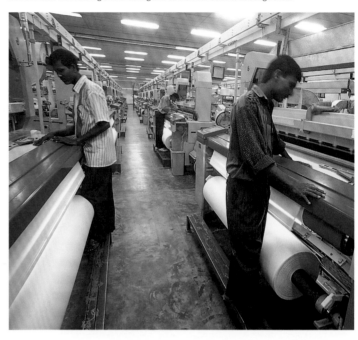

Below: Inside the weaving and finishing mill of Beximco Textiles in Bangladesh.

Beximco

The first of CDC's direct investments in Bangladesh was in the Bangladesh Export Import Company (Beximco). This had been set up in 1972 by brothers Sohail and Salman Rahman. CDC had got to know Sohail well in his capacity as one of the directors of IPDC and supported Beximco through a programme of expansion during the 1980s and 1990s that led to it becoming the largest private sector industrial conglomerate in Bangladesh, employing a workforce of over 20,000 people in more than twenty companies spread across six divisions, including pharmaceuticals, basic chemicals and jute. In 2004 the group's ten listed companies dominated the market capitalisation of the Bangladesh stock exchanges, accounting for a fifth of the total.

Meanwhile, CDC had also backed Sohail Rahman's first venture into textile manufacturing. His Padma Textiles was one of the companies that helped to lay the foundations of what has since become a major industry in Bangladesh, the country being a principal supplier of finished garments to the world market. Taking full advantage of plentiful labour and export incentives offered by the government, Padma started producing cotton and cotton polyester yarn in 1990, with CDC taking twenty per cent of the equity and also providing a loan before then injecting further funds for expansion in 1991. Padma was listed on the local stock exchanges in 1992 and declared its first dividend the following year, at which time CDC agreed to support Beximco Textiles, set up to establish a weaving, dyeing and finishing mill for shirting and other fabrics.

Top and above: The Karnaphuli Fertilizer Co Ltd plant, located on the banks of the Karnaphuli River at Chittagong, Bangladesh's industrial port city on the Bay of Bengal, and (bottom) the company's housing estate a few kilometres away where most of the 600-strong workforce and their families lived. As well as housing, the estate included its own schools, medical and recreational facilities.

It was in 1988 that CDC at last took the plunge in India and Pakistan, opening offices in Delhi and Karachi and making the first investment in Pakistan later that same year. It is said that HRH The Prince of Wales, a CDC board member for nine years from January 1979 to December 1987, had played a part in helping to start the ball rolling in the direction of the two most important countries in South Asia by posing the simple question: "Why not?"

The first reconnaissance missions duly went out in 1985 for consultations with local business leaders, industry gurus, civil servants and politicians, involving many rides through crowded streets in cream-coloured Ambassadors, overnight stays in Oberoi hotels and meetings in Bombay high rises and Lutyens New Delhi buildings. Expectations were high. In 1986 David Killick was appointed as the first deputy general manager (India and Pakistan) and the following year an ambitious investment target was set for the next five years.

This early optimism was understandable. With India and Pakistan enjoying a period of relative political calm and stability and with both countries starting to dismantle the ponderous bureaucracy that had been stifling entrepreneurial business activity and deterring foreign investment since independence, CDC's entry came at an opportune time. And thanks to the legacy of the Raj, the environment was one in which CDC felt very much at home. English was spoken and the legal system was familiar and understandable even if investment was still mired in red tape.

By 1987 one investment in Pakistan had already been approved by the CDC board, while another eleven were under investigation; in India, three approvals were on the books with another eleven being worked up. It was all systems go and a series of very capable and energetic regional representatives soon built up two of the biggest portfolios anywhere in CDC's world.

In this headlong rush there might seem on the face of it to have been an element of the over-enthusiasm that had characterised the earliest days of CDC under Trefgarne, with quite a number of the initial approvals falling by the wayside. There was a difference, however. Here, the failure rate was largely accounted for by improved due diligence and of those that did actually get the go-ahead, only a handful ended in failure. These included the very first venture in Pakistan – a small investment in Mubarik Dairies, a company that was involved in the production of UHT milk. Going into the textile industry in Pakistan also proved to be a mistake, most of the early investments in that sector failing.

Even when appraisals were very thoroughly carried out, projects occasionally ended up going wrong. This was partly because, being new to the game in South Asia, CDC made errors of judgement early on, sometimes getting into partnerships with small, family-led business groups whose long-term interests were not fully aligned with its own. At the same time, the proportion of failures was relatively small and the actual losses suffered were far outweighed in monetary terms by the successes. And even some of those businesses that were marked down as poor investments are still trading today, thirty years later, using plant paid for by CDC and continuing to deliver development.

Among the most successful early investments in India was Apollo Tyres, supported by CDC in 1989-90 with equity and loan finance to build the second of its plants in Baroda in Gujarat. Apollo has gone on to become one of the leading tyre producers in India, selling to over one hundred countries globally.

The most significant of CDC's early ventures in Pakistan were in the chemical fertiliser industry. This came about firstly, in 1989, through the Fauji Foundation, a vast and rather unusual welfare organisation run by retired military men from the Pakistani armed forces and funded by its controlling interests in a large and wide-ranging group of companies, and then secondly, in 1991, through a ground-breaking deal involving Engro Chemicals.

"**By 1987 one investment in Pakistan had already been approved by the CDC board, while another eleven were under investigation; in India, three approvals were on the books with another eleven being worked up.**"

Working with The Fauji Foundation

The Fauji Foundation of Pakistan was originally set up by the British in 1942 as a fund for servicemen who had served with the armed forces and their families but has since grown to the extent that it now provides support for around five per cent of the entire population of Pakistan in the form of pensions, medical assistance, educational scholarships, vocational training and other welfare facilities. Among other things, it runs eleven hospitals and ninety-eight schools. In the absence of grants of any kind, it funds itself through a group of businesses in various sectors spread right across the spectrum of Pakistani enterprise, all of which it controls either wholly or through majority shareholdings.

At the time when CDC got involved with it, the chairman of the foundation always used to be a retired Lieutenant-General and the CEOs and general managers of the Fauji Group companies were Major Generals, Commodores and officers of similar rank. They were straightforward and honest and knew enough about what they were doing to recruit qualified commercial and technical managers whom they then allowed to manage without unnecessary interference. And because they were known as fair employers, they attracted capable people.

CDC's first investment with Fauji consisted of a loan plus a small equity stake in Fauji Fertilizer, helping to finance a second plant alongside the existing one at Goth Machhi in Punjab, where the country's natural gas resources were being utilised in the production of urea fertiliser – something of which CDC had experience as a result of its successful KAFCO investment in Bangladesh, which was in exactly the same business.

Next, CDC invested $40 million in a new plant set up as a joint venture by Fauji Fertilizer and Jordan Phosphate Mines to produce another type of phosphate-based fertiliser. Here, technical difficulties, cost over-runs and other financial problems later brought the project close to collapse, whereupon a CDC team then played a leading role in sorting out a refinancing arrangement with the shareholders, banks and government. This, combined with better management, led to eventual recovery, so that by the time CDC eventually sold its share in 2006 its original $40 million stake was worth $114 million.

CDC also invested in Fauji Cement and the Fauji Oil Terminal and Distribution Company. FOTCO operates Pakistan's largest petroleum handling facility (above) at Port Qasim, east of Karachi, built at a cost of $100 million and capable of managing nine million tonnes of oil per annum. It continues to operate profitably. Altogether, the four investments did well over the next few years, allowing CDC to double its total investment of $111 million.

Engro Chemicals Pakistan Ltd had meanwhile provided another exciting landmark in CDC's investment history, the result of its first ever management buy-out. This bold new venture – it was also the first management buy-out in Pakistan and by far the most significant in any developing country at the time – owed much to the inspired vision of one remarkable and yet ultimately tragic figure, Shaukat Raza Mirza.

While the Engro buy-out provided an impressive demonstration of how to tie up a complicated deal quickly, the long drawn-out and often painful process of setting up the Hub Power power station project in Pakistan was a prime example of the exact opposite. However, this is perhaps not surprising given the scale and international funding complexity of what was in its way a much more innovative and important development project. Arguably the first and largest power station in the developing world to be financed by the private sector, it involved the leading national companies and governments of the United States, the UK, Japan, France and Italy as well as Pakistan, with the World Bank also playing a role.

The project had first been conceived in the mid-1980s, the World Bank and the Pakistan government agreeing proposals to promote private sector power generation to meet the demand of a growing economy. The first companies to answer the call in 1985 were Hawker Siddeley Power Engineering and Xenel Industries of Saudi Arabia, each of them proposing to build a 600 MW oil-fired power station on the Hub River site in Baluchistan, forty kilometres outside Karachi. They agreed to combine forces, re-submitted their proposals in 1987 and then, with the help of a myriad of consultants, spent the next two years producing a mammoth nine-volume feasibility study. CDC, meanwhile, having been part of the potential financing group from the very start, had already been given board approval for an equity investment and a loan.

In 1990, just when it seemed to be a case of all systems go, Hawker Siddeley suddenly pulled out and the construction consortium broke up. At the same time a declaration by Pakistan's Federal Shariat Court confirming that the payment of interest was against the laws of Islamic banking worried international lenders. Undaunted, the remaining parties pushed on, led by the World Bank and CDC. The UK's National Power, now Engie Energy International, stepped in as a lead sponsor and the all-important contract was signed agreeing the price-per-kilowatt that Pakistan's national Water and Power Development Authority (WAPDA) would pay for the electricity that was generated. CDC's loan agreement was signed in 1993 and $33 million was disbursed to the construction contractor the following year. The plant was built and started producing power in 1997, CDC having played a major supporting role that went far beyond its financial input.

That, however, was not the end of it. No sooner had the plant come on stream in 1997 than the new government led by Prime Minister Nawaz Sharif, which had replaced that of Benazir Bhutto, began to question the tariff that had been agreed with WAPDA, suggesting that WAPDA officials must have been bribed to accept it. The CEO of National Power and his No 2 were hounded out of the country and pressure was put on the local managerial staff. In the end, it took three years for the tariff re-negotiation committee on which CDC was represented to hammer out a new deal and it wasn't until 2002 that things really settled down.

Hub Power is now at last very successfully doing what it was meant to do, supplying over 1,600 MW of power to the people of Pakistan – ten per cent of the country's total – from three plants. It is well-established, efficient and financially sound. By the time CDC sold its shares and its loans had been repaid in 2005, it had received total returns of $90 million on its $46 million investment, but it had certainly earned that reward. Without CDC's help, Hub Power might never have happened. The CDC team had been instrumental in pulling together the finance and in then dealing with the tariff issues, which was all about maintaining good relationships on the ground. Unlike the World Bank, CDC had held a seat on the board and had played the role of honest broker, using its local and international networks to bring parties together and resolve differences.

The success of the Hub Power project bore many of the hallmarks of what was CDC best practice, including the exploitation of its global brand image, its status and its skills in managing emerging market risk to encourage private sector investment, and acting as a catalyst to prompt other investors to go where they might otherwise have feared to tread.

This was again very much in evidence in another, similar power project in the Philippines in which CDC became involved at the same time that it was working overtime to get Hub Power off the ground. Fortunately, although based on exactly the same business model, this proved to be a great deal more straightforward.

Left: An eye-catching night time picture of the Engro Chemicals fertiliser plant at Daharki in Pakistan's Sind province. The management buy-out conceived by president and chief executive Shaukat Raza Mirza when Exxon decided to sell all its fertiliser plants in 1990 was the first such venture in which CDC had been involved, the first buy-out in Pakistan and, at the time, probably the largest in any developing country. CDC took a ten per cent equity stake and Engro's other shareholders included 450 employees.

Below: Engro Chemicals plant lights up the night sky.

Below: The control room at Engro Chemicals.

Above: Shaukat Raza Mirza, the president and chief executive of Engro Chemicals Pakistan Ltd.

Shaukat Raza Mirza and Engro Chemicals

Shaukat Raza Mirza was the president, CEO and chairman of what, before the buy-out, was known as Exxon Chemical Pakistan Ltd, a subsidiary of American oil multinational Exxon, now ExxonMobil. The company had been set up in 1965 and three years later started producing urea fertilisers at its plant at Daharki in the Sind province. This was located less than fifty kilometres from Fauji Fertiliser's plant at Goth Machhi on a narrow strip of land on the banks of the River Indus and bordered by the desert, conveniently close to the country's natural gas fields. Exxon had established an attractive and comfortable company town around its plant.

Shaukat Raza Mirza had been an Exxon company man since joining Esso Eastern in 1962. With an MA from Birmingham University in the UK and Exxon experience in the US and Hong Kong, he was transferred back to Pakistan and Exxon Chemicals in 1984 and within four years had been appointed president and CEO and elected chairman. He soon proved an inspiring leader and a visionary, a man with integrity, enthusiasm and energy. While Daharki had been the largest plant when built in the late sixties it had not expanded and its share of the Pakistan fertiliser market had fallen from seventy to twelve per cent. Shaukat Raza Mirza had plans for expansion, but Exxon had other ideas and decided in 1990 to sell its seventy-five per cent shareholding to any fertiliser company that was interested, the other twenty-five per cent being held by the public and institutional investors.

Concerned for his ambitious expansion plans under new ownership and even more anxious about the future welfare of the employees who not only worked for the company but lived in the company town, he conceived a virtually unique buy-out plan in that it involved not just the management but also the entire workforce. At the same time he needed to raise the finance for the major expansion he had in mind.

Local financial institutions shied away, but the International Finance Corporation, who had already been approached about financing Shaukat Raza

Mirza's planned expansion, were excited by his buy-out plan and invited CDC to get involved. In October 1990 Exxon gave them a few months to come up with a deal and what followed between then and May 1991 when the deal was signed shows what can be done when the will is there. It involved 450 employees and seven other groups taking equity. CDC took ten per cent and, along with ten other institutions, provided a loan to help finance the expansion. It also worked long and hard against tight deadlines in order to get the details of the buy-out completed and all the loose ends tied up, dealing with complex legal issues along the way.

Renamed Engro Chemicals Pakistan Ltd – Engro being a contraction of Energy for Growth – the company grew and diversified much as Shaukat Raza Mirza had envisaged, establishing itself as a highly respected member of Pakistan's business and industrial community and an inspiration for others contemplating their own buy-outs. It became the second largest producer of urea in Pakistan after Fauji Fertiliser, entering into a $60 million joint venture with Royal Vopak, the Dutch global leader in the storage and handling of chemicals, to form Engro Vopak Terminal Ltd in 1998, operating a jetty at Port Qasim, Karachi, the construction of which was supported by a loan from CDC. Until it sold its shares in 2002, doubling its investment, CDC remained on the board in an advisory capacity. Later the fertiliser business was demerged and Engro Chemicals became Engro Corporation, which has continued to expand and diversify.

Shaukat Raza Mirza retired as CEO of Engro in 1997, although remaining as chairman and in 2000 he became the first non-political appointee to the managing directorship of the Pakistan State Oil Company. Tragically, he was then murdered by sectarian terrorists a year later, aged sixty-two. The nation was stunned, such was the stature of this charismatic man and the esteem in which he was held. President Pervez Musharraf honoured him posthumously with the Hilal-e-Imtiaz, one of the highest awards in the Pakistani honours system.

A team of maintenance workers at the top of the main chimney at Engro Chemicals plant, seen on the previous page. The painter (centre) has just completed his work on the top, and has red, white and blue paint spatters on his overalls to show for it.

By the late eighties and early nineties there was a desperate shortage of electricity in the Philippines, with regular day-long blackouts. No new power stations had been built for a decade. In 1991, the government kick-started a crash programme by inviting private investors to come in on the same build-operate-transfer terms that had been applied at Hub – in other words, the private sector would construct the power station and produce the electricity for a defined period, selling it under contract to the National Power Corporation.

The contract to build the 700 MW power station on Pagbilao Island in Quezon province that would feed the Luzon grid and help to light up Manila eventually went to the Hopewell Group of property and infrastructure development companies controlled by Hong Kong-based entrepreneur Gordon Wu. Hopewell estimated the cost at $888 million – a figure perhaps just slightly manipulated to include nothing but the lucky Chinese number, eight.

This was in the early days of financing power stations with private sector money and Hopewell needed development finance institutions such as CDC to take the riskiest end of the investment spectrum as a demonstration of confidence to other private financiers. CDC duly did its bit, along with the International Finance Corporation and the Asian Development Bank, providing some equity and a loan to the Hopewell Power (Philippines) Corporation.

The project was a success and CDC's involvement led to an invitation to invest in a second, larger 1,000 MW power station at Sual in Pangasinan province a few years later. Both investments proved financially rewarding while also satisfying the British government's requirement at this time for CDC's investments to demonstrate 'additionality' by bringing something special to the party. They also delivered much needed social and economic benefits to the Philippines at local and national levels.

Left: Hopewell's 700 MW Pagbilao power station in the Philippines. Financially remunerative for CDC, which invested alongside IFC and the Asian Development Bank, Hopewell and a second power station at Sual, provide much needed social and economic benefits for the Philippines, both locally and nationally.

Elsewhere in the South East Asia region during the late eighties and early nineties, CDC decided that the time had come to start selling its mature oil palm plantations in Malaysia, cashing in on the success of these investments so as to be able to recycle the proceeds in new investments. The need to maintain a constant turnover of equity investments was becoming that much greater at a time when, given the constraints imposed by the government on its borrowing facilities, CDC found itself increasingly having to rely on self-generated funds to finance its own continuing growth.

Sarawak Oil Palms was first to be sold, followed by BAL. With SOP, in particular, the decision to offer the company to the public with a listing on the Kuala Lumpur Stock Exchange was prompted not just by the feeling that the time was right for CDC to exit but also by the idea that SOP should be given the opportunity to raise funds from elsewhere in order to finance further diversification. The decision to seek a listing was made in July 1989, but with poor palm oil prices that year and the first Gulf War in 1990 causing uncertainty, the process was delayed for another two years. It turned into a marathon effort for SOP's then managing director Mike Workman and his financial controller Chan Kam Fatt. Working closely with staff in CDC's office in Kuala Lumpur, whose job it was to liaise with the Kuala Lumpur-based advisers and listing authorities, they had to produce seven revisions to the corporate plans and nine different timetables.

When it did eventually go ahead in August 1991 the listing was a great success, being many times oversubscribed. The twenty-four per cent of the company that was sold to the public introduced 14,000 new shareholders, including a number of employees. CDC retained forty-three per cent and the remaining thirty-three per cent was held by CDC's partner, the Sarawak government's Land Custody and Development Authority. Everybody benefited.

By the time CDC finally sold all its shares in 1995 they were worth five times what they had been when the company was floated. And SOP was able to launch a major expansion and diversification programme.

BAL was sold in 1996 to the large, Malaysia government-controlled Golden Hope Plantations as a mature mid-sized estate of 16,400 hectares, half of it planted with oil palms, most of the rest with cocoa. CDC had every reason to take pride in what had been one of its great flagship enterprises, one with which it had stuck through thick and thin, only finally exiting when the time was right, at which point it proved to have been a financial as well as a developmental success. Together with the income received over the years, the price paid represented a financial return of thirteen per cent for each of the forty-eight years of CDC's holding.

BAL had been one of the very first ventures under Trefgarne, pioneering the introduction of two crops in Sabah and becoming a centre of excellence for plantation management, training and research. CDC's final departure was viewed with sentimental sadness by the management, staff and residents of the now prosperous town of Tawau, which owed its development to CDC. In many senses, it marked the end of an era.

Solomon Islands Plantations, on the other hand, survived until 2004, despite taking a terrible and almost terminal battering in 1986 from one of the most ferocious cyclones in living memory. The damage was so extensive that closure had to be seriously considered, but thanks to some remarkable crisis management and a lot of determination, SIPL's staff brought it back to profitability. Thirteen years later, ethnic unrest throughout the island led to it being mothballed for five years and when the fighting eventually died down CDC, having considered the options, sold it to Kulim (Malaysia) Berhad, a major Malaysian listed plantation group.

Left: William Tully OBE, managing director of BAL (seated, centre), pictured in 1993 with the rest of his management team who, between them, chalked up 257 years of service.

Back row, from the left:
Robert Yeow Cheng (chief estates manager, 37 years), David Lim Hong Kee (scientific development officer, 35 years), Joseph Chan MBE (engineering and production controller, 34 years), Thong Ho Yen (Mostyn Estate manager, 35 years) and Alan Lim Meng Seng (personnel manager, 19 years).

Front row, from the left:
Lim Fook Hin (finance controller, 12 years), William Tully OBE (managing director, 42 years) and Mok Tai Yin (chief accounting manager, 43 years).

Cyclone Namu in the Solomon Islands

Records showed that cyclones were rare in the Solomons. There had been a handful in the late sixties, but you had to go back as far as 1952 to find the last big one. Cyclone Namu – it means 'Big Mosquito' – therefore came as a complete surprise when it struck on Sunday 18 May 1986. The violent storm raged for three days, during which time the highest rainfall ever recorded fell on the steep, heavily forested mountain slopes, undermining and uprooting trees and washing them down onto the plains below in a swirling torrent. They jammed under the road bridges over the three main rivers running through Solomon Islands Plantations Ltd's estates, creating dams that caused all three rivers to overflow their banks. The relentless battering of the logs then caused two of the bridges to collapse, releasing a further pent-up tidal wave that swept the plantations.

Brian Woodhead, SIPL's general manager, was busy supervising operations in the head office at Ngalimbiu at the time and in a later report he gave a graphic description of what happened:

"In the office quadrangle a trickle of water unexpectedly appeared across the walkway tiles. Then people from a nearby village came running towards the office, carrying children and babies and what few belongings they had managed to save and took shelter from the rain in the back of the mill truck in the carport. Suddenly, the mill men saw, coming over the riverbank, a tidal wave, carrying with it huge logs and vast amounts of debris that bore down on the office.

"Within seconds the muddy water rose to five feet and the truck started to float. The men pushed women and children onto the carport roof and scrambled up after them and onto the office roof, shouting to me and the others in the quadrangle and reaching down to haul us to safety. The sight from the roof was unforgettable as tree trunks and debris swept past, carving out a path of destruction some 200 yards long into the palms beyond. Although doors burst like balloons with the pressure of water and logs battered the building, it held."

When the storm finally abated and the damage could be assessed it emerged that landslides and mudslides had buried whole villages, the homes of a third of the entire population had been destroyed and more than a hundred people had lost their lives.

Although nobody associated with SIPL was killed, the whole project was badly hit. The head office at Ngalimbiu was flooded close to ceiling height and left surrounded by logs while seventy houses in the village were totally destroyed and every one damaged to some extent. The executive housing at Mbalisuna was also badly affected. Power and fresh water supplies were off, communications had been knocked out, floods were impassable and vehicles had been destroyed. In the plantations, seven per cent of the mature palms were killed outright and only a third came through unscathed.

Some thought that the infrastructure, the palms and the business generally would never recover. Amazingly, thanks to a Herculean mopping up effort by the staff, harvesting actually went ahead on the less seriously affected areas of the plantation within a matter of weeks. And although it took nine years to recover the losses arising from the cyclone – over and above the $7 million claimed on insurance – profitability was restored and dividends paid. It was an extraordinary and inspiring example of leadership in a crisis and survival against the odds.

Cyclones are a much more regular occurrence a little further south in the New Hebridean islands nation of Vanuatu, located between the Solomons and Fiji, but the elements were not the only problem that CDC faced there. Feeling that it was under-represented in the smaller South Pacific island nations, CDC had sent out a series of missions from Suva to investigate a number of what sounded like dream locations. But although it was exciting to meet the Queen of Tonga and drink kava with the elders, no feasible projects could be identified until the government of the Republic of Vanuatu, the administration of which had been shared by France and Britain prior to independence in 1980, issued an invitation to look at the possibilities there.

Having been granted permission to work there by the British government in 1982, after Vanuatu had joined the Commonwealth, CDC wasted no time in setting up Metenesel Estates Ltd a year later to plant cocoa. In 1985 it added a second managed project, Tanna Coffee.

Sadly, both investments failed. Although the cyclones certainly contributed, constantly blowing down the coffee bushes and the cocoa plants, there were all sorts of other difficulties, ranging from the volcanic ash that defoliated the plants to the alien work culture of the people, who weren't really interested in being part of a cash economy. They were happy to work for cash, but once they'd got enough they would go away to enjoy spending it, leaving their work undone. By 1992, both the cocoa and the coffee businesses had been sold to the government for $1. Both survived, but in a scaled-down form. Despite the best of intentions and valiant efforts to make a success of these ventures, they ended up as classic examples of CDC being unable to deploy its own skills on the ground effectively as a result of failing to identify economic opportunities appropriate to the local economy. Fretting over these failures and others like them in countries that desperately needed successes, John Eccles endeavoured to learn lessons for the future from such mistakes.

Back in the Solomons, CDC fared much better with the forestry business it established in 1989 on the volcanic island of Kolombangara, one of the New Georgia islands group that forms part of the Solomon Islands. It was just off Kolombangara during World War II that John F. Kennedy's PT109 motor torpedo boat famously went down after being hit amidships and cut in two by a Japanese destroyer, leading to the dramatic rescue of JFK and the surviving members of his crew after they had swum to safety.

More familiar with the Solomons as a result of its long years of experience with SIPL, CDC understood the possibilities and the challenges involved and Kolombangara Forest Products turned out to be a success both developmentally and environmentally. New sustainable hardwood plantations were established on land that had been logged out and abandoned by a previous, exploitative, timber company, conservation areas were created to protect the remaining indigenous forests, an improved infrastructure was put in place, including a new wharf to be used for exporting timber products, and local people were provided with long-term employment opportunities.

CDC managed all this, holding the majority of the equity and financing the business in a joint venture with the Solomon Islands government. It eventually sold its stake in Kolombangara Forest Products to another private equity investor in 2006. Now a joint venture between the Taiwanese Nien family and the Solomon Islands government, it continues to manage its 14,000 hectares of plantations and 25,000 hectares of natural forest sustainably under FSC certification guidelines, with its FSC-certified wood being used to make veneer, plywood, sawn timber and blinds and shutters, sold internationally under the Norman brand and in the UK under the Hillarys brand.

While much of CDC's more innovative and pioneering activity under John Eccles's leadership was focused on South and South East Asia, there was plenty of positive development in Africa after a long period of widespread uncertainty in many countries as a result of political instability and economic problems throughout the seventies and early eighties. In West Africa, Ghana was emerging from twenty years of unrest and CDC, which had closed down its office there in 1970 because there was so little opportunity, returned in 1991. By the end of 1992 it already had a portfolio of fourteen investments and by the mid-nineties this number had risen further to the point where it equalled that of any country in Africa. These investments included the landmark CDC-managed Ghana Venture Capital Fund, the first fund in which CDC managed other people's money, and colourful cottage industries such as Divine Seafoods and Astek Fruit Processing.

Above: The car phone looks bulky, but it was state-of-the-art back in the early nineties when CDC financed Ghana's first mobile telecoms service, Millicom.

Right: A remarkable satellite image of Kolombangara, the volcanic island in the New Georgia islands chain, part of the Solomon Islands, where, in 1989, CDC established a sustainable hardwood forestry business (indicated by the lighter shaded area), that was both developmentally and environmentally successful. Sold by CDC in 2006, Kolombangara Forest Products' 14,000 hectares of plantations and 25,000 hectares of natural forest continue to be managed sustainably.

Customary
Land

Tombulu

Vanga
Mission

Poitete Division

Poitete
(KFPL Township)

Pulisingau
Wharf

Ring Road

Manighisi

Customary Land

Ringgi Division

Customary
Land

Kuzi

Head Office
Ringgi

Ringgi Wharf

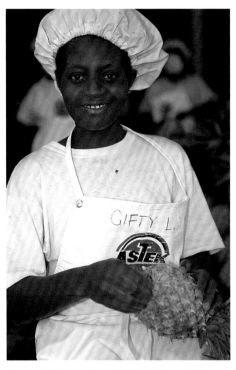

Above and left: An employee at Astek Fruit Processing in Ghana (above) preparing one of the pineapples that, along with other fruit grown locally, went into the company's most popular product, a drink named Refresh. The majority shareholder and manager Mrs Celestine Diji of the delightfully-named Divine Seafoods selling fish in the market in Ghana (left). CDC provided Astek Fruit Processing with a loan to finance the installation of Tetra Pak container equipment and also to target and develop export markets. The project was implemented smoothly and Refresh gained an even higher profile. Divine Seafoods, on the other hand, took over two years to get to the starting blocks. The business was conceived with the highly developmental aim of adding value to locally caught fish by processing them, using a cooperative of local women. CDC's approval probably owed as much to the persuasiveness and charm of Celestine Diji than to the underlying viability of the Divine Seafoods' business plan.

Below: A tea plucker working for Tanzania's East Usambara Tea Co Ltd.

The rehabilitation of tea estates in Tanzania and Uganda

In Tanzania, where the Arusha Declaration of 1967 had brought in a socialist state that regarded any foreign investment as a form of exploitation, curtailing CDC's activities, the nationalised tea estates in the mountains of Usambara had been allowed to run down. At the same time, lack of foreign exchange meant that like its neighbours, Tanzania was struggling to service its debts. CDC came up with a mutually advantageous recycling solution, agreeing to accept repayment in Tanzanian shillings that it would then reinvest in high priority, labour intensive ventures.

As a result of this arrangement CDC took control of the East Usambara Tea Co (EUTCO) in a joint venture with the Tanzania Tea Authority and embarked on a comprehensive rehabilitation of the estates at Kwamkoro and Bulwa that included restoring and improving the infrastructure and building new houses, a school and a medical clinic. As an investment the project was never a great financial success, but it did go some way towards meeting the targets set by the British government for investment in renewable natural resources and in poorer countries.

One thousand kilometres away in Uganda, the tea estates financed by CDC in the late sixties and early seventies had also suffered, first under Idi Amin and then during Milton Obote's second presidency. Following Obote's downfall in 1983, CDC then resumed business in the country, rehabilitating estates and factories at Mityana, Toro-Kahuna and Kiamara. Later, in the mid-eighties, it considered an invitation to take on the restoration of five nationalised estates, including those it had previously financed, but without the prospect of privatisation and with ongoing security problems, declined. In 1990, however, the Ugandan government changed its tune and offered the estates for sale and CDC bought them, forming the Rwenzori Highlands Tea Company in a joint deal with James Finlay, the long-established international tea business. CDC took control, providing corporate management and loan finance, and James Finlay took a slightly smaller equity stake and supplied technical advice.

Under the leadership of CDC's Simon Hill, Rwenzori proved to be a greater commercial success than EUTCO for all involved. At the time of the takeover in 1990, the level of production was about 1,000 tonnes of black tea per annum, but by the time CDC sold its investment to James Finlay in 2001 it was running at 9,000 tonnes and providing employment for 7,000 permanent workers. In 2010 it was acquired by the Indian tea company McLeod Russel.

In Zambia, also, the economy was starting to pick up as a result of the liberalisation that followed the defeat of Kenneth Kaunda and his replacement by Frederick Chiluba in the election of 1991 and in 1993 negotiations began between CDC and the Zambian Privatisation Agency that led the following year to CDC increasing its stake in Chilanga Cement to 50.1 per cent and taking over the management of the company for the third time in its history. Kenneth Kaunda, out of office and not involved, remarked that it was a "rum privatisation" that saw Chilanga bought by "an instrument of the British government"!

A few years earlier, with the economy ailing under Kaunda's presidency as a result of nationalisation, mismanagement and price controls, CDC had found itself holding large amounts of blocked funds in kwacha, the local currency – investment returns on earlier loans that could only be spent within the country, since the government simply did not have the foreign currency reserves to service them in sterling. In 1989, therefore, in response to an approach from the government, CDC agreed to recycle some of this debt into a new investment in a failing 9,000-hectare agricultural estate, Nanga, which included coffee and cotton plantations, arable land and a cattle ranch, the idea being to turn the kwacha into dollars by producing crops for export.

It was again the lack of foreign exchange in Zambia, along with the aim of boosting local food production, which initially prompted CDC's involvement in what was to become one of the biggest arable farms anywhere in sub-Saharan Africa. In order to reduce its foreign import bills, the Zambian government encouraged its nationalised copper mines to establish large farms on which to grow their own food to feed the workforce. The first such venture was an irrigated wheat and soya bean farm at Munkumpu. The CDC board approved a fifty per cent equity investment and the provision of management but the offer was turned down by the management of Nchanga Consolidated Copper Mines, which, politically, was still in the mood to prove that it could go it alone, without outside help.

Undeterred by this rebuff, CDC, alongside various other development finance institutions, then took a small equity stake and provided a small loan to help finance the creation of another such farm just twenty kilometres away at Mpongwe. Instigated by the state investment company ZIMCO and run for them by agricultural managers Landell Mills Associates (LMA), the plan here was to grow soya, maize, coffee and flowers on 4,000-hectares that had previously been the site of a government-owned experimental wheat project.

Within a few years LMA-managed Mpongwe found itself in trouble. The development was costing more than expected, money was running out and, as a result, loans were not being repaid on schedule. When financial restructurings failed to resolve the problems CDC agreed to step in, buying out all the other investors and establishing a 50:50 joint venture with ZIMCO, to be managed by CDC. Five years later, in 1995, the government's privatisation agency invited CDC to take a majority stake and as this fitted with its policies at the time of building and managing world-scale businesses, CDC agreed.

It was the start of a developmental success story. Munkumpu came up for sale the same year and CDC bought it and merged the two. It also set up Mpongwe Milling Ltd to build and operate a wheat flour mill at Kitwe. The result of all this was that, altogether, Mpongwe Development owned 60,000 hectares of land of which 13,000 hectares were under cultivation and by the time the assets of the business were eventually sold in 2008 it was producing around 100,000 tonnes of wheat, soya and maize annually, representing fifty per cent of Zambia's total soya demand, twenty per cent of its wheat requirement and five per cent of its maize needs. Mpongwe was later bought by Zambia's major diversified agribusiness company Zambeef but came to CDC's attention again in 2016 when CDC invested in Zambeef's equity.

Elsewhere in Africa during the eighties and nineties it was often much the same story of picking up the pieces of earlier projects and investments that had suffered during the years of political instability and worldwide economic recession. In the poorer parts of CDC's world, countries were grappling with the realities of debt management and trying to meet the demands made by the World Bank for structural change to their economies. New policies towards privatisation and rehabilitation recognised the benefits of direct foreign equity investment, which didn't add to the countries' debt burden while bringing in technical expertise and management skills.

"By the time the assets of the business were eventually sold in 2008 it was producing around 100,000 tonnes of wheat, soya and maize annually, representing fifty per cent of Zambia's total soya demand, twenty per cent of its wheat requirement and five per cent of its maize needs."

Two local children, lit by the setting sun, stand beside a field of wheat at Mpongwe in Zambia where CDC took over an ailing 4,000-hectare farm and developed it into a successful 60,000-hectare agribusiness concern.

In Zimbabwe, where CDC had shut up shop following UDI in 1965, independence in 1980 opened the way for a welcome return. A new office was opened in Harare in 1982 after the British government had granted permission to work there and CDC had agreed operating conditions with Robert Mugabe's administration.

Early investments included a power project, a development bank and a building society. This was fine as far as it went, but what CDC was really looking for was an opportunity to demonstrate its ability to make a difference in rural areas, as it was already doing so successfully in other parts of Africa at the time. The chance arose in 1984 with an invitation to invest in and take over the management of the Rusitu Valley Development Company, a government-sponsored dairy farm linked with a mixed agricultural small farmer settlement.

While Rusitu was CDC's only managed project in Zimbabwe during the first fifteen years following its return, there were a number of other bread-and-butter investments, including loans and minority equity stakes mostly aimed at helping to develop the country's industrial base. Perhaps a rather more attractive investment, at least from an aesthetic point of view, was the Victoria Falls Safari Lodge.

Rusitu Valley Development Company

Located amid beautiful, lush, rolling green hills in the east of the country, close to where the Chimanimani Mountains form Zimbabwe's border with Mozambique, things started well and the project grew under CDC's management to become, initially, a major regional producer of milk, building up a prime, selectively-bred herd of dairy cattle that grew to 1,500-head at one point with modern dairy facilities. However, with domestic milk prices controlled by the Zimbabwe government and other imported dairy products sold at lower prices than locally-produced goods it was difficult to turn a profit. The herd was therefore halved and the farm diversified into cultivating coffee, tea, macadamia nuts and arable crops. As part of this development, dams were built to irrigate the fields. High development costs meant that the company was regularly on the borderline of financial viability.

The end came in 1998 after attempts to acquire parts of the 7,000-hectare development as part of Robert Mugabe's land acquisition programme, ironic given that it was a joint venture with the state-controlled Agricultural and Rural Development Authority. This happened to coincide with a change in CDC's policy towards agricultural investments and, as a result, Rusitu was sold to a Zimbabwe-based agribusiness company.

"Nevertheless, the Mohale Dam has brought huge benefits to Lesotho in terms of income, power, infrastructure and other developments and it has helped to ease South Africa's drought-related water shortages."

In Southern Africa, the most significant development in the region during this period was in Lesotho, where the Lesotho Highlands Water Project was set up to exploit the country's only real natural resource – the water that fell on the Maluti Mountains. Nearly forty years earlier, CDC had first considered an ambitious scheme to channel this water from what was then Basutoland to South Africa's Free State and Gauteng Provinces, but at that time the idea had to be dropped for various reasons. With South Africa continuing to suffer from water shortages, the plan was revived in the 1980s and in 1991, following a feasibility study and despite it being a large public sector project, which went against the grain of the time, CDC agreed to lend £20.7 million to the Lesotho Highlands Development Authority. This helped to fund the construction of the 185 metre high Katse Dam across the Malibamatso River as the first phase of a scheme that involved altering the watershed and tunnelling through mountains to create canals.

The Katse Dam and reservoir were completed in 1997 and the 110 MW Muela Hydroelectric Power station was opened two years later, a forty-nine-kilometre transfer tunnel linking the two. A second dam, the Mohale Dam, was inaugurated in 2003. Involving literally ground-breaking engineering feats on a grand scale, the scheme has not been without its harsh critics and has involved a range of environmental, social and governance issues. Nevertheless, it has brought huge benefits to Lesotho in terms of income, power, infrastructure and other developments and it has helped to ease South Africa's drought-related water shortages.

Victoria Falls Safari Lodge

"Low volume, low density tourism, which enables tourists to participate in the unspoilt environment," was how the promoter described the 72-bedroom lodge prior to its opening in 1995. Featuring traditional materials, including probably the largest expanse of thatched roof to be found anywhere in the country, and with all existing trees carefully preserved, the lodge was designed to merge so well into its surroundings as to be quite invisible from a distance. From its elevated location looking out over flooded gravel pits, around which the natural landscape and flora had been restored, visitors could enjoy a grandstand view of the elephants and other animals that would come in to drink from the unfenced Zambezi National Park beyond.

With IFC, CDC took an equity investment and made a loan to the company which built and operates the lodge. Despite the catastrophic mismanagement of the economy under Robert Mugabe, the lodge remained open and managed to maintain reasonable occupancy rates, winning the Association of Zimbabwe Travel Agents annual Best Safari Lodge/Best Resort Hotel Award for 21 consecutive years, from 1996 to 2017.

There was one other major African investment during this period that became notable for all the wrong reasons and that was in Malawi. Here, the smallholder agricultural authorities that had been promoted so enthusiastically by CDC during the late seventies had fallen out of favour as the more commercial approach demanded by John Eccles took root. Instead, the focus was shifted to the creation of large managed agribusinesses. Ironically, however, this proved to be too great a challenge.

What was to become the Sable Group conglomerate started in 1984 with CDC's acquisition of over 4,000 hectares of rolling green hills south of Mzuzu to form Kawalazi Estates. The land had previously been owned by Spearhead Enterprises, the commercial arm of President Hastings Banda's Malawi Youth Party that had been established to teach farming techniques and to set up farms in remote areas. Spearhead remained a minority shareholder in Kawalazi Estates, which set about rehabilitating the existing tea and macadamia nut plantations while also growing coffee.

Kawalazi then merged with the neighbouring Kavuzi Tea Company, a state-owned estate and factory, the expansion of which CDC had supported with loan finance before going on to amalgamate with two other farm groups to form the Sable Group in 1991. The two other groups, both of which had also been set up by Spearhead but had become run down and were losing money, were Sable Farming Ltd, which was mostly devoted to coffee plus dairy, macadamia, arable and tobacco interests, and the Impala Farming Company, a collection of arable farms and tobacco plantations. Altogether, the resulting conglomerate involved a widely scattered mosaic of estates up and down the country that added up to a total of 18,600 hectares.

At £42 million, Sable represented CDC's single largest investment anywhere in the world in 1995 and provided employment for 10,000 people. And yet it was also one of CDC's largest sinkholes, proving to be a financial disaster. CDC had gone into it for all the right reasons and there was a lot of all-round support for a project that ticked a lot of the developmental boxes. At the same time, Malawi was always a difficult place in which to make money out of agriculture. The financial viability of the project was low, the risks were high – and they kicked in. No amount of restructuring, reorganisation, cost-cutting and further investment could save it and the conglomerate was eventually broken up and sold piecemeal at knock-down prices. However, some individual estates remained in business.

Meanwhile, back in London, John Eccles and his team were having to deal with a series of government reviews and investigations to which CDC was subjected in the seven years between 1986 and 1993. As well as two routine quinquennial reviews in 1986 and 1992-3 in which the Treasury and the Overseas Development Administration jointly reviewed CDC's performance and decided on its future direction, there was a separate review in 1992 by the Monopolies and Mergers Commission, responsible for examining the efficiency and effectiveness of public sector bodies.

Sir Peter Leslie

Born in 1931 and educated at Stowe before then serving with the Argyll and Sutherland Highlanders, Sir Peter Evelyn Leslie succeeded Lord Kindersley as chairman of CDC in 1989 following a distinguished career in international banking, during which he was successively, chief general manager, managing director and deputy chairman of Barclays Bank and then deputy chairman of the Midland Bank.

His fifteen years experience of overseas banking with the dominions, colonies and overseas section of Barclays, which saw him working in Sudan, Algeria, Zaire, Kenya and the Bahamas, qualified him as an ideal choice as chairman of CDC alongside John Eccles as chief executive.

Having always argued strongly that improving investment and ending trade protection was better than any amount of aid and subsidy in helping developing countries, he was right behind John Eccles in steering CDC towards the private sector investment, which increased from fifty to ninety per cent of all new investments during his five years as chairman.

Keenly interested in history, he wrote a book in retirement detailing the friendship between his wife's father, Sir Edwin Chapman-Andrews, an ambassador, and Emperor Haile Selassie of Ethiopia. He died in September 2007, aged 76.

As it happened, the Monopolies and Mergers Commission report was very positive, concluding that CDC was providing a most effective form of development assistance in line with international best practice and calling for a Development Report to publicise its good work. However, fending off these often vaguely hostile and potentially harmful investigations while at the same time fighting for adequate government funding was not only time-consuming but also inevitably absorbed a great deal of energy and attention that might have been better directed elsewhere. There was also the added pressure of constantly having to jump through endless hoops set up for it by various arms of government that seemed to be forever setting new targets and financial restrictions.

As Eccles noted pointedly on the final page of his very last annual report in 1994: "Perhaps the most testing challenge to CDC's management has always been the maintenance of a positive relationship with HMG (Her Majesty's Government). This is a theme which runs through the history of CDC. Securing a blend between support for CDC's work and the operating independence to ensure its success is not easy."

His frustration was understandable. John Eccles had undeniably left CDC in better shape than he found it. Annual investment had more than doubled from around £90 million to £217 million and the total portfolio of investments stood at £1.3 billion, spread over 348 enterprises in fifty-one countries. It was regularly hitting all the investment targets set for it. And from 1992 it was increasingly able to pay its own way, funding new investments from its own sources – loan repayments, realisations, dividends and interest – to the extent that it was actually returning more to the government in repayments and interest than it was borrowing. Despite all this, it seemed CDC still needed to justify its existence.

"The Monopolies and Mergers Commission report was very positive, concluding that CDC was providing a most effective form of development assistance in line with international best practice."

CDC's investments in 1994

- The output from 27 managed businesses includes 283,900 tonnes of palm oil and 312,000 tonnes of cement. The companies employ 44,000 in sixteen countries.

- India, Pakistan, Jamaica, Costa Rica, Tanzania, Zambia, Indonesia, Malaysia, Thailand and Papua New Guinea all have large country portfolios.

Global investment (£m)

- Americas
- Africa
- Asia & Pacific Islands

Sector of investment (£m)

- Basic development
- Primary production & processing
- Commerce & industry

- # 348 investments
- # £1,304 million invested

(£2.5 billion in 2018 terms)

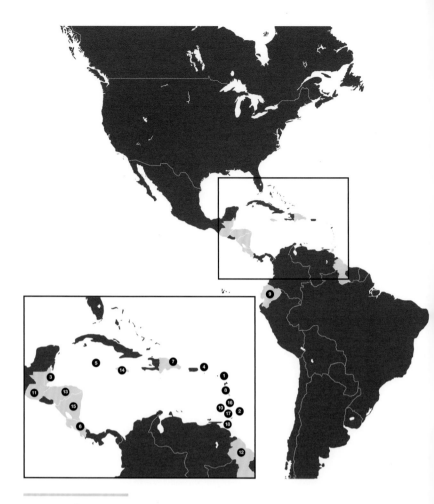

Americas

1. **Anguilla**
   Power
2. **Barbados (Country Office)**
   Power, Hotels and Tourism and Financial Institutions
3. **Belize**
   Power, Transport, Agribusiness, Financial Institutions
4. **British Virgin Islands**
   Power
5. **Cayman Islands**
   Power
6. **Costa Rica (Country Office)**
   Power, Water, Agribusiness, Manufacturing and Commerce, Hotels and Tourism, Financial Institutions
7. **Dominican Republic**
   Hotels and Tourism
8. **Dominica**
   Power, Property and Housing Finance, Agribusiness, Financial Institutions
9. **Ecuador**
   Water, Agribusiness, Financial Institutions
10. **Grenada**
    Hotels and Tourism
11. **Guatemala**
    Agribusiness
12. **Guyana**
    Transport, Agribusiness, Minerals, Oil and Gas
13. **Honduras**
    Property and Housing Finance, Water, Minerals, Oil and Gas, Manufacturing and Commerce, Financial Institutions
14. **Jamaica (Country Office)**
    Power, Property and Housing Finance, Transport, Agribusiness, Manufacturing and Commerce, Hotels and Tourism, Financial Institutions, Telecoms and IT
15. **Nicaragua**
    Transport, Agribusiness
16. **St Lucia**
    Power, Property and Housing Finance, Agribusiness
17. **St Vincent**
    Power, Manufacturing and Commerce
18. **Trinidad & Tobago**
    Minerals, Oil and Gas, Manufacturing and Commerce, Financial Institutions

Africa

19. Botswana
Power, Property and Housing Finance, Water, Agribusiness, Hotels and Tourism, Financial Institutions, Telecoms and IT
Cameroon
Water, Agribusiness, Manufacturing and Commerce

20. Côte d'Ivoire (Country Office)
Agribusiness

21. The Gambia
Agribusiness

22. Ghana (Country Office)
Power, Property and Housing Finance, Agribusiness, Minerals, Oil and Gas, Manufacturing and Commerce, Hotels and Tourism, Financial Institutions, Venture Capital Funds, Telecoms and IT

23. Kenya (Country Office)
Power, Property and Housing Finance, Agribusiness, Manufacturing and Commerce, Hotels and Tourism, Financial Institutions

24. Lesotho
Property and Housing Finance, Water, Manufacturing and Commerce, Financial Institutions

25. Liberia
Water, Agribusiness

26. Mozambique (Country Office)
Minerals, Oil and Gas

27. Malawi (Country Office)
Power, Property and Housing Finance, Transport, Water, Agribusiness, Manufacturing and Commerce, Hotels and Tourism, Financial Institutions

28. Mauritius (Country Office)
Agribusiness, Manufacturing and Commerce, Hotels and Tourism, Financial Institutions, Telecoms and IT

29. Namibia
Agribusiness

30. Nigeria (Country Office)
Agribusiness

31. Seychelles
Power, Hotels and Tourism

32. Sierra Leone
Water, Minerals, Oil and Gas, Financial Institutions

33. South Africa (Country Office)

34. Sudan
Financial Institutions

35. Swaziland (Country Office)
Power, Agribusiness, Manufacturing and Commerce, Financial Institutions

36. Tanzania (Country Office)
Transport, Agribusiness, Manufacturing and Commerce, Hotels and Tourism, Venture Capital Funds, Financial Institutions

37. Uganda
Power, Property and Housing Finance, Agribusiness, Financial Institutions, Telecoms and IT

38. Zambia (Country Office)
Power, Agribusiness, Minerals, Oil and Gas, Manufacturing and Commerce, Hotels and Tourism

39. Zimbabwe (Country Office)
Power, Property and Housing Finance, Agribusiness, Minerals, Oil and Gas, Manufacturing and Commerce, Hotels and Tourism, Venture Capital Funds, Financial Institutions

Pan Africa
Property and Housing Finance

Asia and Pacific Islands

40. Bangladesh
Minerals, Oil and Gas, Manufacturing and Commerce, Financial Institutions

41. Fiji
Property and Housing Finance, Agribusiness, Financial Institutions

42. India (Country Office)
Power, Property and Housing Finance, Transport, Manufacturing and Commerce, Venture Capital Funds, Financial Institutions, Telecoms and IT

43. Indonesia (Country Office)
Power, Transport, Agribusiness, Manufacturing and Commerce, Venture Capital Funds, Financial Institutions

44. Malaysia (Country Office)
Agribusiness, Minerals, Oil and Gas, Manufacturing and Commerce, Venture Capital Funds

45. Pakistan (Country Office)
Power, Property and Housing Finance, Water, Agribusiness, Minerals, Oil and Gas, Manufacturing and Commerce, Hotels and Tourism, Financial Institutions

46. Papua New Guinea (Country Office)
Power, Property and Housing Finance, Transport, Agribusiness, Manufacturing and Commerce, Venture Capital Funds, Financial Institutions

47. Philippines (Country Office)
Power, Agribusiness, Manufacturing and Commerce, Venture Capital Funds, Financial Institutions, Telecoms and IT

48. Solomon Islands
Property and Housing Finance, Agribusiness

49. Sri Lanka
Power, Agribusiness, Venture Capital Funds, Financial Institutions

50. Thailand (Country Office)
Property and Housing Finance, Agribusiness, Manufacturing and Commerce, Financial Institutions

51. Vanuatu
Property and Housing Finance, Agribusiness

Journey to private equity

Journey to private equity
1994–2004

World events...

1995
- Dayton Agreement ends the Bosnian War.

1996
- The Taliban take power in Kabul.

1997
- Tony Blair becomes Britain's prime minister, heading a Labour government.
- Norfund, Norway's development finance institution, is formed.
- The Asian Financial Crisis starts with the devaluation of the Thai Baht and continues into 1998.
- Hong Kong is handed back to China by Britain.

1998
- A difficult year for emerging markets, with stock market indices dropping 22%.

CDC events...

1995
- Lord Cairns takes over as chairman.
- Offices open in Bangalore, Dhaka and Kampala. CDC makes its first investment in South Africa.
- Commonwealth Development Corporation Act removes interest payable on government loans.
- Chilanga Cement is successfully floated on the Lusaka Stock Exchange.

1996
- Commonwealth Development Corporation Act extends powers to participate in financial institutions, privatisations and invest in and improve existing assets.
- The Commonwealth Private Investment Initiative (CPII) is launched by CDC and the Commonwealth Secretariat.
- BAL Plantations is sold for £100m.

1997
- Tony Blair announces that CDC will become a Public Private Partnership.
- Offices open in Santa Cruz, Bolivia; Havana, Cuba; and Mumbai, India.
- CDC invests in SOBOCE, Bolivia's leading cement company.

1998
- Offices open in Colombo, Lima and in Port of Spain, Trinidad.
- CDC first invests in Celtel (formerly MSI International), which establishes a very successful pan-African mobile phone network.
- CDC backs Sify, the first Indian IT company to be listed on the NASDAQ stock exchange.

Right: Bangalore, India. In the 1990s, operating from its offices in Delhi, Mumbai and Bangalore, CDC initiated a number of ground-breaking transactions that helped build the private equity industry in India. CDC's recent strategies have focused on helping the poorer states, with investments to promote financial inclusion and healthcare most prominent. In 2013, CDC reopened an office in Bangalore.

1999

- *Nigeria returns to democratic rule under Olusegun Obasanjo.*
- *The Argentine economic crisis starts and continues to 2002.*

- Dr Alan Gillespie is appointed as chief executive.
- CDC Act changes CDC from a statutory corporation into a limited company incorporated in the United Kingdom whose shares are not publicly traded. On 8 December CDC becomes CDC Group plc.
- Mpongwe Development Co, Zambia, is one of Africa's largest arable farms.

2000

- *The eight Millennium Development Goals are agreed at the United Nations Millennium Summit.*
- *Vincente Fox is elected president of Mexico ending 71 years of rule by the PRI.*

- Offices open in Beijing, Cairo, Miami, Virginia and Mexico City; and reopen in Singapore.
- CDC's portfolio is split into two - the historic and the private equity portfolios.
- CDC's remaining investment in Usutu Pulp is sold.
- CDC helps to rehabilitate Colquiri, a Bolivian tin mine.

2001

- *China accedes to the WTO.*
- *War in Afghanistan starts.*
- *Terrorists attack New York's Twin Towers and other targets in the United States.*

- Aureos is formed as a joint venture with Norfund, to manage SME funds; Colombo, Port Louis, Maputo, Accra and Port Moresby offices are transferred from CDC to Aureos.
- CDC sells Pan African Cement, the holding company which includes Chilanga Cement, to Lafarge.
- Mbabane, Manila, Mexico City, Port of Spain, Lima and Suva offices close.

2002–03

- *Invasion spear-headed by US troops, marking the start of the Iraq war.*

- Paul Fletcher is appointed chief executive in 2002.
- The power generation company, Globeleq, is formed in 2002.
- CDC's prepares for split through 'Project Atlas'. Internally, CDC demerges into management and investment companies in 2003.
- CDC leads the first private equity backed privatisation in India, of Punjab Tractors in 2003.

Chapter six

Journey to private equity

John Eccles was succeeded as chief executive
in May, 1994, by Dr Roy Reynolds and, as so often
in the past, the change of leadership led to a
radical reappraisal of CDC's aims, ambitions,
organisation and culture.

Before officially taking over from John Eccles, Roy Reynolds went on a whistle-stop tour of
CDC's world, taking a close look at a wide cross-section of investments in order to get a feel
for exactly what was going on in the various regions and to see for himself what might be
done to improve performance. On his return he then instigated a full-scale strategy review,
causing a few raised eyebrows by calling in top management consultants McKinsey to help
in carrying it out.

Charged with making some recommendations for future investment policy, the review
inevitably found evidence of both good and bad investments among what was now a
vast and extremely diverse portfolio, the bad ones dragging down the overall return on
capital and thereby contributing to the financial restraints on expansion; some judicious
weeding out was urgently needed, including a reduction in the number of mature managed
businesses, if forward impetus was to be maintained. It was also noted that the portfolio
was still dominated by loans, despite CDC's declared intention of moving more towards
equity investments; on the other hand, there was an acknowledgement that the policy
switch from the public to the private sector had been effectively followed through. Several
new up-and-coming regions were identified as being ripe for an investment initiative.

Based on the findings and recommendations of the review, the proposed way forward
centred on 'focus'. This was to involve targeting a set of those countries, sectors and
financial products that would give CDC the best chance of meeting what remained its
central challenge – that of somehow reconciling the two often competing aims of achieving
both development impact and high returns. CDC needed to be more pro-active and
professional in seeking out and structuring fresh investments and individuals were to be
more accountable for results.

**"Suitably re-motivated and re-energised, the
new organisation swung into action."**

'Focus' was not the only example of a new jargon that entered CDC's vernacular at this time. The countries to be focused upon were those deemed to be at the 'turning point' in 'pre-emerging' markets, namely those that had introduced reforms, especially in terms of good governance, but which were still perceived by investors as being too risky. And in each new investment, CDC must seek to give a clear demonstration of 'additionality', some positive contribution arising out of its participation. This might quite often be achieved indirectly, by assessing and reducing risks and thereby encouraging other investors to follow with technical skills and further finance.

To implement this overall strategy, Roy Reynolds introduced a completely new organisational structure that was redolent of his Shell background, appointing a trio of managing directors to head three core operational units – CDC Industries, CDC Financial Markets and CDC Investments.

CDC Industries, headed by former ICI Explosives executive Bob Clark, took charge of the managed businesses, with a brief to grow them into world-scale concerns; CDC Financial Markets, with ex-Morgan Grenfell investment banker Robert Binyon as MD, took over the regional and country managed funds, building on the foundations laid by the Devcos in supporting SMEs; and CDC Investments, led by CDC's former finance director, Nick Selbie, assumed responsibility for everything else – making, monitoring and also selling investments, especially the controlled and managed businesses that were assessed as being ripe for realisation. These core divisions were serviced by three main support units – structuring and appraisals, business development and legal services. At the same time, Lord Cairns took over as chairman from Sir Peter Leslie, who had retired after five years in the post.

Dr Roy Reynolds

Dr Roy Reynolds trained as a chemical engineer at Birmingham University and Imperial College, London, where he studied for his doctorate. Immediately prior to joining CDC, he had been working as a consultant to the World Bank. Previous to that, he was with Shell for twenty-eight years, having joined the company in 1964. During that time he had gained wide overseas experience with the company in Holland, Curaçao, Brunei (where he was manager of the world's first large LNG plant) and Singapore. He moved back to the UK in 1984 as director of supply and manufacturing, going on to become managing director of Shell UK Oil four years later in 1988. He brought experience of a large multinational to CDC and, perhaps not surprisingly, believed that good management was equally as important as investing cash.

Suitably re-motivated and re-energised, the new organisation swung into action. Following the recommendation from the strategy review that the number of mature managed businesses ought to be slimmed down, and also in line with new chairman Lord Cairns' comment in his first chairman's statement in 1995 about the need to sell old investments "perhaps more rapidly than before" in instances where CDC had completed the job it set out to do, the two major palm oil managed businesses in Malaysia – Sarawak Oil Palms Bhd and CDC's 'flagship' BAL Plantations Sdn Bhd – were sold in 1995 and 1996 respectively – both at the top of the market cycle, thanks to a more buoyant world economy.

Not that managed businesses generally were out of favour at this stage. Far from it. Roy Reynolds firmly believed that one of CDC's greatest strengths was its long experience in managing businesses, a strength he wished to maximise, convinced that good management was as important as cash in developing businesses in poorer countries and that CDC had the ability to pull businesses together to give them the critical mass that would enable them to survive and prosper in a globalised world. So, while SOP and BAL were sold, along with some failing companies, CDC Industries set about developing a string of other world-scale businesses.

The first of these resulted from the merger and expansion of CDC's oil palm interests in a more under-developed part of the Asia Pacific region, based on its established plantations in Papua New Guinea. The process was initiated on New Year's Day, 1995, when Higaturu Oil Palms Pty Ltd was renamed Pacific Rim Plantations (Pacrim), the estates at Milne Bay and Poliamba being brought into the new company. CDC also set up a marketing company in Singapore to sell the palm products. The plan was to use Pacrim to expand regionally. Two years later a foothold was duly gained in Indonesia through a loan made to PT Harapan Sawit Lestari, a plantation company in Kalimantan that CDC then took over in 1999, at which point it formed Pacific Rim Palm Oil Ltd (PRPOL) as the holding company for all the plantations. In 2000, the group was further expanded with the purchase of a majority share in PT Asiatic Persada, an established company with 20,000 hectares of plantations in Sumatra. By the time PRPOL was sold in 2005 it extended to over 56,000 hectares of planted land altogether.

Above: The 1996 AGM of Chilanga Cement, two years after CDC had taken control of the company for the third time during an involvement that lasted more than fifty years altogether. Those pictured here are (from left to right): Knox Karima, operations manager; Patrick Gorman, general manager; Mathew Shitima, director (GM of Civil Service Pension Board); Andy Mazoka, director (chairman of Zambian Anglo American Corporation Ltd); Richard Beacham, chairman; and David Johns, CDC regional manager.

Pursuing the same policy of growing world-scale businesses, the first moves were also made towards expanding Chilanga Cement to create the Pan African Cement group. Having taken control of Chilanga once again in 1994, CDC listed Chilanga Cement plc on the newly-opened Lusaka Stock Exchange in 1995. The first company to be listed there, it helped to encourage the development of capital markets in Zambia. By the end of the year there were 4,350 shareholders and the first AGM the following year attracted hundreds of first-time capitalists, some of whom were disappointed when their expectations of special shareholder benefits such as travel expenses and personal loans were dashed!

Over the next few years CDC refurbished Chilanga's plant and by combining high environmental and social standards with exemplary corporate governance appropriate to a plc provided an excellent role model for other large Zambian businesses. CDC then participated in the privatisation of two other African cement companies that it also went on to manage, starting in 1996 with Portland Cement, Malawi's only cement producer, adding Tanzania's Mbeya Cement two years later. In 2000, CDC's controlling shareholdings in the three companies were transferred into the Pan African Cement group, now the major regional cement player, which was sold to Lafarge the following year.

Other significant developments of existing managed businesses in the mid-nineties included the major expansion of the Mpongwe arable farming project in Zambia and the establishment of East Africa Teas in Kampala to manage all CDC's tea operations in Uganda, Tanzania and Malawi as an integrated business. Private equity transactions initiated by CDC-managed Tanzania Venture Capital Fund also helped to lay the foundations of what was to become one of the world's largest suppliers of Fairtrade teas – Tanzania Tea Packers, better known as Tatepa.

New businesses managed by CDC ranged from aquaculture on Zimbabwe's Lake Kariba and Del Oro fruit juice production in Central America through to flower and vegetable producer York Farms, which became Tesco's sole supplier in Zambia, exporting the bulk of its ten million rose stems and 1,850 tonnes of courgettes, baby corn, green beans, mange tout, squash and chilli peppers for sale in the supermarket chain's UK stores.

Slamet the Tiger

Slamet the Tiger provides a striking symbol of CDC's commitment to environmentally friendly development and conservation.

Slamet – meaning 'Lucky' – is one of a sadly dwindling number of Sumatran tigers, an endangered species of which about four hundred are believed to survive in the wild.

When CDC took over the management of oil palm company PT Asiatic Persada in Jambi, Sumatra in 2000, it called in the Zoological Society of London (ZSL), with the support of the Indonesian government, to help manage the 20,000-hectare plantation's tiger population that, at the time, included seven males and three breeding females.

As part of the three-year Jambi Tiger Project, carried out in partnership with the Indonesian Institute of Science, the ZSL team succeeded in the tricky task of fitting a radio tracking device to Slamet, a mature male, so that they could then chart his movements in order to find out more about the tigers – their habits, their prey and the relationship between the oil palm production patterns and tiger density locally.

One of the main objects of the exercise was to work out how best to establish an effective network of land-use zones, connected by wildlife corridors through the plantation from one section of forest to the next, in an effort to boost the chances of the tigers' survival.

In addition, PT Asiatic Persada designated fifteen per cent of its land to conservation and also set up a team of anti-poaching scouts who worked closely with the local Ministry of Forestry office to prevent the illegal activities that were going on when they first arrived, including the snaring and trapping of wild pigs and deer.

A member of the ZSL team was quoted on BBC News Online at the time: "If every business in the world did the same as PT Asiatic Persada it could have a great effect on forest connectivity and potentially on wildlife".

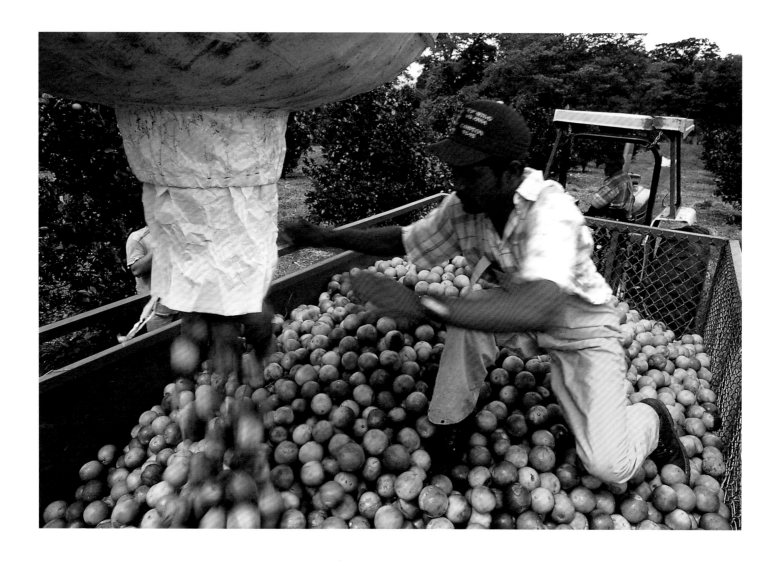

Del Oro

Del Oro, meaning 'of the gold', proved to be far from a golden investment for CDC.

CDC had been involved in growing citrus fruit in Costa Rica since 1989, when it took a fifty-one per cent controlling interest in Inversiones Guanaranga, a company started by an eccentric American from North Dakota called Irwin Wilhite. Wilhite had been planting orange groves on his company's 7,000-hectare estate near the extinct volcano of Orosi, close to the border with Nicaragua, and needed finance to expand.

By 1993, CDC had increased its holding to one hundred per cent, meanwhile planting 3,000 of the 7,000 hectares with orange trees, leaving the rest as a conservation area. In order to add value to its products it then decided to build a new processing plant to produce juice for export and also set up a separate, wholly-owned company to run it.

Keen to expand even further in pursuit of its ambition to become a premier player in the juice industry, CDC started looking round for other opportunities in the region and found them in Belize, where it had participated in the local citrus industry for some years through a small loan to the government-owned Development Finance Co for on-lending to the Citrus Growers Association, later taking over the management of a 750-hectare orange grove.

In 1998 and 1999 it bought both the Citrus Company of Belize and Belize Food Products, the country's two juice processors and, with various other acquisitions, formed Del Oro (Belize) Ltd, which became the sole processor in Belize with 3,000 hectares of orange groves. The result was a more efficient company, which probably saved the industry in Belize – and, with it, some twenty per cent of the country's export earnings. However, the venture was far from a financial success for CDC.

Altogether, CDC invested more than $100 million in trying to build a world-class business, but as things turned out it was not money well spent. Del Oro was never able to compete in a market dominated by the US and Brazil, even though it enjoyed duty-free access to the US market through a government-to-government agreement. The Belize operation, into which $46 million had been poured, was sold to the Citrus Growers Association after just three years for a token $1. In Costa Rica, the decision was taken to expand the Del Oro factory in order to keep pace with increased fruit supply, a move also aimed at maximising the company's appeal to potential buyers. With plant capacity doubled, Del Oro expanded both its orange and pineapple juice production and also diversified into passion fruit juice. Even so, it wasn't until 2008 that the company was eventually sold, recovering a reasonable part of the investment.

Lake Harvest

Lake Harvest was a pioneering tilapia fish farming project on Lake Kariba that grew out of a link with the commercial arm of Stirling University's Institute of Aquaculture. This had originally been established in 1993 when CDC, whose previous investments in shrimp farming in Thailand and Nicaragua and tilapia farming in Costa Rica had run into problems, sought the institute's expert help in setting up its first managed aquaculture project in Malta. Malta Mariculture, CDC's one and only investment in Malta, involved using offshore cages to farm sea bream. The connection with Stirling was then reinforced when one of its MSc graduates, Patrick Blow, joined CDC, becoming Lake Harvest's first general manager.

The project was sited close to the small town of Kariba itself, on the Zimbabwe side of the lake. A series of ponds were dug just inland from the lake shore in which the young fish were raised to a certain size before being transferred to large net cages out in the lake to be grown to market size. They were then brought back to a state-of-the-art factory to be filleted, packed and chilled and sent for export, mostly to Europe.

The use of the word 'pioneering' to describe the venture is perfectly justified given the challenges involved. These included transplanting new technology, establishing a process operating to the highest environmental and hygiene standards demanded by investors and buyers and learning the art of air-freighting fresh produce – all this against a background of local economic, political and legal problems. As if that weren't enough, there were also the wild animals. Elephants were regular and potentially destructive visitors, tiger fish menaced the caged tilapia until stronger nets were introduced and CDC-seconded ponds manager Shivaun Leonard was gored by a buffalo on site and had to be invalided out to London for treatment.

After CDC decided to divest itself of its managed projects, Patrick Blow led a management buy-out in 2002, since when the business has flourished despite the subsequent political problems in Zimbabwe. It expanded its farmed fish production into Uganda and Zambia and the group now produces over 8,000 tonnes of whole fish per annum and employs around 650 people. Today the business is focused on selling into African markets, where the Lake Harvest brand has become a household name in several countries. The business has developed multiple wholesale and retail outlets in its markets, as well as a distribution and fish trading business. Lake Harvest's success as a pioneer has encouraged others to invest in tilapia aquaculture in Africa, so much so that a rapidly expanding industry of fish farms and their supporting aquafeed factories and hatcheries now exists.

With regard to new destinations and new non-managed investments, attention was duly focused on countries in the three regions targeted by the strategy review as having the best potential – South Asia, Africa and Latin America.

In the latter, after the initial build-up of activity in Costa Rica that included the highly successful CDC-managed Aqua Corporación International fish farming venture, CDC was to extend its presence over the next few years from Mexico in the north to Chile in the south, with offices in Mexico City, Miami, Cuba, Trinidad, Bolivia, and Peru. By the end of 2000, partly due to the lack of opportunities elsewhere owing to the fall-out from the Asian financial crisis, this vastly-expanded and now far-flung Americas region accounted for forty per cent of the entire new private equity portfolio, involving a great deal of effort in several territories unfamiliar to CDC.

The greatest presence continued to be in Costa Rica, where the $26 million CDC-managed Central American Investment Fund (CAIF), in which CDC invested $8 million alongside other finance from local and international banks and development finance institutions, was the first investment fund in Central America to be aimed at financing the SME sector. First to benefit was a software company, Exactus, CAIF's injection of capital and expertise at boardroom level making possible rapid expansion into South American markets. CAIF soon opened a second office in San Salvador to manage business in El Salvador, Honduras and Nicaragua and went on to make ten investments in businesses as varied as a Guatemalan flower exporter, a Panamanian-based data transmission company and an El Salvador-based pharmaceuticals company.

Of the many other financial institutions that CDC supported in Central America, its equity investment in ProFund International SA stands out as being its first exposure to microfinance, providing very small loans to help the poorest entrepreneurs. ProFund International later joined CDC in another microfinance investment in the Banco Sol in Bolivia. As well as finance, CDC was active in investing in other diverse sectors in Central America, including cement, property, industrial parks and hotels.

A whistle-stop north-south tour of CDC's interests throughout the region might start in Mexico, where it supported the local management buy-out of a Mexican subsidiary of Betterware, the British company with a long history of selling household and cleaning products door-to-door through catalogues. As well as an equity stake, CDC provided sales and management advice and the company grew so successfully that when it was taken over four years later CDC's stake brought a high return.

Travelling east from Mexico, the CDC tour would take us next to Cuba. This was not an easy place in which to operate – bureaucratic, lacking in transparency and subject to disruptive interference from Castro's government. However, CDC did establish a financial institution – Caribbean Finance Investments Ltd, known as Carifin – which it founded in partnership with the Grupo Nuevo Banco, part of the Banco Nacional de Cuba, and managed it for a decade, turning it at one point into the largest foreign-run financial institution operating in Cuba's domestic market. When the government later introduced significant restrictions, CDC sold its sixty per cent stake to Grupo Nuevo Banco and, despite all the difficulties that had been experienced, again made a good return on the investment.

"Of the many other financial institutions that CDC supported in Central America, its equity investment in ProFund International SA stands out as being its first exposure to microfinance, providing very small loans to help the poorest entrepreneurs."

Above: Harvesting bananas at the Favorita Fruit Company, one of CDC's investments in Ecuador. A major concern that eventually expanded to cover every aspect of production, packaging and export of bananas, providing employment for 9,000 people, it not only yielded a good return but was also a model of social and environmental responsibility.

Above: Outside the La Paz headquarters of Banco Sol, one of Bolivia's leading microfinance institutions.

Further south in Ecuador, where CDC had started working in a small way in 1977 before then stepping up its involvement with a development finance institution in 1994, the outstanding investment was in the Favorita Fruit Company. This was an umbrella company that CDC helped to form in 1998 in order to bring together the various interests of the Wong family group with whom it had been working closely since providing a $5 million loan to help expand their original banana plantation business, Rey Banano del Pacifico, four years earlier. By 1998 the Wongs had set up associated companies involved in every stage of the process of growing and exporting bananas, from fertilisers to packaging and from air fumigation to port facilities at Guayaquil and they were employing 9,000 people. CDC, which had taken equity in Favorita along with the International Finance Corporation and which also provided strategic and financial advice to help with the expansion, again achieved a good return when the Wongs bought back its equity stake in 2004. Apart from that, CDC was particularly proud of the social and environmental aspects of Favorita's operations, which it had helped to promote. This included conservation of the remaining rainforest, the control of water pollution, reduced use of chemical fertilisers and pest control, recycling and disposal of waste and improvements in pay, health and educational facilities for the farmers and their families.

In Bolivia, CDC was especially active, innovative and bold, identifying and participating in some developmentally significant enterprises. As well as its support for many small and medium-sized enterprises through the highly respected and award-winning Banco Sol, which remains one of the country's leading microfinance institutions, it was involved in a wide variety of sectors from mining to cement, along with a hydro-power generation company through its one hundred per cent acquisition of Compañía Boliviana de Energía Eléctrica SA, serving La Paz.

Down at the end of the line in Peru there was a rather novel investment in a railway. In 1999 CDC brought together the Railroad Development Corporation, a US private train operator and a group of Peruvian investors to form Ferrocarril Central Andino for the purpose of purchasing the thirty-year concession to operate the 591-kilometre line from the Pacific port of Callao to the Peruvian capital, Lima before climbing nearly 5,000 metres to the mining industry terminals high in the Andes at Cerro de Pasco and Huancayo. Vital to the Peruvian economy as a freight link, the line also offers tourist trips from Lima to Huancayo in carriages with panoramic observation windows providing spectacular views as the train chugs up through the foothills and on up into the mountains, over sixty-one bridges, through sixty-eight tunnels and over nine switchbacks. CDC sold its stake in 2004, but RDC is still involved.

In both Peru and Chile, CDC went to the cinema. On returning from university in the United States, a group of young Peruvians had decided that cinemas could be a growth area. Statistics showed that cinema visits in Peru had declined from sixteen million in 1981 to just three million in 1995, the reason being the threat of terrorism and the downturn in the economy. However, this trend was changing and the young entrepreneurs could see that the new style of multiplex cinemas, non-existent in Peru at the time, were what was needed to attract the mass audience back. They decided to buy an existing group that owned three old-fashioned cinemas as a base from which to expand. CDC bought into the idea, investing equity in the Nexus Film Corporation, alongside the management team and Interbank Peru and also providing a $2 million shareholder bridging loan facility to buy the long-term lease of the existing cinemas and to build new ones.

Above: The Bolivian tin and zinc mine in the hills at Colquiri. CDC and the Bolivian mining company Comsur took over the run-down mine in 1999 and completely rehabilitated it before selling it on.

Meanwhile, back in Africa in the mid-nineties offices were opened in South Africa, where CDC was able to operate for the first time following the end of apartheid, and in Mozambique, which was just emerging from two decades of civil war. The first small investment in Mozambique was in a graphite mining and processing business in Cabo Delgado in the north of the country in 1995, while in South Africa one of the first major investments linked the two countries in a literal sense, involving as it did an equity stake and loans to Trans Africa Concessions (TRAC) to finance the creation of a 440-kilometre-long toll motorway between Witbank, just east of Pretoria and Maputo, Mozambique's capital and its main port.

The $400 million project, in which CDC was the single largest investor, involved upgrading the existing N4 road to motorway and installing toll plazas. The aim was to encourage the development of the Johannesburg/Pretoria-Maputo corridor, to the commercial and social advantage of both South Africa and Mozambique, while one of the main risks was whether enough drivers would actually pay the toll on what was previously a free road, especially as there would be plenty of opportunities to leave the motorway and skirt around the booths. In fact, drivers welcomed the new and reliable infrastructure, the income from low daily commuter tariffs exceeding expectations by seventy per cent in the first three years. Soon established as one of the safest roads in Africa and later extended from Witbank to Pretoria, it created over a thousand jobs and enabled small businesses to flourish in communities along the way that benefited from the better transport links.

For CDC it was a hugely successful investment, showing an annualised return of just below thirty per cent on its equity of $19 million when it was sold in 2006. But CDC brought much more to the project than just money. For a start, its Johannesburg-based investment manager Remy Hassenforder served as chairman of TRAC, working with the management and fellow directors to resolve the considerable challenges that were encountered along the way, including the need to refinance $230 million of debt. The $400 million of new debt that was raised as a result made it the first private-public partnership to be refinanced in Africa and one of the largest transport deals anywhere in the continent at the time, enabling TRAC to expand and improve its services.

CDC went on to establish a significant presence in South Africa as one of its core emerging markets, with investments that ranged from hotels to healthcare and which also included the first purpose-built shopping centre in the historic Johannesburg township of Soweto. Investments in the healthcare sector, which included the benefits administration company Medikredit, a chain of Prime Cure Clinics, and Medscheme, now South Africa's largest third-party administrator of medical schemes, provided major developmental benefits even if the financial returns weren't especially healthy.

By contrast, investments in platinum mining in the areas north and north east of Johannesburg and Pretoria – first through Aquarius Platinum and then, later, through a $35 million equity investment in Platmin – proved extremely rewarding.

Left and right: Toll booths on the 440-kilometre-long TRAC motorway linking Pretoria, in South Africa with Maputo, Mozambique's capital and main port. Fears that many drivers would refuse to pay the toll, taking advantage of ample opportunity to skirt round the booths by leaving the road and driving cross-country, proved unfounded and the motorway not only improved transport links but helped to boost local economies all along the route.

In Mozambique, the initial small investment in Grafites de Ancuabe SARL was significant for two reasons; firstly, because the project probably would not have gone ahead without CDC and, secondly, because it satisfied that other important CDC requirement of encouraging others to invest in the country. Among other things, this paved the way for the creation of the massive aluminium smelting business, Mozal. Here, CDC participated alongside the International Finance Corporation. At $1.2 billion, the total cost of setting up Mozal was equivalent to the whole of Mozambique's GDP at the time.

Elsewhere in Africa, CDC continued to be busy in destinations old and new. In Swaziland, where it had been involved so successfully for so many years, it oversaw the merger of its long-established flagship Mhlume Sugar with the Royal Swaziland Sugar Corporation, retaining an equity stake that was subsequently sold to neighbouring South African sugar producer, TSB. It went fishing and grape-growing in Namibia and in Tanzania it went prospecting with East Africa Gold Mines, helping to re-launch the Tanzanian mining industry after being absent from the sector since Rendell's day. And, most notably, it started making valuable and very worthy connections in countries all over Africa via its Celtel mobile phone networks.

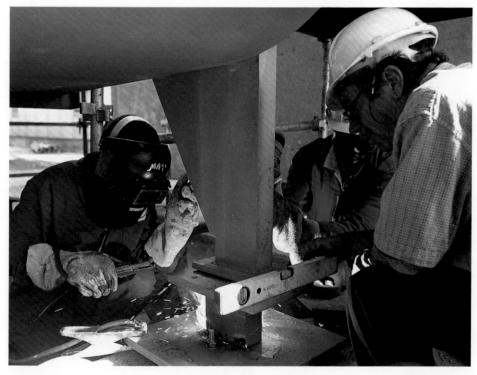

Above: Welders working with an engineer at Mozal, the massive aluminium smelting business in Mozambique that was set up at a cost of $1.2 billion, part-financed by CDC alongside IFC.

Celtel

The story of CDC, Celtel and Dr Mohamed 'Mo' Ibrahim, the visionary, dynamic and inspirational force behind the company's success, is probably worth a book in itself. In terms of its developmental impact, its social, communal and environmental influence, its widespread geographical location in some of the poorest countries throughout Africa and its pioneering private sector status, Celtel was an outstanding success. On top of that, it proved to be a highly profitable investment.

The hero of this extraordinary story is undoubtedly Mo Ibrahim. Born in Sudan in 1948, he first made a name for himself in the telecom sector when he was brought in as technical director of BT subsidiary Cellnet to establish the first analogue mobile phone network in the UK. He then set up his own company, Mobile Systems International (MSI), in 1989.

He and CDC first came into contact in Uganda, where, in 1995, CDC had made a ten per cent equity investment in Clovergem Celtel Ltd, which had been given a government licence to develop the country's mobile telecoms service. MSI had also taken some shares in lieu of payment for providing the network planning software.

Mo had already started to develop his vision for similar networks throughout Africa. The old fixed telephone lines were failing to provide a satisfactory service and African governments were starting to liberalise their telecoms sectors, enabling outsiders to come in, but the big operators were pre-occupied with Europe and the more developed markets such as South Africa and either didn't spot the opportunities or were risk averse or both. Mo, on the other hand, could clearly see the possibilities and in 1998 he formed MSI Cellular Investments – later re-branded as Celtel – with the aim of developing a pan-African telecoms company.

With its long experience of working throughout Africa, CDC was an obvious natural partner. There was some nervousness on CDC's part, but impressed by Mo and the board he had put together, including individuals from BT, Vodafone and a professor of private equity from Harvard, it decided to take the plunge. Under the committed guidance of its telecoms expert, Adrian Robinson, CDC worked very closely with Mo over the next seven years as he pursued his ambitious masterplan, providing not only finance but also boardroom, management and investment support at every level and making full use of its unrivalled contacts network throughout Africa.

By 2005, when Celtel was bought for $3.4 billion by the Kuwait-based Mobile Telecommunications Company – earning CDC a return of $330 million on its $76.5 million investment over the years – it was operating in thirteen African countries.

Along the way, Celtel, later to be rebranded as Zain, had established an exemplary reputation for responsible corporate governance, making it clear from the start that it was not going to do anything that lacked transparency. Having adopted the motto 'Making Life Better', it helped to renovate schools and clinics, provided scholarships and promoted educational journalism. It helped protect endangered species, promoted community use of mobiles in rural villages and took HIV issues seriously.

Although the promotion of mobile phones in Africa was seen as controversial initially, its development value is now recognised. A Vodafone policy paper published in 2005 entitled 'Africa – The Impact Of Mobile Phones' highlighted the many ways in which having access to telephones for the first time had improved the lives and livelihoods of individuals and the fortunes of small businesses in the poorest communities where, previously, the only way to communicate with someone was to travel to see them. And it added: "At a macro level, a country with better communications attracts more foreign investment and a higher GDP".

"Although the promotion of mobile phones in Africa was seen as controversial initially, its development value is now recognised."

Above: Rick Phillips, the manager of Takura Ventures, one of CDC's most successful country funds in the mid-1990s in the days before Zimbabwe's economic meltdown, with Phibion Makoni of Stuttafords Holdings. Takura's first deal enabled Phibion to expand his removals business by helping to finance his acquisition of a rival company.

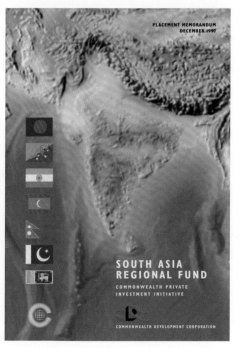

Above: Information memoranda issued in 1996 - 1997 launching the two largest regional funds of the Commonwealth Private Investment Initiative, Commonwealth Africa Investment Fund (Comafin) (left), and the South Asia Regional Fund.

CDC Financial Markets, meanwhile, was especially active in the years immediately after Roy Reynolds' reorganisation. Fulfilling the drive for more venture capital and private equity investment and also for the development of capital markets, it set up six new managed country funds in 1996 alone. This brought the total number of the funds worldwide to twenty-four, of which half were managed. At the same time, it became involved in the Commonwealth Private Investment Initiative – a new idea for a series of much larger regional funds, with many external investors. The first of these, the $64 million Comafin Fund, served African countries and was followed by the Kula Fund and then the $108 million South Asian Regional Fund (SARF). While these were of variable financial success, they enabled CDC to explore on a bigger scale what it subsequently decided to do in the future.

Of the six new country funds, the most successful were those started up in Zimbabwe and Kenya. Ironically, given what was to come, Zimbabwe in 1996 was advertising itself as one of the most attractive places to invest in all of Africa, with the second largest economy south of the Sahara. It could boast political stability, liberalisation of market controls, a favourable attitude to privatisations, an excellent infrastructure and a skilled workforce. On top of that, it was a great place to live and work. No surprise, then, that it was already attracting significant investment interest from around the world, including South East Asia. South African businesses, liberated by the post-apartheid era, were looking north, and thriving Zimbabwe was seen as a stepping stone to the rest of the continent. CDC, too, expected great things by this time, anticipating that its portfolio in Zimbabwe would soon become one of the top three by value in the whole of Africa.

Given this highly confident, optimistic environment, a number of local businesses were looking for injections of cash in order to rehabilitate, innovate or expand, creating fertile ground for a private equity fund. In 1993 CDC had taken a small stake in the Venture Capital Company of Zimbabwe but it was clear that there was room to do far more business, so in January 1996 Rick Phillips was transferred from DFCU in Uganda to prepare the launch of Takura Ventures in Harare in November 1996. CDC managed the company and subscribed thirty per cent of the fund's $13.5 million capital alongside two European development finance institutions and Zimbabwean banks and pension funds.

Takura's first deal helped the owner of Stuttafords, a removals business to expand through the acquisition of one of his main rivals. But the big breakthrough came in 1997 when Takura did a deal with the corporate buyer of a long-established mining supplies company. The buyer did not want two divisions of the company – the scaffolding manufacturer supplying Zimbabwe's then booming building industry and a supplier of crop-spraying equipment to the country's then thriving commercial farms. Recognising that both companies had capable managers and strong positions, Takura encouraged the idea of management buy-outs. Both deals were finalised on the same day and Formscaff and AgVenture were formed.

The business community in Harare was impressed – a new young team had pulled off a most innovative financial transaction. The managements of Formscaff and AgVenture became motivated owners of their new businesses and their success inspired others to do the same. Over the next few years Takura backed fifteen other ventures, of which twelve were management buy-outs. The companies involved ranged from PG Industries, the biggest fibre board producer in central Africa; Dairibord, the national dairy; Commercial Refrigeration, the leading producer of chilled cabinets; to Charhons, a confectionery business. Altogether, they employed over six thousand people and the managements were forty per cent white, forty per cent black and twenty per cent mixed race at a time when many Zimbabwean management teams were still overwhelmingly white.

Sadly, this momentum was checked all too soon by Robert Mugabe's policies, but Takura didn't pull out. There could be no question of that; after all, demonstrating how to manage 'emerging market risk' had been identified as part of CDC's new raison d'etre. Rick Phillips and his team just got cleverer in identifying opportunities and helping investee companies to weather the storms. By 2003, when CDC once again closed its offices in Harare, four of Takura's portfolio of investments had been sold with an excellent average annualised return of thirty-three per cent in US dollars – a remarkable achievement in the circumstances. Meanwhile, most of the businesses managed to struggle on through the mounting economic crisis, still delivering positive US dollar returns.

The success of the Acacia Fund in Kenya, led by Michael Turner, was not quite so spectacular – certainly not in the years immediately following its launch when riots over political change, worsening corruption and the terrorist attack on the US Embassy in Nairobi in 1998 conspired to cause economic stagnation. It is to the credit of the fund managers, CDC-managed Kenya Capital Partners, that Acacia was nevertheless able to invest $15.6 million in eighteen different companies spread broadly across all sectors of the Kenyan economy, ranging from Micro Kenya – now part of the largest regional provider of microfinance – to Mount Elgon Orchards, a profitable exporter of roses.

A later review estimated that Acacia investee companies had made a significant contribution to Kenya's GDP. And in the best CDC tradition of leading by example, it had changed perceptions towards investment in small and medium-sized companies in a country where, previously, larger companies had monopolised all the attention. It had also helped to change attitudes in small companies generally towards what private equity had to offer; until Acacia came along these businesses had feared that in giving away equity they would lose control for ever, but the fund's exits demonstrated the opposite. Overall, Acacia's steady progress undoubtedly helped to change the investment scene in Kenya, while also producing a satisfactory return.

At the same time as CDC's regional and country-based private equity fund managers were managing other investors' funds with the aim of transforming markets, CDC itself was contemplating a transformation of its own, embarking on a journey that would ultimately lead to it, too, adopting a private equity model.

The roller-coaster train of events leading up to that eventual development was set in motion in 1997. By then, the new-look CDC under Roy Reynolds was brimming with confidence, boosted by record income, realisations and investments and further encouraged by signs of continuing economic growth worldwide, even in Africa. There were two nagging concerns. The first related to calls for it to be 'the investor of last resort' – for it only to invest where the private sector would not venture. Pressures on CDC not to invest government money in competition with the private sector were as old as CDC itself, but in the absence of clear evidence, demonstrating conclusively that CDC would not actually be competing was sometimes difficult. This inevitably led to frustration when some of its big and innovative ideas had to be shelved as a result.

The other nagging concern was the perennial one of funding. CDC wanted to do more development – to invest more and, by example, encourage others to invest more in the developing world – but felt that it was being held back by restrictions on the way in which it was financed.

It had been lobbying for years for a fundamental change that would free it from reliance on government loans and give it access to the substantial extra funds that it needed in order to expand as it would like to do, but these pleas always seemed to fall on deaf ears. Then, in October 1997, less than six months after New Labour's election victory, a sudden and earlier than expected announcement by Prime Minister Tony Blair brought a dramatic change that addressed both concerns.

The prime minister chose a speech to the Commonwealth Business Forum at the InterContinental Hotel in London to unveil the government's plans to launch its first Public Private Partnership (known as a PPP) – and that this was going to involve CDC. PPPs had been around for years in the United States, but this was the first one in the UK. It was one of the few occasions when CDC found itself featuring in the national television news headlines.

The timing of this announcement had much to do with the fact that Blair was due to attend his first Commonwealth Heads of Government Meeting (CHOGM) in Edinburgh three days later. Here was an opportunity to announce something new to do with the Commonwealth, Economics, Investment and Sustainable Development – all headline themes for CHOGM – and link it with Labour's election promise to deliver improvements in public services.

In his speech to the Commonwealth businessmen, Blair, having made a point of acknowledging how well CDC was doing, went on to add: "But despite this, I believe it is an under-used asset. It can do more. It has the capacity to play a much greater role in mobilising new private finance for poor countries. One of the most important developments in New Labour is the breaking down of public-private barriers. I am less interested in whether an institution is public or private than whether it works. CDC is a public institution. I believe it can be improved by becoming a public-private partnership."

He then outlined how it would work. Legislation would allow private investors to invest equity in CDC and also lend to it, effectively turning the state corporation into a PPP. The government would retain a minority holding of at least twenty-five per cent as well as a so-called 'golden share' – enabling it to make sure that CDC preserved "its unique character and special skills". All funds arising from the sale would go back for recycling to the Department for International Development (DFID) – the new name for what had previously been the Overseas Development Administration.

In almost every respect this was very good news for CDC, the only slight problem being that it came so quickly. Since the new government had come to power, there had been a fair amount of brain-storming between Roy Reynolds and John Vereker (later Sir John), the permanent secretary at DFID, during which they explored the concept of introducing a PPP, an innovation in Britain at the time. But while Clare Short, the new secretary of state at DFID, was keen that CDC should be doing more, the message was that there would be no more money forthcoming from government. At the same time, she indicated her enthusiastic support for the idea of a reorganisation aimed at bringing in investment from the private sector, allowing CDC to undertake private equity investment that would help to build profitable businesses and lead to sustainable economic development. The prime minister's announcement nevertheless came almost out of the blue, its suddenness catching everyone at CDC by surprise, including Lord Cairns.

As one senior member of the staff commented, it was rather as if Blair had given CDC the all-clear for take-off while the plane was still in bits in the hangar, awaiting construction. The matter of who was going to build it, own it and fly it had yet to be finally decided and the exact flight path was still uncharted. When Roy Reynolds put forward the concept of a PPP, he had visualised working only with investors that shared CDC's goals and values. But while he had ideas about who those private investors were likely to be – such as development-focused charitable foundations – what they might expect from CDC in terms of returns and other deliverables was unknown. What was recognised, however, was that development is a long-term business, and that finding the right partners was always going to be the challenge, and would take time.

All these things had yet to be worked out in detail. In the meantime, plans went ahead for CDC to become a public company, with all its shares initially to be owned by DFID until such time as they were sold on. And One Bessborough Gardens became a hive of activity as the organisation threw itself into the task of preparing for its brave new world.

During the next two years there was an intensive period of re-shaping and re-skilling that included the recruitment of new staff – expert professionals in their field who were also dedicated to sustainable development – along with the re-training of existing employees to make them more commercially-minded and equity-focused. This approach was reflected in the fact that sixty-three per cent of the total invested in 1998 was in risk capital, compared with an average of twenty-three per cent for the previous three years.

While CDC was re-aligning and re-equipping itself to be able to operate effectively in the world of private equity investment, one of its great strengths was still perceived to be its on-the-ground presence, its network of local offices and its managed businesses. These aspects of CDC had been grown significantly prior to the introduction of the PPP model and, with a sharpened sense of commerciality, they were seen as being key to bringing like-minded investors on board.

In announcing the change to a PPP model, Blair had made it clear that safeguards to protect CDC's unique development role would remain in place. CDC would continue to invest in, or for the benefit of, low and middle-income countries as defined by the World Bank and, measured over a five-year period, seventy per cent of the investments would be in 'poorer countries', defined in terms of a specific GDP per head of population. Half of all CDC's investments in any one year were to be in South Asia or sub-Saharan Africa, reflecting the strong belief that this was where CDC was most needed. The new investors would be expected to sign up to these aims.

Lord Cairns

Simon Cairns succeeded Sir Peter Leslie as chairman of CDC in 1995 and held the post until 2004, providing continuity for CDC during a period of momentous change when no less than five chief executives came or went as the organisation tried to establish a new identity for itself. In that respect, he was instrumental in helping to shape CDC's future.

A development economist by training, he had a distinguished business career in investment banking. This included leading S.G. Warburg, one of the UK's most successful investment banks, of which he was CEO. He subsequently became chairman of British American Tobacco and of the insurance group Allied Zurich.

Alongside Cyril Ramaphosa, Lord Cairns founded and chaired the Commonwealth Business Council at the request of Prime Minister Tony Blair and South Africa's President Thabo Mbeki.

It was at the council's inaugural meeting in London that the plan for CDC to become the Labour government's first PPP was announced. The council continues to provide a platform for governments and the private sector to work together to increase trade and investment across the Commonwealth, with a particular focus on Africa.

Between 1981 and 1992, Lord Cairns chaired Voluntary Service Overseas and from 1990 to 1997 he also served as chair of the Overseas Development Institute, which more than doubled in size under his guidance and significantly increased its range of activities. He has also been chairman of Celtel, one of CDC's most successful investments, staying on in that capacity even after CDC sold its equity.

He was a board member of the Mo Ibrahim Foundation until 2016 and serves on the advisory board of Satya Capital, an investor of long-term growth capital in African businesses.

CDC also agreed with DFID that all investments were to follow ethical best practice. In 1998, the private sector was not seen to take corporate responsibility as seriously as it does today and there were question marks over whether potential investors in CDC could be trusted. CDC therefore established its own set of core values and business principles, which were set out in new guidelines dealing with business integrity, health and safety, environmental and social issues. These were then embedded in the investment appraisal and monitoring processes, which were revamped. Roy Reynolds was also keen to ensure that the 'development impact' of each investment was measured before CDC made a commitment. Alice Chapple undertook much innovative work internally on this to identify what to measure and how and then making sure the results were evaluated.

If the government's sudden announcement of the PPP plan had caught CDC somewhat on the hop, its timing generally soon turned out to have been even more unfortunate in that it coincided with the Asian financial crisis. Starting in Thailand with the collapse of the baht in July 1997, this spread rapidly through the region, affecting investors' confidence in emerging stock markets around the world, which dropped by twenty-two per cent in 1998.

Falling commodity prices and severe devaluations of some of the regional currencies had a considerable knock-on effect on CDC's income. CDC had just sold Sarawak Oil Palms and BAL Plantations, the largest of its mature managed businesses in South East Asia, reducing its exposure there. However, its substantial portfolios in Indonesia and Pakistan were badly affected by foreign currency devaluation and shortages, while many companies that had taken hard currency loans were unable to make interest and capital repayments. The whole of CDC's universe was affected to a greater or lesser degree, as was the case with other financial institutions at the time. Mountainous provisions against possible losses – £155 million in all compared to £55 million the year before – had to be put through the books in 1998, leading to the first annual deficit of costs, provisions and taxes over income since 1954. The return on CDC's capital over the three years 1996-8 slumped to 3.6 per cent, well below DFID's target of eight per cent.

Dr Alan Gillespie

Dr Alan Gillespie was born in Northern Ireland in 1950 and was educated at Grosvenor High School, Belfast, and Cambridge University, where his PhD subject was the role of growth centres in regional economic development. He then embarked on an international banking career, serving ten years with Citibank and fifteen years with Goldman Sachs before taking up the role of chief executive at CDC, aged forty-nine. At Goldman Sachs he had been a partner and managing director, responsible for UK investment banking – specifically mergers and acquisitions and corporate finance – and had also opened their office in South Africa.

While in office with CDC he was also chairman of the Northern Ireland Industrial Development Board and since then he has been non-executive chairman of the Ulster Bank Group and a member of the Advisory Board of the Judge Institute of Management at the University of Cambridge. Since leaving CDC, he has continued to work in international development, becoming the founding chair of the International Finance Facility for Immunisation (IFFIm), a $5 billion fund established under the leadership of DFID and five European countries as part of the Make Poverty History campaign. He has been awarded two honorary degrees and is an honorary fellow of Clare College, Cambridge. He has been chair of the Economic and Social Research Council since 2009 and was a board member of United Business Media until 2017. He has also been Old Mutual's senior independent director since 2011.

Despite these setbacks there were reasons to be positive: the fundamental financial position of CDC was still strong and in 1999 there was a welcome improvement in the economic climate. Recognising that it was a means of enabling CDC to move to the next stage of its development, based on all the strengths it had built up over the years – it was therefore decided to push ahead with the plan for a PPP, and after fifty-one years as a statutory corporation, CDC duly became a public limited company on the appointed day in December 1999, at which point Roy Reynolds stepped down. He had steered CDC successfully through a five-year period of dramatic change and as he handed over the reins he could be proud, having further built on its reputation as a dynamic and trusted organisation, with a good track record of positive returns – one that was respected internationally and also valued by DFID, who recognised that it was punching above its weight in managing funds and businesses and taking initiatives that were not available to other DFIs. He also considered he had created the platform for CDC to build a new future, but it was clearly going to be a challenging prospect. There was still much to be done.

Roy Reynolds was succeeded by Alan Gillespie, who took over just in time for the dawning of the new millennium. An investment banker with a background in development and a deep commitment to issues of social justice, Alan Gillespie accepted the job as CEO believing that he could make a real contribution to the new CDC, but his vision for its future was different from that of his predecessor. He regarded CDC as having been too focused on the industrial production and processing of raw materials and crops, and on capital investment in traditional sectors. And while acknowledging that it managed businesses well, he questioned what he saw as its long-term approach of holding onto them rather than looking to sell them as soon as the time was judged to be right. With his career in finance, he was more interested in liquidity, in making and selling relatively short-term equity investments and nimbly moving on.

Alan Gillespie's views were shared by his chairman, Lord Cairns, who, like him, was an experienced investment banker. He also received the support of Secretary of State Clare Short, who could see the merits of CDC as an equity investor in modern, progressive sectors such as real estate, telephony and healthcare that would be relevant to the long-term future of developing countries; and in industries that supported agriculture rather than in agriculture itself.

This altered brief not only involved establishing new directions for CDC's business, but also required the reshaping of the organisation. Among other things, it entailed a considerable amount of major restructuring, and within CDC's London office staff numbers were cut by nearly a third, a redundancy programme that Alan Gillespie nevertheless handled with characteristic tact and understanding. At the same time, he enlivened and refreshed the management by recruiting a new team including Richard Laing, Paul Fletcher and Andrew Reicher, who became, respectively, the heads of CDC, Actis

and Globeleq. Bright young people with MBAs were also recruited, many of whom later became Actis partners. But such changes very quickly created a sense of 'us' and 'them', even though many of the existing staff accepted that the world was changing and were excited by the new ideas.

The new management considered that if CDC was to attract new investors – now identified as investment banks, institutional investors and global private equity players – it would need to generate the sort of higher returns that the capital markets would expect; and that given the added risk premium for investing in what, at the time, were less attractive emerging markets, plus a further risk premium for liquidity, CDC would need to be aiming at a risk-adjusted rate of return of fifteen percent per annum, rather than the eight percent previously asked of it by DFID.

To this end a new strategy was devised. Unveiled early in 2000, this basically involved splitting CDC's portfolio of investments into two. The older investments – the 'legacy', which included all the old loans and most of the managed agribusinesses – were to be moved to a separate division known as CDC Assets, managed by a group of seasoned professionals. And while the Assets team would continue to manage £160 million of public sector debt for a fee, ownership of this would be transferred back to DFID, meaning that CDC's portfolio would effectively consist only of private sector investments.

New investments made since 1 January 1998 went into the CDC Capital Partners portfolio along with some of the earlier investments, such as Engro Chemicals, that fitted the risk capital mould, plus those managed businesses that qualified as being of international scale, such as the oil palm plantations of South East Asia, Pacific Rim Palm Oil Ltd. This was to provide the starting point from which the 'track record' of investment returns could be established.

The most dramatic aspect of this 'rationalisation' process was the board's decision to sell off those managed businesses that were not doing well, or which had little or no chance of meeting the returns criteria that CDC was setting for itself. The list of those that were earmarked almost inevitably included most of the agricultural investments.

In the past, financially less rewarding investments in renewable natural resources had effectively been subsidised by CDC, which was prepared to accept lower-than-commercial returns from investments that were considered worth doing simply for developmental reasons, mostly in the tropical agriculture sector, balancing this against the higher returns made elsewhere. Already, under the businesslike stewardship of John Eccles, this thinking had started to change and only investments that might be expected to produce higher returns were able to survive the more rigorous appraisals that had to be passed before board approval was given. Many agribusiness prospects and many projects that might have stayed the course in earlier times were lost along the way.

These changes understandably caused unease among those who still believed in agricultural development as the most direct and effective way of helping the poorest peoples and, predictably, the move to sell most of the agricultural investments was therefore highly controversial and was opposed both from within and from outside the organisation. CDC's reputation in many of the developing countries in which it operated rested on its management of these businesses and the governments of some of the smaller African countries felt abandoned. Past board members expressed their concerns. DFID received petitions, questions were asked in the House of Commons and, in July 2002, a team from CDC had to explain the reasoning to an International Development Select Committee. Alan Gillespie, personally, had to bear the brunt of much criticism from the old guard and the British press who believed that the organisation was no longer fulfilling its true purpose.

Alan Gillespie was sensitive to this disapproval, recognising that CDC's departure would leave a gap in the fight against rural poverty and he later regretted not including agriculture in the list of sectors.

CDC Industries was duly broken up and a dedicated team from CDC Assets went out and sold those managed businesses and other older investments that had been identified for disposal, sometimes at low prices designed to make them affordable to local purchasers. However, the substantial total raised from the sale of hundreds of investments over the next few years was beyond expectations and helped to fuel CDC's continuing growth, even, ironically, back into African agribusiness.

CDC Capital Partners was rolled out in 2000, the name carefully chosen to suggest an association with some other leading private equity firms operating at the time and its new logo using a palette of colours, including dark blue and lime green, that were then fashionable. All the new private equity investments went into the Capital Partners portfolio. As a private equity investor, CDC would not only be investing money, properly structured so as to give it rights and good prospective returns; it was also acting as a business partner to its investee companies, providing expert advice, introducing and sometimes imposing experienced and skilled managers, guiding strategic decisions, improving corporate governance and if necessary forcing through other change. The aim was to build enduring and profitable businesses that would lead to sustainable development.

To ensure this happened, Alan Gillespie introduced a much more rigorous and challenging in-depth quarterly investment review process, where each investment manager individually would sit with a review team, scrutinising how the business was going and deciding what changes should be made, and how, and planning how CDC would sell its investments.

Meanwhile, Alan Gillespie had also undertaken an overall review of CDC's activities on which to base a detailed plan of action, identifying the regions and the sectors in which the new divisions should be seeking to invest.

Mengniu China Dairy

Mengniu China Dairy was founded by Mr Niu Gensheng, who set up the company in 1999 with two colleagues from one of the Mongolian state milk production companies. They started Mengniu with $12,600 between them and within two years the company's milk, yoghurt, ice cream and other products were notching up sales of $87 million! By 2006 this figure had risen to an even more staggering $1.8 billion, making Mengniu the largest supplier of dairy products in China, if not in the world.

It was in 2002 that CDC got involved, meeting Mr Niu and offering to help his ambitious expansion plans, which included listing the company on the Hong Kong stock exchange. Having satisfied itself that there would indeed be enough cows to supply the milk to the collection points, CDC invested $3 million in 2002 and a further $4 million the following year. The milk came from cows grazed on the wide grassy plains of Inner Mongolia and other Chinese provinces. Mengniu paid a fair market price to its suppliers and also offered contracts, encouraging independent herdsmen, some with only one or two cows, to sell to them.

These herdsmen established themselves around the milk collection centres, where more contracts were on offer for milking and delivery to the factory. The company helped farmers to access finance and, for a fee, would provide advice on how to improve milk yields. The network grew to several thousand collection centres from where the milk was sent to more than twenty processing and production complexes, the foremost of which is the world-class, state-of-the-art centre on a campus-like industrial park in an otherwise undeveloped area in the steppe lands 40 kilometres to the south of Hohhot, the capital of Inner Mongolia. Here, a whole community has grown up around the manufacturing and office complex, including houses, apartments, gardens, fountains, pools and sporting facilities. Mengniu's permanent workforce numbered over 30,000 and, altogether, the company was estimated to support up to 300,000 herdsmen and farm workers.

The China team did much to support the company through its expansion, before exiting in 2007, helping to prepare it for listing on the stock exchange by overseeing changes to the organisational structure and financial reporting and information systems and also advising on compliance with international standards on environmental, health and safety and corporate governance issues. In the final run-up to listing, assistance was also given in identifying the underwriters and advisers for the public offering. Mengniu was successfully listed on the Hong Kong stock exchange in June 2004, the share price rising by twenty-five per cent on the first day. Half of CDC's shares were sold at the time and the remainder in 2007, realising $40 million for a $7 million investment.

Right: One of Mengniu's state-of-the-art automated milking units.

Above: A Computer Aided Design (CAD) operator at Square D Software (later renamed DSQ Software). The Chennai-based company, in which CDC made its first IT investment in India in the early nineties, was part of the first wave of the Indian IT revolution.

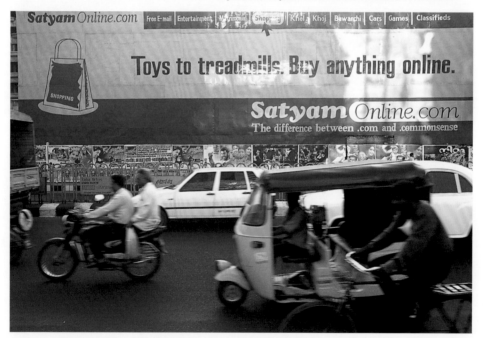

Above: An advert for Satyam Online.com in India. CDC invested $12 million in Satyam Infoway Ltd (Sify) through SARF in 1999. CDC helped Sify to list its shares on the New York-based NASDAQ stock exchange, the first Indian IT company to do so.

As a result, it was decided that the six core sectors should be minerals, oil & gas, telecommunications & IT, infrastructure, fast-moving consumer goods (including some agribusiness) and financial institutions. The four regions – or 'strategic business units' as they were now called – were the old, familiar stamping grounds of Africa, South Asia, Latin America and Asia Pacific. In Latin America there was to be expansion away from the old Caribbean and Central American areas and in Asia the focus was to be on India and China. Managing directors were appointed to head each of the SBUs. The review team had also concluded that if CDC was going to describe itself as an investor in emerging markets with any conviction then it needed to be working in the larger growth economies within its regions. These included Nigeria, where CDC concentrated its efforts on building up a private sector portfolio, and North Africa, where it opened an office in Cairo and started making investments in mining, telecoms and the food industry. One of the most obvious targets, however, was China.

Private equity in China was still in its infancy, so the approach was to identify and then work with a private sector partner. Shortly after opening an office in Beijing in 2000, having signed a memorandum of understanding with the Chinese government the year before, CDC entered into a joint venture with CGU, the British insurance giant that is now part of Aviva, whereby each of them committed $49.5 million to the CGU-CDC China Investment Company. They also formed China Capital Partners, managed by CDC, to find, make and manage the investments. Given nervousness about investing in Chinese businesses due to concerns about the ways in which they were managed and uncertainty about the continuing role of the state, the strategy of the fund was to invest in expansions, buy-outs and companies that were poised – ready, willing and able – to list on stock markets in the region or beyond.

The China National Offshore Oil Company (CNOOC) provided an opportunity to start understanding how to do business in China, to make contacts and to build networks. CNOOC wanted to expand into overseas oil and gas markets but an earlier attempt to offer shares to the public had failed. At the time, the markets were sceptical as to whether Chinese companies could meet the international listing requirements for corporate governance and CNOOC needed international investors on board to demonstrate confidence before it tried again. CDC paid $25 million for a small stake in the company, alongside several hundred million dollars of international investment from Hong Kong, Singapore and the US. There was still a risk of further failure, but in the event the listing on the Hong Kong and New York stock exchanges went ahead successfully and when CDC sold its equity less than two years later, it achieved a healthy return. The deal also had the added bonus of helping CDC to establish a bond of friendship and trust with CNOOC that was to pay extra dividends later on.

Other investments included the cellular telecoms manufacturer China Grentech and the solar panels manufacturer Suntech. Both these were very successful, especially Suntech, which went on to be listed on the New York Stock Exchange, not only boosting CDC's green credentials in so far as its products were helping to combat global warming by reducing carbon emissions but also enabling CDC to make a return of twelve times the money invested.

However, the cream of CDC's Chinese investments was Mengniu China Dairy. Mengniu – it translates as 'Mongolian Cow' – could justifiably claim that its product was truly out of this world, Chinese cosmonauts having taken Mengniu milk with them when they went into orbit. For CDC, investment in the company not only brought stellar returns but also satisfied its most cherished developmental aims, helping 300,000 independent farmers in one of the poorest parts of China.

While setting out its stall in China, CDC, under the exceptional leadership of Donald Peck, had also been stepping up its activities in India, the other major emerging market at the time. By focusing on the technology, media and telecommunications industries, CDC effectively hit the bull's eye of some of CDC's main regional and sector targets. And until the dot.com bubble burst one particular investment saw a spectacular increase in value.

The $12 million investment in Satyam Infoway Ltd (Sify) – a company offering internet and electronic data interchange services to corporate clients and the first Indian IT company to be listed on the NASDAQ stock exchange – was actually worth a hundred times that amount on paper at the peak of the dot.com boom, more than all the rest of CDC's worldwide portfolio put together. Regrettably, CDC couldn't sell its stake at that point, even if it had wanted to, because, along with the other founding investors, it owned shares that had been issued in India rather than American Depository Receipts (ADRs) on NASDAQ, and the government wouldn't allow their conversion.

"**While setting out its stall in China, CDC, under the exceptional leadership of Donald Peck, had also been stepping up its activities in India, the other major emerging market at the time.**"

However, Sify survived the dot.com crash and, with help and a lot of hard work from CDC's investment manager, went on to become India's first private internet service provider, launching internet access for home users via dial-up and i-Way and later establishing 1,725 franchised internet cafes in sixty-three Indian cities. Combined with its success in consistently upgrading its technology and services to the corporate sector, this made Sify a household name in India. When CDC sold its equity in 2004 it still doubled its original investment. Not bad at all, although not quite as good as 10,000 per cent!

CDC enjoyed a steadier ride with Daksh eServices. As part of the Indian IT revolution, four experienced Indian IT specialists saw the huge untapped potential in providing business process outsourcing services. Having put together a convincing business plan, they set up Daksh in January 2000 but needed a financial partner who would give them credibility when they offered their services to international businesses and who would stay with them and help each time they needed more money for expansion. CDC became its first investor, putting in $1.8 million in March 2000 before providing further financing in 2001 and 2002.

Within a year of starting up with a staff of just seven it was employing six hundred-and-fifty people at its Delhi call centre, attracting young, motivated business graduates. By the time IBM bought the whole company in 2004 for $170 million, Daksh had created more than six thousand jobs and had established call centres in four Indian cities as well as one in Manila in the Philippines. CDC's exit returned $14 million, eight times its total investment, an annualised rate of return of sixty-eight per cent. IBM Daksh has since gone from strength to strength and, at the last count, had 20,000 employees.

Sify and Daksh were just two of a dozen or more investments made by CDC in the IT and telecoms sectors in India in the late 1990s and early 2000s. Not all of them were successful and CDC lost most of its $60 million investment in BPL Mobile, one of its largest anywhere in the world at the time. However, this was balanced by a number of commercial and award winning successes in other sectors. And under Donald Peck's management, CDC became one of the most respected private equity investors in India.

Three investments in particular – UTI Bank, Punjab Tractors and Glenmark – demonstrate the way in which CDC had matured as a private equity investor by this time.

UTI Bank was already India's fourth largest bank in 2001 when CDC, having identified the sector as failing to keep up with the demand for banking services in the country's rapidly expanding economy and looking for an opportunity to make an entry, invested $32 million for twenty-six per cent of the equity. Acting on recommendations resulting from CDC's due diligence, UTI Bank then increased its retail banking operations – making loans to individuals and extending its branch and ATM network – and also established a risk management arm, with staff recruited with help from CDC. Overall, CDC took an active role in planning strategy through its two seats on the board and provided expert assistance in several specific areas such as the creation of an anti-money laundering policy and the vetting of credit proposals. After two years, CDC then set about looking for a strategic investor to take it on to the next stage and identified HSBC, to whom it sold most of its shares in 2004. In 2008, having changed its name to Axis Bank, the bank had over five hundred branches in India and one each in Singapore and Hong Kong.

Punjab Tractors was the second largest manufacturer of tractors in India, the country with the biggest tractor market in the world. State-owned, it also produced combine harvesters and forklift trucks and had management control over three subsidiaries, one of which was the country's third largest manufacturer of light commercial vehicles. Through its managed South Asia Regional Fund (SARF), CDC first bought a small five per cent holding on the stock market before then going on to buy a controlling interest in the company in 2003 when a majority holding of shares came up for sale, the first privatisation in India won by a private equity investor.

Again, CDC worked as part of the company's core management team, introducing Punjab Tractors to dealers and component suppliers in the US, Europe and Africa, and driving through improvements in operational areas such as new product development, procurement processes, cost reduction and working capital management while also making changes to the management team and introducing new non-executive directors to the board. When it sold its stake four years later to the Mahindra Group – one of India's largest companies, which was looking for global scale – CDC got back three times its original investment.

Having done its homework, the CDC office in Mumbai had identified the pharmaceutical industry as another good prospect for investment. India offered a large, expanding domestic market and, internationally, there was the potential to export more generic drugs to regulated markets such as the US. So, when Glenmark Pharmaceuticals announced it was looking for finance to fund expansion along these lines, CDC was able to react quickly, investing $11.6 million in July 2002 to buy fourteen per cent of the company.

Glenmark delivered on its strategies for growth. It obtained approvals from the US Federal Drugs Administration for the generic formulations and CDC helped it to expand its generics business in North and Latin America. Glenmark opened and acquired new manufacturing and research & development facilities, the latter doing exciting work on new drugs for the treatment of asthma and diabetes. CDC also worked with the company to define and implement world-class health and safety polices and to introduce new members to the board with the experience to turn Glenmark into a world-class pharmaceuticals business. Acting in self-interest as well as for the benefit of other investors, a liquidity action plan made the stock better known, increasing its turnover. It became of interest to institutional investors. In a rising market, CDC's investment was sold in blocks and eventually received ten times what it had originally invested. It was a short-term investment, but CDC had a long-term vision shared by Glenmark's management and this was duly delivered.

Below: Aerial view of the Compañía de Electricidad de Puerto Plato power generating plant in the Dominican Republic, showing barge-mounted and land-based power units, along with the Spanish sixteenth century fort (in the bottom right of the picture).

Above: Maintenance workers adjusting controls to the plant at Compañía Boliviana de Energía Eléctrica SA (COBEE). Globeleq acquired control of COBEE in 2004, a power generating company based in La Paz, Bolivia. Its capacity of 203 MW came mainly from run-of-the-river hydroelectric power stations using the water from two local river systems originating high in the surrounding Andes.

Globeleq

Globeleq Ltd – the name formed from Global, Electricity and Equity – was set up in 2002, bringing together CDC's portfolio of nineteen investments in power companies in Asia, Latin America and Africa. Included among the nineteen were several in the Dominican Republic and one in the Leeward Islands in Domenica, where Dominica Electricity (Domlec) was the oldest of CDC's electricity ventures and the first of the so-called 'Eveready Batteries'.

The failure to attract private investors following 9/11 and the collapse of Enron did not deter CDC from moving forward with Globeleq as a wholly-owned subsidiary. Between 2002 and 2006, working from London and Houston, it developed and managed power stations throughout CDC's markets in Asia, Latin America and Africa, building new plants in Africa and investing and acquiring existing ones from international power companies that were withdrawing from the emerging markets because of the general downturn at the time. This programme of expansion, which brought in new outside investors and introduced expertise where it had previously been lacking, was funded by selling almost all CDC's old, original minority stakes in power companies.

By 2006, the major international power companies were showing renewed interest in the emerging markets as the general economic situation improved and the prices they were prepared to pay started moving up. In keeping with CDC's record of selling developed assets, the decision was then taken to put Globeleq's investments up for sale. On this occasion the timing was perfect and all but three were sold in 2007 as part of a record realisation for CDC that brought in £1.2 billion of cash and resulted in an annualised rate of return of eighteen per cent in sterling. The three generating companies that were retained were Songas in Tanzania, Azito Energie in Côte d'Ivoire and Tsavo Power in Kenya and they formed a platform upon which the renamed Globeleq Generation Ltd then rebuilt a fresh portfolio of investments in power projects aimed at providing reliable electricity supplies to Africa and Central America.

While CDC had gradually been implementing the changes to its investment policy around the world, the organisation itself had been undergoing a series of rapid and radical changes back at London Office as it moved towards its new identity as a private equity investor, remodelled and fit for purpose.

By 2001, it had become clear that the PPP model envisaged by the New Labour government in 1997 was not going to work in the short term. CDC had failed to attract the private investors it needed, partly due to general uncertainty in the world economic environment which had worsened again since the brief respite in 1999, the dot.com crash and other factors, but also due to lingering concerns about the lack of a 'track record' of consistent returns, worries about the adverse effect on earnings potential of the restrictions governing CDC's investment policy and about the perceived threat of continuing government interference.

It was at this point, in an attempt to address the matter of building confidence in CDC's investment potential, that CDC formed Globeleq. It was an idea whose time had come. Over the previous five years CDC had built a sizeable portfolio of nineteen investments in the power sector, mainly in the Americas and mostly minority equity stakes in independent power producers that sold electricity into national grid systems, and valued at $272 million. The delivery of reliable and uninterrupted power supplies is a fundamental requirement for the development of any country's economy and CDC had supported the sector ever since the very early days, starting with the 'Eveready Batteries' in the Caribbean. CDC had already identified the opportunity to bring these together into a single power generation company that would serve as a platform for expansion by acquiring majority stakes and developing greenfield sites.

Even more to the point at this juncture, given what CDC was trying to do, was that investment in private sector power was arguably less risky than in most other sectors because the revenues were spelled out in legal agreements between the power producers and their customers, who were usually government-owned utilities and therefore government-guaranteed.

The plan was to form a separate company which would hold all CDC's power sector equity stakes. Investors would then be invited to subscribe and the money that was raised would be used to make fresh investments. This would be like a microcosm of what CDC wanted to do with the whole of its business and, it was to be hoped, would provide a good example of what it could do and what could be achieved.

A good idea was unfortunately ruined when, for reasons completely beyond CDC's control, its timing turned out to be terrible thanks to the combination of 9/11 and the spectacular fall from grace and into bankruptcy of Enron. Enron was a power company, other power companies also collapsed in a general downturn of demand and, suddenly, power equalled major risk. On top of that, emerging markets were still out of favour. Given such a triple whammy, who would want Globeleq? In fact, Globeleq turned the down-turn to its own advantage, buying power stations from international power companies who were forced to sell because of financial problems in their home markets. Globeleq went on to be a very successful power operating company, but as a wholly-owned subsidiary of CDC.

Paul Fletcher

Born in 1956 and educated at Oxford University, where he took a degree in geography, Paul Fletcher began his career trading commodities for Cargill in Minneapolis and London and spent eight years working as a corporate finance professional in New York, Tokyo and London before joining the commodities division of Bankers Trust. He next became general manager for Citibank in Kenya, based in Nairobi, and then moved back to the bank's London Office. It was from there that he joined CDC in 2000. He is a director of the Emerging Markets Private Equity Association. He led Actis as the firm's senior partner and is now its non-executive chairman.

While moving its power sector investments into Globeleq, CDC was doing much the same thing with its small private equity country funds, separating them out into another offshoot that it named Aureos. These funds had not been performing quite as hoped. They had performed good developmental work, supporting SMEs, often helping local entrepreneurs to get started and to expand. But they were mostly operating in small economies from which CDC was gradually exiting. The risk was believed to be high and many of the investee companies floundered, meaning that the expected financial returns of the funds were uninspiring – not good news when CDC was trying to improve its track record overall. Creating Aureos Capital was a way of getting them out of the portfolio. Happily, the Norwegian development finance institution Norfund was quite prepared to invest because of the strong developmental impact and it formed a joint venture with CDC, bringing with it $50 million of additional funds, enabling Aureos to grow. Aureos, the name carefully chosen to hint at the dawn of a golden age, went on to become the leading independent private equity investor in low-to-mid cap businesses in emerging countries.

Meanwhile, with CDC having stalled in its efforts to deliver a successful PPP model within the planned time frame, but with its leaders keenly aware of the need to press on with the task of finding and implementing a solution, it was a case of back to the drawing board at One Bessborough Gardens. In early 2002, a dedicated 'Project Atlas' team was appointed to tackle the truly Herculean task of working out and finalising the details of a viable and acceptable solution to the challenge of CDC's structure and funding. This was to be based on the private equity model that was normal in the United States and Europe and to which CDC had inexorably been moving bit by bit in which the ownership and management of investments were separated.

The proposal was that DFID would wholly own the investment company, which would hold all the existing investments of CDC. The working title for this organisation was Investco, although it was later decided that it should retain the name CDC.

A new management company, provisionally known as Manco but later named Actis, would be set up to manage the investments and would also launch new funds in which investments by others would be invited, thereby meeting the prime objective of enabling more development.

Songas

Songo Songo, an island off the coast of southern Tanzania, is the spectacular setting for the Songas gas processing plant. Gas is extracted from Songo Songo's underground and undersea reserves and then piped to the Ubungo power station in Dar es Salaam, where it is either converted into electricity for supply to the national grid or used to supply natural gas for industrial processes. Presenting a considerable civil engineering challenge, the pipeline first runs for twenty-six kilometres along the seabed to the shore and then for a further 217 kilometres underground to Ubungo, passing under fourteen rivers and 172 roads along the way.

Opened in 2004 and operated by Globeleq's majority-owned company, Songas Ltd, Songas currently provides one third of all Tanzania's electricity, with further expansion planned for the future, thereby reducing the country's dependence on drought-sensitive hydroelectric facilities and expensive imported fuel oils. That dependency was restricting the country's expansion, especially for power-hungry industrial processes such as the production of cement and the extraction of metals from ores. The project cost £320 million and Globeleq led the consortium of investors and banks in what was the first public private partnership of its size in Tanzania, partnering with the Government of Tanzania, the Tanzania Electrical Supply Company (TANESCO) and the Tanzania Petroleum Development Corporation, to provide the first natural gas fired generation plant and associated infrastructure in the country. By utilising the country's own natural gas resources, the Songo Songo gas-to-electricity project has substantially reduced operating costs for TANESCO and other industries in Tanzania. It has been estimated more than $5 billion has been saved since commercial operations commenced in 2004.

Actis would be structured as a partnership, owned sixty per cent by its partners and an employee benefit trust and forty per cent by DFID. This would calm the fears of potential investors that the British government might impose restrictions on their investments. CDC, however, would continue to be governed by the targets set for it by DFID of seventy per cent in poorer countries and fifty per cent in South Asia and sub-Saharan Africa, confirmed by the then Secretary of State for International Development, Clare Short. It was deemed to be an elegant solution.

Once the new structure had been agreed with DFID, Alan Gillespie stepped down as chief executive, the board and DFID satisfied that his job was done and that the new management team, mainly recruited by him, was ready to pick up the baton.

Under Alan Gillespie, the operating environment in CDC had been transformed. The processes and people needed to take it forward had been put in place, and many good private equity investments had been responsibly made that were growing sustainable businesses and delivering positive development impact. The building blocks were in place for the next step of attracting investors into the funds that would multiply the amounts available for development in traditionally capital-starved regions.

Alan Gillespie was replaced in December 2002 by Paul Fletcher, who had joined CDC in 2000 as managing director for Africa and co-ordinator for the six core sector groups. The following July he was earmarked as the senior managing partner of Actis while Richard Laing, who had also been with CDC since 2000, as finance director, was named chief executive designate of CDC.

Early in the process another team of management consultants from McKinsey was called in again to advise on where the future funds should be set up. It confirmed the focus on Africa, South Asia and China, with power as the sector on which to concentrate. The targeting of these three major markets was at the expense of Latin America and South East Asia, where CDC's commitment was reduced. This policy was later reversed by Actis, which set up new operations in both regions.

The new structure was formally confirmed on 7 July 2004, although to all intents and purposes it had already been in operation for a year by then through a soft internal split that had effectively helped to sort out how things were going to work. The changes involved a massive reduction in staff at CDC, reflecting the fact that it was doing a radically different job. By the beginning of 2003, employee numbers had already fallen to 241 worldwide, from 664 three years earlier, a drop accounted for by transfers to the separate entities of Aureos and Globeleq plus redundancies and resignations. Most of those who remained transferred to Actis contracts in 2004, twenty-six becoming partners. With CDC's overseas offices also transferred to Actis, only twenty-five stayed with CDC.

All four London-based teams – CDC, Actis, Globeleq and Aureos – shared the existing headquarters at One Bessborough Gardens which was, by then, half empty. New premises were called for and appropriate. In March 2004 Actis, Aureos and Globeleq moved to the top two floors of a new glass-clad building on the south bank of the Thames, part of the More London development next to London's City Hall. This boasted an awe-inspiring view, taking in St Paul's Cathedral, the City of London, Tower Bridge and, right opposite, the Tower of London. CDC, meanwhile, moved into one of the floors of a small, renovated building at 6 Duke Street, St James's, just off Piccadilly in London's West End – and just a short stroll from Lord Trefgarne's old office in Dover Street. As things turned out, this was not to be the only way in which the organisation proved to have come full circle. As had been the case with Trefgarne at the helm, CDC under its new chief executive would start off enthusiastically only later to find itself increasingly under pressure.

actis

Actis

Actis, which means 'sunbeam' in Greek, adopted the strap line 'The positive power of capital', to reflect its style and aims.

Formed in 2004 as a partnership to take over the management of CDC's investments, it at first managed only CDC's funds, plus that of investors who had committed to CDC-managed funds – such as the South Asia Regional Fund. All the investments in CDC's old portfolio were allocated to one or other of Actis's funds and were then gradually sold off, returning substantial cash to CDC.

Actis was established with the primary aim of attracting other sources of investment into the developing markets, seen as the most effective means of stimulating economic independence in the long term. With anchor support from CDC, which committed to investing in all its funds during its first five years – it went on to achieve this objective with great success, attracting commitments from over 200 pension funds, governments, family funds and other financial institutions in addition to CDC. When Actis was formed, DFID initially took a forty per cent share of its equity and this was held until 2012 when, with the original development aims having been achieved, this was sold to Actis's partners for a negotiated sum and a share of future returns.

Actis now has a team of over 100 investment professionals in 13 offices worldwide and has pioneered a string of landmark investment 'firsts' in the realm of private equity across emerging markets – achievements recognised by the private equity industry. By 2017, it had invested approximately $7.8 billion in over 200 businesses in its selected sectors of consumer, energy, financial services, healthcare, infrastructure and real estate and had realised $9.3 billion from 160 exits.

Its energy funds have committed over $5 billion in over 32 companies across more than 25 countries, generating 18GW of energy capacity and directly impacting 80 million consumers. Actis's real estate business closed its third fund in 2016 – to date, the largest private real estate fund targeting sub-Saharan Africa – and, among its showpiece developments, the real estate team has built the first certified green buildings in Lagos, Nairobi and Accra. Within private equity, Actis has invested over $5.5 billion in mid-market, high-growth companies across consumer, financial services and healthcare sectors.

Its latest strap line – 'Values drive Value' – reflects Actis's belief that investing responsibly creates businesses that are more resilient, more innovative and better able to deliver societal benefits – and are therefore, ultimately, more valuable. At the heart of its responsible investing ethos is the idea that managing environmental, social and governance issues is not simply about mitigating risk, but about value creation.

Aureos

Aureos was set up in 2001 as a joint venture between CDC and Norfund to manage CDC's SME-targeted funds in emerging markets, which were not generally thought to be attractive to private investors at the time. It initially took over responsibility for the 139 investee or portfolio companies that were in the funds originally invested and managed by CDC between 1989 and 2001 and which had been valued at $72 million when Aureos took over.

Its focus was on the more difficult and developmental segments of the market – encouraging small and medium-sized enterprises in some of the poorest countries of the world. The single country funds, such as the Ghana Venture Capital Fund and the Acacia Fund in Kenya – which had provided the platform for the creation of Aureos in 2001 – had been set up by CDC in the 1990s, mainly in Africa, at a time when no one else was making this kind of bold commitment. Early performance had been mixed, but the idea caught on and CDC can claim that Aureos had been the trailblazer for private equity in Africa. CDC therefore continued to support Aureos through investing in its funds, including its new generation of substantial regional funds in each of its main regions of Africa, Asia and Latin America.

Based in Old Bond Street in London, Aureos's global team of investment executives led by Sev Vettivetpillai grew from an initial 33 to 140, working out of a network of twenty-five offices in Latin America, Africa and Asia – that had expanded from an initial ten – to cover fifty countries altogether, a network that gave it an unrivalled coverage of SMEs in the emerging markets. At the end of 2008 Aureos had around $1 billion of funds from various sources under management and after its managers undertook a spinout, CDC considered that its work in incubating a profitable manager of SME funds in the emerging markets had been achieved.

CDC's investments in 2003*

- Adopting private equity as the route to delivering sustainable development results in a smaller, more focused investment portfolio.

- Expansion in the Americas and in South Asia leads to geographical balance.

- Power regains its number one position as the largest of CDC's sectors.

Global investment (£m)

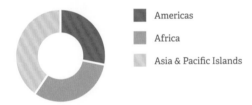

- Americas
- Africa
- Asia & Pacific Islands

Sector of investment (£m)

- Basic development
- Primary production & processing
- Commerce & industry

- ## 228 investments
- ## £1,340 million invested

(£2.1 billion in 2018 terms)

* Note: 2003 was the last full year before CDC was restructured.

Americas

1. **Antigua**
   Hotels and Tourism
2. **Argentina**
   Power, Transport, Telecoms and IT
3. **Belize**
   Agribusiness
4. **Bolivia (Office)**
   Minerals, Oil and Gas, Manufacturing and Commerce, Financial Institutions
5. **Chile**
   Power, Manufacturing and Commerce
6. **Costa Rica (Office)**
   Power, Property and Housing Finance, Agribusiness, Manufacturing and Commerce, Hotels and Tourism, Private Equity Funds, Financial Institutions, Telecoms and IT
7. **Cuba (Office)**
   Financial Institutions
8. **Dominica**
   Power
9. **Dominican Republic**
   Power, Property and Housing Finance, Agribusiness, Manufacturing and Commerce, Financial Institutions
10. **Ecuador**
    Transport, Agribusiness, Manufacturing and Commerce, Financial Institutions
11. **El Salvador**
    Manufacturing and Commerce, Telecoms and IT
12. **Grenada**
    Hotels and Tourism
13. **Guatemala**
    Power, Manufacturing and Commerce
14. **Guyana**
    Agribusiness
15. **Honduras**
    Property and Housing Finance, Manufacturing and Commerce
16. **Jamaica**
    Power, Hotels and Tourism
17. **Mexico**
    Manufacturing and Commerce
18. **Nicaragua**
    Power, Agribusiness
19. **Peru**
    Power, Transport, Manufacturing and Commerce
20. **St Lucia**
    Power
21. **Trinidad & Tobago**
    Financial Institutions

Pan Americas
Transport, Manufacturing and Commerce, Private Equity Funds

Africa

22. Botswana
Agribusiness

23. Cameroon
Manufacturing and Commerce

24. Côte d'Ivoire (Office)
Power, Agribusiness

25. Egypt (Office)
Manufacturing and Commerce

26. Ghana
Transport, Private Equity Funds, Financial Institutions

27. Kenya (Office)
Power, Property and Housing Finance, Transport, Agribusiness, Hotels and Tourism, Private Equity Funds, Financial Institutions

28. Liberia
Financial Institutions

29. Malawi
Hotels and Tourism

30. Mauritius
Private Equity Funds

31. Mozambique
Transport, Manufacturing and Commerce

32. Namibia
Agribusiness

33. Nigeria (Office)
Property and Housing Finance, Private Equity Funds

34. South Africa (Office)
Power, Property and Housing Finance, Transport, Minerals, Oil and Gas, Manufacturing and Commerce, Hotels and Tourism, Private Equity Funds, Financial Institutions

35. Swaziland
Agribusiness, Manufacturing and Commerce, Financial Institutions

36. Tanzania (Office)
Power, Property and Housing Finance, Agribusiness, Hotels and Tourism, Private Equity Funds, Financial Institutions, Telecoms and IT

37. Uganda
Property and Housing Finance, Agribusiness, Financial Institutions

38. Zambia (Office)
Property and Housing Finance, Agribusiness, Manufacturing and Commerce, Private Equity Funds, Telecoms and IT

39. Zimbabwe
Agribusiness, Hotels and Tourism

Pan Africa
Private Equity Funds, Telecoms and IT

Asia and Pacific Islands

40. Bangladesh
Power, Transport, Minerals, Oil and Gas, Manufacturing and Commerce

41. China (Office)
Manufacturing and Commerce, Private Equity Funds, Telecoms and IT

42. Fiji
Financial Institutions

43. India (Office)
Power, Property and Housing Finance, Transport, Agribusiness, Private Equity Funds, Financial Institutions, Telecoms and IT

44. Indonesia (Office)
Property and Housing Finance, Agribusiness, Manufacturing and Commerce, Financial Institutions

45. Laos
Hotels and Tourism

46. Malaysia (Office)
Property and Housing Finance, Private Equity Funds

47. Pakistan (Office)
Power, Transport, Minerals, Oil and Gas, Manufacturing and Commerce, Financial Institutions

48. Papua New Guinea
Agribusiness, Private Equity Funds

49. Philippines
Power, Agribusiness, Manufacturing and Commerce, Private Equity Funds

50. Singapore (Office)
Power, Transport, Private Equity Funds

51. Solomon Islands
Agribusiness, Minerals, Oil and Gas

52. Sri Lanka
Power, Transport, Private Equity Funds, Financial Institutions

53. Thailand
Manufacturing and Commerce, Financial Institutions

Pan Asia
Transport, Private Equity Funds

Fund of funds

Fund of funds
2004–2011

2005

- *Live 8 international concerts raise interest in the Make Poverty History campaign.*
- *Britain sets the priorities for Africa's economic development at the G8 meeting at Gleneagles.*
- *Hurricane Katrina floods New Orleans and causes enormous loss of life and damage.*
- *The Paris Declaration sets out five fundamental principles for making aid more effective.*

2006

- *Saddam Hussain is hanged.*
- *Conflict in Sudan's Darfur region escalates.*
- *Douglas Alexander replaces Hilary Benn as secretary of state at DFID.*

2007

- *Gordon Brown becomes Britain's prime minister, continuing to lead a Labour government.*
- *Dramatic falls in the Shanghai stock exchange in February signal the beginning of the change in the world's financial markets.*

2004

- *Conflict begins in Darfur, Sudan.*
- *The Tsunami on 26 December kills over 225,000 people in eleven countries bordering the Indian Ocean.*

World events...

CDC events...

- **Actis is split out of CDC, becoming its main fund manager, and CDC's remaining overseas offices are transferred to Aureos or Actis.**
- **Richard Laing is appointed chief executive and Malcolm Williamson as chairman; and CDC moves to 6 Duke Street, St James's, London.**
- **Globeleq's Songas project opens, utilising Tanzania's natural gas to provide half of Tanzania's electricity.**
- **The Palms, financed by CDC, is the first modern shopping centre in Nigeria.**

- **CDC invests in ShoreCap International, the first of many new funds managed by fund managers around the world.**

- **Richard Laing is appointed chairman of EDFI, the Association of European Development Finance Institutions.**

- **By the end of the year CDC works with 42 fund managers and has committed capital to 100 funds and four co-investments spread across its target geographies.**

Right: Dhaka, Bangladesh. CDC has been investing in Bangladesh since 1981, mainly in sectors such as textiles, fertiliser and power generation, while also helping telecoms service provider Grameenphone to expand in the late 1990s. Grameenphone was the first company to introduce digital mobile technology in Bangladesh, going on to build a cellular network that reached 99 per cent of the country. In 2013, CDC provided a $25 million loan to Grameenphone, part of a facility altogether totalling $345 million made along with IFC, other DFIs and Standard Chartered Bank. The funding is helping modernise the Grameenphone network and increase its coverage in rural areas, acting as a driver for wider economic growth.

2011

- *Protests against the Syrian Government of President Bashar al-Assad mark the beginning of the Syrian Civil War.*
- *Resignation of Egyptian President Hosni Mubarak after weeks of protest across the country.*
- *Osama Bin Laden killed by US forces.*
- *Libyan leader Colonel Gaddafi killed as his hometown of Sirte is overrun by forces of the National Transitional Council.*
- *South Sudan gains its independence from Sudan.*

2010

- *Haiti's earthquake kills 230,000 – one of the deadliest natural disasters on record.*
- *The Deepwater Horizon drilling rig explodes and sinks, causing a massive oil slick and an environmental disaster in the Gulf of Mexico.*
- *Chinese human rights activist Liu Xiaobo awarded the Nobel Peace Prize.*

2008

- *Violence in Kenya and Zimbabwe follows disputed elections.*
- *Global financial crisis leads to the collapse of major financial institutions, the introduction of palliative monetary and fiscal policies, and global recession.*

2009

- *Inauguration of Barack Obama as US president.*
- *UN food agency reports that a record one billion people around the world don't have enough to eat.*
- *Sri Lanka's military declares victory in its decades-old conflict with rebel Tamil Tigers.*

- **CDC moves to 80 Victoria Street, London.**
- **CDC celebrates its 60th anniversary.**

- **CDC commits to new targets set by DFID, focusing investment on countries with gross per capita national income of $905 per annum, down from $1,750, with more than fifty per cent going to sub-Saharan Africa.**
- **Malcolm Williamson is succeeded as chairman by Richard Gillingwater.**

- **Andrew Mitchell takes over as secretary of state at DFID following the general election that results in a Conservative/Lib Dem coalition and makes a written parliamentary statement announcing "The Reform of CDC Group plc".**
- **The International Development Committee launches an inquiry into CDC, alongside DFID's three-month public consultation process into the proposed reforms.**

- **Andrew Mitchell makes another written statement to Parliament, outlining a new strategy for CDC, including a return to direct investing.**
- **Richard Laing steps down as chief executive and Richard Gillingwater effectively takes over as executive chairman for an interim period until the appointment of Diana Noble as the new CEO.**
- **CDC joins the International Aid Transparency Initiative, the first bilateral DFI to do so.**

Chapter seven

Fund of funds

The CDC that set about adapting to its new role as a fund of funds, pioneering development through specialist investment in emerging market funds, was a very different organisation from what it had been before, having undergone a structural change more radical than anything attempted previously in its history.

CDC's incoming chairman, Malcolm Williamson, a former CEO of Standard Chartered Bank, described it in CDC's annual review for 2004 as a "bold departure in development finance ... the results of which will be followed with interest by its peers...". However, the mission statement Britain now adopted for its development finance institution – "to generate wealth in emerging markets, particularly in poorer countries, by providing capital for investment in sustainable and responsibly managed private sector businesses" – remained very much in line with its foundational aim of fostering economic development in its poorer overseas territories and would have been recognised, at least in spirit, by any one of CDC's past chairmen.

In introducing the changes, Secretary of State for International Development Hilary Benn acknowledged this continuity in stating the new intention: "CDC already has a ground-breaking track record of assisting in the development of private sector businesses in poor countries. This new approach aims to significantly increase this effect, benefiting regions such as Africa and South Asia."

"CDC's incoming chairman, Malcolm Williamson, described the new model as a 'bold departure in development finance ... the results of which will be followed with interest by its peers'."

An aerial view of hills in the eastern Democratic Republic of the Congo taken in 2009, the location for the Twangiza gold mine opened by Banro Corporation, an Actis investment.

213

Sir Malcolm Williamson

Malcolm Williamson was appointed chairman of CDC in 2004. Like his predecessor, Lord Cairns, he came from a banking background, having started his career with Barclays and then going on to be both group chief executive at Standard Chartered Bank and managing director of Girobank before becoming president and CEO of Visa International immediately prior to joining CDC. Knighted in 2007 for services to the financial services industry, he served as chairman until March 2009 and played a vital supporting role in helping to establish and build CDC as a fund of funds in the early years.

Having served on many boards, Sir Malcolm's current non-executive roles are as chairman of Newday, Chartered Court Financial Services Ltd, Youth Business International, and The Centre for the Study of Financial Innovation.

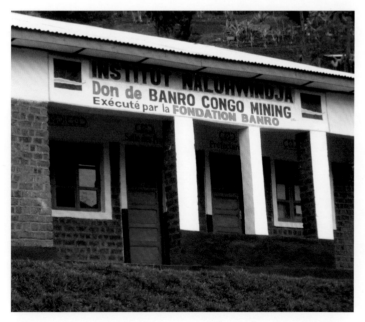

Above: Part of a new 150-student secondary school in Luhwindja, opened in 2009 and funded by the Banro Foundation, a charity set up to support the local community by Banro Corporation, an Actis investment in the eastern DRC.

Splitting the ownership and management of CDC's investments – with CDC retaining ownership, but with management entrusted to its two offshoots, Actis and Aureos – involved the introduction of a completely new business model. Under the leadership of new chief executive Richard Laing, staff numbers at CDC were reduced to just twenty-five and occupied a renovated office in Duke Street. The rest of the two hundred or so former CDC staff members moved to Thames-side offices opposite the Tower of London that Actis and Aureos shared with Globeleq, CDC's power business now managed by Actis. This reorganisation and transfer of personnel was logical given that Actis and Aureos, between them, would now be responsible for managing all existing investments as well as making new ones, labour-intensive tasks for which CDC agreed to pay a fee, plus a share of any profits made.

The perceived advantages of the new structure were that it would enable decisions to be made at grassroots level through the network of Actis's and Aureos's local and regional offices – seen as being the key to successful private equity investment when dealing on a regular day-to-day basis with portfolio companies – while also giving these fund managers an added incentive to get best value from their investments, hopefully leading to better performance, both developmental and financial.

Richard Laing

Born in 1954 and educated at Rugby School and Cambridge University, where he studied engineering, Richard Laing's varied and interesting career began at Marks & Spencer. He then qualified as an accountant with PricewaterhouseCoopers before moving to Booker Tate, working in agribusiness in developing countries, and jointly with CDC on projects in Kenya, Sri Lanka and Papua New Guinea. Prior to joining CDC in 2000 as finance director, he spent fifteen years with De La Rue, holding a number of positions overseas and in the UK, latterly as group finance director.

Promoted from within, Richard was CEO from 2004 to 2011, longer than any of his three predecessors, and during that time he oversaw the transformation of CDC into a financially successful fund of funds, generally recognised among fund investors and other bilateral DFIs as the place to go to for investments in funds in the world's poorer countries. Inspired by his strong personal commitment to development and to finding new ways in which to deliver genuine development impact, CDC under his leadership was instrumental in nurturing a new generation of fund managers, providing them with anchor investments along with the expertise and training that raised ESG awareness and standards, strengthening the foundations of the private equity business in some difficult and capital-scarce markets, notably in Africa.

While CEO, he also served as chairman of EDFI (the Association of European Development Finance Institutions) from 2006 to 2007 and director of the Overseas Development Institute from 2004 to 2016. He has, since leaving CDC, been chairman of 3i Infrastructure plc, an Invesco investment trust and Miro Forestry, where CDC is a shareholder and which operates in Sierra Leone and Ghana. He has also served as a non-executive director of J P Morgan Emerging Markets Investment Trust and as a trustee of Plan International UK, a children's charity operating in developing countries and a member of the UK's Disaster Emergency Committee.

The longer-term objective was that as Actis and Aureos became established, CDC would find various other fund managers around the world through which to invest its capital, while Actis and Aureos would, in turn, diversify their sources of funding away from CDC. The hope here was that in the process the amount of investment capital going to the poorer and traditionally capital-starved economies of the developing world would be encouraged to multiply dramatically and that, as a result, the private sector in these poorer areas would be developed, creating jobs, generating tax revenue and stimulating further economic growth that would lead to a reduction in poverty, following a pattern already successfully demonstrated in a number of once poor, now prospering countries worldwide.

In order to focus attention on the poorest countries, CDC and DFID had agreed on two five-year rolling targets for its investment strategy during the period 2004-2008. The first was for at least seventy per cent of CDC's new investments to go to the very poorest countries, defined as those having a gross national income of less than $1,750 per head, with a maximum of thirty per cent going to less poor countries where the GNI was under $9,075 per head. The second objective was for at least fifty per cent to be invested in sub-Saharan Africa or South Asia, where the need was greatest. This combination of objectives allowed for investment to continue in wealthier countries such as South Africa and China and parts of Latin America, where private equity investment, especially in support of their poorest peoples, was still hard to attract.

Although the terms of the five-year umbrella agreement drawn up by DFID to cover the relationship between CDC and Actis recognised these developmental targets, they actually applied contractually only to CDC and not to Actis, whose primary aim was to attract new third-party investors into poorer countries, while also maximising the value to be returned to CDC from its old, existing portfolio, now under its management. However, the mobilisation of third party capital in poorer countries at a time when most private equity investors remained wary of emerging markets could not have been successfully achieved by Actis without new government funds, so it was reliant on CDC as its major cornerstone investor. CDC's business plan envisaged that it would commit £1.14 billion to Actis funds during the first five years – compared with just £52 million allocated for CDC to grow its own portfolio of fund managers – and this was agreed on the understanding that Actis would support CDC in achieving its targets.

In line with this joint understanding, CDC made anchor commitments to Actis's new second-generation funds, the Fund 2 series (2004-2007) – the first successfully to attract third parties. While these many funds included those that were focusing on China, South East Asia and Latin America, maintaining CDC's presence in these geographies, over these years the lion's share of $330 million was committed to Actis Africa Fund 2, with a further $204 million committed to its two South Asian-focused Fund 2s. These were invested in a range of innovative private equity transactions, followed up by close hands-on management. In investing the funds, Actis applied an investment policy that rested on two pillars: growing personal wealth and domestic consumption by an expanding middle-class, and satisfying the need for domestic infrastructure. Opportunities were looked for in six principal sectors: in business and financial services, consumer business, healthcare and education, industrials, infrastructure and real estate. Applying skills learned by CDC in the 1990s, this approach led to sophisticated investments based first on understanding the potential of private equity in its various markets.

In India, particular specialist expertise was developed in the automotive components sector, with investments in companies such as Sandhar and AVTEC, respectively suppliers and manufacturers of engines and transmissions, as well as in other industrial and consumer businesses such as Halonix, manufacturers of energy efficient lamps. One of its most successful investments was Paras Pharmaceuticals, an Indian healthcare company that Actis helped to professionalise and to expand overseas. Elsewhere in South Asia, it invested in Pakistan's LMKR, an information services provider to the oil and gas industry.

Above: Electric motors await servicing in the workshops at Savcio, a management buy-out supported in 2004/5 and sold to Actom in 2012, both Actis investments to support South Africa's electricity infrastructure.

Banque Commerciale du Rwanda

CDC had received permission to operate in Rwanda as far back as the 1970s, but did not actually have an investment there until 2004, when Actis used its funds to take control of the state-owned Banque Commerciale du Rwanda in what was the country's first privatisation of a financial institution. Rwanda was still feeling the after-effects of the civil war of the early 1990s, the most horrifying aspect of which had been the atrocious genocide of ethnic Tutsis and moderate Hutus by extremist Hutu militias. To take over and transform a long-established public sector bank at that time was a bold venture. In a model privatisation, undertaken in competition with others, Actis's newly ex-CDC staff purchased 80% of BCR's equity and then proceeded to modernise the bank's operational systems and management, expanding its branch network and range of financial products and transforming its governance and internal controls. The Actis team helped to recruit the managing director, chief financial officer and most of the senior managers and introduced experts from their network to offer leasing services from CDC's long-established DFCU in Uganda as well as mortgage finance. BCR grew in size, market share and profitability, partly through its focus on the expanding SME sector, offering quality business banking. The makeover was to have a positive effect on transforming the Rwandan economy and when Actis sold the investment in 2012, it was able to return substantial proceeds to CDC for reinvestment.

Above: Kilombero Valley Teak, located in the Morogoro region of southern Tanzania, was set up by CDC in 1992 to establish sustainable teak plantations and protect and manage over 20,000 hectares of native forests and wetlands and their flora and fauna. This photo shows the process of high pruning to improve log quality.

In Africa, Actis invested CDC's funds throughout the continent, from Egypt – in support of Sinai Marble, a commercial exporter of marble products – all the way down to South Africa, where it backed one of the country's largest management buyouts, involving the diversified financial services business, Alexander Forbes. In Nigeria, it worked to support the expansion of one of the country's leading banks, Diamond Bank, while at the other end of the scale it acquired a majority stake in the previously family-owned company Mouka, transforming and expanding its business of making and selling foam-filled mattresses manufactured to the highest international environmental standards. Elsewhere in Africa, businesses were supported in several countries new to CDC investment – with backing for mineral, oil and gas exploration in Senegal, Tunisia and the Democratic Republic of the Congo and for the expansion of mobile phone coverage in Algeria. These ventures demonstrated a willingness to push boundaries, as did its first investment in Rwanda.

Responding to CDC's determination to push ahead with overtly challenging and developmental initiatives in sectors that failed to appeal to other investors at the time, including other DFIs, Actis also worked closely with CDC's management to establish three development-focused funds where CDC was the sole investor in each. These were the Actis Africa Empowerment Fund, the Actis Africa Agribusiness Fund, and the Actis Africa Real Estate Fund. The objective here was to demonstrate that these sectors could be profitable as well as developmental.

The $50 million Actis Africa Empowerment Fund was the first fund focused on helping black economic empowerment groups to buy shares in transforming businesses in South Africa. There was a shortage of suitably structured risk capital for new BEE groups, in part because of the perceived risks in financing these types of early stage companies as a result of past failures. Actis established a fund that would finance those newly emerging BEE groups with the skills and management to add value to investments in which it was directly investing through its Actis Africa Fund 2, improving the prospects of their success. It supported, for example, BEE participation in Alexander Forbes; in Savcio Holdings, a business repairing and servicing electric motors; and in Fuel Logistics (now RTT), a supply chain and logistics services group.

To provide the $93 million wholly CDC-funded Actis Africa Agribusiness Fund with extra heft, it was seeded with the transfer of several of the old legacy agricultural businesses still held by CDC, including Tatepa Tea, Tanwat and Kilombero Valley Teak in Tanzania, Mpongwe and Nanga Farms in Zambia and Cavally in Côte d'Ivoire. The fund proceeded to invest in one of Africa's poorest countries, Sudan. In 2006, the fund took a controlling stake in Equatoria Teak, a company set up to take over an 18,000-hectare teak and natural woodland concession on long-established plantations in Western and Central Equatoria regions that had been planted by the government from the mid-1970s with aid finance and which had then been simply left to grow, largely without any form of specialised silvicultural management. Ironically, given the war-torn environment of the country, the result was some of the highest quality plantation teak wood in the world. Actis took on the rehabilitation of the plantations, establishing added-value processing facilities and undertaking both replanting of harvested areas and new planting elsewhere. It sold the fund's stake in 2011 to Maris, an investment management company with diverse interests ranging from mining to agriculture that continues the work in what soon became the new country of South Sudan.

The new investments made by these first two funds achieved varying degrees of success and after discussion no successor funds went ahead. But, by contrast, Actis's efforts in investing the $154 million Actis Africa Real Estate Fund pioneered the "international standard" real estate market in Africa, providing a powerful demonstration effect to other would-be developers and investors.

CDC's role as a developer in this area dated back to the early 2000s, when it built up a small portfolio of African real estate assets, including shopping malls and other developments. These developments, and those that have followed, were well done, setting world-class benchmarks for construction, environmental and social standards. They included, originally, the first A-grade shopping malls in Zambia, Kenya, Nigeria and Ghana. A number of these seeded the Actis fund.

CDC played a key role in shaping Actis's real estate strategy and, equally, the Actis team, led by long-serving ex-CDC Actis partner David Morley, shared a strong alignment with CDC on development impact. Both saw the significant development value of high-quality shopping malls, built to 'best in class' standards, not only in creating jobs during their construction and operation, but also through the new markets they generated, the entrepreneurs they encouraged and the other benefits they brought, such as formalising the economy and additional tax receipts. Attracted by the quality infrastructure, African regional supermarkets would become anchor tenants and establish, maintain and raise the standards of local supply chains for goods and services sold, which, in turn, would supply the entrepreneurs setting up smaller retail outlets. The presence of malls and other first class real estate also helped to ensure that the affluent middle classes, who might otherwise take their talents for wealth creation elsewhere, would be encouraged to stay put, enriching the local community. And, likewise, the provision of such facilities attracted others from outside, including the returning entrepreneurial African diaspora, who would come back from developed markets expecting such basic facilities and services.

The fund proved both developmentally and financially successful and Actis's team proved itself to be the strongest in the market, its developments leading the growth of the sub-Saharan African real estate market and generating marked impact. This proven alignment with CDC's key objectives meant that when a second fund was raised in 2011, CDC invested $50 million – and this time it was joined by IFC. CDC then followed this up with another $75 million specifically aimed at more challenging countries and Actis used these funds to make investments in greenfield developments in Nigeria, Zambia, Kenya and Ghana, with CDC taking direct co-investments in two of these – Nairobi's Garden City and Accra's The Exchange. Garden City set the benchmark for others to follow, being the region's first development to meet international standards for green buildings, including, notably, Africa's largest solar panel covered car park. Within a decade the asset class had been so well established, that in 2016 CDC severely limited its participation in a third fund, instead using its connections to encourage Actis towards more developmental assets and newer, more challenging countries.

Right: Sitting in the shade at the Equatoria Teak plantation nursery near Nzara in South Sudan, a group of workers prepare teak tree seedlings for planting out. This process involves seedlings that have germinated in the nursery and have grown to a height of about sixty centimetres over a period of three or four months being converted into bare root stems by having the leaves and tap root sliced off to encourage transpiration – the absorption of water – before being replanted in the main plantation.

Umeme

While Songas and Tsavo generated power, Umeme was pioneering in that it distributed power. Umeme had been formed in 2005 to take over a twenty-year concession, following privatisation, and it then undertook the challenging task of modernising, managing, operating and extending Uganda's electricity distribution network. It inherited a network of sub-stations, poles and lines stretching over 20,000 kilometres that had not been properly maintained, leading to losses of electricity and a danger to life. Because of fallen poles and the attempted theft of electricity, fatalities were very high. Customers were also failing to settle their accounts, with only about 70 per cent of potential revenues being collected. And connection levels were low.

Uganda's distribution systems were transformed by Umeme. Under Actis's management, the focus was on cutting distribution losses and improving both the consistency of supply and safety standards. In the decade from 2005 – during which CDC's $13 million of patient capital was employed – it replaced rotten poles and cut losses resulting from theft and other technical failings from 40 to 20 per cent, comparable to the cost of building a new power station; it also quadrupled its connections to the grid. Deaths of members of the public, which in 2007 had totalled seventeen, including children, had been reduced to zero six years later. And Umeme was instrumental at Bujagali, on the Nile, connecting the hydroelectric power station commissioned in 2012 and the largest in Uganda at the time, the power from which contributed to Uganda's nation building.

A CDC-commissioned report in 2016 concluded that the modernisation of electric power in Uganda had created about 200,000 jobs – directly in the power industry itself and indirectly through helping businesses of all shapes and sizes to thrive – and at least 20 per cent of these had come as a result of Umeme's work.

There had been very few examples of private sector power distribution in Africa, but Umeme showed that it could be done. And Actis, which had managed the work through Umeme, had demonstrated that it could successfully handle major and very complex infrastructure development projects – a distinctive quality among its private equity fund manager peers – and that alone justified CDC's continued support for Actis's management of CDC funds invested in infrastructure. Umeme remained part of CDC's portfolio until 2016, when its remaining stake was sold four years after a public listing on the stock exchanges in Kampala and Nairobi.

A nursery growing teak and other valuable hardwood species at Kilombero Valley Teak Co, Tanzania, one of the most innovative forest management companies in Africa. Set up by CDC in 1992, CDC's holding in KVTC is now held through the GEF Africa Sustainable Forestry Fund, in turn a pioneering initiative by CDC.

CDC's expertise in energy investment was also used to good effect by the ex-CDC Actis team. This was another sector in which CDC's commitment and funds continued to be needed, as other investors remained unconvinced as to its merits. After 2004, CDC's still wholly-owned power generation company Globeleq's management took the opportunity to develop new power plants and, with Actis's expertise in managing investments, undertook a series of acquisitions in emerging markets worldwide while asset prices were low. When the market then improved the majority were sold, leaving a core of three African power investments by 2007 – Songas in Tanzania, Tsavo in Kenya and Umeme in Uganda, the first two of which formed a new Globeleq that proceeded to expand anew throughout Africa. Actis thus continued with CDC's tradition of undertaking major projects to address Africa's under-investment in energy infrastructure and consequent lack of access to electricity, a role that CDC was to take back under its own aegis a decade later.

Despite such close cooperation and plenty of examples of where their overall objectives were aligned, Actis and CDC had differing aims and, consequently, developed different strategies over the years. CDC remained Britain's independent bilateral DFI, with development in poorer countries as its primary concern, whereas Actis's aim was to invest responsibly in order to demonstrate 'the positive power of capital' and build successful businesses that would attract new investors, with the goal of becoming a leading private equity fund manager in its markets. Through a combination of CDC's legacy and anchor support, careful management and fortunate timing in a period of strong global growth, it was able swiftly to achieve these objectives.

By mid-2008, Actis had over $5.7 billion of funds under management, and by year-end its first global emerging markets fund, Actis Emerging Markets 3, had closed at $2.9 billion. Since its inception, Actis's investor base had grown to 100 investors, drawn from across the globe. And while CDC had committed $2.7 billion to its new funds between 2004 and 2008, a similar amount of $2.9 billion had been raised from third parties, the majority of whom had never before invested in emerging markets. Meanwhile, Actis's team of initially ex-CDC staff had successfully continued CDC's tradition in making responsible and often pioneering investments, using sophisticated structuring and pushing for the highest ESG standards, albeit in increasingly larger businesses and funds in middle-income emerging markets. This meant that after the end of the five-year umbrella contract and with the change in its investment objectives in 2009, CDC then necessarily became very selective in choosing which Actis funds in which to invest, focusing on Africa in general and on real estate, infrastructure and energy in particular, judging that the Actis teams were the most effective among its peers in these areas.

In some ways, what was being undertaken by the Aureos team was even more closely aligned with CDC's objectives, with a focus on the difficult and highly developmental segments of the market – encouraging small and medium-sized enterprises in some of the poorest countries of the world. The single country funds, such as the Ghana Venture Capital Fund and the Acacia Fund in Kenya – which had provided the platform for the creation of Aureos in 2001 as a joint venture between CDC and Norfund – had been set up by CDC in the 1990s, mainly in Africa, at a time when no one else was making this kind of bold commitment. Early performance had been mixed, but the idea caught on and CDC can claim that Aureos had been the trailblazer for private equity in Africa. CDC therefore continued to support Aureos through investing in its funds, including its new generation of substantial regional funds in each of its main regions of Africa, Asia and Latin America. By the end of 2008, Aureos had around $1 billion of third-party capital under management and after its managers undertook a spinout, CDC considered its work in incubating a profitable manager of SME funds in the emerging markets to have been achieved.

Keen to push ahead with developing the private equity industry in its geographies beyond what Actis and Aureos were doing, the small team left at CDC in 2004 had decided very early on to grow its own portfolio of fund managers, with a distinctly pioneering aim – specifically to become a developer of private equity fund managers in the world's poorest countries. Given the relatively small amount of money it had been allocated for investment with new fund managers of its own, this would have been a tall order had it not been for high global economic growth during the years before the financial crisis of 2008, combined with the terms of the agreement with Actis. The upswing in the world's economies meant that Actis and Aureos were able to sell many of CDC's old 'legacy' investments for substantially more than envisaged, a prime example being the sale in 2005 of its stake in telecoms company Celtel that yielded an extraordinary £162 million in cash. This and other profitable sales meant that Actis quickly found itself holding more cash than envisaged, for which suitable new investments were not immediately available. And in accordance with a 'use it or lose it' clause in the agreement, Actis passed any unused surplus back to CDC. As a result, CDC had plenty of cash to invest with new fund managers.

The two main criteria CDC used in choosing a new fund were that it should be either 'best-of-breed' in its geography or sector – the fund's manager already having established credibility – or that it should be a pioneer, investing in some innovative or developmental way. This might include situations where the manager itself was a novice in the field, with CDC providing support. US-based ShoreCap International, which, in December 2004, became CDC's first manager outside the Actis and Aureos stable, was chosen principally for its pioneering fund, ShoreCap I. This invested in microfinance institutions and banks specialising in small business ventures, notably in Africa and Asia. By becoming the largest investor in ShoreCap, CDC was able to underline the fact that it would continue to be pioneering, with an emphasis on seeking out investments aimed at alleviating poverty.

Above top: A gathering of potential customers in the Gambia listen intently as representatives from Reliance Financial Services, an investment by ShoreCap, explain how a microfinance company like Reliance can help the smallest businesses and even sole traders and entrepreneurs to expand by providing them with development finance.

Above: A Gambian fruit stallholder, one of Reliance's many small business clients, proudly showing off the produce on her market stall.

Microfinance continued to be one of the sectors of particular focus, with a total of seven fund managers specialising in supporting microfinance institutions by 2008. CDC was an early supporter of the sector and one that stuck with its Indian institutions through the crisis of confidence that followed the crash in Andhra Pradesh in 2010 and the exposure of widespread bad governance. Equally, CDC continued to invest in subsequent ShoreCap funds, supporting the fund manager through a difficult period of change following the financial crisis, during which the team managing CDC's funds became Equator Capital. These examples illustrated a continuing theme – that of CDC supporting its business partners through the tough times.

In the twelve months after its commitment to ShoreCap, CDC followed up with investments – either committed or given board approval – made by a further seventeen new fund managers, so that by the end of 2005 it was already describing itself as a fully operational fund of funds. And from then on the total number of managers increased year-by-year, varying widely in size and style. At the larger end, commitments were made to Helios Investment Partners in Africa, ICICI and India Value Fund Advisors in India, Patria in Brazil and CDH in China.

Helios and Patria were both committed to buy-and-build strategies, which have had transformative effects on the telecommunications and extramural teaching industries in their respective markets; ICICI pioneered the first leveraged buyout deal and the first mezzanine deal in India; and CDH focused on privatising state-owned enterprises in China.

On a smaller scale, commitments were made to many funds, such as Atlantic Coast Regional Fund in West Africa, Africa Capital Alliance in Nigeria, GroFin and Business Partners Kenya in Africa and VenturEast, Lok Capital and Ambit Pragma in India. These were all investing in the difficult but important SME sector, and many of the funds were pioneering in nature. CDC was an anchor investor in every one of them.

Africa was the main destination for CDC's capital and by the end of 2007 sixty per cent of the businesses invested by all its funds worldwide were located there. African businesses found it difficult to raise capital as the regulatory environment and other risks to doing business in many African countries were unfavourable and deterred would-be investors. Meanwhile, most local stock markets were simply unable to meet the demand for investment. CDC played a leading role in getting Africa more connected to the international capital markets by taking a lead in investing in most of the private equity funds that were being raised, notably in Nigeria. The availability of CDC's investment prompted many experienced and skilled financial specialists – including quite a number among the returning diaspora of African professionals – to look afresh at the opportunities in Africa and to consider setting up new private equity funds rather than simply working for existing banks and financial institutions. CDC encouraged and supported these first-time fund managers and many of the resulting companies went on to thrive, building the capacity of the private equity industry in their respective fields, a notable example being Helios Investors.

Above: A mobile branch of the Equity Bank, headquartered in Nairobi, Kenya, which was an early investment by Helios.

Helios Investors

Helios Investors was founded in 2004 by two Nigerian nationals, Tope Lawani and Babatunde Soyoye, both of whom had enjoyed successful careers with leading international private equity investor Texas Pacific Group. Their initial concept was to raise a small West Africa fund to invest primarily in a select group of greenfield businesses supplying large markets that were either underprovided or dominated by structurally expensive imports. CDC worked with Helios' two principals over a period of eighteen months to refine their proposal and make it attractive to international investors, resulting in a fund of $305 million, much larger and more wide-ranging than originally envisaged. CDC's commitment of $50 million was its largest to a new fund at that time and reflected its desire to help well-founded pioneering initiatives coming from promising teams in Africa. The fund's investments included a business providing mobile phone towers in Nigeria, a large telecommunications company in Angola and two banks – one in Nigeria and the other in Kenya – providing SME finance and other financial services to the underserved low-income market. The latter, Equity Bank, went on to become the Africa Regional winner of the Emerging Markets Sustainable Bank of the Year Award in 2008.

A second Helios Investors fund was successfully launched in 2009, with CDC committing $75 million, which attracted other investors, thereby enabling businesses that might otherwise have not been financially supported to go ahead. CDC's funds were not needed later when Helios came to raise its third fund, although CDC did go on to work with Helios on ideas for a more recent credit fund. In a relatively short time Helios had earned a reputation as a pre-eminent pan-African private equity firm managed by African professionals, one which, from inception, demonstrated a strong commitment toward improving business principles and standards of governance in Nigeria and elsewhere in Africa. And there was another connection when ex-CDC Henry Obi became a partner.

In Asia, it was a similar story of directing CDC's capital where it was most needed, supporting fund managers that invested responsibly with the aim of helping businesses to flourish and bringing overall economic growth. Geographically, as well as in the sectors it invested in, CDC was ambitious, backing fund managers in countries that were new to it. In Central Asia, ShoreCap invested in XacBank, Mongolia's largest microfinance institution, and in Afghanistan, CDC made a brave commitment to the Afghanistan Renewal Fund, which, while made during an interlude of optimistic calm in that fraught country, failed to be followed up with an investment once the long-standing conflict resumed. Not as challenging, but still with significant risks, CDC committed to two Pakistan-focused funds with the aim of supporting the nascent private equity industry there, but while one of these funds made investments in a range of businesses, its performance was disappointing and CDC did not achieve its objective of re-engaging in the country in a positively developmental way at this time, although some of its other regionally-based fund managers, including Actis, did make some investments there.

Mapping the market in India in 2004, CDC identified India Value Fund Advisors to be one of the top three fund managers operating there, its strong focus on governance issues and hands-on approach to investment differentiating it from its peers and its sector-agnostic fund strategies having the potential to return strong development impact. CDC invested $5 million through IVF in 2005, $25 million in 2007 and $40 million in a successor fund in 2009, each time being the only DFI invited to do so. Encouraged by IVF, CDC added value in providing advice on fundraising, strategy, team alignment and fund governance matters. It was the incorporation of global best ESG practices into its portfolio companies that distinguished IVF, while its pioneering use of internal operations-focused professionals to act as business partners to portfolio companies demonstrated to other Indian private equity managers what was achievable in control/buyout transactions, few of which had been completed by private equity firms at that time.

CDC later backed Rajeev Agrawal, one of the partners managing IVF, when he struck out on his own, taking with him the experience and values of IVF to set up Ambit Pragma, a fund focused on control or significant minority stakes in India's SME sector. CDC's pioneering development of the private equity industry in this way, through assisting experienced individuals working in corporates to become independent, was to be repeated in the ensuing years, notably in helping the most prominent woman working in private equity in India, Renuka Ramnath, to leave established CDC-backed ICICI Ventures and establish her own fund management company, Multiples, which has subsequently grown to manage $1 billion of funds invested in Indian businesses.

In China, where CDC was also one of the pioneers of the private equity industry, it continued to make investments in funds that were instrumental in transforming China's low income, agriculturally-based economy into one that was more market-oriented and prosperous. Capital Today, a Shanghai-based growth capital fund managed by Kathy Xu, and Qiming, a tech fund also based in Shanghai, were stand-out examples of successful fund investments.

The team at CDC that achieved all this within a few years was small, ambitious, focused and hardworking. There was a collegiate atmosphere, with a marked lack of bureaucracy and everyone sharing the small open-plan office, including the CEO, who was accessible to all. Meanwhile, diversity both in gender and nationality was increasing, with fourteen nations represented. It was an exciting time, finding, assessing and working with new fund managers – many of them first-timers – as well as with old and new colleagues at Actis and Aureos. Through its own re-skilling and recruitment, CDC was becoming recognised in the development finance world as a skilled fund investor, with deep due diligence skills. It had also established itself as the largest supporter of private equity funds in sub-Saharan Africa and India and had a larger proportion of its funds committed to the world's poorest countries than any of the European development finance institutions or IFC. The feedback it received was that if a fund had CDC as an investor, this created a halo effect and other institutions would follow.

"If a fund had CDC as an investor, this created a halo effect and other institutions would follow."

Above: A congested street scene near the business and financial hub of Karachi, Pakistan. CDC committed to two Pakistan-focused funds with the aim of supporting the nascent private equity industry there. However, performance was disappointing, and CDC did not achieve its objective of re-engaging in the country in a positively developmental way, although some of its other regionally-based fund managers, including Actis, did make some investments there.

As its commitments and the number of fund managers increased, the size of the team grew steadily, although only to around forty; but even that expansion meant that it had outgrown its premises at Duke Street, St James's. In March 2008 the head office moved once again, back in the direction of its old Bessborough Gardens address, to Cardinal Place, a new combined office and retail development at 80 Victoria Street, located close to DFID's offices at the time.

One of DFID's objectives for the CDC team in these post-restructuring years was to rebuild the balance sheet that had lost much of its value following the financial crisis and global downturn that started in Asia in 1998. During the first three years following the reorganisation, this was quickly achieved. CDC went rapidly from strength to strength financially, so much so that the annual review for 2007 showed net assets of £2.7 billion, up from £1 billion in March 2004, more than restoring the balance sheet. Altogether, the cash generated by this and other sales and sources of income in 2007 amounted to £1 billion, which was described as a "wall of cash" coming back to CDC in one year, thanks largely to gains realised due to good investments by CDC in the late 1990s and early 2000s. Even with investments made into funds of £412 million, what it meant was that CDC ended 2007 with £1.4 billion in cash, double the amount of the year before. All this gave CDC the confidence and the cash to continue its mission.

The same year saw other positive and significant developments for CDC, with the team drawing up its own method for comprehensively assessing development impact through the collection of a range of indicators such as taxes paid, jobs created, training provided, mobilisation of third-party capital and the sustainability of its businesses. Private equity in general was under attack at the time for lacking accountability and transparency and CDC, by asking its fund managers for this type of information and reporting on it, was breaking new ground. CDC was also ahead of the curve in introducing a code of practice for fund managers, setting out guidance on how to assess, address and monitor environmental, social and governance (ESG) issues, a step up in what was expected from fund managers and more closely aligned to meeting the international standards of best practice.

Also, in these years, CDC made its first co-investments directly into businesses, with three commitments going to financial services in Africa and to renewable energy in Asia in support of fund managers investing in businesses that for various reasons had failed fully to secure their funding plans. This debt offering, although small-scale to start with, was to form part of an alternative investments strategy in the years ahead, and, along with its initiatives in assessing development impact and addressing ESG issues, also demonstrated that CDC was continuing to be looking to add value and be more than a provider of finance to equity funds.

Above: An imposing mountain landscape near Freetown. The Sierra Investment Fund in Sierra Leone was the first private equity fund to be raised in the country as it recovered from a decade of conflict, but the market proved too small for Manocap, which was managing SIF, to be a great success.

Meanwhile, even though the first casualties of the credit crunch had appeared in 2007, unsettling the international banking system and the developed markets, the emerging markets weren't immediately affected, and CDC continued to achieve record highs in its investment levels. As the global financial crisis really took hold in 2008 its results did inevitably start to be hit – and yet it still had a good financial story to tell. That year was the last in the five-year period of the umbrella agreement with Actis and in its annual review it chose to give prominence to the performance over those five years as a whole.

During that time, £2.5 billion in cash had been generated by sales of legacy investments and this had been returned to CDC for reinvestment, meeting the targets set by DFID. Commitments had been made to 127 funds, with fifty-nine managers supporting 681 businesses, amounting altogether to £2.7 billion. The commitments were diverse in nature – to funds of all sizes, with differing aims and throughout the geographies and across all the sectors in which CDC was enabled to operate. The thinking was that by increasing the amount of capital available to fund managers for investment in profitable businesses, while also providing advice to both fund manager and investee companies that would improve the chances of success, development would be delivered. And even in 2008 itself, when the world economic tide turned, CDC still managed to notch up record new investments of £436 million and record outstanding commitments of £2 billion.

These were impressively high numbers. And, significantly, not one of the new fund commitments made in 2008 was through Actis, which now managed only half of CDC's entire portfolio, a proportion that was falling annually. CDC had come a long way towards establishing its independence.

CDC had also far exceeded DFID's target for the mobilisation of $1 billion of outside finance for the period, its fund managers reported as having raised $21 billion of third party capital. While no one was claiming that CDC's participation was solely responsible for mobilising this amount, it was increasingly backing first-time fund managers with anchor investments. Backing inexperienced managers – whether in private equity in general or in specific geographies or markets – was not without its risks: the funds tended to be smaller and less likely to succeed, while the close supervision provided for fund managers and their portfolio companies in the locations where they operated had opportunity costs for the small CDC team now that it no longer had its own network of overseas offices, it meant that the CDC team had to conduct frequent visits around the world.

However, long-term rewards came with the resulting development of first-time local fund managers whose success then attracted others to the same markets, increasing the pool of capital and the options for entrepreneurs seeking private equity finance and thereby creating a virtual upward spiral. The managers of Africa Capital Alliance, Helios and Catalyst in Africa and Ambit Pragma, Lok Capital, IDFC Project Equity (now IDFC Alternatives) and Multiples in India were all examples of fund managers whose early steps were supported by CDC.

This sort of hand-holding was not restricted to first-time fund managers. If a first-time fund was taking a long time to invest, or its investee companies were struggling, CDC would provide assistance in identifying the problem and redirecting the strategies, so that when its managers came to raise a further fund they were better prepared. An example of CDC doing exactly this was the help it gave to Catalyst, a locally-based first-time team established to support the growth of private equity in East Africa. CDC also helped teams that had become experienced in private equity to move into other sectors, such as real estate, a prime example here being Kotak, in India. CDC built on its relationship with Kotak Private Equity to become the largest investor in the Kotak India Realty Fund. Later, CDC worked with them on their entry into the affordable housing market. This demonstrated another common thread, CDC leveraging a good relationship to explore new avenues together.

When it came to deciding investment targets for the next five-year plan, 2009-2013, DFID called for CDC to increase even further its focus on poorer countries and, in particular, on Africa. This was in line with the thinking of the Labour government, whose new leader, Gordon Brown, was pro-Africa, as was his Secretary of State, Douglas Alexander. It was also prompted by the fact that CDC's portfolio had been growing in places that were no longer perceived to be so much in need of development support, such as some of the Latin American countries and, especially, rapidly-growing China, where eleven per cent of the total portfolio, in terms of value, was invested at the end of 2008. DFID therefore reset the targets, stipulating that more than seventy-five per cent of CDC's investments from new commitments should be in countries with gross national income per capita of under $905 per head per annum, down from the previous $1,750, and more than fifty per cent in sub-Saharan Africa.

"**The managers of Africa Capital Alliance, Helios and Catalyst in Africa and Ambit Pragma, Lok Capital, IDFC Project Equity and Multiples in India were all examples of fund managers whose early steps were supported by CDC.**"

This further narrowing of the target range for investments, with its low setting of the GNI bar, meant that there could be few new investments in China, South East Asia, Asia Pacific, Central Asia and Latin America and that the relationships with fund managers established in these less poor regions would no longer be followed through to successor funds. It also raised broader challenges, such as the need to manage an increased portfolio risk from less diversification. As something of a compromise, it was agreed that CDC could, in addition, commit up to £125 million over the five years to funds supporting SMEs in countries with a GNI of up to $11,115, recognising that there were many millions of people within these relatively well-off countries who were still living in great poverty.

Meanwhile, despite all the impressive financial figures and developmental successes that were being reported, not everybody was happy with the way things were going. In November 2008, CDC marked its diamond anniversary with an event at London's magnificent Lancaster House – but the mood wasn't as celebratory as had been hoped. Those invited naturally included former CEOs, past board members and retired senior management, many of whom had had lengthy careers within CDC and had then been highly critical of its transformation into a fund of funds, regretting the loss of its regional organisation, its direct investing capability and its managed businesses, feeling that investments were no longer as closely tied to development as they should be and that the culture had become too driven by financial incentives.

These critical views were shared by a number of politicians and other individuals concerned about CDC's limited role in the private equity model, which was also coming under attack in the media. In particular, it was the British satirical fortnightly magazine *Private Eye* and the tenacity of its investigative journalist, former tax inspector Richard Brooks, that brought CDC into an unflattering public spotlight and, in turn, stimulated others to air their views. In the autumn of 2007, Brooks had claimed that KPMG's valuation of Actis, used as a basis on which to assess the amount to be paid by its new partners for their sixty per cent share of the business, was too low and based on an overly conservative valuation of the portfolio, the inference being that the partners had negotiated an excessively generous deal for themselves at the expense of the British taxpayer and the world's poorest peoples.

A series of critical articles by Richard Brooks was published in the magazine throughout 2008, reporting on further investigations into CDC, Actis and DFID, and these reports were often followed up by others in the media, including the BBC's Radio 4 investigative programme *File on Four*. Among other things, the programme questioned the replacement of long-term directly-invested and managed businesses – such as the recently-sold arable farms at Mpongwe in Zambia – by shorter-term investments in funds with potentially high financial returns but less obvious developmental value, too many of which were considered to have supported business enterprises in regions that were relatively well-off, rather than those in the poorest countries. CDC's use of offshore financial centres, a common feature of private equity investment, also came under fire as being inappropriate for a government-owned DFI charged with alleviating poverty. Once the remuneration that was accruing to some senior managers in 2007 – the year of plenty preceding the financial crash – was then revealed, these critical voices became so loud that they could no longer be ignored. As a result, the National Audit Office undertook a review of DFID's oversight of CDC, while *Private Eye's* campaign reached a peak in October 2008 with a collection of articles published under the banner headline: 'The Actis-CDC Sell-Off – The Full Background'.

Although the NAO report, published shortly afterwards, recognised that "CDC has made a credible contribution to economic development in poor countries while also encouraging other foreign investors to engage with them", it questioned whether its development impact could not be better measured. Addressing *Private Eye's* charge that Actis had been undervalued, it found that the valuation had been reasonable and that Actis had performed well, but added that the incentive-based remuneration structure meant that there were no residual profits for distribution to Actis's shareholders, denying DFID, which owned forty per cent of Actis's equity, any reward. DFID was also criticised for failing to give sufficient attention to other details, including the remuneration framework at CDC. Parliament's Public Accounts Committee reviewed the NAO report in its role of holding the government and its public servants to account. Like the NAO, it challenged both DFID and CDC to consult more, and encouraged DFID to pay more attention to ensuring that CDC was focused on poverty reduction in deprived areas. These points were taken on board by both CDC and DFID.

"**Meanwhile, despite all the impressive financial figures and developmental successes that were being reported, not everybody was happy with the way things were going.**"

Richard Gillingwater

Born in 1956 and educated at Chesterfield Grammar School and St. Edmund Hall, Oxford, where he studied law, Richard Gillingwater first qualified as a solicitor with Lovells before changing to a career in banking, initially at Kleinwort Benson, during which time he completed an MBA at IMD, Lausanne. Moving to BZW, he rose to be joint head of Global Corporate Finance, and after BZW's takeover by CSFB he ultimately became chairman of European Banking. In this role he acted as adviser to the UK government, which led to his appointment as chief executive of the Shareholder Executive, the body created in September 2003 to improve the government's performance as a shareholder in government-owned businesses. In April 2007 he became dean of Cass Business School, a position he held until 2012.

Appointed a non-executive director of CDC in January 2009 and chairman three months later, he adopted a diplomatic and conciliatory approach when it came to overseeing CDC's dealings with DFID, Parliament and the media. Having identified Diana Noble as Richard Laing's successor as CEO, he gave her his full support as she worked on developing and implementing the new business model. He retired in 2013, having successfully guided CDC through a challenging period in its history. Awarded a CBE in 2008 for services to the financial services industry, he remains on the boards of Janus Henderson and Scottish and Southern Electricity and in 2015 took up the role of pro-chancellor of the Open University.

In March 2009 Malcolm Williamson stepped down as chairman, having successfully worked with his chief executive to implement the fund of funds strategy, and was replaced by Richard Gillingwater, who had not long left the Shareholder Executive, the government body he established in 2003-04 to professionalise the management of government shareholdings in organisations such as CDC. In that capacity he had had some late involvement with the formation of Actis and was familiar with CDC.

The immediate priority at this time, however, was to navigate the fallout from the global financial crash, which had created a critical cash flow situation that, had it not been handled as assiduously as it was by CDC's management, could have had existential consequences. The then general fund of funds business model was essentially to over-commit in the confident expectation that income from the returns coming from funds would help to cover the new commitments, but the dramatic drop in CDC's income that came in the wake of the crash meant that the inherent risks of the over-commitment policy came home to roost, necessitating some emergency cutbacks and economies. Unlike others, CDC succeeded in getting through the next few difficult years by renegotiating some existing commitments – notably with Actis – by clear and careful cash management, by reining in new commitments and by seeking and achieving Treasury agreement for a new standby borrowing facility.

Despite these necessary cutbacks, CDC still managed to commit to eleven new funds in 2009, while also investing with six more fund managers. Several of those that were being investigated during the year were especially significant in terms of potentially strong development impact. They also marked a move towards more specifically focused funds. These included funds investing in Indian agribusiness, renewable energy in Asia, SMEs in Sierra Leone and Bangladesh, and sustainable forestry in sub-Saharan Africa.

The India Agribusiness Fund, managed by Rabo Equity Advisers, part of Rabobank, was the first private equity fund focused on the Indian food and agribusiness sector. It invested to build the infrastructure across the agricultural value chain, including food processing and rural retail and cold chain logistics. The Renewable Energy Asia Fund, managed by Berkeley Energy, supported a new sector dedicated specifically to mitigating the effects of climate change through clean energy infrastructure or 'cleantech'. Two principals of its manager, Berkeley Energy, had come to CDC in 2007 with the idea of investing in renewables and CDC had worked with them over two years to develop this into a workable proposition with their partners and to build a team in South East Asia. CDC had to step back from taking it forward in the region because of the change in strategy, but later, in 2014, CDC then was to transfer the model to Africa, with a commitment to the Africa Renewable Energy Fund, based in Nairobi.

Above: Textile workers in Bangladesh. Ananta Apparels was one of the earliest investments by Frontier Fund, Bangladesh's first private equity fund, to which CDC committed $10 million in 2010 as an anchor investor. Ananta has grown to be one of the country's leading garment exporters, providing jobs to 17,000 workers in factories maintaining high standards of corporate responsibility and producing ready to wear clothes for well-known international brands.

The Sierra Investment Fund in Sierra Leone, recovering from a decade of conflict, and Bangladesh's Frontier PE Fund, which was committed in 2010, were the first private equity funds in those countries. It was brave of CDC to investigate and support fund managers in these places at a time when there were more established markets elsewhere that were more able to absorb capital. The market for private equity in Sierra Leone proved too small for Manocap, which was managing SIF, to be a great success, but the Bangladesh-based fund managers fared much better. After a great deal of groundwork by CDC's team, working together with IFC, DFID and other partners in assessing the regulatory environment and then, at their request, helping the Bangladesh authorities to prepare for private equity investment, the fund made a series of seven investments. These were mainly in businesses in the manufacturing sector, involved in making a wide range of products from motorcycles to textiles and white goods. In each case, CDC made it a priority to ensure that decent standards were maintained for low-paid workers.

The GEF Africa Sustainable Forestry Fund was a pioneering initiative by CDC itself. Wanting to support sustainable forestry in sub-Saharan Africa and finding no fund managers already doing this, or prepared even to consider it, CDC went out and invited tenders, as a result of which the contract to manage the fund was awarded to US-based GEF Management, managers of a series of funds under the Global Environment Fund banner, which had operations near Stellenbosch in South Africa.

CDC naturally became the anchor investor, seeding the fund with its existing and long-standing CDC teak plantations and sawmilling business, Kilombero Valley Teak in Tanzania, formerly in the Actis Africa Agribusiness Fund, and into which it continued to invest.

The proposition attracted others – mainly fellow DFIs – willing to invest alongside it mainly because of the expected sustainable environmental and ecological benefits, irrespective of the long-term nature of the investment and the propensity of the sector to deliver low, although consistent, financial returns. The manager proved an effective choice and the fund became respected as one of the premier forestry funds in Africa. Over time, investments in forestry plantations and in one natural forest were made in accordance with the initial plan. These included Peak Timbers in northern Swaziland (now eSwatini), a 31,500-hectare timber and sawmilling business that became the largest employer in the region, with one-third of its total area managed for conservation purposes, the remaining part growing Forest Stewardship Council (FSC) certified pine and eucalyptus. From a sustainable forestry perspective the investments are proving successful, delivering demonstrable development impact, although financial returns are, as expected, long-term and, to an extent, unrealised.

Above: A post-harvest log handling yard at Kilombero Valley Teak Company, Tanzania. From here the logs go to an integrated processing plant to be sawn, dried and be value-added.

Bearing in mind that in 2009 CDC's staff still only numbered 46 and that they were managing investments with 65 fund managers in 134 funds and supporting 794 underlying portfolio companies in 71 countries, such innovation and dedication to searching out new opportunities was highly creditable. Sixty-one per cent of the new investments were in Africa, easily exceeding DFID's fifty per cent target. And $1.2 billion of other capital had been mobilised, an estimate that was well on its way to meeting another new DFID target, for mobilisation, agreed at two hundred per cent of CDC's investment over a three-year period, with priority given to investment with first-time fund managers, in the expectation that subsequent funds would then find it easier to attract investors. At the same time, the hard-pressed CDC staff were also working on a comprehensive and all-encompassing development report, entitled *Growth for Development*, that was launched in July 2009. This set out the thinking behind its new monitoring and evaluation system for measuring the development effects of its work and the results of the evaluations already undertaken. Indicators of development performance were reported on along with regional and sector reviews describing the work CDC was doing and why.

The report also introduced CDC's new Investment Code – updated ESG guidelines expanded to explain how sound policies could be used to add value to investments and how ESG risks should be managed while also addressing matters such as climate change and gender equality management. Published subsequently on the website in 2010, this work to promote responsible investment and business practices was accompanied by a series of training sessions given by CDC in eight cities around the world and attended by forty-five of its fund managers. In so doing, CDC built a reputation as a leading trainer for fund managers worldwide in the practical application of the IFC's performance standards on social and environmental sustainability.

All this effort was recognised by the European DFI community generally and by those benefitting overseas. However, it did little to improve CDC's public image and those in the UK who considered the fund of funds model to be inappropriate for CDC continued to criticise its work. With bankers and financial institutions generally under heavy fire from all sides in the wake of the 2008 financial crisis, the media continued to investigate and publish articles relating to CDC and its fund managers' investments, shining a spotlight on anything that suggested financial returns were being prioritised over development outcomes.

Among those reading these articles were ministers and MPs at Westminster, including those on the opposition front bench who, with an election due in the spring of 2010, could soon become CDC's political masters, the most prominent and influential among this group being the Shadow Secretary of State for International Development, Andrew Mitchell. He'd been shadowing the post for four years and with a long-standing interest in development issues was passionate about assuming the role, should the Conservatives win the election. He had a particular interest in CDC that went back to the 1980s, when, as a young man, he was employed at the investment bank, Lazard, of which Lord Kindersley, CDC's chairman at the time, was managing director. This had led to him touring CDC's projects with Lord Kindersley and he had been impressed by its work.

Still caring deeply about CDC, he had nevertheless come to regard it as having assumed a diminished role relative to its history and its status as a world-leading DFI. Using what was to become an oft-repeated phrase, he talked of CDC having "lost its way", believing strongly that the narrowness of having just one fund of funds strategy and the inherent limitations of private equity investing were too restrictive. The view he shared with others was that without the ability to make direct investments, its capacity to achieve significant development impact was compromised; that the tendency of private equity to tie up strategies and make investments for set periods was too inflexible and led to a reduction in control; and that the desire to attract other outside investors encouraged fund managers to seek the highest financial returns for the lowest risk.

The election, on May 6, 2010, duly confirmed Andrew Mitchell as secretary of state at DFID and he wasted no time before taking action. The first CDC board meeting following the election discussed and welcomed a paper entitled 'CDC Report' which envisaged the evolutionary expansion of CDC's activities. The paper had been written by Jeremy Sillem, a colleague of Andrew Mitchell's from the days when they worked together at Lazard, who had then gone on to become the managing partner and founder of Spencer House Partners, an asset management advisory business. The report was clear and straightforward in its analysis. And even though certain parts of it were the subject of some debate within CDC, it presented an overall vision that all were in agreement with, of "a more proactive, directly involved organisation".

The proposals called for CDC to develop the capability to make direct investments again, initially through co-investment, accelerating and ramping up the work CDC was already doing in making co-investments directly to its fund managers' investee companies. They also called for an increased range of financial instruments. To an extent this was building on CDC's alternatives strategy that had been developing since 2008 and which had already planned for $275 million of long-term debt investments and $100 million in co-investments between 2010 and 2013, but the ambition to scale up was significant in its scope.

Above: Andrew Mitchell, Secretary of State for International Development (2010-2012), visiting the operations of Prasanna Purple in 2010.

Above: One of the buses operated by Prasanna Purple, a company invested by Ambit Pragma Ventures, the fund manager of AFP1, an Indian fund in which CDC committed $20 million in 2008. The investment helped Prasanna Purple expand its operations, introducing a modern fleet of buses to improve the quality and safety of journeys for passengers in formerly underserved cities. By 2018, it was carrying 240 million passengers in its city buses and 1.5 million passengers on intercity buses.

The paper also supported the continuation of investment through funds, although suggesting that CDC should be more active in selling them when their development job had been done, and where there were private sector investors willing to buy. Other interesting ideas included working with other like-minded sources of capital, such as interested investors in the City of London, arguably the world's financial centre for investment in the emerging markets; developing flexible criteria for choosing investments that were more closely aligned with development objectives than offered by the current broad-brushed poorer 'Africa and South Asia' approach; and engaging a chief investment officer to take responsibility for delivering these objectives – something that did subsequently happen in 2014.

Three weeks later, on June 16, 2010, CDC unveiled its *Development Review* for 2009 at an event held in London's Cabinet War Rooms. This updated and extended the analysis contained in *Growth for Development*, its predecessor of the year before and included the perspectives of external commentators and a survey of the added value that CDC had determined it was bringing.

Nonetheless public debate about CDC continued, with the media closely examining various aspects of CDC's operations. This included, later in the year, another powerful critique by *Private Eye*, with the release of a second compilation of previously published articles in the form of a special seven-page colour supplement, with the banner headline 'THAT'S RICH'. It was a testing time for the staff at CDC, who continued to work conscientiously throughout, believing that the original mission was still being delivered, albeit through a different model, and who considered that they had the evidence to demonstrate this. Respecting its chief executive Richard Laing for doing his best to protect them from these distractions, they pushed ahead with what they believed to be highly developmental new funds, while at the same time working on the launch of a further revised ESG Toolkit, with training sessions for fund managers, throughout the world.

CDC made commitments totalling £231 million during 2010, of which fifteen were to new funds. These included support for first-time fund managers Cauris Croissance, targeting SME businesses in Francophone West Africa, and Multiples, investing across all sectors in India. And performance far exceeded the targets set by DFID in 2008, with ninety-two per cent of the new investments being in the poorest countries, as against a target of seventy-five per cent, and eighty-four per cent in sub-Saharan Africa, where the target had been for over fifty per cent.

Meanwhile, the senior CDC staff worked with Jeremy Sillem, Andrew Mitchell and his team at DFID to flesh out a strategy for CDC's new future. The result was effectively a new working business plan, whereby CDC pledged to introduce a new programme of direct investments, debt products and guarantees to markedly increase its effectiveness, commercially and developmentally. The plan was also comprehensive in addressing topics such as transparency and additionality, the added social and environmental and other benefits that could accrue indirectly from responsible and well-thought-out investment.

A week later, on October 12, Andrew Mitchell made a written statement to Parliament, declaring 'The Reform of CDC Group plc'. The reforms he listed were all those already agreed with the board: CDC was to be reconfigured and reinvigorated in order to increase its development impact and to realise its potential to be what he defined as "the jewel in the crown of the UK's support to the private sector in developing countries". He also called for it to become "more pro-poor focused than any other development finance institution, doing the hardest things in the hardest places". Greater flexibility would again be given to CDC to use a range of actively-managed, directly-invested financial instruments appropriate to the needs of its target countries – now limited to those in sub-Saharan Africa and the poorer parts of Asia – with the aim of producing a more diversified, innovative, risk-taking portfolio, with clearly measured development impact and additionality to ensure that its supported businesses could be seen to be improving working conditions, managing environmental issues, acting transparently and stamping out corruption. The statement went on to say that DFID would be launching a public consultation before finalising its decisions.

On the day that the statement was issued, DFID held an event at the London School of Economics to launch its own private sector strategy and also to introduce the CDC reforms and consultation process. A keynote address at the event was made by Sir Paul Collier, Oxford professor of economics and a leading authority on international development, whose book *The Bottom Billion* looked at why the poorest countries in the world were failing and what could be done about it. The professor spoke in support of the reasons for change, and Andrew Mitchell gave a speech that left no doubt about his determination to drive through the transformation of CDC.

Left: Wananchi engineers installing and maintaining telephony infrastructure in Kenya. An investment by Emerging Capital Partners, one of CDC's pan-African fund managers, in Wananchi provided capital for the company to provide broadband internet, cable television and voice telephony services to customers in Kenya and Tanzania. The company has since expanded to other parts of Africa and extended its services.

Above: A $20 million commitment in 2008 to VenturEast Proactive Fund, a fund investing in early-to-growth stage technology businesses, enabled an investment of $3.5 million to be made in Atyati, a company involved in developing mobile technologies to support the provision of mobile banking facilities for the benefit of India's rural poor. The platform allowed the Indian government and banks to administer financial services remotely through the use of thousands of 'agents' – for example, making pension payments and providing banking services that created new jobs as well as serving those without access to bricks-and-mortar accounts, while also encouraging opportunities for new enterprises.

Above: CDC chairman Richard Gillingwater (sitting) leads a board visit to Bangladesh, with non-executive director Fields Wicker-Muirin talking to local women. Each year the CDC board would travel to a different country where CDC worked, meeting the local fund managers and their investee company teams, and gaining first-hand insights into operations there and the impacts being made.

At the same time, it had been announced that the International Development Committee was also going to be looking at CDC. Launching the inquiry – under its long-serving chairman, Liberal Democrat Malcolm Bruce – it invited written evidence from interested parties in advance of hearings planned for December. This was within its investigative remit as the House of Commons Select Committee charged with monitoring the work of DFID and its related public bodies. As well as examining the likely success of DFID's proposed reforms, 'The Future of CDC' was to consider CDC's effectiveness vis-à-vis other development finance institutions and DFID's shareholding in Actis.

DFID's three-month public consultation process was formally opened on November 5 with the issue of a questionnaire, followed by a workshop and four independent studies, the results of which were published on its website. Many of CDC's fund managers with whom CDC had built core relationships over the years responded to the consultation, recognising CDC's recent contribution to development and its demonstrable track record. Altogether, about a quarter of those who responded were from the investment and fund management community, giving a balance to those who criticised the way CDC was working.

With the consultation still going on, the IDC inquiry held three public hearings in one of the Palace of Westminster committee rooms, during which a variety of witnesses were questioned. The first session included Sierra Leone-based fund manager, Manocap's Tom Cairnes, Oxfam's Penny Fowler and Richard Brooks, each of whom had both good and bad to report. The second meeting examined CDC's management, represented by Richard Laing and Richard Gillingwater along with Rod Evison, long-time CDC-staffer and at the time managing director for Africa. The third hearing, held in early January, questioned Secretary of State Andrew Mitchell. DFID's consultation period ended late that month, and the IDC's report was published two months after that.

In many ways, the findings of the report were seen by CDC to be constructive and reasonably positive and they also received some favourable comment in the press. The report acknowledged CDC's success in becoming uniquely well-known and highly regarded for its experience in investing through funds that encouraged others to invest alongside them; and, with the important proviso that its capital should only be used where its participation brought additional value either directly, or indirectly through encouraging further investment from outside, the continuation of the fund of funds model was recommended. Overall, its recommendations resonated with those of DFID, and there was much with which CDC was also in agreement – such as the need to give more thought to how development impact could be explicitly measured.

On 7 June 2011 Andrew Mitchell made another written statement to Parliament, having agreed the new way forward with CDC. CDC had been given the go-ahead for another metamorphosis, one that would see it grow significantly in size once again, with enough flexibility to enable it to extend its reach.

While Richard Gillingwater remained as chairman and was instrumental in helping to facilitate the transition overseen by Andrew Mitchell, its chief executive, Richard Laing, having already announced his retirement in February, stepped aside in July to allow the implementation to be carried on by a new pair of hands. He had undertaken the role for seven years – longer than any of his three immediate predecessors – and his diligence and commitment to CDC and a strong overall focus on development had helped to deliver the private equity model, transforming CDC into a financially successful fund of funds. It had become recognised among fund-raisers and other bilateral DFIs as the pre-eminent place to go for investments in funds in the poorer countries and had nurtured a generation of new fund managers ready to invest again. In so doing, it had achieved much good development, creating sustainable businesses and jobs, helping to prove the validity of the private equity model outside developed markets and, specifically, making Africa, India and China more attractive places for private sector investment. CDC had also sought to invest proactively in funds in sectors that it believed to have potential for overt development impact when other more cautious investors were shunning them, while also finding new ways to measure that impact and to promote best practice among fund managers with regard to ESG issues, initiatives of which Richard Laing was particularly proud. Furthermore, CDC under his leadership had built a store of value that was to give his successor a firm foundation for taking it forward. And all of this had been achieved with a small team numbering less than fifty, among whom he had come to be regarded with great respect.

Following Richard Laing's departure, Richard Gillingwater effectively became executive chairman, with Rod Evison as acting CEO. While the new CEO was being recruited, Evison and his team worked closely with DFID in deciding how the high-level business plan could be implemented, and also on the drafts of the new governance documents. Acting to fulfil one of these requirements, CDC quickly joined the International Aid Transparency Initiative, the first bilateral DFI to do so, and put in place a new disclosure policy involving the release on its website of information about its operational policies, investments, fund managers, organisation, accounts and remuneration. Announcing CDC's membership was to be the subject of the new CEO's first press release.

The interim team also got on with the business of making investments in innovative funds, until the new investment strategy came into force in 2012, replacing that set out in the original 2009-2013 five-year plan. In 2011, CDC made twelve new commitments totalling £188 million, of which ten were in new funds, bringing the total to 152 funds managed by 80 different fund managers. The new undertakings included further funds in the microfinance sector in Africa and India, addressing issues of financial inclusion that reached the 'bottom of the pyramid' – in Silverlands, an African agribusiness fund; a fund specialising in Vietnam; and notably, the first private equity fund focusing on India's eight poorest states. Also of note, while not committed until the following year, the investment recommendation establishing the first private equity fund in Ethiopia was presented to CDC's board in November 2011.

In the months before Andrew Mitchell himself also moved on – leaving DFID in September 2012 to take up the post of chief whip – he continued to give time, energy and hands-on attention to CDC. He asked it to find a way to invest in the Indian states where poverty was at its greatest, but CDC had found that none of the Indian fund managers with whom it had a relationship was willing to do that: there was not enough economic activity and no teams were based there. CDC had no option but to look elsewhere for a suitable investment team and eventually found an investment banker of Indian origin with a successful career in New York and London, who then set up Pragati Equity Advisers. The Pragati Fund, supported by CDC and IFC, made several investments in the poorest states, but wasn't as successful as had been hoped and the team had to be replaced by UTI, given the job of managing the portfolio.

Although CDC had an office in Addis Ababa in the 1970s and had made an unsuccessful attempt at growing tea, it had not attempted an investment there since then until, more than thirty years later, an anchor investment of $15 million was made in the Ethiopia Growth and Transformation Fund. This was the result of an exercise much like that in Bangladesh, CDC working with DFID and other interested parties to explore the market opportunities and regulatory environment for private equity in the country, finding them lacking, and then making something happen. In this instance it was Gabriel Schulze, a US citizen with strong Ethiopian connections, partnering with Berhane Demissie, a consultant to the Ethiopian prime minister's family office, who made the running. Set up by Berhane as Schulze Global Investment's local manager, it became the leading fund manager in Ethiopia, making investments across a range of sectors. Berhane Demissie later left to co-set up Cepheus Growth Capital Partners, developing an Ethiopian SME-focused fund in which CDC invested in 2017.

Meanwhile, the lengthy process of identifying and recruiting exactly the right candidate to take on the challenge of leading CDC forward ended with the recruitment in November 2011 of the highly-respected international investment specialist Diana Noble as its new CEO. This ended another chapter in CDC's history during which it had established itself as a bold and dedicated investor in funds; it also marked the beginning of its reconstruction as a DFI providing a 'full-service' range of development finance instruments – more like its DFI peers, once again. The fund of funds episode had demonstrated, nevertheless, that investments in funds – or 'intermediated equities' as they were becoming known – had every right to be retained as one of the principal arrows in its quiver to be aimed by CDC at its overall target – identified in its revamped 2011 mission statement – to support the "building of businesses in the poorest countries, creating jobs and making a lasting difference to people's lives".

CDC's investments in 2011

- Through a fund of funds strategy CDC supports more businesses and is invested in more countries than ever before.

- Seventy per cent of businesses are in Africa or South Asia.

- No one sector dominates, with the highest (twenty per cent) in infrastructure.

Global investment (£m)

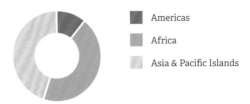

- Americas
- Africa
- Asia & Pacific Islands

Sector of investment (£m)

- Basic development
- Primary production & processing
- Commerce & industry

- ## 1,126 businesses
- ## £1,913.3 million invested

(£2.3 billion in 2018 terms)

Note: Investments are shown at valuation.

Americas

1. **Argentina**
   Agribusiness & Food
   Extractive industries
   Health care
   Infrastructure
2. **Belize**
   Agribusiness & Food
   Real Estate
3. **Brazil**
   Consumer Services
   Education
   Financials
   Health care
   Industrials
   Business services
   Infrastructure
4. **Colombia**
   Consumer Services
   Financials
   Health care
   Industrials
   Infrastructure
5. **Costa Rica**
   Consumer Services
   Financials
   Health care
   Industrials
6. **El Salvador**
   Consumer Services
   Financials
   Real Estate
7. **Grenada**
   Consumer Services
8. **Guatemala**
   Consumer Services
   Infrastructure
9. **Honduras**
   Infrastructure
10. **Jamaica**
    Infrastructure
11. **Mexico**
    Consumer Services
    Education
    Financials
    Health care
    Industrials
    Business services
    Infrastructure
    Real Estate
12. **Panama**
    Industrials
    Real Estate
13. **Peru**
    Consumer Services
    Extractive industries
    Financials
    Industrials
14. **St Lucia**
    Business services

Latin America Region
Financials

Africa

15. **Algeria**
    Agribusiness & Food
    Financials
    Health care
    Industrials
    Business services
16. **Angola**
    Industrials
    Business services
17. **Botswana**
    Financials
18. **Burkina Faso**
    Extractive industries
    Financials
19. **Cameroon**
    Agribusiness & Food
    Extractive industries
    Financials
    Health care
20. **Democratic Republic of the Congo**
    Extractive industries
    Financials
    Business services
21. **Côte d Ivoire**
    Agribusiness & Food
    Extractive industries
    Financials
    Business services
    Infrastructure
    Real Estate
22. **Djibouti**
    Extractive industries
23. **Egypt**
    Agribusiness & Food
    Extractive industries
    Financials
    Health care
24. **Gabon**
    Business services

25. Ghana
Agribusiness & Food
Consumer Services
Extractive industries
Financials
Health care
Industrials
Infrastructure
Real Estate

26. Kenya
Agribusiness & Food
Consumer Services
Extractive industries
Financials
Industrials
Business services
Infrastructure
Real Estate

27. Liberia
Extractive industries
Financials
Business services

28. Libya
Agribusiness & Food

29. Madagascar
Agribusiness & Food
Extractive industries
Financials
Industrials
Business services

30. Malawi
Business services

31. Mauritania
Extractive industries

32. Mauritius
Agribusiness & Food
Health care
Industrials
Business services
Real Estate

33. Morocco
Agribusiness & Food
Extractive industries
Industrials
Business services
Infrastructure

34. Mozambique
Extractive industries
Health care

35. Namibia
Agribusiness & Food

36. Nigeria
Extractive industries
Financials
Industrials
Business services
Infrastructure
Real Estate

37. Rwanda
Financials

38. Senegal
Consumer Services
Extractive industries
Industrials

39. Sierra Leone
Agribusiness & Food
Financials
Business services
Infrastructure

40. South Africa
Agribusiness & Food
Consumer Services
Extractive industries
Financials
Health care
Industrials
Business services
Infrastructure

41. Tanzania
Agribusiness & Food
Extractive industries
Financials
Industrials
Infrastructure
Real Estate

42. Togo
Financials

43. Tunisia
Agribusiness & Food
Extractive industries
Financials
Health care
Industrials
Business services

44. Uganda
Financials
Business services
Infrastructure
Real Estate

45. Zambia
Agribusiness & Food
Extractive industries
Financials
Industrials
Real Estate

46. Zimbabwe
Extractive industries

East Africa Region
Financials

West Africa Region
Financials

Pan Africa
Agribusiness & Food
Financials
Industrials
Business services
Infrastructure

47. Afghanistan
Financials

48. Azerbaijan
Financials

49. Bangladesh
Consumer Services
Financials
Health care
Industrials

50. Cambodia
Financials

51. China
Agribusiness & Food
Consumer Services
Education
Extractive industries
Financials
Health care
Industrials
Business services
Infrastructure
Real Estate

52. Fiji
Business services

53. India
Agribusiness & Food
Consumer Services
Education
Extractive industries
Financials
Health care
Industrials
Business services
Infrastructure
Real Estate

54. Indonesia
Agribusiness & Food
Consumer Services
Extractive industries
Financials
Industrials
Business services
Infrastructure
Real Estate

55. Kazakhstan
Financials
Industrials
Business services

56. Kyrgyzstan
Consumer Services

57. Malaysia
Consumer Services
Extractive industries
Financials
Industrials
Business services
Infrastructure

58. Pakistan
Agribusiness & Food
Consumer Services
Extractive industries
Financials
Health care

59. Papua New Guinea
Agribusiness & Food
Extractive industries
Industrials

60. Philippines
Consumer Services
Extractive industries
Financials
Health care
Business services

61. Samoa
Agribusiness & Food

62. Solomon Islands
Extractive industries

63. Sri Lanka
Agribusiness & Food
Financials
Health care
Industrials

64. Tajikistan
Financials

65. Thailand
Agribusiness & Food
Consumer Services
Education
Health care
Industrials
Business services

66. Tonga
Industrials

67. Vanuatu
Consumer Services

68. Vietnam
Consumer Services
Industrials

69. Yemen
Industrials

Asia Region
Extractive industries
Financials
Industrials
Business services

Note: Excludes Europe.

241

An ambition for impact

An ambition for impact
2012–2017

2012

World events...

- *London hosts the Summer Olympics.*
- *Rio 2012 – the UN Conference on Sustainable Development – is the third international conference on sustainable development aimed at reconciling the economic and environmental goals of the global community.*
- *Worst power blackout in world history leaves 620 million people in India without electricity.*
- *Barack Obama re-elected for a second term as US president.*

2013

- *Death at the age of 95 of Nelson Mandela, South Africa's first black president.*
- *Death of former prime minister Margaret Thatcher followed by funeral at St Paul's Cathedral.*
- *Ukrainian police break up student protest camp in Kiev's Independence Square marks the beginning of the crisis in Ukraine.*

2014

- *Mysterious disappearance of Malaysian Airlines Flight 370.*
- *Narendra Modi leads Bharatiya Janata Party (BJP) to victory in India's parliamentary election, first party in thirty years to win an absolute majority.*
- *Ebola outbreaks peak in West Africa.*
- *Emergence of Islamic State of Iraq and Syria (ISIS).*
- *Russia annexes Crimea.*

CDC events...

2012
- Publication of CDC's strategy for 2012-2016, along with a new mission statement and the return to direct investing.
- Rapidly-growing CDC moves to new, larger premises at 123 Victoria Street.
- Justine Greening becomes secretary of state at DFID.
- CDC takes on management of DFID's £75 million Impact Fund.
- CDC supports over one thousand businesses.

2013
- Thirteen new direct investments contribute to a record-breaking total of sums committed by CDC in a single year, amounting altogether to over $1 billion.
- Richard Gillingwater succeeded as chairman of CDC by Graham Wrigley.
- CDC and Standard Chartered Bank sign a Master Risk Participation Agreement for $50 million, increased to $150 million in 2014, to support businesses in the poorest countries, including those hit by the Ebola crisis.

2014
- DFID agrees a long-term capital increase of £735 million to help fund CDC's rapid and continuing growth.
- Annual report shows that equity funds dropped from fifty-one per cent to twenty-nine per cent of the total number of CDC investments.
- Harvard professor Josh Lerner appointed to produce a report evaluating the development impact of CDC's funds strategy 2004-2012. It concludes that CDC had had "a transformative effect on its markets of interest".

Right: Lilongwe, Malawi. In 1948, Lord Trefgarne established three regional offices to cover Africa – that for Central Africa being in Nyasaland at Zomba, the small colonial capital and attractive university town. In 1949, the office moved down the road to Blantyre, the country's commercial heart. Some of CDC's most pioneering ventures at that time – as epitomised by Operation Ploughshare and the Lindi Convoy – were located in the country that became Malawi. Seventy years later, CDC is returning to its roots by investing meaningful amounts of money in catalytic projects, where there is the opportunity to make a real difference and accelerate development.

2015

- *The Sustainable Development Goals – a collection of 17 goals covering social and economic development issues – are set by the United Nations, aimed at transforming the world by 2030.*
- *Earthquake in Kathmandu kills 8,000 and triggers avalanche on Mount Everest, killing 18 climbers.*
- *Russian intervention marks a turning point in the Syrian Civil War.*

- Africa and Asia funds teams adopt new 'Intermediate Equity' strategy aimed at mobilising human capital.
- Diana Noble introduces The Africa List to develop the business, management and leadership skills of young African men and women working in the private sector.
- Introduction of the DFID-funded 'Development Impact Accelerator Facility'.

2016

- *The migration crisis reaches a peak with refugees, asylum seekers and other displaced persons flooding into Europe from Syria, Afghanistan and Africa, posing mounting problems for the EU.*
- *Referendum results in the UK voting to leave the European Union, after which prime minister David Cameron steps down, to be replaced by Theresa May.*
- *Donald Trump elected president of the US against the odds, defeating Hillary Clinton.*

- Staff numbers increase by thirty-nine per cent over the year, from 161 to 224 – the steepest rise in recruitment since Lord Trefgarne was first building CDC in the late 1940s.
- Priti Patel becomes secretary of state at DFID.
- New Bill introduced in Parliament to enable DFID to provide additional capital when needed by CDC to fund higher levels of investment.

2017

- *Snap election returns Theresa May and the Conservatives, but with a reduced majority.*
- *Robert Mugabe steps down as president of Zimbabwe and is replaced by Emmerson Mnangagwa.*
- *An estimated 400,000 Rohingyans flee mass killings and persecution in Myanmar, creating a refugee crisis.*
- *Global growth starts to pick up after nearly ten years of recession following the financial crisis of 2008.*

- A new Commonwealth Development Corporation Act 2017 raises the limit on government assistance from £1,500 million to £6,000 million with the facility to raise this again to £12,000 million.
- New five-year strategic framework for 2017-21, entitled Investing to Transform Lives, puts special emphasis on pioneering and innovative strategies.
- Diana Noble steps down as CEO and is succeeded by Nick O'Donohoe.
- Penny Mordaunt becomes secretary of state at DFID.

Chapter eight

An ambition for impact

When first approached about taking over as CDC's next CEO, Diana Noble was well aware in advance of what would be expected of her because DFID and CDC had already, on 31 May 2011, announced a new seven-point business plan for 2011-2015 that Richard Laing's successor would be required to flesh out and implement.

The plan signalled significant organisational change and expansion, to the extent that in many ways it was as if a whole new development finance institution were being constructed from scratch. There were to be new ways of investing, a new investment universe, new development objectives, an innovation division, greater transparency, an updated investment code and a revised remuneration framework.

The job of overseeing such drastic restructuring clearly presented a considerable challenge, but after some deliberation, as well as discussions with the board of CDC based on a paper she had written setting out what she saw as her direction of travel, the highly-regarded former partner in private equity firm Schroder Ventures decided that it would nevertheless be well worth undertaking. Part of her reasoning was that because of the pioneering direct investments that it had made in the past, CDC remained highly respected in its markets. And the strong balance sheet that she would inherit would provide a financial safety net if things did not straightaway go exactly according to plan.

"The plan signalled significant organisational change and expansion, to the extent that in many ways it was as if a whole new development finance institution were being constructed from scratch."

Above: The sun rising over Globeleq's Droogfontein Power plant in South Africa, located near the town of Kimberley in the Northern Cape, and one of the first utility scale solar plants in Africa. The plant uses 168,750 PV panels to generate electricity that is exported into Eskom, South Africa's national grid. Producing 85 GWh per year, it supplies enough clean renewable electricity to meet the needs of nearly 19,000 average-sized homes.

The first six months after taking up her post in November 2011 were spent working almost full-time on developing the new strategy, confirming and building upon the business plan. This involved amending the original drafts worked upon by the interim team in conjunction with DFID, a process so time-consuming in itself that the five-year plan period had to be pushed back a year to 2012-2016.

DFID had given Diana Noble three clear overall guidelines for the new strategy: to make new investments only in Africa and South Asia, to get the balance right between developmental impact and financial return and, most significantly, to start investing directly in businesses again, rather than only through the medium of fund managers.

Investing only in Africa and South Asia generally provided a welcome strategic focus, but it also raised the difficult issue of what to do about India. The problem there was that while there was still great poverty in many areas of the country, the overall growth of its fast-emerging economy meant that it did not seem to some to be in real need of CDC's investment. This had been one area of specific concern for Andrew Mitchell. Meeting this particular challenge was achieved through the creation of a management tool that would help address the dual mandate of balancing developmental impact and financial return.

What became known as the Development Impact Grid was the result of some brainstorming by the lead team at CDC, aimed at coming up with a simple formula that would help to clearly identify those investment possibilities with the greatest impact potential without long subjective debate. This was deemed an essential task. The new CDC had to be able to demonstrate objectively that it was targeting the right, tougher investments and to define what that meant. The key underlying factor here, it was decided, should be job creation. Every government needs to create jobs, especially those with rapidly increasing populations. And putting a human face on stories of impact through job creation could inspire the wider CDC team.

To help in deciding where to invest to achieve the greatest development impact in this respect, the grid featured a system of grading countries in terms of the difficulty they had in attracting investment and rating the various sectors by their propensity to create jobs, the combined ratings providing a measurement by which potential investments could be filtered and monitored. In this process, manufacturing, agribusiness, infrastructure, financial services, construction, health and education, were identified as the priority sectors.

Designing a strategy for the third of DFID's directives – a return to significant direct investing – was initially challenging. Since 2004, CDC's core competence had been in selecting fund managers so that now, with few staff having any direct investing expertise and without the benefit of its former regional network, it was difficult to set a timescale within which to effect the turnaround. The markets needed to be understood in depth if the possibilities for the future were to be properly identified, but this would take time. To deal with this, Mark Pay – a returnee from Actis and CDC, brought in by Diana Noble to lead on direct equity investing – developed a 'platform' strategy that involved investment with successful partners who might be encouraged, with CDC's support, to venture into the targeted, more difficult countries. The total sum to be allotted for direct equity was initially set at $1 billion over the first five years – a figure that the board thought lacked ambition, doubling it to $2 billion.

Bringing all these various strands together, CDC's revised strategy for 2012-2016 was published in May 2012. It included a lengthened, more explicit mission statement, namely: "To support the building of businesses throughout Africa and South Asia, to create jobs and make a lasting difference to people's lives in some of the world's poorest places". This statement was also embedded in the new investment policy, part of a set of integrated governance documents forming the rules by which CDC would be run that, while they were not finally signed off for another year, were comprehensive, clear and simple and have stood the test of time. They included CDC's objectives of sustainable development and economic growth, demonstrating the possibility of successful investment to would-be but reluctant private investors and, where possible, mobilising private investment alongside its own. A new code of responsible investing, setting out how CDC would apply strict business integrity, social and environmental standards, was also part of this foundational work.

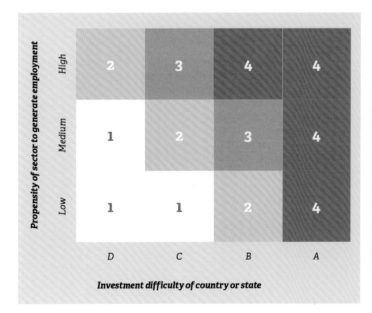

Above: The Development Impact Grid was designed to be a simple tool to identify potential investments without long subjective debate. Grading countries by their difficulty of investment and sectors by their propensity to create jobs. The combined ratings provided a measurement by which potential investments could be filtered and monitored.

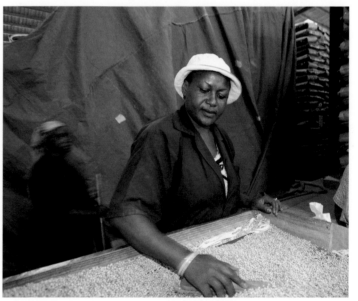

Above: Pigeon peas being processed at the Export Trading Group's quayside facility in the Tanzanian port of Dar es Salaam. With more than 300 warehouses, procurement, processing and distribution centres throughout Africa, ETG buys crops such as pigeon peas, chick peas, soya beans, cashew nuts and sesame seeds from literally millions of subsistence farmers in some of the continent's poorest countries, notably Malawi, Mozambique and Tanzania. After processing and packaging, these commodities are either marketed locally and in neighbouring African countries, or exported worldwide. As well as providing a livelihood for its suppliers, ETG directly employs more than 7,000 people.

Diana Noble

Diana Noble was educated at Sherborne School and at SOAS, where she studied law. Joining the investment bank Schroders as a trainee, she became a partner of Schroder Ventures, remaining there for twelve years before leaving to take the role of founder CEO of eVentures, a private equity firm company backing start-up Internet businesses. She then went on to become the founding MD of Reed Elsevier's venture capital fund. Immediately prior to joining CDC she worked for the Clinton Foundation's Health Access Initiative in a number of roles, including that of executive vice-president for operations, overseeing the expansion of a global programme for the scaling up of children's access to HIV and AIDS treatment in poor countries.

CEO and executive director of CDC from November 2011 to June 2017, she took on the challenging task of providing leadership in the reshaping and rebuilding of CDC after some difficult years. She did this with energy and commitment, and in a collegiate style that made working for CDC during those years an enjoyable experience, even when it involved very long hours. In many ways she embodied the aspirational values and identities she later identified as capturing the essence of working for CDC – those of being compassionate, thoughtful, fast-moving and non-defensive, facing up to tough challenges and recognising that while the work that CDC was trying to do wasn't easy, it was enormously worthwhile. As she often pointed out, the aim was never just about investment, but about making a real difference to people's lives in some of the poorest places on earth.

Her achievement in helping to re-confirm CDC's reputation as one of the world's most effective DFIs was recognised in June 2017, shortly after she stepped down as CEO, with the award in the Queen's Birthday Honours list of a CBE for services to international development. Since leaving CDC, Diana has taken up roles as a non-executive director of the Bank of England, the Business Growth Fund (the UK and Ireland's most active investor in growing businesses), and of MedAccess (CDC's new provider of financial guarantees to manufacturers of drugs and diagnostics). She has also founded Kirkos Partners, which offers advice to leaders of private equity firms.

In September 2012, CDC and DFID unveiled the new policy at an event held at Church House, the London base of the Anglican Church. Even though the existing fund investing team and its support staff formed a core from which to build, it really felt as if a new development finance institution were being created and this was both challenging and exciting. An ambitious recruitment drive got underway, new processes had to be established and new, larger premises found, with an eventual move across the road to 123 Victoria Street. With so much to be done, it was frustrating but hardly surprising that when Diana Noble came to review 2012 after her first year in office there was little hard evidence to report of impact from the new strategy at work.

The one and only direct equity investment had been made in November 2012 through a facility of $32.5 million provided to the founders of a pan-African agribusiness, Export Trading Group, to enable them to expand their operations, to build food-processing factories throughout sub-Saharan Africa. ETG ran a supply chain, buying from smallholder farmers and then processing, warehousing and selling their produce, employing 7,000 people. This satisfied all the demands of CDC's new investment strategy – prioritising agribusiness, helping smallholder farmers and being both commercial and developmental – that had been so loudly called for in recent years.

Of the year's eight other new commitments, six had been to equity funds, proving that those remaining from the funds team were still diligently delivering the goods, while managing the existing 155 funds with 84 different fund managers, who, between them, were overseeing investments in 1,250 businesses. The new funds were to support businesses in the priority sectors, including African housing and real estate, Indian microfinance and funds focusing on SMEs. The $20 million commitment to the Phatisa Pan-African Housing Fund was for building middle and lower-income housing in Eastern and Southern Africa. The $75 million commitment to African real estate was to Actis's Africa Real Estate Fund 2 and although investing in real estate, especially shopping malls, had come in for criticism, CDC strongly believed in its development value and it was one of the strategies that CDC and Actis continued to share in common.

The two remaining new commitments – to Investec Africa Credit Opportunities, a sub-Saharan African credit fund, and a follow-up loan to Diamond Bank in Nigeria – came from a new team that had been formed under Holger Rothenbusch, another CDC alumnus, brought back into the fold from DEG, the German DFI, to develop strategies for direct debt and financial institutions. CDC had done some lending since the change of investment policy in 2008, but this had been small-scale, limited to a relatively small number of co-investments and investments in debt funds. Because it was no longer set up to manage direct debt investment – one of its mainstream routes to investing of old – the strategy that CDC initially adopted was to borrow the best ideas and processes from others, through developing close relations and then co-lending with fellow DFIs including IFC, DEG, FMO and Proparco. Thereafter, as confidence built, the plan was for the growing debt team to partner with these other DFIs and develop mutually-beneficial relationships with commercial banks in providing trade finance, before going on to extend its capability.

The following year, 2013, turned out to be much busier. Thirteen new direct investments were investigated and negotiated, which, when added to investments in another thirteen funds, amounted to a record-breaking total of sums committed for one year of £608 million. The commitments varied widely and included Bridge International Academies, helping to provide affordable education for low-income families in Kenya; Equitas, supplying microfinance loans to clients in the poorer Indian states; Rainbow Healthcare, expanding its chain of paediatric hospitals in India; and the largest ever investment in an Indian fund, with $200 million going into the India Infrastructure Fund II, managed by part of IDFC, with which CDC had a long history. A bold re-entry into Zimbabwe was made with Takura, a commitment of $15 million to its Takura II fund going to support exceptional local managers. Takura II helped to rescue businesses such as Cairns Foods, a company providing livelihoods not only for its direct employees but also for the thousands of smallholder farmers supplying it with raw foodstuffs. With Robert Mugabe still very much in control as president, it was brave of CDC to contemplate such an initiative.

Elsewhere, what really stood out was the first direct investment for a very long time in an oil palm plantation. The $18 million committed to buying twenty-seven per cent of the equity of Feronia, a large agribusiness primarily producing palm oil in the Democratic Republic of the Congo, was the most ambitious and challenging investment of these early years – one with the potential to be hugely developmental.

Meanwhile, during 2013, DFID was looking for a new CDC chairman. Richard Gillingwater had held the position since 2009, steadying CDC through a difficult period of upheaval immediately before and after the change of government and the implementation of the new incoming Conservative vision that followed. Having then to find a high-quality replacement for Richard Laing had not been easy, but, along with Andrew Mitchell, he'd been instrumental in identifying an outstanding candidate and persuading her to take on the demanding job. Hardworking and committed, he had regularly led board visits to CDC's areas of operations overseas to meet with fund managers and portfolio companies. On standing down, he could look back with some satisfaction over his spell as chairman, having successfully overseen the re-set of CDC's strategy and having also recruited a talented new team to drive it through.

After a duly diligent search, the person asked by the new Secretary of State Justine Greening in July 2013 to succeed him was Graham Wrigley, who, as a former Aureos chairman, was already familiar with CDC. His interest had been stimulated by DFID's future vision, outlined to him during preliminary discussions with its Permanent Secretary Mark Lowcock that included the prospect that as long as the demand for capital in its markets in Africa and South Asia could be demonstrated, substantial government funding would be available to support CDC's return to direct equity and debt investing.

Graham Wrigley

As a founder partner of private equity investor Permira, Graham Wrigley shared a career background with Diana Noble at Schroders. He was a member of the firm's management board as it grew into one of the world's leading private equity firms, with over $20 billion under management. He was appointed to be chairman of CDC by Justine Greening in August 2013.

Born in 1962 and educated at Simon Langton Grammar School in Canterbury, Kent before studying law and economics at St John's College, Cambridge, Graham had decided by the age of eighteen that he wanted to make a contribution to international development at some stage in his career. After working for Bain & Co and gaining an MBA from INSEAD, he acted on this, stepping down from Permira in 2006 and enrolling at the School of Oriental and African Studies in London to take a Master's degree in development economics, his dissertation focusing on investing in microfinance in India. He then went on to work in microfinance and SME investing, including four years as chairman of Aureos from 2008-2012, during which time he also advised CDC on its largest new direct equity investments.

In addition to his chairmanship of CDC, he also works with several charities, including Sir Edmund Hillary's Himalayan Trust UK, where he serves as chairman, and has volunteered for them for over 35 years.

With his knowledge and first-hand experience of global investment businesses, a passion for development and also a reputation for being strong on building relationships and trust at all levels, Graham Wrigley was ideally suited to chart and navigate the organisation's journey going forward after the challenges of the previous years.

Right: In 2013, CDC invested $17.3 million of equity in Rainbow Hospitals, India's largest specialist paediatric and maternity care provider, providing high-quality facilities throughout India. With a further $15 million invested to date, CDC has supported the group's expansion into key new locations in Indian cities such as Delhi, Bangalore and Chennai. It continues to expand and aims to treat over 1 million patients every year. It is pioneering paediatric care in India and providing specialist services that were previously not available in the country.

Feronia

The first of Feronia's three remote oil palm plantations had originally been developed as long ago as 1911 by Lever Brothers, now Unilever, which had built a far-flung and now ageing infrastructure that provided the only source of income for 100,000 people in a war-torn country with an increasing population. Operations had suffered significantly during the two Congo wars that took place between 1996 and 2003, when a lack of management and investment meant that each plantation was left to keep going as best it could, in virtual isolation from the head office. With no input from overseas during this time, senior management in the DRC kept the business running, often at great personal risk. Unilever, had already disposed of a number of its DRC plantations over time and in 2009 it sold out to a Canadian-listed company, Feronia Inc.

Four years later, in 2013, the potential to achieve significant development impact by stepping in to save Feronia was clear to see. Here was the largest and oldest private sector employer in one of the world's hardest places, producing edible oil – vital for healthy life – and it was in a dire situation. The company was producing palm oil wholly for domestic use in a country where the demand from a large and growing population hugely exceeded supply, as a result of which the consumption of vegetable fat per head was low, with poor nutritional effects. Although admittedly a high-risk investment, CDC reasoned that money had already been ploughed in by others in an effort to turn the ailing business around and that with an extra injection from CDC the cash flow would eventually turn positive. And if that took longer for any reason, CDC's strong balance sheet meant that it could, if necessary, make further investments. On that basis it went ahead, making a commitment in 2013, and did indeed follow up in the following years with further money.

Within a few years, CDC was to be in control of the distressed company, with yet more funds still needed before it might break even. Out of necessity it stepped in again, providing leadership to a restructured management and board, which took on the huge task of continuing with the rehabilitation of the old palm oil mills and the replanting of the three widespread and not easily accessible plantations, totalling some 107,000 hectares. CDC also persuaded its understandably sceptical fellow DFIs to provide critically-needed loan finance and to share the financial burden.

To help its already hard-pressed management tackle the massive task of improving health and safety for workers while also engaging with the dependent local communities, CDC's environmental and social responsibility team worked very closely with Feronia to define the company's E&S policies and practices and has since remained closely involved with their implementation throughout the investment. Because the locations were so remote, the DRC government had not been able to provide the normal services, such as housing, roads, healthcare, education, water, power and telecoms. Palm oil economics had changed irrevocably in the interim and managing the communities' high expectations of what could be provided and maintained in the way of infrastructure and services when the funds available were still not unlimited has had to be done in a sensitive and purposeful manner. However, a massive transformation has already been achieved. Where there was dereliction, there is now renewal. The plantations, mills, offices, houses, water boreholes, schools and clinics are being cared for once more. People are going about their business and everywhere there are signs of life returning – new flowerbeds as well as fruit and vegetable gardens are being planted and many goats and cockerels are audibly making their presence known. In all respects, CDC has been doing exactly what it was asked to do – assisting development and making a real difference to people lives in the hardest and poorest places.

Above: Office workers at Equitas, a leading Indian microfinance institution based in the south Indian state of Tamil Nadu. CDC made direct investments in 2013 and 2015 to support its work reaching poor and unbanked customers with a broad range of financial services.

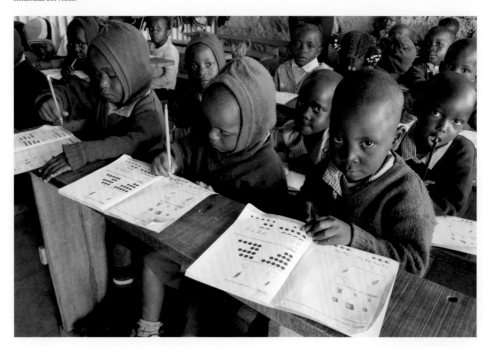

Above: An investment in 2013 helped Bridge International Academies to provide affordable education for low-income families in a number of African countries.

CDC had not received any government funding for twenty years, but in that time the requirements of international development aid worldwide had changed considerably. The establishment of the Millennium Development Goals for improving the lives of the world's poorest peoples, along with calls to respond to the effects of climate change, had underlined the fact that the needs of developing countries were such that they could not be met by public sector finance alone; private sector investment needed to be harnessed and promoted. In early 2012, DFID had therefore introduced its own pioneering private sector strategy, whereby it planned to extend its work beyond grant aid to investment of returnable capital in development projects. This being CDC's area of expertise, it was hoped that it would eventually play a major role, initially by managing DFID's innovative, albeit relatively small, 'impact facility', aimed at identifying fund investments that were borderline commercial but with high impact potential. At this time, the character and aims of 'impact investing' were in the early years of being formulated.

The idea of 'impact investing' had first been proposed by DFID to CDC in the autumn of 2011, when CDC was asked to manage a relatively small pot of money for investment with the managers of impact funds – identified as those that while offering little likelihood of a financial return would have high social impact by targeting small businesses that would benefit poor people as consumers, producers, suppliers or employees. CDC initially had reservations. Given that it was already at that time hiring professionals to build strong sustainable businesses of scale in what Andrew Mitchell defined as "the hardest places", with an emphasis very much on impact rather than financial return, it was concerned that if it now started looking for investments where the expected returns were even lower and the risk of failure higher, this could damage its reputation for high quality investing, even if some exciting impact resulted. Nevertheless, discussions continued throughout 2012 and were finalised by the end of the year, with CDC taking on the management of the DFID Impact Fund of £75 million.

The small new team formed to specifically implement the Impact Fund sat with the team managing CDC's investments in funds and over time the funds team embraced the new team, as it became clear that they were going through similar processes and making sensible judgements, but just further down the risk reward curve.

Realising the continuum, CDC itself was to embrace the concept of impact investing, and this led directly to later impact initiatives and to an important new strand of the next investment policy. But it took until 2014 for the DIF team to make its first investment, simply because there were so few fund managers with experience of impact investing in emerging markets. This initial investment of $15 million went into Novastar Ventures, a fund managed by a team based in Kenya and Ethiopia that aimed to invest in early stage businesses that supported the very poorest – those earning less than $2 a day – with essential goods and services.

For Graham Wrigley, these were exciting and inspiring propositions at both ends of the investing scale. Here was the chance for CDC to be part of the wider policy debate on investment within the overall aid agenda. At the same time, there was the opportunity to widen CDC's development impact further and to grow it substantially through a potential increase in funds available for investment in the years ahead. Having agreed to become chairman, and while waiting to take over, he prepared a memorandum calling for a review to consider all the possibilities for what CDC, building on the achievements since 2012, might look like in the future. On the agenda were the considerations of how large and fast it should grow, how it should avoid the over-commitments of the past, and how the growth should be funded, including an evaluation of the potential for a large capital increase.

Diana Noble and the management team had been initially cautious about even faster expansion, arguing that there could be a danger in growing too quickly and that CDC should stay on the path already agreed until a firm foundation had been established. With the heavy workload involved in rebuilding the organisation and making new direct investments there was already more than enough to do, and plenty that could go wrong, stretching the resources of the restructured CDC. However, the arguments in favour were persuasive, the strength of DFID's will to support the private sector giving CDC a potential for growth that could transform it now and for the future, presenting it with opportunities that could not be ignored. This proved convincing and the review went ahead with full management support. Its findings led to discussions followed by more detailed studies which were in turn to define CDC's future shape, size and funding in the ensuing years.

In 2014 CDC really started scaling up its activity. The record of what was achieved during that year is impressive, not so much in terms of the total amount of new investment commitments – which actually undershot the target, due to the unexpected delay in some negotiations – but more in the increased momentum of the organisation. The board, the management and the investment and support teams were working flat out, doing much hard thinking while also building the organisation and its processes for the future and engaging fully both with its shareholder, DFID, and the Treasury. Things actually began moving so quickly at this stage that there were times when there simply wasn't the capacity to take on any more. This was despite the fact that there had been a major recruitment exercise and that the number of committees had been expanded using external expertise, brought in to ease the pressure on the internal teams. At the same time, the number of investments being transacted and those in the pipeline clearly demonstrated that CDC needed more capital.

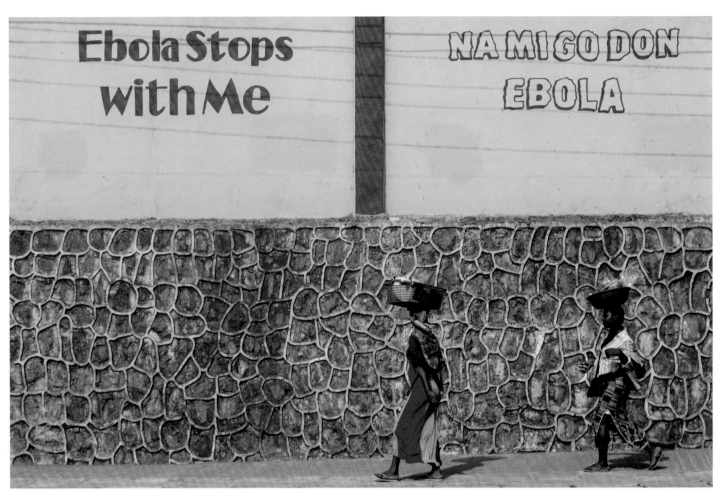

Above: CDC displayed fleetness-of-foot in responding speedily to the Ebola crisis in West Africa by setting up a risk-sharing agreement with Standard Chartered Bank to support dozens of businesses in Sierra Leone, one of the countries worst hit by the epidemic and one of the hardest places in which to operate. In the midst of the crisis, with the Sierra Leone economy in free fall and SCB's business clients there desperate for cash loans that the bank alone could not afford to take on, CDC offered to match all SCB's new loan finance up to $25 million, thereby helping to save threatened businesses and preserve jobs that might otherwise have been lost.

With her financial background, Secretary of State, Justine Greening, saw the value of private sector development, understood CDC's mission and championed its work, with the result that government support was readily forthcoming when needed. And it was urgently needed in the spring and summer of 2014 when the combination of a record number of commitments the previous year and a slowing of income from the sell-off of old legacy investments meant that CDC found itself facing potential cash flow difficulties. However, demonstrating the goodwill of DFID and the Treasury, CDC was rapidly able to get support for both a liquidity policy and a $1.2 billion debt facility with ten commercial banks, which together eased the situation, although in the event the debt facility was not actually used. Also, in the summer of 2014, DFID agreed with CDC's proposition that it needed a long-term capital increase to fund its growth and prepared the business case for a recapitalisation of £735 million, taking it up to the limit allowed by the Commonwealth Development Corporation Act of 1999. The recapitalisation was announced in July the following year.

The annual report for 2014 showed that, at £297 million, the commitments were less than half the previous year's record £608 million. While the drop was not of concern – CDC was working to five-year targets, finding annual measures unhelpful – it also contained evidence of a much more significant trend, this being the first year since 2004 in which funds accounted for less than half of the total number of completed investments, coming down from fifty-one per cent in 2013 to twenty-nine per cent in 2014. This trend was confirmed by the split of new commitments, with thirteen going directly into businesses and only five to funds. CDC could confidently say that it was primarily a direct investor once again.

The direct equity investments forged some new and mutually rewarding strategic partnerships with, among others, Grindrod, a South African transport logistics company that was planning to expand its operations northwards; Narayana Health, another provider of affordable healthcare in India, and RBL Bank, one of several institutions transforming the access of the poor in India and other countries to financial services. Later, in 2017, CDC was to publish a case study analysing the effect of hundreds of loans made by RBL to SMEs over the period 2013-2017, looking primarily at how the SMEs were performing before and after, and the results made the case in favour of DFIs such as CDC investing in such financial institutions. Also noteworthy was the renewed provision of trade finance through a risk-sharing agreement with another major strategic partner, Standard Chartered Bank. Towards the end of the year, during the West African Ebola crisis, this relationship sparked an initiative to support suffering businesses in Sierra Leone, undoubtedly one of the world's hardest places in which to operate. This was something of which CDC was particularly proud.

The Ebola virus epidemic that caused more than 10,000 deaths between 2013 and 2016 peaked in October 2014, with Sierra Leone one of the two countries most affected. That autumn, CEO Diana Noble attended the IMF meetings in Washington at which the international community searched for possible responses.

Discussing this later between themselves, she and Diana Layfield, CEO of the Africa Region for Standard Chartered Bank, explored what their two organisations together might be able do. CDC was not a relief organisation and neither was SCB, but a meaningful response was found in a risk-sharing agreement to support dozens of businesses in Sierra Leone.

The year before, CDC had looked at the problems faced by commercial banks following the reform measures put in place to strengthen the risk management of the banking sector known as Basel III. While well-intentioned, these measures were forcing banks in CDC's geographies to reduce their risk appetite, which often meant turning down loan requests from businesses they had previously supported. Partnering with DFIs was an option for the banks, but the DFIs' reputation for being slow and difficult to deal with put them off. Keen to challenge this perception, CDC and SCB had, in May 2013, signed a Master Risk Participation Agreement for up to $50 million, to share risk with private sector banks in trade finance, enabling transactions essential for oiling the wheels of international trade, and with the potential for high development impact. Such was the appetite, particularly in Bangladesh, that the sum was increased to $75 million later in the year and to $150 million in 2014. The two Dianas now built on this mutually supportive foundation in Sierra Leone.

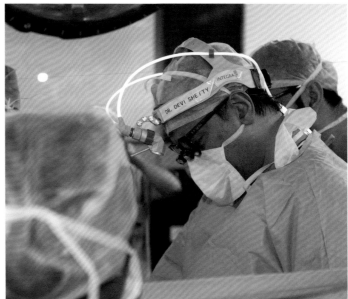

Above and right: The Indian hospital groups Narayana Healthcare and Rainbow Hospitals provide outstanding examples of CDC investments adding value in terms improving overall operational efficiency. After CDC's E&S team had first helped with energy, waste and water management in existing hospitals, paying for environmental audits to demonstrate how small changes could lead to big savings, the management of both groups adopted all these ideas with enthusiasm, calling for more audits and designing the results into their new hospitals, the first in India to meet international green building standards.

SCB had had an office in Freetown for a hundred years and knew that its customers, who would normally have been good risks, were running out of cash to continue their operations because, in the midst of the Ebola crisis, few people were able to make payments. And, given that the economy of Sierra Leone was in free-fall, the bank was neither able nor willing to take on much further risk. To provide the needed working capital, CDC offered to match all SCB's new finance up to $25 million. The debt team worked swiftly in reviewing the risk of a pre-agreed list of 15-20 companies with SCB, which agreed to take on the portfolio management. The two organisations pushed the deal through their respective decision-making processes, taking a mere six weeks to reach a formal legal agreement, and the funds were deployed quickly. It demonstrated CDC's fleetness of foot in helping the threatened businesses in Sierra Leone through the crisis and thereby securing jobs that might otherwise have been lost. Building on the partnership, a phase two was agreed in 2016, with more capital, more companies and longer loan periods. By strengthening the local operations of international banks, CDC can claim to be protecting them from closure or sale.

While the decrease in the number of investments made in funds in 2014 was significant, this did not mark the scaling down of the work of the two funds teams operating in Asia and Africa – quite the opposite, in fact, it actually prompted a fresh start. The calls for CDC to curtail this form of investment were still there, being considered too much at arm's length, with CDC unable to exercise sufficient control, add value or point to development impact. However, it knew the reality to be very different and was proud of the fact that CDC was generally recognised among investors as the pre-eminent funds investor in its geographies. An example of an innovative fund being committed at this time can be found in the Africa Renewable Energy Fund, managed by Berkeley Energy and building on the relationship built earlier by CDC in South East Asia. To justify carrying on investing in funds, CDC's management was therefore determined to establish and defend their credibility. To this end, it commissioned an eminent Harvard Business School academic to undertake a study of the past, while also bringing back another alumnus to develop a visionary strategy for the future.

Appointed in late 2014 to investigate the outcome of the funds invested between 2004 and 2012, Professor Josh Lerner and his team went on to produce a report, published the following year, verifying the positive contribution that CDC had made. Among other things, it pointed to the mobilisation of an impressive amount of other capital to work alongside that invested by CDC itself and the anchoring and mentoring of new locally-based fund managers, who then became established and successful in their markets. The report also highlighted the promotion of a culture change among fund managers, encouraging them to take an active and serious approach to ESG and business integrity issues. Indicating the widespread development impact that had been achieved, it concluded: "The organisation, in short, has had a transformative effect on its markets of interest".

In early 2015 Murray Grant returned to the CDC fold from Actis to head up the Africa funds team, and six months later he was in charge of the Asia team as well, instigating a re-badging and a new strategy. The aim of what was re-named 'intermediated equity' was to push the boundaries beyond simply investing in private equity funds to include the mobilisation of human capital. This entailed finding and supporting as many local entrepreneurs and skilled managers as possible, who would then develop businesses of all sizes, from vast numbers of informal businesses at the bottom to a few very large companies at the top. Investments through closed-end funds would be only one method. Freed from their time limits, traditional and new forms of 'intermediated' vehicles – investment holding companies akin to conglomerates, where centralised management facilities would support smaller local group businesses – would be promoted as well. The aim was to increase the number of formal-sector, mid-sized and large-scale businesses, notably in sub-Saharan Africa, where they were few in comparison to the informal sector and to other areas of the world.

Right: Feronia. The large oil palm fruit bunches are harvested using a traditional long-handled sickle with a chisel-shaped blade to dislodge them from the tops of the trees. Each dense fruit cluster can weigh up to 25kg, so harvesters, who will each work on up to several hundred trees in a day, have to make sure they stand well clear as the fruit falls to the ground.

The mobilisation of human capital was also the driving force behind another new enterprise established at this time. Thinking through how to develop people in CDC's geographies, recognising that it was always a challenge to find the right local people to manage investee companies and that without decent management, no amount of money would lead to impact or returns, CDC's answer was to identify and bring together a network of aspiring business leaders in key areas, focussing on the smaller countries in Africa where the need was perceived as being most critical and where such networks were lacking. As well as encouraging the personal development of the individuals involved, The Africa List aimed to provide CDC with insights into the countries and their investment opportunities, promoting CDC's development mandate in a new way.

While some at CDC had expected that 2015 might see a change of pace from new initiatives to consolidating, completing and embedding the work already started, the reality couldn't have been more different. At DFID's offices, Justine Greening was also promoting innovation. Under her leadership, and as part of its new private sector strategy, the department had announced that it was going to make available a large pool of capital available for undertaking new development opportunities, using new returnable instruments aimed primarily at making impact. The DFID team started coming up with ideas for such opportunities, while also considering which organisations, such as IFC and other European DFIs, might undertake them. However, questions were asked as to why it should be doing this externally when Britain had its own, wholly government-owned DFI, which by this time was relatively small compared to its European counterparts. Acting on this, DFID approached CDC's chairman in late spring to open a discussion on the subject of CDC doing even more.

Left: Site preparation in readiness for planting. In early 2015 CDC invested $15 million into Miro Forestry, operating sustainable forestry plantations in Sierra Leone and neighbouring Ghana, planting only on degraded and unused land and selling its timber mainly for local construction.

Above: Occupying a spectacular coastal location in the Eastern Cape between the townships of Jeffreys Bay and Humansdorp, Globeleq's Jeffreys Bay Wind Farm consists of sixty 80-metre high turbines spread over a total area of 3,700 hectares, just four per cent of which is covered by the turbines while the rest is cultivated farmland.

Opened in 2014, the farm produces 460GWh of electricity, serving the needs of more than 114,000 households. A percentage of the operating revenues are used to benefit the local community through socio-economic and enterprise programmes.

The Africa List

At a meeting of the heads of European DFIs, Diana Noble noted that everyone was talking about money and investments, but no one was talking about people. Wanting CDC to be different, and believing passionately that it is great leaders and management rather than capital alone that determine successful businesses, she launched a project to look at how CDC could best support the next generation of business leaders in the markets it serves. This led to the recruitment of Dirk Holshausen, who, as part of his MBA, had developed a network of aspiring leaders in his native Zimbabwe, and who was now asked to build something similar for CDC in other African countries.

The Africa List he set up comprises a network of young African men and women who are working in the private sector and whose achievements suggest that they have the potential to attain senior leadership roles as the heads, CEOs and non-executive directors of one of the top 100 companies in their respective countries, if they have not already done so. CDC's contribution is to orchestrate the ongoing search for such leaders, using its own extended networks, and then to provide them with opportunities to develop and share their talents, skills and professional networks in order to improve their leadership capabilities and to help them build better businesses faster.

The Africa List network was launched in Uganda in 2014 and by late 2017 had been extended to Zambia, Tanzania, the DRC and Ethiopia, altogether including 500 top companies and 1,000 leaders across five of Africa's fastest growing markets. Courses and continuous learning opportunities have been provided through partnering with top tier business schools and strategy firms, among which are Saïd Business School at Oxford University, London School of Economics, McKinsey, Deloitte, Bain & Company and PwC. The aim is to continue to expand to countries carefully selected as the next growth centres of the continent, supporting the leaders in those markets who are responsible for shaping the next decade of growth.

Following this up, the chairman wrote a note to his CEO entitled 'Tectonic Plates', to capture the seismic implications of what he saw as a pivotal moment in CDC's history. And he told his board that it brought CDC to "a remarkable crossroads ... with enormous opportunities (but with real risks)". The board was initially hesitant, concerned that CDC was in danger of trying to run before it could walk, but was eventually persuaded after it was acknowledged that CDC would only embark on a new venture where the case had been convincingly made beforehand. It was therefore agreed that the management should consider which, if any, of these development opportunities it would be prepared to take on, while at the same time coming up with its own ideas for impact investing by CDC, along with the implication of managing more capital over and above the £735 million that Justine Greening had just announced.

This led to a process, starting in October 2015 and lasting a year, that used a set of provisos known as the 'Three Green Lights' for deciding which of DFID's and which of its own proposals CDC would take on, as well as any others put forward for consideration from elsewhere. To qualify for CDC's acceptance, any proposals would have to be highly developmental and sustainable; CDC would have to have the ability to carry them through; and – very importantly – CDC had to believe that they would actually work and would lead to meaningful impact. Only those that both CDC and DFID mutually agreed had the potential to qualify on all three counts would go ahead.

It soon became clear that these innovative strategies would not only carry higher risk, but would also achieve impact in ways that were different from those associated with CDC's core business, where there was a requirement for financial returns as well as impact. As such, they needed careful thought and discipline, and it was decided that they should be considered apart from CDC's continuing investment approach. This separation marked the start of the journey towards establishing CDC's strategy for 2017-2021, with two distinct strands to its investment policy, one covering the ongoing commercial approach and the other directed towards the pioneering more targeted and higher-risk strategies.

Within CDC's management, attitudes towards the more challenging sort of impact investing had already changed considerably. The work that the team managing the small DFID Impact Fund was doing alongside the commercial fund of funds selection teams had inspired the MD for direct equity, Mark Pay, to develop an equivalent team to work alongside the direct equity team, identifying high quality but higher risk investments. With the board's support, he set about looking for the right person to lead it, who, once identified, was encouraged to write a proposal for DFID. Following a successful pilot, DFID duly provided the finance. The £40 million CDC-managed DFID-funded Impact Accelerator Facility was underway.

Charged with managing DFID's pot of money, the DIAF team, which grew from a one-man band in 2015 to a staff of fifteen two years later, would only recommend an investment if there was a compelling impact story that could be told in advance, with a clear challenge and solution involving CDC's participation, but where it was also clear that the risk of failure would normally rule out CDC's investment. Early investments in Rwanda, the DRC and Malawi demonstrated this to good effect.

The first of these, in 2015, was Africa Improved Foods. With planned state of the art facilities in Rwanda (and with an aspiration to expand to Ethiopia), AIF was proposing to process raw materials from local smallholders to produce foodstuffs used by the World Food Programme for fighting malnutrition in infants and lactating mothers, but the carefully constructed plan, with many parties involved, was in danger of failing when CDC came to its rescue with an investment of $4.5 million.

The next investment, in 2016, was Virunga Power, a hydro-power business providing energy to the communities living in and around the Virunga National Park in the eastern DRC, a challenging post-conflict zone known for its mountain gorillas that were protected by the Virunga Foundation, the charity that had set it up. CDC's mezzanine loan of $9 million was the first repayable finance to have been invested in the area since 1984, with a limited amount of supplementary grant funding also available for the purpose of building capacity and providing technical expertise to the management team. CDC assisted with the preparation of documentation such as tariff agreements, and, in doing so, helped to instil in Virunga Power's managers the business disciplines that would prepare it for attracting fully commercial investment in the future, as well as improving health and safety.

In Malawi, 14Trees was a joint venture with cement multinational LafargeHolcim (which had purchased CDC's Pan African Cement) to produce environmentally friendly soil-stabilised bricks in Lilongwe and, by doing so, saving the trees used to fire traditional clay bricks. This venture kick-started the team to make a run of investments in Malawi with $32 million invested to the end of 2017. Included among them was a macadamia farm north of Mzuzu, where irrigation was provided to nearby smallholders growing chillies and paprika under contract to Nando's; a poultry business in Blantyre; and Agricane, a project to support smallholder farmers growing sugar cane in the Shire Valley. To those sceptical about the wisdom of such concentration, the DIAF team argued that in Malawi CDC was taking the lead in what was one of the poorest countries in the world, with an agriculture-based economy in which few other people were investing. Through making it a focus of attention by investing meaningful amounts of money in really catalytic projects, there was a chance to turn the dial – to make a real difference and accelerate development. To anyone who recalled the level of past investment by CDC in Malawi that had ceased in the late 1990s, this would be a demonstration that CDC was returning to its roots.

Elsewhere in CDC's world, there were twenty-seven new commitments in 2015, amounting to £713 million, more than double the year before, of which two-thirds was directly invested in businesses. Included among them were several firsts. To support the construction and operation of telecommunication towers, debt of $20.3 million invested in the Irrawaddy Green Tower Project represented CDC's first ever investment in Myanmar, with its environmental and social responsibility (E&S) team working alongside other DFIs to improve health and safety standards in a country where these had been noticeably lacking. Another investment – in Zambia – also helped to develop telecoms towers with the aim of improving coverage.

"To anyone who recalled the level of past investment by CDC in Malawi that had ceased in the late 1990s, this would be a demonstration that CDC was returning to its roots."

Left: CDC's first-ever investment in Myanmar, Irrawaddy Green Towers is rolling out telecom towers across the country, establishing a mobile communication network that will help to end decades of isolation. As an important part of CDC's involvement, the E&S team has been working alongside other DFIs to improve health and safety standards in a country where these had previously been noticeably lacking.

Top and above: As a company engaged in managing container freight terminals in India – a business that involves the potentially hazardous manual transfer of goods from trucks to containers – Pristine Logistics has benefitted hugely from the improved standards encouraged by CDC's E&S team. Working conditions have been transformed as a result and the company has received its Integrated ISO for quality, environment and health and safety.

A further two investments in Pakistan were the first direct investments by CDC since the 1990s. One of these re-kindled a relationship with the Aga Khan Foundation, an investment of $122 million going to support the privatisation of Habib Bank, Pakistan's largest commercial bank. The re-establishment of the partnership with the foundation would also see CDC investing in AKFED in order to develop and build power stations in Africa, another example of CDC working with its partners to expand into new geographies. Another investment was in Pristine Logistics, a rail-freight infrastructure developer and operator in the poorer states of India, where CDC again helped to transform health and safety standards and professionalise ESG management.

That £713 million total for the year's new commitments would have been even more impressive – up to nearly £1 billion - had it not been for the exclusion of the takeover, alongside fellow DFI, Norfund, of Globeleq Africa, which had become sub-Saharan Africa's largest independent power producer. Valued at $426 million (£277 million), the deal was the largest in CDC's history, but because it involved transfers of its assets back to CDC from Actis Infrastructure Fund 2, it failed to register as a new commitment. It was, nevertheless, a bold and ambitious undertaking and the great effort that it involved was justified by the development potential.

Every country needs power, but there were very few experienced and appropriately funded risk-takers, trusted by African governments, who could be relied upon to develop new greenfield power stations from scratch in the poorest countries of Africa, which was where they were most needed. The deal that was finalised in mid-2015 saw CDC take a controlling seventy per cent stake, the first significant directly-held majority holding taken on since the change in strategy. It was also a project that fitted well within CDC's platform strategy, the cash flows from existing power stations providing a strong foundation for undertaking risky and uncommercial projects elsewhere, especially in the hardest countries, so as to multiply Globeleq's power portfolio in the long-term, with huge developmental benefits.

CDC and Norfund together then set about making major changes to Globeleq's management and board and overhauled its systems to equip it for managing a portfolio that included some of the very first renewable wind and solar power stations in the region, and also to fire up the fresh strategy of promoting the development of new projects, as well as the expansion of existing ones, throughout sub-Saharan Africa. By 2018 it was managing eight operational power stations using various technologies and was in the process of developing five more new or enlargement projects in a number of sub-Saharan countries, each of which would add much needed megawatts to the respective national grids, with the determination to do much more.

Appointing Globeleq's board and the executive team and controlling strategy, while maintaining its status as an investment, was what Graham Wrigley characterised as a "CDC-managed business of old, but with a twenty-first century twist". Globeleq was to become an anchor investment within CDC's portfolio, and successfully completing such a major and complex transaction demonstrated the growth of the team's knowledge, confidence and ambition at the time.

CDC was already convinced of the powerful linkages between the availability of electricity, economic growth and wider job creation, and it commissioned the UK's Overseas Development Institute to carry out a systematic and independent review by way of confirmation. Thinking through how investment in power generation could, in turn, deliver development impact wasn't easy, but it was indicative of the ambitions of the new-look CDC to establish its thought leadership in the development arena. In the past CDC had not been known for pushing at the boundaries of development theory; it had been more about applied development, showing in practice what could be done and using anecdotal evidence of this to point to thriving businesses among more-educated, healthier and wealthier communities. The ODI review was another example of CDC seeking to provide verifiable evidence of the development impact it was claiming.

"Graham Wrigley characterised Globeleq as a 'CDC-managed business of old, but with a twenty-first century twist.'"

It was with growing confidence and a sense of achievement that Diana Noble sat down in early 2016 to write her annual review of the past year. In contrast to the previous years of hard slog and uncertainty, there was a feeling that the new 'full-service' CDC had already accomplished something of substance. There was a growing fund of very positive stories to report and a good working relationship with DFID in the regular meetings; she had a strong and loyal team delivering results; and she was supported by a fully engaged board, led by a popular, can-do chairman.

A second review was published soon after the main report came out. This showcased the work of the E&S team, which presented the evidence to support CDC's claim that it provided more than just money. In the review's introduction, Diana Noble explained that on top of clarifying and maintaining ESG standards, there was innovative development work to be done by taking a proactive approach to creating value through improvements in environmental and social areas – working with investment managers to promote such issues as energy efficiency and waste and water management. While carrying out due diligence, the E&S team would frequently negotiate an action plan that would map out improvements in E&S performance over a defined period, with the aim of both mitigating risks and enhancing opportunities to create impact.

Where the risks were high, CDC usually insisted that there was an ESG committee of the board with a CDC representative participating as a member or observer. This encouraged ESG matters to be taken seriously by its investee boards and managements, who often then appointed professional ESG managers for the first time. In the case of funds, strategic tailored advice was also offered in addition to the long-standing provision of training in standards. The team also engaged in thought leadership, undertaking or commissioning and sharing research on topics relevant to its work, such as the management of supply chains in agribusiness and the challenges of land acquisition where titles were contested.

After several years of regular debate, CDC had also decided that all its investment proposals, without exception, must be able to point to some sort of genuine additionality – where CDC could be seen to be adding value by its participation – and to this end it had appointed an ex-IFC staffer to consult widely and come up with a set of specific guidelines to support this mandate.

Additionality

As a publicly-funded DFI committed to adding value in developing countries rather than crowding out private sector funds, the question 'Why is CDC needed?' was always in mind. Answering this question in a focused and rigorous way had been considered alongside questions of development impact and financial return. Prior to 2012, CDC, as a fund of funds, had considered itself already to be highly additional in nurturing fledgling fund managers and mobilising others to invest. However, with CDC investing directly once again, it became important, both for CDC itself and for prospective investees, to provide greater clarity about what additionality meant as a practical matter, when applied to individual transactions. The result was a document setting out the key principles of additionality, along with guidance as to their application. 'Practical guidelines for determining additionality' became one of the most rigorous and comprehensive statements about additionality among DFIs, with whom it has been shared.

The guidelines highlighted two distinct types of additionality: financial and value. Financial additionality refers to the concept of providing capital (as either debt or equity, directly or through funds) where capital is either not offered by the private sector at all, or is not offered in sufficient quantity or on terms that reflect both the needs and realities of clients in CDC markets. Value additionality recognises that DFIs such as CDC often provide non-monetary services – such as knowledge and advice in regard to governance, environmental and social issues, improvement in corporate processes and standards, design of sustainable business strategies – which the commercial market typically doesn't offer, but which are important contributions to commercial sustainability.

Above: CDC is working with RBL, one of its financial intermediary investments in India, on a programme to increase financial inclusion and literacy. The programme has supported 25,000 women in Madhya Pradesh and is now delivering a second phase in Bihar, where it aims to support 35,000 women via a similar programme. Pictured above is one of the Madhya Pradesh workshops, with CDC's joint head of the Environmental & Social Responsibility team, Mark Eckstein, at the back and (front left, in white) Asha Rajan from CDCs India Office.

Above: Founded in 1939, Shankerdas & Sons, is one of Sierra Leone's longest-running manufacturing businesses. The Ebola outbreak that began in 2014 caused so much disruption to its operations that the company was faced with either running at a loss or cutting its workforce.

A loan from the facility set up by Standard Chartered and CDC enabled Shankerdas & Sons to continue operating at full capacity throughout the crisis. In 2016 the company received a second loan to fund the construction of a new bottled drinks factory, providing a further 250 jobs.

Meanwhile, the further acceleration of investing activities made possible by the availability of new capital from DFID meant that human capital was needed more than ever within CDC itself. The resulting recruitment drive led to the steepest gradient in the intake of new staff since the days when Lord Trefgarne was first building CDC in the late 1940s, the total more than trebling from 49 to 161 between 2011 and 2015 and going on to rise another thirty-nine per cent to 224 by the end of 2016.

Hiring on this scale was quite a challenge in itself. To transform the organisation from a funds-investing to also include a direct-investing business meant first finding people with the right skills to achieve that. Alongside the appointment of frontline investment experts and managers with specialist sector expertise, support teams were set up to advise on everything from the delivery and measurement of development impact and environmental and social responsibility to business integrity and governance issues, corporate strategy, portfolio analysis and risk assessment. Other teams, such as the legal and tax team, were enhanced. Without the skills, energies, commitment, ideas and output of those who decided to join the growing team, the restructured CDC could not have been successfully created.

It had been recognised all along that regional knowledge and trusted local guidance are vital factors when it comes to investing wisely in the hardest markets in the world. This was initially addressed by having three advisers in East, West and Southern Africa and one, Srinivasan Nagarajan, who started as regional director for India before going on to become head of South Asia, based in Bangalore.

Srini had returned to CDC from Actis, as had several other key members of the leadership team. Without these pivotal people and the experience and expertise they provided, Diana Noble's job would have been immeasurably more difficult. In this respect, another key appointment was that of Colin Buckley, hired in 2012 as chief operating officer, responsible for building several of the teams from scratch, as well as dealing with all corporate functions and being the main interface with DFID.

These committed people also contributed to the development of a new internal culture through the introduction of a set of aspirational values and identities designed to capture what it would mean to work for CDC – being compassionate, thoughtful, fast-moving and non-defensive, facing up to tough challenges and recognising that while the work that CDC attempted to do in some of the world's poorest places wasn't easy, it was hugely worthwhile. It was hoped that this would help to create a fulfilling work environment that would attract recruits who were passionate about the mission and who would make it their life-long careers, job satisfaction helping to compensate for the lower pay dictated by the remuneration framework. Being able to recruit and hold on to high quality staff was essential if CDC was to keep pace with planned growth and all the new opportunities that were increasingly presenting themselves.

In 2016, it became clear that there was a convergence of thinking in DFID and CDC in regard to CDC's future direction. DFID noted the new air of confidence in CDC, its growing annual investment record and its increasing appetite for impact investing; CDC was keen to do more. At the same time, a DFID-commissioned independent review of CDC had supported the continuation of the investment policy that had been introduced in 2012.

Attention therefore turned to how CDC should be funded for a large, sustained increase in its own annual investment rate. DFID had the vision that the department would be Britain's grant-giving body, with CDC as its investment arm, both playing to their strengths. CDC would again become the largest DFI working in Africa and South Asia, and while it would still be required to show a return on its balance sheet, it would also have the space to do some thoughtful and strategic impact investing. The hope was that it would continue to mobilise third party capital while also drawing in other British capabilities, especially from the City, making London the major capital market for Africa. Fundamentally, this approach built on the ambitious developmental principles established by the United Nations Global Goals for Sustainable Development and the Addis Ababa Accord on Financing for Development, which together called for a massive mobilisation of investment by the private sector in support of achieving the goals that they had set by 2030.

All this was very much in accord with CDC's thinking on where it should be heading, confirming its ambition for impact and recognising that its role in economic development and in mobilising others' money were to be increasingly important within the overall aid agenda.

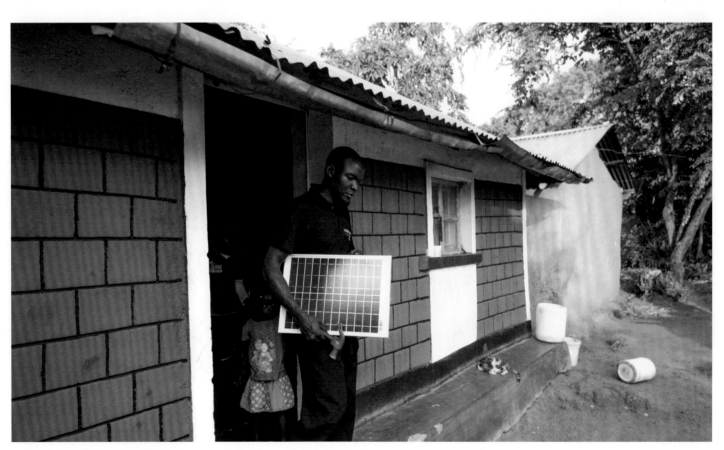

Above: A solar panel supplied by M-KOPA, the leading off-grid solar power company selling electricity and low-energy appliances to homes in Kenya, in which CDC made a commitment in 2016.

With its financial projections carefully thought out and prepared, with input from CDC's CFO Clive MacTavish, DFID then sought time in the Parliamentary timetable for a new CDC Bill that would enable DFID to provide additional capital, when needed, for CDC to continue with the much higher levels of investment that it was already now achieving. The scale of the upgrade was such that it could not be financed solely by self-generated income in the form of returns from current investments along with the sale and recycling of old legacy investments. DFID was constrained by the Commonwealth Development Corporation Act of 1999 that limited the size of the government's investment in CDC to £1.5 billion, a cap that had already been reached with the £735 million recapitalisation. Without additional funds, CDC would have to scale back its investment rate fairly swiftly. The bill therefore proposed to raise the cap by £4.5 billion to £6 billion, with a proviso for another £6 billion, should the secretary of state for international development decide that it was justified.

The bill was put before Parliament in November 2016 by Priti Patel – who had replaced Justine Greening as secretary of state as part of a post-Brexit referendum ministerial shuffle in the preceding July. The proposed legislation was actually introduced earlier than first planned, due to the availability of parliamentary time and with an eye to the anticipated tsunami of Brexit-related legislation that was then thought likely to be tabled sooner rather than later. The timing caught many by surprise, including *The Financial Times*. "Britain's overseas aid budget is set for an 'astounding' overhaul that would allow billions of pounds of development funding to be channelled into the government's controversial private equity arm," it reported on November 25. Such reaction meant that extra effort was needed to explain the purpose of the bill during its passage through Parliament.

One of the key points that had to be made clear was that raising the cap didn't automatically mean CDC would receive more funds and that it was a cumulative, not an annual figure. Each time CDC requested more capital in the future, it would first have to present a rigorous business case to DFID, setting out the cash-flow reasons for the extra funding. CDC would also need to justify how it would invest the funds. A further important point to be stressed was that any extra capital was not going to be used to ramp up investment, but was simply to sustain it at the level already reached.

The bill coincided with the release of a new report by the National Audit Office entitled 'DFID: investing through CDC', the NAO's first assessment of CDC since 2008 when it criticised DFID for its lack of oversight. The report recognised CDC's achievement while making reasonable recommendations on improving measurement of development impact, many of which were already in the process of being implemented. The resulting Public Accounts Committee hearing took place in February 2017, with Graham Wrigley, Diana Noble and DFID's Mark Lowcock giving evidence.

In the week before the PAC meeting, DFID had published its new economic development strategy with Priti Patel writing: "Our ambition must be to create an unprecedented increase in the number and quality of jobs in poor countries; enable businesses to grow and prosper; and support better infrastructure, technology, connectivity and a skilled and healthy workforce". CDC was explicitly stated as being an integral part of the strategy.

Above: Principally involved in the production, processing, distribution and retailing of beef, chicken and pork, as well as milk, dairy products, eggs, maize, soya beans and wheat, Zambeef aims to become one of the most accessible and affordable protein food providers in southern Africa.

"DFID noted the new air of confidence in CDC, its growing annual investment record and its increasing appetite for impact investing."

Above: In 2016 a commitment of $15 million was made in Afghanistan by the CDC team managing the DFID-funded Impact Fund. InFrontier was a private equity fund set up to support businesses vital to the growth of the economy there. Pictured here are flat-roofed houses in part of Kabul.

With cross-party support, the bill received Royal Assent as the Commonwealth Development Corporation Act 2017 on 23 February. At this stage DFID, with the support and engagement of Priti Patel, decided to listen and think carefully before firming up CDC's new strategic framework for 2017-2021. This led to an intensive evaluation of the differing views expressed by a wide range of organisations and individuals, including politicians of all parties, NGOs and academics. Three messages came through clearly: that development impact still needed to be better measured; that CDC had to improve its transparency still further; and that special attention had to be given to helping the poorest of the poor, with the aim of leaving no one behind. This latter entreaty chimed with Shadow Secretary of State Kate Osomor's call for a reduction not just of world poverty but also of inequality, later enshrined in Labour's policy document on international development, entitled 'A World for the Many, Not the Few'.

As a result of all of these discussions, the strategy was amended and refined. In March 2017 it was ready to be publicly announced by Priti Patel, but in the event was delayed until July, following the snap June general election of that year. Broadly speaking, it maintained CDC's general direction, with more of the same, projecting an average investment of £1.2 billion per annum over the five-year strategy period, with a focus on sectors in Africa and South Asia with the highest potential for job creation. In addition, however, there was to be a further £0.6–£1.6 billion available over the five years for investment in new, innovative strategies.

Mid-2017 saw another new beginning for CDC. Diana Noble had announced towards the end of the previous year that she would be leaving. She had overseen the transformation of CDC from a fund of funds back to a full-service DFI, highly respected by its peers and with a new relevance in the markets. This had involved almost six years of sustained heavy lifting and she had done exceptionally well in meeting the huge operational challenge of re-growing CDC, with all that this entailed. It had been a continual juggling act of recruiting to fill the vacancies on an expanding organisational chart to take on the new directions and scale, while at the same time making the changes to the operational systems and processes needed for CDC to operate smoothly as it grew.

Above: 14Trees, Malawi.

Innovative strategies

The innovative strategies announced in 2017 as part of the five-year plan for 2017-21 built on the experience gained by CDC from running the DFID Impact Fund and Impact Accelerator. In addition to bringing both of these onto CDC's balance sheet rather than DFID's, four specific examples were quoted to illustrate how innovative strategies were being developed. These key initiatives had emerged from the selection process undertaken by CDC to determine which of the team's innovative investment ideas were agreed to be the most achievable and to have the greatest potential.

The first was a resource efficiency facility that would provide the E&S and debt teams with a vehicle to meet CDC's climate policy objectives through the provision of low cost loans for increasing energy and water efficiency and the phasing out of fossil fuels in favour of renewable energy sources. The facility also has a grant component to support portfolio companies in conducting audits and feasibility studies to identify potential resource efficiency improvements. Second was a facility that would guarantee the market demand from users of healthcare commodities, such as medicines and diagnostic aids, with the aim of encouraging manufacturers to produce to scale and lower their unit prices, leading to more affordable healthcare and healthier lives. The third would provide a local currency debt facility for off-grid solar companies and where suitable loan finance was lacking. The intention here was to promote the growth of a responsible market for off-grid solar products, ranging from solar lanterns to community mini-grids supplying power to multiple domestic appliances in places that were far from mains electricity supplies. The fourth example was also power-related, with the goal of building a structure to support the operation and expansion of transmission and distribution utilities, specifically in African countries where these had suffered under-investment.

At the same time, she had been determined throughout to make sure that CDC was focused on making a beneficial impact on people's lives, rather than thinking just about investment. And although, in this respect, the long-term success of those investments is not yet proven, there are reasons to be optimistic. The publication setting out the strategic framework for 2017-2021 that she had worked on before she left was entitled 'Investing to Transform Lives' and this aim was echoed in the title given to her last annual review, for 2016: 'Supporting the Potential of People'.

Released in mid-2017, the 2016 review reported thirty-eight new commitments totalling £1.2 billion, up from £713 million in 2015, of which three-quarters was directly invested. Notable among them was a loan of $103 million to the Sirajganj 4 power project to support a dual-fuel combined-cycle power plant in Bangladesh. An equity investment of $65 million into the Zambeef Group, a major diversified agribusiness company, marked CDC's welcome re-entry into the sector in Zambia, was also noteworthy in that it meant engaging again with Mpongwe, the large CDC-managed arable farm that Zambeef had acquired following CDC's exit in 2008. The partnership with AKFED and its infrastructure arm, Industrial Promotion Services, to develop new power generation, marked CDC working again with the Aga Khan in Africa, with an investment of $68.5 million committed to the AKFED power platform to form a partnership to develop challenging power projects such as the Ruzizi III hydro-power project in the Great Lakes region.

Another notable investment was in M-KOPA, the leading off-grid solar power company selling electricity and low-energy appliances to homes in Kenya, with customers able to settle their bills online via their mobile phones. CDC's $11.6 million was earmarked to expand the company's reach and product range.

Elsewhere, a commitment of $15 million was made by the CDC team managing the DFID-funded Impact Fund in a very challenging country – Afghanistan. InFrontier was a private equity fund set up to support businesses vital to the growth of the economy there. It wasn't the first time that a CDC team had recommended investing in the conflict-ridden state: a decade earlier, in 2006, CDC had committed money to the Afghanistan Renewal Fund with similar aims, but the environment at that time was too overwhelmingly hostile and it had been wound up a year later. However, it serves as another reminder that CDC's ambition for meaningful impact has been ever present.

Above: Another view of Globeleq's Jeffreys Bay wind farm in South Africa helps to illustrate one of CDC's newest investments elsewhere that combines both its commercial and innovative strategies. In 2017, CDC established fully-funded Ayana Renewable Power to invest in wind and solar power projects in the poorest parts of South Asia, including areas of India, Pakistan, Sri Lanka and Myanmar. A community development strategy linked to each of the projects will ensure that the power that is generated reaches those people who will benefit most, either directly, as consumers, or indirectly through job creation. Ayana will also provide training in skilled trades such as carpentry and plumbing, as well as supplying renewable energy products such as roof-top solar panels for use in powering homes, businesses and farms.

As 2016 marked the end of the existing five-year strategy, the opportunity was taken in the annual review to present some statistics to show how far it had come during that period. Perhaps most significantly, these stats revealed that the proportion invested in the poorest and most challenging countries had almost doubled, from twenty-three per cent in 2009-2011 to fifty-three per cent in 2012-2016. At the same time, the proportion invested in priority sectors – those with the highest potential for job creation – had risen from just over half to three-quarters. A similar upward trend was also reflected in the measures of developmental impact.

Taxes paid by portfolio companies in 2012 had almost doubled to $4.1 billion in 2016. Gigawatt hours produced by CDC's power generation businesses totalled 69,310 GWh, nearly quadrupled from 2012. Loans and advances supplied by financial institutions in its portfolio amounted to $140 billion, more than six times that provided in 2012, and supported many millions of jobs. Further millions were supported through direct employment and indirectly through supply chains, local informal income and better access to infrastructure. Precisely how far all this can be attributed solely to CDC's participation is difficult to calculate, but the incontrovertible truth is that a great many people's lives will have been changed for the better.

Nick O'Donohoe took over as CDC's chief executive in June 2017, after an exhaustive recruitment process, during which he was one of 300 candidates considered. A two-month tour of CDC's operations was then followed by a smooth handover. Coming from an investment banking background, he had made his name in establishing Big Society Capital, the UK government-inspired social investment bank. Earlier, while at J P Morgan, he had been asked in 2007 to take a part-time role in supervising a social finance group and, through this, became inspired to explore ways in which capital could be used for a higher purpose, a thought-process made more acute by the disillusionment with capitalism precipitated by the financial crisis. Co-authoring a report, 'Impact investments: an emerging asset class', published by J P Morgan and The Rockefeller Foundation in 2010, he was influential in bringing attention to the idea of 'impact investing', which he helped to define as a concept that investment should seek both financial and social returns. The report recognised that CDC had been doing just that "for quite some time", implying that it was the original impact investor. It is therefore unsurprising that he came to be recruited to CDC and that he was so keen to take up what he considered to be "one of the great jobs".

His ambition for the future of CDC under his leadership, agreed with DFID and the CDC board and following through on the approved strategy for 2017-2021, was fourfold. First, to continue to build CDC as a distinctive high-performing DFI, growing its portfolio, headcount and regional representation in order to play a larger part in meeting the huge need for capital to aid development in the poorest and most difficult places in the world. Secondly, to take on more risk in areas that mainstream investors still saw as too risky, and to do this in very innovative ways that would be highly developmental and bring about sea changes in undeveloped markets through deepening CDC's expertise in sectors. Thirdly, to raise the bar in thinking about development impact, about what CDC was doing, and for whom, and to measure how well it was working. And fourthly, to bang the drum for CDC and the other DFIs, improving the wider understanding and support for their work, engaging with mainstream financial institutions and also with development NGOs, all of them working together with the aim of partnering, sharing data and providing support to achieve the world's development goals. This was an inspiring ambition for even more impact from a man who recognised that the re-building of CDC was still very much a work-in-progress.

To head up CDC was now perceived as an increasingly significant leadership role, offering the prospect of even more meaningful public service in a rapidly-growing DFI that found itself, once more, at the centre of the international development stage. The opportunity for growth offered to CDC by its shareholder, DFID, had excited Graham Wrigley, the board and the management team with the vision of greater development impact and, together, they had embraced the challenge of how to bring it to fruition. But while the turnarounds in CDC's headcount, scope of operations and corporate persona had indeed been profound, there was still a way to go before it could be declared 'job done'.

From 2018, it was estimated that it would require a further four or five years of expansion, funded by new tranches of capital drawdowns, for CDC to regain the desired comparability in size with other DFIs, relative to their countries' aid budgets. CDC could then consider reverting to a strategy of growth through self-financing, paying its own way, something that it had done so successfully over the years and to which it remained committed. At the same time, the build-up would have to be achieved only through investments made in those poorer parts of Africa and South Asia where the genuine need and potential benefits remained demonstrable; and only as long as DFID continued to support economic development, using CDC to complement its own work in providing aid. That was why the increased reserve of available government capital was to be allocated in tranches, with a convincing business case having to be made before each tranche; and why no annual investment targets were to be set.

This concern for thinking things through and analysing each potential investment with the utmost care in order to ensure making the right decisions continues to characterise the deliberations of CDC's board and management. They remain very conscious that the challenges CDC will undoubtedly face in the years ahead – economic, political and investment-related – could, in all likelihood, be no less testing than those that had confronted earlier generations of its leaders. And, equally, they know for certain that they will need to persist in wrestling with answers to the question of how to succeed in improving the lives of those of the world's peoples most in need – the ambition for impact that continues to drive CDC.

Nick O'Donohoe

Born in 1957, Nick O'Donohoe was educated at St Conleth's College and Trinity College, Dublin, graduating with a degree in Mathematical Economics and Statistics, after which he studied for an MBA at Wharton School, Pennsylvania. After fifteen years at Goldman Sachs he joined J P Morgan, running its European equity business, and latterly becoming its gobal head of research.

In 2011, having taken a lead at J P Morgan in helping to promote 'impact investing' as an idea and an asset class, in 2011, with founder of private equity firm Apax Partners, Sir Ronald Cohen, he was asked to set up Big Society Capital, an independent financial institution conceived by David Cameron's government to use unclaimed bank accounts to invest in social impact funds, and hailed as the world's first social investment bank. He was CEO of BSC until the end of 2015, moving to become a senior adviser for the Bill and Melinda Gates Foundation, where he gave guidance on the application of blended finance – combining government and philanthropic funds – to international development.

Nick O'Donohoe has also served as chairman of the UK Dormant Assets Commission, is a board member of the Global Impact Investing Network (GIIN) and deputy chairman of the Global Steering Group on Impact Investment.

Taking over the role of CEO in June 2017, Nick brought to CDC his experience of financial institutions, both in the private and the public sector, and his expertise in 'impact investing', which looks for social as well as financial returns. While this term was only coined around 2007, he freely admits that CDC, by investing for both financial and development impact since its early days, was the original impact investor.

In 2018 CDC marked its seventieth anniversary. Passing such a milestone is a time to celebrate an institution's achievements and CDC did this in the warm late spring at the Serpentine Sackler Gallery in London's Hyde Park. In the presence of a succession of former secretaries of state for international development from both sides of the Houses of Parliament, Penny Mordaunt, who had taken over the role from Priti Patel in the previous November, gave a speech confirming CDC's place in DFID's work. As an organisation it had survived and thrived through many challenging episodes over the years, but it was the pioneering development impact that its alumni had helped to achieve, in association with its stakeholders, the peoples of the countries where it had worked and other DFIs, that was recalled with most pride. This was the impact that had transformed lives, communities, economies, infrastructures and capital markets; that had introduced new technologies and crops; had formed and nurtured businesses to sustainable maturity; and had given successive generations the opportunity for a more prosperous future. Back in 1963, William Rendell, CDC's longest-serving chief executive (1953-1973) and author of the first book on its history, had written to his staff, proudly claiming: "There are few indeed, within our area of operations, where life would be quite the same if CDC had not existed". Fifty-five years later, it is hoped the same may be said.

Three years after CDC's pioneering creation in 1948, its chairman and chief executive, Lord Reith – who was to appoint William Rendell to take over from him as CEO - wrote in his annual report for 1951 that CDC's raison d'etre, as declared in its founding Act's motif, was "to do economic good; just that; but to do it without losing money". Shortened to "to do good without losing money", this became his oft-repeated maxim and remains CDC's dual mandate, shared by other DFIs. Reith wrote in another annual report that "there are many difficulties still to be met, risks to be run", adding that CDC "realises its responsibility and its opportunity; it will do its best".

It was a much later chairman, Graham Wrigley, who, only half-jokingly, used the phrase 'perpetual paranoia' to describe the concerns experienced by successive generations of CDC's leaders in dealing with a constantly changing and often conflicting kaleidoscope of political, economic and financial pressures. Making long-term illiquid investments in the world's poorest countries is both difficult and risky and before making a final decision it is necessary to weigh and juggle four characteristics of any project or investment; the potential for financial return, for development impact and for added value, along with the reputational risk to CDC itself should things go awry – all these factors have to be considered. Getting the balance right has never been easy, and never will be. But CDC, as of old – and echoing Lord Reith again – remains as committed as ever to doing the most good it possibly can to make a lasting difference to people's lives in some of the world's poorest places.

Left: The stunning colourful designs of Vlisco's West African-made fabrics illustrate an initiative to support the economic empowerment of women in the Democratic Republic of the Congo. Born in Kinshasa, Monique Gieskes returned to the DRC after an international business career to set up the regional operations for Vlisco, manufacturer and distributor of the iconic branded fabrics. In 2012, as part of this job, she set up the Vlisco Tailor Academy in Eastern Congo to support underprivileged, talented and motivated young women to gain financial independence, later expanding the initiative to Ghana and Nigeria. CDC is invested in Vlisco through Actis, which took control of Vlisco in 2010. Monique is now also a non-executive director of CDC's controlled DRC-based oil palm plantation company, Feronia, that CDC first invested in 2013. Together Vlisco and Feronia reflect the strategies of CDC as fund of funds and direct investor, both with the same objective, of working to improve lives in one of the world's hardest places.

Above: Getting together with CDC to celebrate its seventieth anniversary at London's Serpentine Sackler Gallery in May 2018 were seven of the eight secretaries of state for international development to hold the post since it was created by Tony Blair in 1997. L to R: Priti Patel (2016-2017), Douglas Alexander (2007-2010), Penny Mordaunt (2017-), Nick O'Donohoe (CEO), Baroness Amos (2003), Clare Short (1997-2003), Andrew Mitchell (2010-2012), Justine Greening (2012-2016) and Graham Wrigley (chairman). Only Hilary Benn (2003-2007) was unable to attend.

"As an organisation it had survived and thrived through many challenging episodes over the years, but it was the pioneering development impact that its alumni had helped to achieve, in association with its stakeholders, the peoples of the countries where it had worked and other DFIs, that was recalled with most pride."

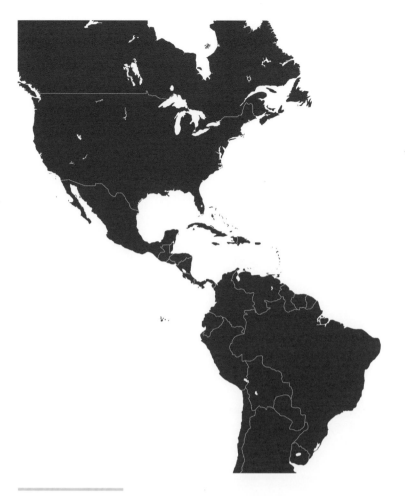

CDC's investments in 2017

- CDC's portfolio includes direct investments again, over 100 having been made since 2012.

- Africa dominates as the destination for investment, with three-quarters of new businesses since 2012.

- India is the country with the highest investment, at thirty-two per cent of the total.

Global investment (£m)

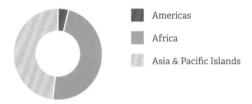

- Americas
- Africa
- Asia & Pacific Islands

Sector of investment (£m)

- Basic development
- Primary production & processing
- Commerce & industry

- **1,277 businesses**
- **£3,940 million invested**

Note: Investments are shown at valuation.

Africa

1. **Algeria**
   Manufacturing
2. **Botswana**
   Financial Services
   Trade
3. **Burkina Faso**
   Infrastructure
4. **Cameroon**
   Construction
   Infrastructure
5. **Cape Verde**
   Agribusiness
6. **Côte d Ivoire**
   Agribusiness
   Business Services
   Financial Services
   Infrastructure
7. **Ethiopia**
   Agribusiness
   Business Services
   Education
   Healthcare
   Infrastructure
   Manufacturing
8. **Democratic Republic of the Congo**
   Agribusiness
   Business Services
   Education
   Infrastructure
   Manufacturing
   Trade
9. **Egypt**
   Healthcare
   Infrastructure
   Manufacturing
   Trade
10. **Gabon**
    Business Services

11. **Ghana**
    Agribusiness
    Business Services
    Construction
    Education
    Financial Services
    Infrastructure
    Manufacturing
    Mineral Extraction
    Real Estate
    Trade
12. **Guinea**
    Infrastructure
13. **Kenya**
    Agribusiness
    Business Services
    Construction
    Education
    Financial Services
    Healthcare
    Infrastructure
    Manufacturing
    Real Estate
    Trade
14. **Madagascar**
    Infrastructure
    Trade
15. **Malawi**
    Agribusiness
16. **Mali**
    Business Services
    Infrastructure
17. **Mauritius**
    Communications
    Financial Services
    Manufacturing

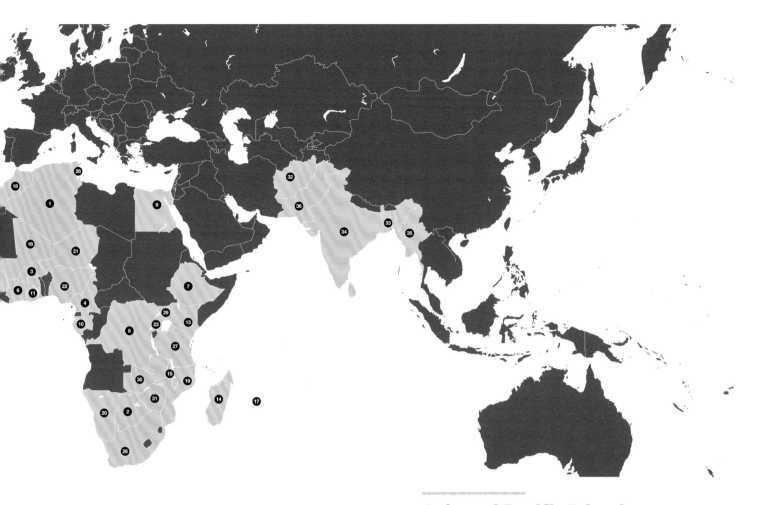

18. **Morocco**
    Business Services
    Education
    Trade
19. **Mozambique**
    Construction
    Trade
20. **Namibia**
    Business Services
21. **Niger**
    Agribusiness
    Business Services
    Communications
22. **Nigeria**
    Agribusiness
    Business Services
    Communications
    Construction
    Financial Services
    Healthcare
    Infrastructure
    Manufacturing
    Mineral Extraction
    Real Estate
23. **Rwanda**
    Agribusiness
    Construction
24. **Senegal**
    Infrastructure
25. **Sierra Leone**
    Financial Services
    Infrastructure
26. **South Africa (Office)**
    Business Services
    Communications
    Financial Services
    Infrastructure
    Trade

27. **Tanzania**
    Financial Services
    Infrastructure
    Manufacturing
28. **Tunisia**
    Manufacturing
    Trade
29. **Uganda**
    Agribusiness
    Communications
    Financial Services
    Infrastructure
    Trade
30. **Zambia**
    Agribusiness
    Communications
    Construction
31. **Zimbabwe**
    Agribusiness
    Business Services
    Education
    Financial Services
    Healthcare
    Manufacturing
    Trade

Africa Region
Business Services
Communications
Construction
Education
Financial Services
Healthcare
Infrastructure
Manufacturing
Trade

West Africa Region
Agribusiness
Business Services
Manufacturing

East Africa Region
Financial Services
Infrastructure

32. **Afghanistan**
    Business Services
33. **Bangladesh**
    Communications
    Infrastructure
    Manufacturing
    Trade
34. **India (Office)**
    Agribusiness
    Business Services
    Education
    Financial Services
    Healthcare
    Infrastructure
    Manufacturing
    Microfinance
    Trade

35. **Myanmar**
    Communications
    Microfinance
36. **Pakistan**
    Financial Services
    Healthcare
    Infrastructure
    Trade

Global
Financial Services
Infrastructure
Trade

Note: The map and country list
exclude those businesses invested
under pre-2012 investment policies.

CDC publications 1948–2018

Annual reports and reviews

1948

1959

1968

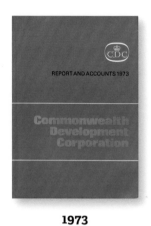

1973

Newsletters, staff bulletins and magazines

1950

1969

1976

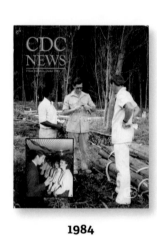

1984

Brochures, books and other publications

1967

1977

1988

1997

1987

1999

2007

2014

1988

1994

1996

1999

2000

2008

2014

2016

Authors' note

As CDC approached its 70th anniversary, it became increasingly clear that the first edition of Pioneering Development, published in 2008 to coincide with its 60th, was in need of an update. The twin aims for the earlier book – to celebrate the momentous sixty-year landmark and to promote a better understanding of CDC's past shape and achievements – had been successfully realised. It was still being used by newcomers to its management and board, its stakeholders and other interested parties to learn about CDC's heritage; and in its stories the team was finding stimulation about what could be accomplished, along with and the realisation that in the past CDC had faced and overcome very similar problems to those that confronted it in the present. Even the book's name inspired the new generation of leaders to seek out investments that continued to be truly pioneering in their way. And while it was not an academic history, historians were finding it to be a source of useful insights that added to their accounts of international development and other DFIs. But such has been the magnitude of the changes that have taken place during the ten years since then that anyone wishing to understand the organisation in 2018 could no longer rely solely on reading the original book. Its final chapter, taking the reader up to 2008, described a CDC that was no longer recognisable to the new generation of staff at 123 Victoria Street. For starters, the team had multiplied six-fold. The chairman and chief executive therefore decided that a second edition was required, telling the story of the last ten years, its release to be part of the 70th anniversary celebrations.

Embarking on this exercise, it soon became apparent that this was going to be more challenging than first envisaged. Simply recording what had happened in only the last ten years without considering both what had happened before and also looking to the future was going to be inadequate. The roots of the changes in 2010-2011 needed to be traced back and the investments made since then, being mostly unrealised, meant that the development story of the new modus operandi was very much a work-in-progress. To address these matters, the new penultimate chapter was rewritten completely, not just from 2008; and with the opportunity to do so and the benefit of a longer time perspective, elements of the preceding chapter, covering the period from 1994-2004, were also revised. And the end of the new closing chapter looks forward to the future with the message that the development outcome is still uncertain.

It also became clear as we undertook the research that such was the depth of the passion felt for CDC, that setting out the competing views of the main protagonists, those key figures among the leadership and the staff, both past and present, would have to be carefully weighed and considered if we were to provide a balanced account and avoid any upset. We have done our best in this respect, but, even so, it has to be acknowledged that some opinions may be perceived as having been imperfectly represented. That, however, is unfortunately almost inevitable, given that we are covering recent events that are still fresh in people's minds and open to different and in some cases contested interpretations. Nevertheless, it is hoped that the outcome will still be seen overall as a positive and adequately-balanced reflection of the background to the changes of the recent past and the sort of development that was being sought and achieved. And that read together with the earlier chapters, the book will provide a satisfying guide as to how CDC arrived in its current form.

Our authors' note to the first edition included a comprehensive list acknowledging those who helped us with its writing and here we repeat our gratitude to them. Those we wish to thank for their contributions to this new work – including the minor updates we have made to the earlier chapters and also material that, in the event, went unused – are listed below. Notable among these are CDC's current and former chairmen, chief executives, board members and the communications team at CDC; and to the design and production team at Honey – Peter Higgins, Lee Smith, Adam Davison, Marisa Allen and Kaye Richardson. The full list of those interviewed, who reviewed drafts and/or provided other information or support, is: Guy Alexander, Michael Anderson, Elaine Brain, Nyika Brain, Ian Brenkley, Colin Buckley, Anna Butler, Torbjorn Caesar, Rhyddid Carter, Robert Comba, Valentine Chitalu, Ronnie Cox, Tim Davidson, John Diess, Jane Earl, John Eccles, Mark Eckstein, Rod Evison, Clarisa de Franco, Alan Gillespie, Richard Gillingwater, Murray Grant,

Barbara Harrad, Mauricio De Jong Oliveira, Mark Kenderdine-Davies, Aaron Kisebe, Ritu Kumar, Richard Laing, Simon le Gassicke, Daudi Lelijveld, Mark Lowcock, Tom Lupton, Sasja McCann, Alex MacGillivray, Frank Maguire, Peter Massey, Clive MacTavish, Innes Meek, Pelayo Menendez, Mike Merrett, Miriam de Lacy, David Morley, Srini Nagarajan, Diana Noble, Nick O'Donohoe, David Osborne, Andrew Palmer, Orde Eliason, Mark Pay, Arpita Raksit, Frances Reid, Roy Reynolds, Holger Rothenbusch, Jeremy Sillem, Sarah Stockwell, Nikolas Stone, Lynsay Taffe, Pierre van Hoeylandt, Fields Wicker-Miurin, John White, Wendy White, Malcolm Williamson, Graham Wrigley, and Mike Young. We sincerely regret any oversights.

Much of the photography remains the same as in the first edition, but to refresh the old chapters, some images have been replaced with others sourced from CDC's historic photograph archive managed by Orde Eliason. The sources for the new chapters are CDC's image archives and stock.

Data on the portfolio for 2011 and 2017 have been compiled with the able assistance of Clare Callender, who has also fact-checked the numbers in the new chapters. The broad economic sector pie-charts have used a classification adopted in the early years, which has been maintained throughout the book to enable comparability. However, some further subjective classifying has been necessary as new sectors have been introduced, and for which the authors are responsible.

As in the first edition, we have included some personal names of CDC staff members in addition to those of the chairmen and chief executives. The caveats given there apply equally to this update, as does the conclusion: that CDC's successes came about through the brains and graft of the thousands who have worked for it and/or supported it positively in some way, and this book is for all these people.

Lastly, it is inevitable that given the often complex subject matter and despite the process of checking our understanding and facts, there are still bound to be some errors that remain, and for these we apologise.

September 2018

Christopher Brain

Born in 1954 and educated at Speedwell School, Bristol and at St John's College, Cambridge, where he read archaeology and anthropology, Christopher Brain joined CDC in 1980. His career with CDC included secondments to several of its managed agribusinesses in Malawi and Solomon Islands, followed later by postings to its offices in Kuala Lumpur as regional head for Malaysia, Philippines and Vietnam and to Harare as country head for Zimbabwe. In CDC's London offices, he held various roles in its investment and operations teams, before transferring in 2004 to Actis, where he directed its valuations function until 2012. More recently, he completed a Masters degree in Research (MRes) in history at King's College, London.

Michael Cable

Born in 1942 and educated at Bedford Modern School and at King's College, London where he edited the London University student newspaper and graduated with a degree in modern history, Michael Cable started a journalistic career in Manchester before moving to Fleet Street in 1966. He later turned freelance, working for newspapers and magazines worldwide, and now also runs his own small publishing business, through which he is involved in writing and producing a wide range of books, including biographies and company histories.

Index

A

Acacia Fund, Kenya 192, 205, 223
Accra, Ghana 205, 218
Actis 123, 195, 202, 203–4, 205, 210, 213, 214–18, 220, 223, 226, 227, 228, 230, 232, 238, 267, 276
Actis Africa Agribusiness Fund 217, 218, 233
Actis Africa Empowerment Fund 217
Actis Africa Real Estate Fund 217, 218, 249
Addis Ababa, Ethiopia 67, 109, 239
ADMARC, Malawi 131
Afghanistan 226, 272, 272, 273
Africa 18, 62, 63, 71, 73, 82–95, 109, 110–12, 126–31, 140, 144, 160–70, 180, 186–92, 201, 204, 205, 212, 215, 216–24, 225, 227, 229, 232–4, 237, 239, 245, 247, 248, 249–50, 252–62, 265, 267, 270, 272, 273, 275
    see also individual countries by name
Africa Capital Alliance 229
Africa Development Bank 66
Africa Improved Foods, Rwanda 265
the Africa List 245, 261, 262
Africa Renewable Energy Fund 232, 258
African Queen factory ship 32, 33
Aga Khan Fund for Economic Development (AKFED) 147, 267, 273
The Aga Khan 147, 147
Agrawal, Rajeev 226
Agricane, Malawi 265
agriculture/agribusiness 9, 12, 14, 18, 20, 24, 26, 28–9, 33, 37, 40, 49–50, 54–7, 62, 73, 86, 90–7, 110–12, 114, 117–19, 123, 126–31, 134, 160, 162, 162, 165, 168, 170, 177, 180–1, 195–6, 218, 232, 239, 248, 250, 265, 273
    see also cocoa plantations; coffee plantations; meat/cattle industry; palm oil production; rubber plantations; sugar industry; Swaziland Irrigation Scheme (SIS); tea industry
Agventure, Zimbabwe 191
Aid, British overseas 98, 101, 106, 108, 112, 113, 271
Akwaeze, Gabriel 85, 85
Albert E. Reed & Co 31
Alexander, Douglas 229, 277
Alexander, Margaret and Harry 132
Allison, Stanley 83
Ambit Pragma, India 226, 229, 235
the Americas 74, 202
    see also Central America; Latin America; individual countries by name
Amin, Idi 67, 87, 164
Amos, Baroness 277
Ananta Apparels, Bangladesh 233
Anderson, George 133
Anglo-Indonesian Plantations 118
Angola 140, 225
Anyaoku, Chief Emeka 123
Apollo Tyres, India 150
Aqua Corporacion International, Costa Rica 183
Aquarius Platinum, South Africa 186
Arusha Declaration (1967) 87, 164
Asia 144, 199, 201, 205, 223, 226, 227, 232, 237, 245, 258
    see also Asia Pacific; South Asia; South East Asia; individual countries by name

Asia Pacific 125, 179, 199, 230
Asian Development Bank 67, 157
Astek Fruit Processing, Ghana 160, 162, 162
Atlantic Fisheries, the Gambia 33
Attlee, Clement 11, 12, 24, 38
Atyati, India 238
Aureos 177, 203, 204, 210, 214–15, 223, 250
AVTEC, India 216
Ayana Renewable Power 274
Azito Energie, Côte d'Ivoire, 201

B

BAL Plantations Sdn Bhd 9, 14, 24, 24, 96, 96, 97, 123, 132, 158, 158, 176, 179, 194
    see also agriculture/agribusiness; Borneo Abaca Ltd; palm oil production
banana plantations 86, 184, 184, 185
Banco Central de Costa Rica 134
Banco Sol, Bolivia 183, 184, 185
Banda, Hastings 170
Bangkok, Thailand 67, 106, 121, 122, 122
Bangladesh 67, 147–8, 149, 149, 151, 232, 233, 238, 257, 273
Bangladesh Export Import Company (Beximco) 148
Banque Commerciale du Rwanda 216
Banro Corporation, DRC 213, 214
Barbados 36, 67, 74, 77
Baring, Sir Evelyn see Howick, Lord
Basutoland 18, 67, 71
    see also Lesotho (Basutoland)
Beacham, Richard 114, 132, 179
Bechuanaland Cattle Ranch 31
Bechuanaland Protectorate 18, 31, 67, 71
    see also Botswana
Belize 9, 22, 74, 107, 181
Belize Food Products 181
Belsham, Alan 121
Benn, Hilary 212, 277
Berkeley Energy 232, 258
Bessborough Gardens office, London 141, 145, 146, 146, 204
Betterware, Mexico 183
Beximco Textiles, Bangladesh 148
Bhutto, Benazir 141
Biafran War 82, 83, 84, 85
Binyon, Robert 179
Blackman, William 42, 42
Blair, Tony 176, 192–3, 277
Blow, Patrick 182
Bolivia 176, 177, 183, 185, 185, 201
Borneo 14, 24, 26, 49, 56, 59
    see also Sabah; Sarawak
Borneo Abaca Ltd 14, 24, 26, 26, 49, 49, 97, 123
    see also BAL Plantations
Borneo Development Corporation (BDC) 37, 39, 56, 123
Borneo Housing Mortgage Finance Ltd 54, 56, 123
Botswana (Bechuanaland) 18, 19, 31, 36, 67, 71, 107
Boyd, Alistair 'Engineering' 75
Boyd, Alistair 'Mortgage' 75, 77

Brazier, Brigadier Clifford 24
Brazil 225
Bridge International Academies 250, 254
Bristol Hotel, Lagos, Nigeria 82, 83
British economy 10, 11–12, 73
British Guiana
    see Guyana (British Guiana)
British Guiana Timbers 17, 23, 23, 33
British Honduras see Belize
Brooks, Richard 230, 238
Brown, Gordon 229
Bruce, Sir Malcolm 238
Brundtland, Gro 140
Brunei 96
Burgess, Jack 59, 72, 86
Buru Buru, Nairobi, Kenya 87, 88, 88–9

C

Caine, Sir Michael 12
Caine, Sir Sydney 12, 12
Cairns Foods, Zimbabwe 250
Cairns, Lord 176, 179, 193, 193, 195
Callaghan, James 106
Cameron, David 245, 275
Cameroon 66, 82, 86, 101, 107
Cameroon Development Corporation (Camdev) 86
Capital Today, China 226
Caribbean Finance Investments Ltd (Carifin) 183
Caribbean Housing Finance Corporation (CHFC) 66, 76, 77, 79
Caribbean Utilities Ltd 74
Caribbean 9, 17, 36, 37, 40, 62, 66, 74–81, 83, 102, 132, 133, 144, 183, 202
    see also individual islands by name
Castries, St Lucia 17, 17, 107
Catalyst 229
catering services, Nigeria 82
cattle/meat industry
    see meat/cattle industry
Cauris Croissance 237
CDC
    The Africa List 245, 261, 262
    Annual Reports and Reviews 36, 40, 45, 57, 72, 72, 101, 109, 125, 171, 256, 268, 274, 276, 280
    background to formation 8, 9, 12–13
    development reports (1994, 2009 and 2010) 171, 171, 234, 237
    Development Impact Grid 247-248, 248
    innovative strategies (2017-2021) 245, 272-274
    logos and name changes 4, 66, 74, 145, 196
    map charting investments in 1959 62–3
    map charting investments in 1972 102–3
    map charting investments in 1982 136–7
    map charting investments in 1994 172–3

    map charting investments in 2003 206–7
    map charting investments in 2011 240–1
    map charting investments in 2017 278–9
    'Practical Guidelines for Determining Additionality' 268
    Project Atlas 177
    quinquennial reviews 106, 107, 113, 134, 140
    Staff Bulletins and other publications 43, 43, 50, 280–1
    Strategic framework 2017-2021 'Investing to Transform Lives' 245, 263, 272-273, 275
    timeline (1948-1950) 8–9
    timeline (1950-1959) 36–7
    timeline (1959-1972) 66–7
    timeline (1972-1982) 106–7
    timeline (1982-1984) 140–1
    timeline (1994-2004) 176–7
    timeline (2004-2011) 210–11
    timeline (2012-2017) 244–5
CDC Assets 195, 196
CDC Capital Partners 195, 196
CDC Engineering Ltd 36
CDC Financial Markets 179, 191
CDC Industries 179
CDC Investments 179
CDC Nigeria Ltd 126
CDH, China 225
Celtel 176, 188–9, 223
cement industry
    Chilanga Cement 9, 18, 24, 24, 25, 44, 45, 66, 141, 165, 176, 179, 179, 180
    Fauji Cement, Pakistan 151
    Nigeria Cement Co Ltd 84, 84, 133
    Pan African Cement 24, 177, 180, 265
    SOBOCE, Bolivia 186
Central Africa Power Corporation 44
Central African Federation 36, 44
Central America 134–5, 180, 183, 199, 201
    see also individual countries by name
Central Asia 226, 230
    see also individual countries by name
Central Hotel, Kano, Nigeria 82, 83
Cepheus Growth Capital Partners 239
CGU-CDC China Investment Company 199
Charusorn family 122
Chilanga Cement, Zambia 9, 18, 24, 24, 25, 44, 45, 66, 141, 165, 176, 179, 179, 180
Chile 185
Chiluba, Frederick 24, 165
China 9, 98, 141, 176, 196, 199, 204, 215, 216, 225, 226, 229, 230, 239
China Capital Partners 199
China Grentech 199
China National Offshore Oil Company (CNOOC) 199
Churchill, Sir Winston 36, 39, 45
Citrus Company of Belize 181
Citrus Growers Association 181

Clark, Bob 179

Clovergem Celtel Ltd 189

cocoa plantations 96, *96*, 97, 112, 117, 118, 158, 160

coffee plantations 110, 111, *111*, 112, 160

Collier, Sir Paul 237

Colombia 134

Colonial Development magazine 32, *32*, 33

Colonial Economic Advisory Committee 12

Colonial Economic and Development Council 12

Colonial Office 12, 37, 38, 45, 60, 61, 68, 70, 72, 73

Colonies, British 12, 14, *15*, 43, 45
   see also individual countries by name

Colquiri, Bolivia 177

Commonwealth Africa Investment Fund (Comafin) 190, 191

Commonwealth 12, 61, 66, 67, 72, 73–4, 98, 101, 147, 160, 176, 192
   see also individual countries by name

Commonwealth Business Council 193

Commonwealth Development Act (1963) 66, 73

Commonwealth Development Corporation Act
   (1978) 106, 145
   (1982) 107
   (1986) 140
   (1995) 176
   (1999) 256, 271
   (2017) 245, 272

Commonwealth Development Finance Company 60, 61

Commonwealth Housing Corporation 86

Commonwealth Private Investment Initiative (CPII) 176, 190, 191

Commonwealth Property Development Services Ltd 78

Commonwealth Relations Office 61, 73

Compagnie Heveicole de Cavally, Côte d'Ivoire 112

Compania Boliviana de Energia Electrica SA 185, 201

Compania de Electricidad de Puerto Plato, Dominican Republic 201

Comsur, Bolivia 185

Connaught Bridge Power Station, Malaya 56, *56*

construction/infrastructure developments 24, 56, 73, 74, 78–81
   Castries, St Lucia 17, *17*, 107
   Kariba Dam 18, 24, 44, 44, 45, *46*, 47
   Lesotho Highlands Water Project 18, 169
   Modern Terminals, Hong Kong 67, 98, *99*
   N4 motorway, South Africa 186, *186–7*
   Nava Nakorn, Thailand 106, 120, *120*, 122
   New Kowloon flatted factories, Hong Kong 98
   Newport Holdings Industrial Estate, Jamaica 78, *78*
   Ocean Building, Singapore 125
   Public Utilities Board, Singapore 125
   Queen Elizabeth Quay, Sri Lanka 148
   Rodney Bay, St Lucia 67, 80, *80–1*, 132

South East Asia Gateway Terminals 148
   Valley Field and Buru Buru, Nairobi 86–7, 88, *88–9*
   see also Actis Africa Real Estate Fund; hotels and tourism; irrigation projects; property and housing finance

Cook, Sir Robin 16, *16*

Cooperativa Agroindustrial de la Reforma Agraria de la Palma Africana (Coapalma) 134, 135

Cooperativa Agroindustrial de Productores de Palma Aceitera 134

Costa Rica 101, 106, 134, 181, 183

Côte d'Ivoire (Ivory Coast) 66, 101, 109, 112, 113, 140, 201

Crown Property Bureau, Thailand 122

Cuba 183

D

dairy industry 150, 168, 196, *197*, 199

Daksh eServices, India 200

Dalton, Hugh 11

Dar es Salaam, Tanganyika (Tanzania) 37, 106, 133, 248

DEG 147, 250

Del Oro, Costa Rica 181

Demissie, Berhane 239

Democratic Republic of the Congo (DRC) 213, *213*, 214, 217, 250, 252, 262, 265, 276

Department for International Development (DFID) 192–3, 194, 195, 196, 203–4, 205, 211, 215, 227, 228, 229, 230, 233, 234, 235, 237, 238–9, 244, 245, 246–7, 250, 255, 256, 261, 263, 269, 270–2, 275, 276

Development Bank of Singapore (DBS) 59, 67

The Development Business (M. McWilliam) 108

development companies, banks and financial services
   Borneo Development Corporation 37, 39, 56, 123
   Caribbean Finance Investments Ltd (Carifin) 183
   Development Bank of Singapore 59, 67
   Development Finance Co, Belize 181
   Development Finance Company (Eastern Nigeria) Ltd 37, 61, 82, 84, 85, *85*
   Development Finance Company of Kenya (DFCK) 86, 87, *87*, 90
   Development Finance Company of Uganda (DFCU) 66, 87, *87*, 216
   Fiji Development Co 98
   Ghana Venture Capital Fund 160
   Industrial Development Leasing Company 147
   Industrial Finance Corporation of Thailand 122
   Industrial Promotion and Development Company of Bangladesh (IPDC) 147
   Malaya (Malaysia) Industrial Development Finance (MIDF) 66, 97
   National Development Bank, Sri Lanka 148
   Northern Nigerian Investment Ltd 61, 82
   Profund International SA 183
   Tanganyika (Tanzania) Development Finance Co Ltd (TDFL) 87, *87*, 133

Urban Development Corporation 78, 79
   see also fund managers; loans and financial support; microfinance; property and housing finance

Development Finance Company, Belize 181

Development Finance Company (Eastern Nigeria) Ltd 37, 61, 82 84, 85, *85*

Development Finance Company of Kenya (DFCK) 86, 87, *87*, 90

Development Finance Company of Uganda (DFCU) 66, 87, *87*, 216

Development Impact Grid, CDC 247–8, *248*

Diamond Bank 217, 250

Divine Seafoods 160, *162–3*, 163

Dominica 9, 74, *74*, 77, 106

Dominica Electricity Services Ltd (Domlec) 74, 201

Dominican Republic 201, *201*

Dover Street offices 8, 14, 16, *16*, 42

DSQ Software 198

Dwangwa Sugar Corporation 110-111

E

Eagle Star 76, 77

East Africa 20, 48, 66, 72, 74, 86, 90, 109, 132, 147, 229, 249
   see also individual countries by name

East Africa Gold Mines 188

East Africa Industries 18

East Africa Teas 180

East Caribbean Housing Ltd 75, 77

East Usambara Tea Co Ltd, Tanzania (EUTCO) 164

Ebola crisis 256, 257–8

Eccles, John 75, 107, 140, 141, 142, 143–5, 146, 160, 170–1, 178, 195

Economic Development Board, Singapore 59

Ecuador 134, 184, 185

education and career support 18, 24, 54, 54–5, 57, 67, 84, 95, 119, 122, 123, 148-149, 164, 185, 189, 214, 225, 252, 268, 276
   the Africa List 245, 261–262
   Bridge International Academies 250, 254
   Mananga Agricultural Management Centre 18, 67, 119, *119*

Edwards, Karl 115, *115*

Egypt 217

Ekona Banana Estates, Cameroon 86, *86*

El Cajon hydroelectric power project 134, *135*

Electra House, Kuching, Sarawak 56, *56*

electricity *see* power sector

Elizabeth II, Queen 36, 114, *114*, 123, 245

Elizabeth the Queen Mother, Queen 47, *47*, 95

Emerging Capital Partners 237

Empresa Nacional de Energia Electrica, Honduras 134

Engro Chemicals Pakistan Ltd 141, 150, *152*, 153, 154, *154*, 155, 195

Engro Vopak Terminal Ltd, Pakistan 154

Enron 201, 202

Environmental & social responsibility 248, 252, 258, 265, 266, 267, 268

Equator Capital 225

Equatoria Teak, Sudan 218, 219

Equitas, India 250, 254, *254*

Equity Bank 225, *225*

Ethiopia 82, 90, 101, 106, 109, 140, 239, 255, 262

Ethiopia Growth and Transformation Fund 239

eucalyptus plantations 95, *95*

Association of European Development Finance Institutions (EDFI) 87, 141, 210, 215

Evelyn Baring: The Last Proconsul (C. Douglas-Home) 71

Evison, Rod 238, 239

Export Trading Group (ETG) 248, 249

Exxon Chemical Pakistan Ltd 153

F

Falkland Islands 9, 14, 33, 107

Falkland Islands Freezer Company Ltd 14, 33

Family Farming Tobacco Project, Zambia 109

farming *see* agriculture/agribusiness

Fauji Cement, Pakistan 151

Fauji Fertilizer, Pakistan 151, 154

Fauji Foundation, Pakistan 150–1

Fauji Oil Terminal and Distribution Company (FOTCO) 151

Favorita Fruit Company, Ecuador 184, 185

Federal and Colonial Building Society, Singapore 24, 59

Federal Land Development Authority (FELDA) Malaysia 37, 54, 54–5, *55*, 56, 57, 109

Feronia Inc, DRC 250, 252, *252–3*, 276

Ferrocarril Central Andino, Peru 185

fertiliser production 148, 150, 151, 154

Fiennes, David 39, 49, 54, 57, *57*, 123, 145

Fiji 98

Fiji Development Co 98

File on Four (BBC Radio 4) 230

The Financial Times 28, 33, 271

First Permanent Building Society 73

fishing industry 33, 182–3, 188

'Five Eveready Batteries' 74–5, 201, 202

Fletcher, Paul 177, 195, 202, 204

FMO 67, 250

forestry 17, 112
   Equatoria Teak 218, 219
   GEF Africa Sustainable Forestry Fund 233
   Guyana Timbers 23, *23*, 33
   Kilombero Valley Teak 217, 222, *222*, 233, 234
   Kolombangara Forest Products 160
   Miro Forestry 260
   Nyika Forestry Development Syndicate 30–1, *30–1*, 41
   Peak Timbers 233
   Shiselweni Forestry Company 95, *95*, 122, *123*
   Tanganyika (Tanzania) Wattle Estates (Tanwat) 9, 18, 130, *130*, 131, 132
   Usutu Forest 18, 60, *60*, 71
   see also agriculture/agribusiness; palm oil production

Formscaff, Zimbabwe 191

Fort George Hotel, Belize 9, 22, 74

Foster, John 97
14Trees, Malawi 24, *107*, 265, 273
Frontier Fund, Bangladesh 233
fruit/juice production 163, 181, *181*, 188
funds/fund managers 228–9, 230, 234–5, 236, 239, 248, 249, 258
  Acacia Fund 192
  Actis Africa Agribusiness Fund 218
  Actis Africa Empowerment Fund 217
  Africa Capital Alliance 229
  Ambit Pragma 226, 229
  Berkeley Energy 232
  Catalyst 229
  Cauris Croissance 237
  CDH 225
  Central American Investment Fund (CAIF) 183
  Emerging Capital Partners 237
  Frontier Fund 233
  Ghana Venture Capital Fund 160
  Helios Investors 225, 229
  ICICI Ventures 225, 226
  IDFC Project Equity 229
  India Value Fund Advisors 225, 226
  Kotak Private Equity 229
  Lok Capital 229
  Multiples 226, 229
  Novastar Ventures 255
  Patria 225
  PNG Venture Finance Pty Ltd 114
  Pragati Fund 239
  Rabo Equity Advisers 232
  ShoreCap International 223–5, 226
  Sierra Investment Fund 228
  Silverlands 239
  Takura Ventures 180, 191
  VenturEast Proactive Fund 238
  see also Actis; Aureos

G

Gambia Eggs Scheme 14, 28–9, 33, *33*, 40
Gambia Rice Farms 33, *33*
The Gambia 9, 14, 28, *32*, 33, 33, 42, 66, 224
Garro-Jones, George Morgan *see* Trefgarne, Lord
GEF Africa Sustainable Forestry Fund 222, 233
George VI, King 36, 95
Ghana 37, 60, 82, 86, 141, 160, 205, 218, 260, 276
Ghana Venture Capital Fund 141, 160, 205, 223
Gibson, William 57
Gieskes, Monique 276
Gillespie, Dr Alan 177, 194, *194*, 195, 196, 204
Gillingwater, Richard 211, 232, *232*, 238, 238, 239, 244, 250
Glenmark Pharmaceuticals, India 200
Globeleq 74, 177, 201–2, *203*, 204, 210, 214, 223, 247, 262, 267
Government, British 12, 14, 24, 45, 61, 70, 72, 73–4, 90, 98, 101, 106, 107, 112, 114, 134, 143, 147, 158, 160, 165, 168, 170–1, 192–4, 204, 211, 230, 255, 256, 271
  see also Colonial Office; Department for International Development (DFID); House of Lords; Ministry of Overseas Development (ODM); Sinclair Committee; individual politicians by name

Gowon, President General 85
Grafites de Ancuabe SARL, Mozambique 188
Grameenphone, Bangladesh 148
Grant, Gavin 135
Grant, Murray 258
Greening, Justine 250, 256, 261, 263, 277
Gregoire, Peter 57, *57*
Grenada 74
Grenada Electricity Services Ltd (Grenlec) 74
Grenadines 107
Grey, Lord 107, 142
Griffith-Jones, Sir Eric 67, 71, 107, 108, *108*, 142
Grindrod, South Africa 257
Groundnuts Scheme 28
Grupo Nuevo Banco 183
Gumaro Tea Plantation, Ethiopia 109
Guyana (British Guiana) 9, 23, *23*, 33, 67, 74, 77, 143
Guyana Housing and Development Co Ltd 23
Guyana Mortgage Finance Co Ltd 23
Guyana State Corporation 23
Guyana Timbers 23, *23*, 33

H

Habib Bank, Pakistan 141 267
Halilu, Alhaji 83
Hall, Eric 83
Hallway Hotels Overseas Ltd 83
Halonix, India 216
Hassenforder, Remy 186
healthcare 18, 24, 49, 84, 95,114, 148-149, 164, 205, 216, 252, 273
  Medikredit 186
  Medscheme 186
  Narayana Health 257, *257*
Prime Cure Clinics 186
Rainbow Healthcare, India 250, *250*
Heath, Edward 67, 101
Helios Investors 225, 229
Higaturu Oil Palms, PNG 106, 114, 116, *116*–17, 179
Hill Street offices, London 42, *42*, 43
History of the Commonwealth Development Corporation, The (W. Rendell) 41
Ho, Ivan 56, 123
Home Finance Company, Fiji 98
Honduras 134, *135*
Hong Kong 59, 67, 98, *99*, 176, 200
Hong Kong Building and Loan Agency 98
Hong Kong Transportation Co. 26
Hopewell Power (Philippines) Corporation *156*–7, *157*
hotels and tourism
  Bristol Hotel, Lagos, Nigeria 82, 83
  Cathay Hotels group, Fiji 98
  Central Hotel, Kano, Nigeria 82
  Eric Hall 83
  Fort George Hotel, Belize City 9, 22, 74
  Hallway Hotels Overseas Ltd 83
  Ikoyi Hotel, Lagos, Nigeria 82, *82*, 83
  Lake Victoria Hotel, Uganda 18, 22, *22*
  Nigeria Hotels Ltd 82

Ocho Rios, Jamaica 78, 79, *79*, 81
  Oriental Hotel, Bangkok 106, 122, *122*
  Rodney Bay, St Lucia 81
  Victoria Falls Safari Lodge, Zimbabwe 169, *169*
House of Lords 12, 14, 29, 40
Housing Finance Co of Kenya Ltd 66, 86
Housing Finance Co of Uganda Ltd 86, 133
Howick, Lord 18, 66, 67, 69, 70–3, 74, 100, *100*, 101, 109
Hub Power power station, Pakistan 153
Hume, Sir Nutcombe 37, 61, 68
Hunt, Paul 22
hydroelectric power 9, 18, 24, 45, 47, *47*, 74, 134, *135*, 148, 169, 185, 201, 220, 265

I

IBM Daksh, India 200
Ibrahim, Dr Mohamed 'Mo' 189
ICICI Ventures, India 225, 226
IDFC Project Equity, India 229, 250
Ighodaro, Adiba 123
Ikoyi Hotel, Lagos, Nigeria 82, *82*, 83
Impact Accelerator Facility (DIAF) 245, 263, 265, 273
Impact Fund, DFID (DIF) 244, 255, 263, 272, 273
'impact investing' 255, 263, 275
Impala Farming Company, Malawi 170
The Independent 109
India 8, 61, 71, 98, 140, 147, 150, 176, 177, 198, 199, 216, 225, 226, 229, 232, 237, 238, 239, 247, 250, 257, 266, 267, 268, 274
India Agribusiness Fund 232
India Value Fund Advisors 225, 226
Indonesia 97, 101, 117–18, 132, 133, 179, 194
Industrial Commercial Developments (ICD), Jamaica 78
Industrial Development Leasing Company, Bangladesh 147
Industrial Finance Corporation of Thailand (IFCT) 122
Industrial Promotion and Development Company of Bangladesh (IPDC) 147, 148
Industrial Promotion Services (IPS), Bangladesh 147
InFrontier, Afghanistan 272, 273
Instituto Nacional de Seguros, Costa Rica 134
Inter-American Development Bank 37
Inter-Continental Hotel, Ocho Rios, Jamaica 79
Interbank Peru 185
International Aid Transparency Initiative 211, 239
International Development Committee of the House of Commons 211, 238
International Finance Corporation (IFC) 37, 73, 147, 154, 157, 185, 188, 218, 233, 239, 250, 261
Inversiones Guanaranga, Costa Rica 181
Investec Africa Credit Opportunities 250
Inyoni Yami SIS (IYSIS) 18, 133
  see also Swaziland Irrigation Scheme (SIS)
Iron Mountain, Ngwenya, Swaziland 69
Irrawaddy Green Tower Project, Myanmar 264, 265

irrigation projects 9, 18, 33, 37, 49, 50, *51*, *52*–3, 53, 66, 67, 71, 94, 94, 95, 119, 126, 127, 133, 168, 265
  see also Swaziland Irrigation Scheme (SIS)
IT (Information technology) 176, 183, 198, 199–200
Ivory Coast (Côte d'Ivoire) *see* Côte d'Ivoire

J

Jamaica 66, 67, 76, *76*, 77, 78, *78*, 79, 141
Jamaica Housing Development Company 77
Jamaica Mortgage Bank 77
Jamaica Telephone Co 141
Jambi Tiger Project, Indonesia 180
James Finlay 164
Java, Indonesia 118
Jeffreys Bay Wind Farm 262, *262*, 274, *274*
Johnson, Dick 96
Johore Palm Processing Ltd, Malaya 57
Jones, Arthur Creech 14
Jurong Town Corporation (JTC) Singapore 59, 125

K

Kafue Textiles, Zambia 128
Kaleya Smallholders Company, Zambia 128, *128*, *129*
Kampala, Uganda 133
Kano Central Hotel, Nigeria 82, 83
Kariba Dam 18, 24, 44, *44*, 45, 46, 47
Karnaphuli Fertilizer Co Ltd (KAFCO), Bangladesh 148, *149*, 151
Kasungu Flue-Cured Tobacco Authority (KFCTA), Malawi 109, 110, 111, *111*
Kasungu Tobacco Scheme, Nyasaland 110
Kathy Xu 226
Katse Dam and reservoir, Lesotho 169
Kaunda, Kenneth 24, 109, 128, 165
Kavuzi Tea Company, Malawi 170
Kawalazi Estates Malawi 170
Kemoli, Richard 123
Kenya 9, 18, 48, 66, 71, 72–3, 86–7, 88, *88*–9, 90, *90*, 91, *91*, 92–3, 93, 106, 109, 112, 123, 147, 191, 192, 201, 218, 223, 225, 237, 250, 255, 270, 273
Kenya Building Society 73
Kenya Capital Partners 192
Kenya Tea Development Authority (KTDA) 66, 90, *90*, 91, *91*, 92–3, 93, 109, 112
Kerwood, Adrian 84, *84*, 133
Kilembe Mines, Uganda 48
Killick, David 110, 150
Kilombero Sugar, Tanzania 132
Kilombero Valley Teak Co, Tanzania 217, *217*, 218, 222, *222*, 233, 234
Kindersley, Lord 107, 141, 142, 144, 145, 170, 235
Kiwi Polish Company, Singapore *58*, 59, *59*
Kolombangara Forest Products, Solomon Islands 160
Kotak India Realty Fund, India 229
Kotak Private Equity Fund, India 229
Kuala Lumpur, Malaysia 9, 37, 54, 133, 158

Kuan Yew, Lee 125
Kuching River, Borneo 39, *39*
Kula Fund 191
Kulai Oil Palm Estate Sdn Bhd, Malaya 9, 55, 57, *57*
Kulim (Malaysia) Berhad, 158
Kwai Chung, New Territories, Hong Kong 98, *99*

L

Lafarge/LafargeHolcim 24, 123, 180, 265
Lagos, Nigeria 13, *13*, 82, *82*, 107, 123, 128, 132, 141, 205
Laing, Richard 195, 210, 211, 214, 215, *215*, 237, 238, 239, 246, 250
Lake Harvest, Zimbabwe 182
Lake Kariba, 182
Lake Malawi 20, 21, *21*
Lake Victoria Hotel, Uganda 18, 22, *22*
Landall Mills Associates (LMA) 165
Lane, Ian 87, 133
Latin America 37, 101, 134, 135, *135*, 183, 199, 200, 201, 204, 205, 215, 216, 223, 229, 230
see also individual countries by name
Lawani, Tope 225
Layfield, Diana 257
Lee, Ek Hua 59, 123
Lennox-Boyd, Alan 48, *48*
Lerner, Professor Josh 244, 258
Lesetho Highlands Development Authority 169
Leslie, Sir Peter 141, 170, *170*, 179
Lesotho (Basutoland) 18, 67, 71, 169
Lesotho Highlands Water Project 18, 169
Lewis, Arthur 107, 142, 144
Liberia 107, 112, 128
Limbang Oil Palm Pilot Scheme, Sarawak 96
Limpasa Dambo farm, Nyasaland 20
Lindi Convoy, Nyasaland 20, *20*, 21, *21*
Lingyangwa Smallholder Tobacco Scheme, Malawi 109
LMKR, Pakistan 216
Lobatse Abattoir, Botswana 18, 19, *19*
Lok Capital, India 229
The Lost World of the Kalahari (L. van der Post) 31
Lowcock, Sir Mark 250, 271

M

M-KOPA, Kenya 270, 273
Macalder-Nyanza Mines Ltd, Kenya 48
Macmillan, Harold 37, 60, 61, 66
maize cultivation *130*, 131, 165
Makoni, Phibion 190
Malawi (Nyasaland) 9, 20, 24, 30–1, *30–1*, 36, 66, 90, 107, 109, 110, *110*, 111, *111*, 130, 131, 170, 180, 248, 265
Malaya (Malaysia) Industrial Development Finance (MIDF) 66, 97
Malayan Electricity Board 56
Malayan Emergency 56, 59
Malaysia (Malaya) 9, *26*, 37, 54–6, 57, 59, 62, 66, 97, 109, 121, 123, 132, 158, 179

Malaysia Building Society 9, 24, 56, 59
Malta Mariculture 182
Mananga Agricultural Management Centre (Mananga Management Centre) 18, 67, 119, *119*
Manocap 228, 233, 238
manufacturing
    Ananta Apparels 233
    Apollo Tyres 150
    AVTEC 216
    Beximco Textiles 148
    East Africa Industries 18
    Engro Chemicals Pakistan Ltd 141, 150, 152, 153, 154, *154*, 155, 195
    Fauji Fertilizer 151, 154
    FOTCO 151
    Halonix 216
    Karnaphuli Fertilizer Co Ltd 148
    Monno Ceramic Industries Ltd 147
    Padma Textiles 148
    Punjab Tractors 177, 200
    Sandhar 216
    Vlisco 276
    see also cement industry, textile industry, palm oil production, development companies
Master Risk Participation Agreement 257
Matalon family 77, 78, 79, 81
Mau Mau rebellion 71
Mauritius 141
May, Theresa 245
Mbeki, Thabo 193
Mbeya Cement, Tanzania 24, 180
Mbeya Exploration Co Ltd, Tanganyika 48
McClean, 'Old Mac' 75
McKinsey management consultants 178, 204
McLeod Russel 164
McNamara, Robert S. 101
McWilliam, Sir Michael 108
meat/cattle industry
    Bechuanaland Cattle Ranch 31
    Lobatse Abattoir 18, 19, *19*
    Molopo Ranch 18, 19, *19*, 36
Medikredit, South Africa 186
Medscheme, South Africa 186
Meinertzhagen, Sir Peter 100, *100*, 106, 108, 109, 112, 113, 134, 140, 142, 144, 147
Mengniu China Dairy 196, 197, 199
Merpati Airlines, Indonesia 67, 101, 118
Metenesel Estates Ltd, Vanuatu 160
Mexico 183
Mhulme Canal, Swaziland 50, 51, *51*, 52–3, 53
Mhulme Sugar 18, *51*, 95, 132, 188
Mhulme Water 37, 50
microfinance 183, 184, 185, 192, 223–5, 226, 239, 249, 250, 254
Millicom, Ghana 160
Mills, David 80, 132
Milne Bay Oil Palms, Papua New Guinea 114, 115, *115*
Minerals/mining industry 48, 69, 82, 128, 151, 165, 177, 185, 186, 187, 188, 217
Ministry of Overseas Development (ODM) 113

Miri, Sarawak, Borneo 97
Miro Forestry, Sierra Leone/Ghana 260
Mirza, Shaukat Raza 153, 154, *154*
Mitchell, Andrew 211, 235, *235*, 237, 238, 239, 247, 250, 255, 277
mobile phones *see* telecommunications
Mobile Systems International (MSI) 189
Mobile Telecommunications Company 189
Modern Terminals, Hong Kong 67, 98, *99*
Mohale Dam, Lesotho 169
Molopo Ranch, Bechuanaland 18, 19, *19*, 36
Monno Ceramic Industries Ltd 147
Monopolies and Mergers Commission 143, 170–1
Monrovia, Liberia 107, 128
Montserrat Electricity Co Ltd (Monlec) 74
Montigny 60
Montserrat 74
Mordaunt, Penny 245, 276, 277
Morley, David 218
Morris, John 118
Mostyn 132
motorways 186, *186–7*
Mozal aluminium, Mozambique 188, *188*
Mozambique 106, 140, 186, 188, 248
Mpongwe Developments Co, Zambia 165, 177
Mpongwe Farm, Zambia 165, *166–7*, 180, 218, 230
Mpongwe Milling Ltd, Zambia 165
Mubarik Dairies, Pakistan 150
Muela Hydro-Electric Power Station, Lesotho 169
Mugabe, Robert 168, 169, 191, 250
Mukonchi East Assisted Tenants Scheme, Zambia 109
Mukonchi Tobacco Training and Settlement Scheme 109
Multiples, India 226, 229, 237
Mumias Outgrowers Company, Kenya 112
Mumias Sugar Co Ltd (MSC) 106, 111, 112
Musharraf, Pervez 154
Myanmar 265, 274

N

Nagarajan, Srinivasan 269
Nairobi, Kenya 66, 72, 86, 87, 88, *88–9*, 123, 218
Namibia 141, 188
Nanga Farm, Zambia 165, 218
Narayana Health, India 257
National Agricultural and Food Corporation, Tanzania 131
National Audit Office (NAO) 230, 271
National Housing Authority, Thailand 122
National Housing Corporation, Kenya 86
National Power (now Engie Energy International) 153
National Seed Company of Malawi (NSCM) 130, 131
Nava Nakorn, Bangkok, Thailand 106, 120, *120*, 122
Nchanga Consolidated Copper Mines, Zambia 128, 165

Ndola Lime, Zambia 128
New Kowloon, Hong Kong 98
Newport Holdings Industrial Estate, Jamaica 78, *78*
Newport West Docks, Kingston, Jamaica 78, *78*
Nexus Film Corporation, Peru 185
Nigeria 9, 13, *13*, 37, 61, 66, 82, 82–5, *84*, 86, 123, 126, *126*, 127, 132, 199, 205, 210, 217, 218, 225, 276
Nigeria Cement Co Ltd (Nigercem) 84, *84*, 133
Nigeria Hotels Ltd 82, 83
Nigeria Industrial Development Bank 126
Nigerian Bank for Commerce and Industry 85
Noble, Diana 211, 232, 239, 245, 246–9, 250, 255, 257, 262, 268, 271, *272–3*
Norfund 176, 177, 203, 205, 223, 267
Northern Nigerian Investment Ltd 61, 82
Northern Rhodesia 9, 18, 24, 36, 44, 66, 109, 128, 141
    see also Zambia (Northern Rhodesia)
Northern Textile Manufacturers 82, *82*
Novastar Ventures, Kenya/Ethiopia 255
Nxumalo, Donald 95
Nyasaland 9, 20, 30–1, *30–1*, 36, 66
see also Malawi (Nyasaland)
Nyerere, Julius 82, 87
Nyika forest plantation, Nyasaland 30–1, *30–1*
Nyika Forestry Development Syndicate 31, 41

O

Obasanjo, General 126
Obote, Milton 87, 164
Observer 38
Ocean Building, Singapore 124, 125, *125*
Ocho Rios, Jamaica 78, 79, *79*, 81
O'Donohoe, Nick 245, 274–5, *275*, 277
Office of the Rubber Replanting Aid Fund (ORRAF), Thailand 122
oil and gas 199, 203, 217
    see also power sector
oil crises, global 106, 107, 112, 127
oil palm production
    see BAL Plantations; Borneo Abaca Ltd; palm oil production
Onosode, Gamaliel 123
Operation Ploughshare, Nyasaland 20
Oriental Hotel, Bangkok, Thailand 106, 122, *122*
Osomor, Kate 272
Overseas Development Administration (ODA) 122, 170
Overseas Development Institute 267
Overseas Food Corporation 12, 28, 29
Overseas Resources Development Act (1948) 9, 12, 28, 45, 60
    (1956) 60
    (1969) 67, 98
Overseas Resources Development Bill 8, 12
overseas staff, lives of 132–3

P

Pacific Islands 74, 133, 150
  see also South East Asia; individual
  islands by name
Pacific Rim Palm Oil Ltd (PRPOL) 114,
  179, 195
Pacific Rim Plantations (PACRIM) 179
Padma Textiles, Bangladesh 148
Pakistan 8, 61, 67, 98, 140, 147, 150–3, 194, 226,
  227, 267, 274
palm oil production 9, 86, 115, 134, 258, 259
    Central America 134
    Coapalma, Honduras 134
    Feronia 250, 252, 252–3, 276
    Higaturu Oil Palms, 106, 114, 116, 179
    Johore Palm Processing Ltd 57
    Kulai Oil Palm Estate 9, 55, 57, 57
    Latin America 134
    Limbang Oil Palm Pilot Scheme 96
    Milne Bay Oil Palms 114
    Pacific Rim Palm Oil Ltd (PRPOL) 114,
    179, 195
    PT Harapan Sawit Lestari 179
    PT Tatar Anyar 118
    sale of plantations in Malaysia 158, 179
    Sarawak Oil Palms Bhd 96, 97, 158,
    179, 194
    Solomon Islands Plantations Ltd 96,
    158
    see also BAL Plantations; Borneo
    Abaca Ltd
Palmoriente, Ecuador 134
The Palms shopping centre, Nigeria 210
Pan African Cement 24, 177, 180, 265
paper/pulp industry *see* pulp/paper
industry
Papua New Guinea 106, 114–16, 117, 140, 179
Paras Pharmaceuticals, India 216
Parliament, British 8, 14, 24, 98, 101, 211, 230,
  232, 237, 239, 271
  see also Government, British
Patel, Priti 245, 271, 272, 276, 277
Patria, Brazil, 225
Pay, Mark 248, 263
Peak Timbers, Swaziland 233
Peck, Donald 199, 200
Pelwatte Sugar, Sri Lanka 148
Permanent Housing Finance Company of
  Tanzania 86
Peru 185
pharmaceutical industry 200, 216
Philippines 153, 157, 200
Phillips, Rick 190, 191
Phillips, Tom 118
Phipson, Stan 20
Pigeon Island, St Lucia 80, 80, 81
Platmin, South Africa 186
PNG Electricity Commission 114
PNG Venture Finance Pty Ltd 114, 140
Poliamba Oil Palms, PNG 114
Port Moresby, Papua New Guinea 115, 140
Portland Cement, Malawi 180
Portmore Land Development Co, Jamaica
  78
poultry farming 28–9, 33

power sector 74–5, 98, 114, 134, 169, 204,
  232, 273
    Actis 205
    Ayana Renewable Power 274
    Caribbean Utilities Ltd 74
    Compania Boliviana de Energia
    Electrica SA 185
    Compania de Electricidad de Puerto
    Plata 201, 201
    Connaught Bridge Power Station
    56, 56
    Dominica Electricity Services Ltd
    (Domlec) 9, 74, 74, 201
    Globeleq 74, 177, 201–2, 203, 210, 214, 223,
    247, 262, 267
    Grenada Electricity Services Ltd
    (Grenlec) 74
    Hopewell Power (Philippines)
    Corporation 157
    Hub Power 153
    hydroelectric power scheme, Sri
    Lanka 148
    Jeffreys Bay Wind Farm 262, 262, 274,
    274
    Kariba Dam 18, 24, 44, 44, 45, 46, 47
    Lesotho Highlands Water Project 18
    M-KOPA 270, 273
    Montserrat Electricity Co Ltd
    (Monlec) 74
    PNG Electricity Commission 114
    Songas 201, 203, 210, 223
    St Lucia Electricity Services (Lucelec)
    66, 74, 75
    St Vincent Electricity Services (Vinlec)
    74, 74
    Tsavo Power 201, 223
    Umeme 220, 220–1, 223
    Virunga Power 265
    see also hydroelectric power;
    solar power
Pragati Equity Advisers, India 239
Prasanna Purple, India 235
Premier Portland Cement Company,
  Rhodesia 24
Prime Cure Clinics, South Africa 186
Prince of Wales, HRH 31, 107, 122, 146, 150
Private Eye 230, 237
Private Property Office, Thailand 122
ProFund International SA 183
Proparco 106, 250
property and housing finance 74, 78, 81,
  88, 114, 120
    Borneo Development Corporation 37,
    39, 56, 123
    Caribbean Housing Finance
    Corporation 66, 76, 77, 79
    Commonwealth Housing Corporation
    86–7
    East Caribbean Housing Ltd 75, 77
    Federal and Colonial Building Society
    24, 59
    First Permanent Building Society 73
    Guyana Housing and Development
    Co Ltd 23
    Guyana Mortgage Finance Co Ltd 23
    Home Finance Company, Fiji 98
    Hong Kong Building and Loan Agency
    98

    Housing Finance Company of Kenya
    86
    Housing Finance Company of Uganda
    86
    Jamaica Housing Development
    Company 77
    Jamaica Mortgage Bank 77
    Jurong Town Corporation (JTC) 125
    Kenya Building Society 73
    mortgage finance Costa Rica 134
    Permanent Housing Finance
    Company of Tanzania 86
    Portmore Land Development Co 78
    Rodney Bay Development Company
    80
    Singapore Factory Development Ltd
    36, 59, 123, 125
    Sinkahakan Credit Foncier 121
    Tanzania Housing Bank 87
    Thai Factory Development Co Ltd 122
    Thailand Housing Finance Co Ltd
    121–2
    Trinidad and Tobago Mortgage
    Finance Company 77
    see also construction/infrastructure
    developments; development funds
    and banks
PT Asiatic Persada, Indonesia 179, 180
PT Coklat Ransiki, Indonesia 117, 118
PT Harapan Sawit Lestari, Indonesia 179
PT Tatar Anyar, Indonesia 118
Public Private Partnership, CDC becomes
  a 192–4, 195
Public Utilities Board, Singapore 125
pulp/paper industry
    Nyika Plateau, Malawi 30, 31
    Usutu, Swaziland 9, 18, 60, 69, 71, 177
Punjab Tractors, India 177, 200

Q

Qiming, China 226
Queen Elizabeth Quay, Sri Lanka 148

R

Rahman, Tunku Abdul 54, 61
Railroad Development Corporation, Peru
  185
railway projects 60, 69, 69, 185
Rainbow Healthcare, India 250
Ramaphosa, Cyril 193
Ramnath, Renuka 226
Ransiki, Indonesia 117, 118, 118
Ransome Kuti, Fela 82
Ratnakar Bank Ltd (RBL), India 257, 268
Razak, Tun Abdul 54
real estate 205, 218, 229, 249
    see also construction/infrastructure
    developments; development funds
    and banks; hotels and tourism
recording studio, Nigeria 82
Reece, Major-General Thomas Wynford
  'Tiger' 20
Reicher, Andrew 195
Reith, Lord 9, 16, 24, 37, 38–41, 39, 42, 45, 49,
  50, 57, 60, 61, 71, 101, 276
Reliance Financial Services, the Gambia
  224

Rendell, Sir William 13, 36, 39, 41, 41, 45, 48,
  49, 50, 57, 57, 60, 61, 68, 70, 72, 74, 81, 90, 94,
  95, 100, 100, 101, 106, 276
Renewable Energy Asia Fund 232
Republic of Cameroon 82, 86
Rey Banano del Pacifico, Ecuador 185
Reynolds, Dr Roy 141, 178, 179, 192, 193,
  194, 195
rice farming 18, 33, 55
road construction 60, 118, 186, 186–7
Robinson, Adrian 189
Rodney Bay Development Company 80
Rodney Bay, St Lucia 67, 80, 80–1, 132
Rothenbusch, Holger 250
Royal Swaziland Sugar Corporation,
  Swaziland 188
rubber plantations 54, 55, 86, 109, 118, 122
    Compagnie Heveicole de Cavally 112, 218
    Office of the Rubber Replanting Aid
    Fund 122
    Societe Africaine de Plantations d'Heveas
    (SAPH) 112
    Rusitu Valley Development Company,
    Zimbabwe 168
Rwanda 141, 216, 217, 265
Rwenzori Highlands Tea Company,
  Uganda 164

S

Saapi 60
Sabah (North Borneo) 9, 26, 37, 49, 56, 66,
  96, 97, 123, 158
Sable Farming Ltd, Malawi 170
Sable Group 110, Malawi 170
Saigon, fall of 106, 122
Sand River Reservoir, Swaziland 67, 94,
  94, 95
Sandhar, India 216
Sarawak 37, 39, 56, 66, 96, 96, 97, 123, 158
Sarawak Oil Palms 96, 97, 158, 179, 194
Savannah Sugar Company 126, 126, 127, 127
Savings and Loan Society, Kenya 73
Schulze, Gabriel 239
Selassie, Emperor Haile 109, 170
Selbie, Nick 179
Senegal 217
Seychelles 83
Sharif, Nawaz 153
Shawcross, Geoffrey 57
Shim Kah Foo 123
shipping/container terminals 98, 148, 267
Shiselweni Forestry Company, Swaziland
  95, 95, 122, 123
ShoreCap International 210, 223–5, 226
Short, Clare 193, 195, 204, 277
Sierra Investment Fund, Sierra Leone
  228, 233
Sierra Leone 82, 228, 232, 233, 256, 257–8, 260
Sify (Satyam Infoway Ltd), India 176, 198,
  199–200
Sillem, Jeremy 235, 237
Silverlands 239
Sinai Marble, Egypt 217
Sinclair Committee 68, 70, 73
Singapore 9, 24, 57, 59, 66, 67, 83, 123, 125, 133,
  179, 200

Singapore Factory Development Ltd 36, 59, 123, 125

Singapura Finance 9, 24, 59

Sinkahakan Credit Foncier, Thailand 121

Slamet the Tiger 180, *180*

Smallholder Coffee Authority, Malawi 110, 111, *111*

Smallholder Sugar Authority, Malawi 110, 111, *111*

Smallholder Tea Authority, Malawi 109, 110, *110*

Smith, Ian 24, 44

Sobhuza II of Swaziland, King 37, 50, 53, 67, 69, 94, 95

SOBOCE, Bolivia 176

Societe Africaine de Plantations d'Heveas (SAPH) Côte d'Ivoire 112, 113, *113*

solar power 199, 218, 247, 267, 270, *270*, 273, 274

Solomon Island Plantations Ltd 96, 133, 140, 158, *159*

Solomon Islands 96, 106, 140, 158, 159, *159*, 160, *161*

Songas, Tanzania 201, 203, 210, 223

South Africa 36, 71, 141, 150, 169, 176, 186, 191, 193, 215, 216, 217, 247, 248, 249, 274

South Asia 147–8, 193, 199, 204, 212, 215, 216, 250, 270, 272, 275

South Asian Regional Fund (SARF) 190, 191, 198, 200, 205

South Atlantic Sealing Company, Falkland Islands 14, 33

South East Asia 72, 74, 96–9, 121, 125, 157, 158, 160, 179, 191, 194, 195, 204, 216, 230, 232, 258
see also individual countries by name

South East Asia Gateway Terminals, Sri Lanka 148

Southern Rhodesia 24, 44, 60, 66, 71, 82
see also Zimbabwe (Southern Rhodesia/Rhodesia)

soya production 165

Soyoye, Babatunde 225

Special Crops Development Authority, Kenya 90

Square D Software, India 198

Sri Lanka (Ceylon) 9, 140, 148, 274

St Lucia 9, 17, *17*, 66, 67, 74, 75, 80, *80–1*, 81, 107, 132

St Lucia Electricity Services (Lucelec) 66, 74, 75, *75*, 77

St Vincent 74, 74, 75, 77, 107

St Vincent Electricity Services (Vinlec) 74, *74*

Staff Bulletins, CDC 43, *43*, 50

Standard Chartered Bank 244, 256, 257–8

Standard Life 77

Stephenson, Christopher 121, 132

Strachey, John 12

Stuttafords Holdings, Zimbabwe 190, 191

sub-Saharan Africa 101, 165, 193, 204, 205, 211, 215, 218, 226, 229, 232, 233, 237, 249, 258
see also individual countries by name

Sudan 218

sugar industry 109
    Agricane 265
    Kaleya Smallholders Company, Zambia 128

Mhulme Sugar Company 18, *51*, 95, 132, 188

Mumias Sugar Company Ltd 106, 111, 112

Pelwatte Sugar 148

Savannah Sugar 126, *126*, 127, *127*

Smallholder Sugar Authority, Malawi 110

Suharto, President 117

Sukarno, President 117

Swaziland 9, 18, 37, 50, 51, *51*, *52–3*, 53, 60, 67, 71, 94, *94*, 95, *95*, 119, 122, 132, 188, 233

Swaziland Iron Ore Development Ltd 69

Swaziland Irrigation Scheme (SIS) 9, 18, 37, 49, 50, *51*, *52–3*, 53, 67, 71, 94, 95, 119, 133

Swaziland National Agricultural Development Corporation 95

Swaziland Railway 60, 69, *69*

Swynnerton, Sir Roger 90, 109

T

Takura Ventures, Zimbabwe 190, 191, 250

Tanah Merah Land Development Board, Malaya 54

Tanganyika 9, 20, 28, 48, 66, 72
see also Tanzania (Taganyika)

Tanganyika (Tanzania) Development Finance Co Ltd (TDFL) 87, *87*, 133

Tanganyika (Tanzania) Wattle Estates (Tanwat) 9, 18, 130, *130*, 131, 132

Tangold Mines, Tanzania 48

Tanzania (Tanganyika) 9, 20, 24, 28, 37, 48, *48*, 66, 72, 82, 86, 87, 90, 132, 147, 164, 180, 188, 201, 203, 210, 217, 218, 220, 223, 233, 234, 237, 248, 262

Tanzania Housing Bank 87

Tanzania Seed Company (Tanseed) 131

Tanzania Tea Authority 164

Tanzania Tea Packers (Tatepa) 180, 218

Tanzania Venture Capital Fund 180

Tate & Lyle 128

Taylor, John 48, 83, 85, *85*, 132, 133

tea industry 18, 86
    East Africa Teas 180
    East Usambara Tea Co Ltd 164
    Kavuzi Tea Company 170
    Kenya Tea Development Authority (KTDA) 66, 90, *90*, 91, *91*, 92–3, 93, 109, 112
    PT Tatar Anya 118
    Rwenzori Highlands Tea Company 164, *164*
    Smallholder Tea Authority 110, *110*
    Tanzania Tea Packers (Tatepa) 180, 218

telecommunications
    Algeria 217
    BPL Mobile 200
    CDC fund managers 225, 237, 238
    Celtel 176, 188–9, 223
    China Grentech 199
    Grameenphone 148
    IHS Zambia Ltd 9
    Irrawaddy Green Tower Project 264, 265
    Millicom 160, *160*

terrorist attack, Kulai Oil Palm Estate 57

textile industry 82, 128, 148, 150, 276

Thai Factory Development Co Ltd 122

Thailand 101, 106, 120–2, 194

Thatcher, Margaret 107, 142, 144, 244

timber industry
    see also forestry

tin and zinc mines 177, 185, *185*

tobacco industry 109, 110, 111, *111*, 131

Totman, Gren 45, 70

tourism *see* hotels and tourism

Trans Africa Concessions (TRAC), South Africa/Mozambique 186

Treasury, British government 73, 101, 170, 232, 255, 256

Trefgarne, Lord 8, 9, 14, 16, 16, *16*, 17, 24, 28, 29, 33, 38, 40, 50, 61, 70, 158, 269

Trinidad and Tobago 66, 77, *77*

Trinidad and Tobago Mortgage Finance Company 77

Tristan da Cunha Development Corporation 14

Tsavo Power, Tanzania 201, 223

Tully, William 123, 158, *158*

Tun Abdul Razak 54

Tunisia 101, 217

Turks and Caicos Islands 9, 143

Turtle Towers, Ocho Rios, Jamaica 79, *79*

U

Uganda 18, 20, 48, 66, 67, 72, 82, 86, 87, 90, 133, 164, 180, 182, 189, 220, 223, 262

Uganda Development Corporation 22

Umeme, Uganda 220, *220–1*

Umuhuali Community, Nkalagu, Nigeria 84, *84*

Unilateral Declaration of Independence (UDI), Southern Rhodesia 24, 44, 82, 168

Unilever 18, 28, 252

Upper Peirce Reservoir, Singapore 125

Urban Development Corporation, Jamaica 78, 79

USAID 122

Usni Pramoj (M.L.) 122

Usutu Forest, Swaziland 18, 60, *60*, 71

Usutu Pulp Co, Swaziland 60, 69, 177

UTI Bank (later Axis Bank), India 200

V

van der Post, Laurens 30, 31, *31*

Vanuatu (New Hebrides) 107, 160

VenturEast Proactive Fund, India 238

Venture to the Interior (L. van de Post) 31, *31*

Ventures and Visions (Lord Trefgarne) 14

Vereker, Sir John 193

Vettivetpillai, Sev 205

Victoria Falls Safari Lodge, Zimbabwe 168, 169, *169*

Vietnam 239

Viphya Tung Estates, Nyasaland 20, 110

Virunga Power, DRC 265

Vlisco 276, *276*

Vuvulane Irrigated Farms, Swaziland 18, 95

W

Walton, Chris 90

Water and Power Development Authority, Pakistan (WAPDA) 153

water supplies 9, 18, 33, 37, 49, 50, *51*, *52–3*, 53, 66, 67, 71, 94, *94*, 95, 119, 125, 126, 127, 133, 168, 169

West Africa 40, 60, 82, 86, 101, 144, 160, 225, 237, 256, 257, 276
see also individual countries by name

West Papua (Irian Jaya) 117

Western Storage Ltd, Jamaica 78, *78*

Western Terminals Ltd, Jamaica 78, *78*

wheat production 165

Wilhite, Irwin 181

Williamson, Sir Malcolm 210, 211, 212, 214, 232

Wilson, Harold 66, 106

wind power 262, *262*, 267, 274, *274*

Wise, Peter 49, *49*

Wong family 185

Wood, David 133

Wood, Lieutenant-General Sir Ernest 14

Woodhead, Brian 159

Workman, Mike 158

World Bank 61, 90, 98, 101, 109, 112, 114, 118, 145, 148, 153, 165

Wrigley, Graham 244, 250, *251*, 255, 267, 271, 275, 276, *277*

Wu, Gordon 157

X

XacBank, Mongolia 226

Y

Yap, Howard 123

Z

Zaire 101

Zambeef Group, Zambia 165, 271, 273

Zambia (Northern Rhodesia) 9, 18, 24, 36, 44, 66, 109, 128, 141, 165, 180, 182, 218, 262, 265

Zambia Sugar Company 128

Zambian Privatisation Agency 165

Zanzibar 66

Zimbabwe (Southern Rhodesia) 24, 36, 44, 66, 71, 82, 107, 168, 182, 190, 191, 250, 262

ZIMCO 165

Zoological Society of London (ZSL) 180